D0036833

THE
KILLING
SCHOOL

THE
KILLING
SCHOOL

INSIDE THE WORLD'S
DEADLIEST SNIPER
PROGRAM

Brandon Webb
with John David Mann

St. Martin's Press 〽 *New York*

www.stmartins.com

The Library of Congress Cataloging-in-Publication Data is available
upon request.

ISBN 978-1-250-12993-2 (hardcover)
ISBN 978-1-250-12994-9 (e-book)

Our books may be purchased in bulk for promotional, educational, or
business use. Please contact your local bookseller or the Macmillan Cor-
porate and Premium Sales Department at 1-800-221-7945, extension
5442, or by e-mail at MacmillanSpecialMarkets@macmillan.com.

First Edition: May 2017

10 9 8 7 6 5 4 3 2 1

This book is dedicated to my fellow warriors turned military authors, who have had the courage, in the face of massive peer pressure, to enter the author's coliseum and engage in literary battle, and who emerge again, their faces "marred by dust and sweat and blood" (as Teddy Roosevelt puts it in the quote on pg vii), knowing they gave their all in the process.

It's ironic that these warriors, many of whom barely managed to survive being shot by the enemy's ranks, arrive back home in the States only to find themselves targeted and shot at in a war of words, often fired their way by members, or former members, of their own units.

Criticism by some in the military community is expected, especially from those who served in the Special Operations community, a group largely in the shadows prior to September 11, 2001. Still, scrutiny is one thing. Trash-talking and outright character assassination is something else. I've experienced this myself, and it's no fun. So have Chris Kyle, Marcus Luttrell, Howard Wasdin, and scores of other colleagues. So, no doubt, will the four men whose stories we share in these pages.

The next time you see one of those "silent professionals" disparaging someone from their own community, on social media or elsewhere, keep this in mind: most critics and would-be character assassins typically share two traits in common—insecurity with their own performance (in this case, with their own military service) and professional jealousy.

More than a century ago, an old cavalry soldier and Medal of Honor recipient, no stranger himself to the slings and arrows of envious resentment, put it far better than I can:

It is not the critic who counts; not the man who points out how the strong man stumbles, or where the doer of deeds could have done them better. The credit belongs to the man who is actually in the arena, whose face is marred by dust and sweat and blood; who strives valiantly; who errs, who comes short again and again, because there is no effort without error and shortcoming; but who does actually strive to do the deeds; who knows great enthusiasms, the great devotions; who spends himself in a worthy cause; who at the best knows in the end the triumph of high achievement, and who at the worst, if he fails, at least fails while daring greatly, so that his place shall never be with those cold and timid souls who neither know victory nor defeat.

—**Teddy Roosevelt**

Contents

Author's Note

All the events in this book are true and are described herein to the best of my knowledge and/or recollection. In several cases, names have been changed. We have at all times sought to avoid disclosing particular methods and other sensitive mission-related information. This book was submitted to, partially redacted, and ultimately cleared by the Department of Defense review board prior to publication.

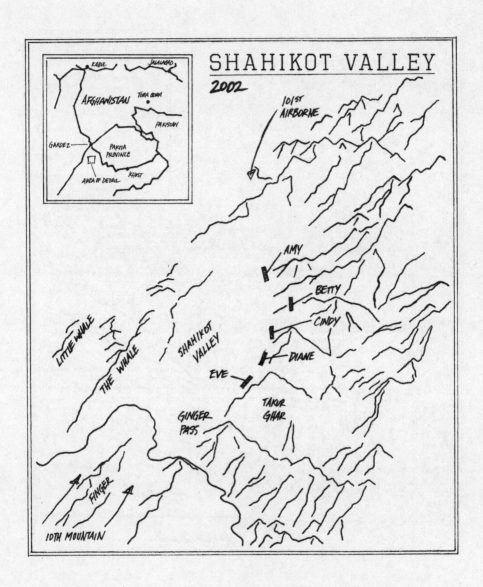

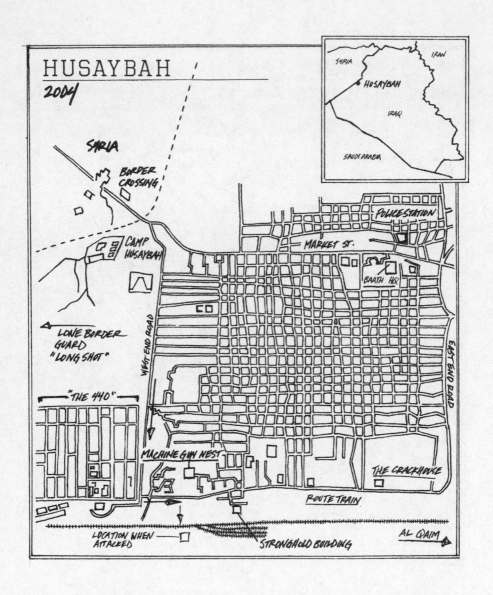

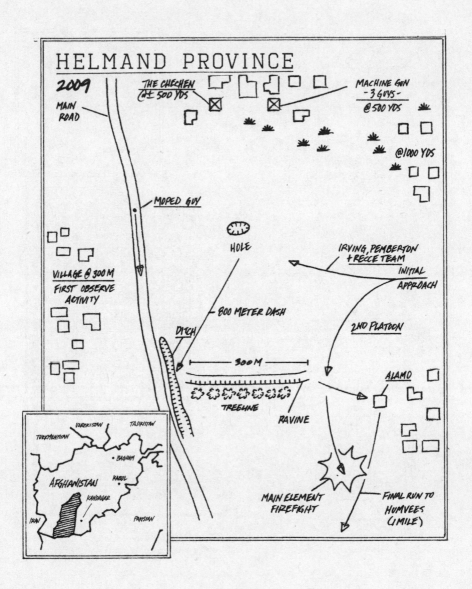

THE
KILLING
SCHOOL

PROLOGUE: LIVING WITH DEATH

Every man owes a death. There are no exceptions.

—Stephen King, *The Green Mile*

I have an unusual relationship with death.

For most of us, death is a mystery, a thing we fear and seek to avoid, evade, or deny, even to the point of pretending it doesn't exist, at least until we reach our sixties or seventies and it starts coming around to claim the lives of those we know and love.

For me, the face of death is as familiar as the barista at my local coffee shop.

In the freezing morning hours of March 4, 2002, I sit with seven of my teammates in an MH-47 Chinook helicopter, code name Razor 1. We're not moving; we're tied down at Bagram Air Base in northern Afghanistan, waiting for the word to go. We have been deployed as a QRF (quick reaction force) to fly out to the Shahikot Valley, near the Pakistan border about a hundred miles south of here, to rescue Neil Roberts, a fellow Navy SEAL who has been shot down on a mountaintop there, along with a team of SEALs who went in to get him out and got pinned down themselves by enemy fire.

Finally the word comes—only it isn't "GO," it's "Get Off."

At the last minute, for reasons we are never told (no doubt political), we are yanked off the bird and replaced by a team of U.S. Army Rangers who fly off in our place while we sit on our hands. Five members of that rescue team—the team that replaced us, the team that should have been us—never come back. Neither does Roberts. Instead, he becomes the first U.S. Navy SEAL killed in the young conflict people are already calling the War on Terror.

A few weeks later, another SEAL named Matthew Bourgeois steps out of a Humvee on the outskirts of Kandahar and onto a land mine. The bizarre thing is, I stood there, on that exact same spot, two months ago, when the Humvee I was riding in parked right there—directly on top of a live antitank land mine. The only reason the damn thing didn't blow us to pieces is that whoever set it up did a lousy job.

But not this time. Unlike the one underneath my Humvee's wheel, the device Matthew just stepped on has been set correctly. A fraction of a second later he becomes Afghanistan's Navy SEAL casualty #2.

You could say I had cheated death once again, but I didn't see it that way. Orpheus may have tricked Hades; Ingmar Bergman may have had Max von Sydow play chess with Death; but those are only stories. In real life, death isn't something you cheat or outmaneuver. Death is like the wind: it blows where it wants to blow. You can't argue with death; you can't stop it. Best you can do, as any sailor will tell you, is your damnedest to harness it.

We never really left Afghanistan, and soon we were in Iraq, too, and many other parts of the world, and more deaths followed. In 2012 I started writing a book, *Among Heroes,* honoring friends of mine who had given their lives in the course of the War on Terror. While I was still working on the first draft, my best friend in the world, Glen Doherty, was killed in Benghazi. Before the manuscript was finished, another SEAL sniper friend, Chris Kyle, died in Texas while trying to help out a suffering vet. I had thought the book was my idea; but death was writing it with me.

As many thinkers over the ages have pointed out, your relationship with death colors your relationship with life, perhaps even determines it. Crazy Horse rode into battle at the Little Bighorn saying, "Today is a good day to die." That's not simply a declaration of balls and bravery. Embracing death is the only thing that allows you to fully embrace being alive. "The fear of death follows from the fear of life," said Mark Twain. "A man who lives fully is prepared to die at any time."

As I said, I have an unusual relationship with death, but then, so does every Special Operations sniper.

The sniper plays many roles in modern warfare. He or she is a master of observation and reconnaissance, often the commander's prime instrument of detailed intelligence behind enemy lines. Snipers are master trackers, often devoting hours or days to following a trail and observing people's movements without ever firing a single shot. They serve as assets of psychological warfare; a single sniper can sow confusion and insecurity in the minds of thousands of enemy troops. Advanced military sniper training, probably the most exacting and excruciating of any course of training anywhere on earth, schools its students in an astonishing range of skills and disciplines, from digital photography and satellite communications to physics to memorization techniques that any Las Vegas huckster would kill to own.

Still, while these are all real and true aspects of what is one of the world's most complex skill sets, the fact remains that the sniper's fundamental task is brutally simple. It is the sniper's job to compose, choreograph, and execute a death.

The experience of killing, of course, is hardly unique to snipers. That is the nature of war; every soldier, sailor, and airman is put in a position to come face-to-face with death, and many do. A line of tanks, a formation of aircraft, a company of infantry: these are all tasked with delivering death—but in a messier, more haphazard, and more massive way. They pour out huge amounts of money and matériel onto the battlefield, slaughtering dozens or hundreds, destroying buildings and towns, despoiling environments.

The sniper's charge is to dole out death to an individual, singularly and instantaneously.

The killing that a sniper delivers is different from that of the rest of war. For one thing, it is vastly more precise, more efficient, and, to be frank, more economical. In Vietnam, killing a single NVA or Vietcong took American infantry firing roughly fifty thousand rounds, at the cost of well over $2,000. For an American sniper to dispatch one enemy fighter took an average of 1.3 rounds. Total cost: 27 cents.

The sniper's kill is also more personal. It's one thing to charge onto a battlefield in the heat of a firefight, or hurl a grenade over a wall, even shoot someone with a sidearm as you run through a building, adrenaline soaking your muscle fibers and nerve endings. But when you sit concealed in a hide site for hours, even days, watching someone, noting his every move, getting to know his daily routine, his mannerisms, assembling an entire profile of his personality and intentions through exhaustive observation, it's an entirely different experience. A sniper may know his target intimately before the moment comes to squeeze the trigger.

Finally, the way a sniper kills another human being is vastly more deliberate. More conscious. "More cold-blooded," you could say—but if you do, then you've never walked in a sniper's shoes. Chris Kyle, arguably the most famous of twenty-first-century snipers, was often asked about how he felt about all the people he'd killed, and Chris always turned it around: it wasn't about the people he killed, it was about the boys he kept from being killed. Most military snipers you talk to will say the same thing. Their goal out there in the field isn't to take lives so much as it is to save them.

But make no mistake: while preservation of life may be the goal, inflicting death is the means. The sniper, possibly more than any other military figure, embodies the inherent contradictions and ironies of war. The aim of war is to squelch or settle conflict; in other words, to enable the people whom the warrior represents to live in peace. When you go to war, your ultimate purpose is to remove barriers that keep societies from going about their normal lives; to promote the peace, to protect and preserve the living.

Which you do by killing.

The sniper's mission is to deliver life by delivering death.

This is the story of the people who do that: who they are, how they do what they do, and the training that produces them.

I.
THE MISSION

You will be inserting in one of the most lethal trouble spots on the face of the planet. You will have been briefed beforehand, to the best of our ability and extent of current intel, but the unknowns will greatly outweigh the knowns.

You will be the eyes and ears, the radar and periscope, of our operation. You will encounter situations where you are the only one who actually knows the full extent of what is going on there on the ground, and will have to make judgment calls about how to respond, even if you do not always have the explicit authority to do so.

To an extent greater than in any previous era of warfare, the course this conflict takes, and the odds for its successful completion, will depend on you. . . .

1

WARRIOR, ASSASSIN, SPY

There is another type of warfare—new in its intensity, ancient in its origin—war by guerrillas, subversives, insurgents, assassins; war by ambush instead of by combat, by infiltration instead of aggression, seeking victory by eroding and exhausting the enemy instead of engaging him.

—President John F. Kennedy

A few miles off the coast of Somalia
Monday, February 27, 1995, close to midnight

I've never drowned to death, but I've come close. I'm not saying we were exactly waterboarded during the course of our training, but let's put it this way: I'm familiar with how it feels to be surrounded, invaded, swallowed by water, that intimate sense of skin-close death. I'd already known it for years. At the age of thirteen, I would dive deep down in the middle of the night, into the inky green blackness, to wrestle free a tangled anchor attached to the boat where I worked. There's something primal about being taken over by water, something deeply peaceful even as it terrifies you. "Ashes to ashes," goes the familiar funeral patter, "dust to dust . . ."—but it's not really like that. Dust isn't where we started. We came from water, and the water is always ready to claim us back.

Right now Alex Morrison was mulling over thoughts about death and water, as he felt their craft heave and plunge in the midnight African sea swell.

Alex had been a SEAL since 1989, graduating from the Naval Special Warfare sniper program in mid-'94, less than a year earlier. The son of a marine officer, he had joined the teams out of an unquenchable thirst for adventure. He had the feeling he was about to get some.

He looked around, craning his eyes in the dark.

There were about forty of them, crammed onto their bench seats in the dark, packed like heavily armed sardines into a corrugated steel MILVAN shipping container fastened to the deck of an amphibious hovercraft, speeding toward the Somali coast, a few miles still to go. They couldn't see out, not that there was much to see at midnight on the ocean; still, if they were out on deck at least they would have been able to see the stars and get a sense of horizon. If something happened, they would have been able to *do* something.

No dice. All they could do was think about the mission in front of them.

"Operation Restore Hope," that's what they'd called it back in 1992 when it started. An international effort to bring order and stability to war-torn, famine-ravaged Somalia. All you had to do was look at the Battle of Mogadishu in October 1993 to know how *that* plan was turning out.

More like Operation Hopeless, thought Alex.

And now that they'd pulled the plug, someone had to go in and get the last few thousand U.N. personnel who were still there, housed in complexes in and around the coastal airport. They couldn't be airlifted out—too many crazy, khat-chewing Somali militia running around with surface-to-air missiles. They couldn't leave via commercial shipping, either: too many mortars, RPGs, and so on. It had to be a military operation, and a delicate one at that. Which was why Alex and his platoon were there.

The operation employed a total of about fourteen thousand personnel, though only a fraction of those were being used in the actual landing force. Most would remain onboard the Coalition fleet of two dozen ships, four miles off the coast, to receive the evacuees and support the mission. It would be the largest amphibious withdrawal under hostile conditions since we'd pulled out of North Korea in 1950.

About half the landing forces would put in at Mogadishu's seaport, just north of the airport, in large landing craft. Hundreds more would roll in on amphibious assault vehicles, essentially large waterproofed tanks. Some were flying in on helos. Not Alex. He and the other sardines were hovercrafting straight onto the beach by the airport runway, where he and their platoon's other sniper would immediately fan out with their support teams and establish overwatch for the duration of the mission. Which should go smoothly—not a shot fired. After all, Mohamed Aidid and the other Somali warlords had been talked with, and had agreed to let the U.N. forces go peacefully. But of course, they had added, they couldn't be responsible for the actions of militias or splinter groups, now could they?

To put it in plain English: once the evacuation began, all bets were off.

Somewhere over eastern Afghanistan
Monday, March 4, 2002, before dawn

Rob Furlong crouched in the freezing cold transport helo, feeling the Chinook's metal hull vibrating against his back. Random thoughts slipped through his head. The smell of jet fuel and rush of frigid air acted like smelling salts, jarring his brain. As if he needed any added stimulation to stay alert. Hydraulic fluid wept down the interior walls of the bird here and there, creating the appearance of a dank cave. Sitting in their retractable pipe-and-webbing red nylon seats, two rows of fighters faced each other across the metal floor. The insistent, high-pitched whine of the Chinook's turbines and *whump whump whump* of its twin rotors made conversation close to impossible, leaving the men largely alone in their thoughts.

Sitting up toward the front of the chopper, near the door gunner, Rob looked to his left, down the row of assorted fighters on his side of the helo, and occupied his mind with trying to work out exactly which units they each belonged to—Delta, 101st Airborne, Tenth Mountain Division? There were about thirty of them, plus an all-terrain four-wheeler loaded by the rear ramp. Seven other Chinooks were flying in the same formation with his, with a total of more than two hundred troops, part of the nearly two thousand being thrown into this operation, the first major offensive of the still new war.

Most of these guys (Rob included) had never seen combat before. This was true of more than 95 percent of U.S. and Canadian armed forces. The world had been at peace, relatively speaking, for a decade.

Rob swiveled his head and looked the other way, toward the front of the craft, where the door gunner sat by his FN MAG M240 machine gun, doing a decent impression of a catnap. MAG: *mitrailleuse d'appui général,* French for "general purpose." The M240 fires 650 to 1,000 rounds per minute. Rob's mathematical mind automatically ran the quick calculation. Once that gunner pulled the trigger, the big gun would be shooting ten to fifteen rounds every second. Not bad, for general purposes.

Those rounds were 7.62s. Unlike the ".50" of the .50 cal rounds Rob carried, which describes the bullet's diameter (or, more accurately, the diameter of the gun barrel that fires it) in inches, the "7.62" denotes diameter in millimeters. A .45, a .38, a .22, those are inch-based calibers, the classic American naming style for firearms and ammunition. The popular 9mm (like the sidearm Rob carried) follows the European metric convention, as did the 5.56 shells that went with Rob's combat rifle, the C8, and its close cousin, the American military workhorse M4, and the ever-popular M16, the standard U.S. service rifle since Vietnam.

Before boarding the chopper, Rob had talked with a young Delta sniper who carried an SR-25. Rob liked that gun. A semiautomatic, the SR-25 is built like an M16 only with a longer barrel, and rather than a 5.56 it shoots a 7.62, which packs that much more punch.

And then there was the massive .50 cal sniper rifle resting its stock on the helo's floor next to Rob's left foot. The .50 cal he would use to make history. Standing on its end, the long gun stood nearly as high as Rob himself, each rocket-ship-like bullet tall as a Coke can. A round from a .50 cal can reach out and touch someone at distances of more than a mile, and do so with a force that can take out an engine block. It is, as Rob puts it, "like a punch in the face from God."

"Ten minutes out!" came the call back into the cabin.

Furlong looked over at the front gunner's pintle-mounted M240 again, and wondered what it would sound like when that big gun exploded into action.

Husaybah, Iraq
Saturday, April 17, 2004, early morning

When Jason Delgado woke up in his bank office on the morning of April 17, his first thought was, *Shit*. He did not have a good feeling about the day ahead. Jason was not a banker, and this was no ordinary bank. He was the chief scout of his marine scout sniper platoon, and the sprawl of deserted offices and warehouses stuck on the ass-crack known as the Iraq-Syrian border were what he and his team had been calling home for a few months now.

He sat up on his cot, swiveled around to plant his feet on the floor, and looked around to find the source of the gunfire that had roused him.

Through the open door he saw the other two snipers in his section, Josh Mavica and Brandon DelFiorentino, sitting on their bunk beds, shooting people.

On their Xboxes. *Grand Theft Auto: San Andreas.*

Boys will be boys. Delgado shook his head. "You guys don't get enough of that shit in your day job?" He nodded in the direction of the city that lay outside the walls of their base camp. Although barely six months their senior, Delgado felt something like a father's responsibility for these two, and for all the other guys in the platoon, too. Not yet twenty-three himself, Delgado was platoon sergeant of the sniper platoon for Lima Company, Third Battalion, Seventh Marine Regiment, in charge of managing the fragile state of this misbegotten city.

It was barely two years since Rob Furlong's predawn helicopter ride into eastern Afghanistan, but the world was now a vastly different place. A year earlier, in March 2003, Delgado had been part of the unit that pushed north through Iraq to take Baghdad away from Saddam Hussein and give it back to the people. Now he was back in country on a new deployment, this time to the Wild West border town of Husaybah, his base of operations a literal stone's throw from Syria.

Husaybah. A three-syllable word meaning roughly "I can't believe the shit we're in." The drug-smuggling, arms-running, corruption capital of western Iraq, Husaybah made Sam Peckinpah's *The Wild Bunch* look like a girls' finishing school.

Delgado reached down and grabbed his M40A3. Not quite the monster of Furlong's .50, but still a serious boom stick. The bolt-action M40 fires a .30-06 cartridge, the *thirty-aught-six* referring to both its caliber (.30) and the year it was adopted by the U.S. military (1906). The bolt action meant it wouldn't provide the rapid-fire performance of a semi-auto, like the M16 or the SR-25, but it delivered a hell of a wallop, and with phenomenal accuracy.

He headed to the porta-john, taking the gun with him. You never knew just when some upright citizen would fire a mortar shell over the wall.

Delgado was frustrated and pissed off. Worse, he was worried. For more than six weeks he'd been saying there was trouble brewing out in the streets, not just normal everyday urban-shithole trouble but the serious kind. Nobody seemed to believe him or see what he was seeing. Just a few days earlier one of his snipers had been shot through both legs. Another marine had died; yet another was back in the States in a coma, and probably wouldn't make it. To Jason, this did not feel like a series of unfortunate events. These were not random attacks.

Delgado grew up in the streets. He knew what it smelled like when something bad was about to go down. He was smelling it right now.

Somewhere in Helmand Province, Afghanistan
Thursday, July 9, 2009, midday

Nick Irving stood up, stretched, and yawned. He looked down at where he'd been sleeping: a spit of desert scrub with a small rock serving as his pillow. Not exactly the Hilton. Still, it was sleep. How long had he been out? He glanced at his watch. More than two hours. Amazing. In the past four days Nick had barely slept at all—a few stolen minutes here and there, a total of no more than three of the last ninety hours.

He bent down and picked up Dirty Diana off the blanket where he had carefully laid her. His beloved SR-25, named, of course, for the Michael Jackson song (released in 1988 when Irving was not yet two). A close cousin to the workhorse M4, the SR-25 was a smaller gun than Delgado's M40. Nick liked it for that reason: it was smaller and lighter, like himself, and he also liked it for its semiautomatic action, which suited the kind of intense, rapid-fire action he'd seen over five deployments as a U.S. Army Ranger in Iraq and Afghanistan. No long slow stalks or one-shot/one-kill Vietnam-style missions for Irving. At least not so far. No, the shit he'd seen had been more like the classic close-quarters-battle (CQB), full-contact, down-and-dirty fighting they'd practiced for days on end in ranger training than what you'd think of as a *sniper* mission per se.

The rangers are a relatively small Spec Ops outfit, numerically speaking, and tend to have an unusually high op tempo. In Iraq Nick's unit had routinely gone out on two missions per night, and sometimes as many as four or five. They'd go hit their target, be on their way back to rest and get some chow, and there'd be the commander on the radio saying they'd just gotten fresh intel on a new target, and they were back out again.

Back in the nineties, rangers served more or less in a supporting role, as in the 1993 Battle of Mogadishu, when the Third Ranger Battalion (Nick's unit) supported the Delta Force fighters. In the new century's asymmetrical warfare that quickly changed, with ranger units working independently, gathering their own intel and mounting their own missions, doing their own high-value target (HVT) hits. Being a ranger sniper had become something like being a sniper on a SWAT team. Fast, hard strikes at short distances, always moving. No sitting out there in a ghillie suit, looking for a target for a week, piss-ing in your pants while you lay in wait. Nick kept Dirty Diana dialed in at three hundred meters, a relatively short range for a sniper, and he'd taken plenty of shots shorter than that.

He strolled over to where a knot of marines were sitting playing poker. Irving and his spotter, Mike Pemberton, were the only two rang-ers here, temporary guests at a marine outpost somewhere out in the middle of the nowhere known as Helmand Province.

Jutting up from the middle of Afghanistan's southern border, Hel-mand was a very different part of the country from the area Rob Furlong had seen seven years earlier, in 2002, when the war was still fresh. No mountains to speak of here, just low-lying scrub, desert, and urban terrain. And poppies. Billions of poppies. Helmand Province had the largest concentration of poppy cultivation anywhere in the world. It was, in other words, heroin central, which meant it was also Taliban cen-tral and, increasingly, a safe haven for foreign radical Islamist forces.

American military presence here had been, up to this point, fairly close to zero.

"Hey, we heard where you guys are headed," one of the marines said. "That's some far-flung shit out there."

It was. Irving and Pemberton were headed deep behind enemy lines, into an area even marines wouldn't go without a full complement of forces, as Nick would soon learn.

"Watch out for the Chechen," said a second marine.

The Chechen? wondered Nick. *Who the hell is the Chechen?*

Somalia 1995. Afghanistan 2002. Iraq 2004. Afghanistan 2009.

Four plot points on a graph of America at war. That decade and a half has redefined the nature of the modern sniper, and Spec Ops snip-ers like Alex Morrison, Rob Furlong, Jason Delgado, and Nick Irving have played defining roles in each of these pivot points.

While Alex sat in the dark, heading for his rendezvous with the Mogadishu coastline, I was stationed in San Diego, working as a rescue swimmer on an antisubmarine helicopter squadron, still two and a half years away from entering BUD/S (Basic Underwater Demolition/SEAL training). The idea of being a sniper was the furthest thing from my mind. When Rob Furlong boarded his Chinook to fly into combat in Afghanistan seven years later, I was there, too, just miles away, now serving as a sniper for SEAL Team Three, Echo Platoon, waiting to hear if we would be sent in after Neil Roberts and the others. By the time

Jason Delgado was waking up on April 17, 2004, in Husaybah, my BUD/S classmate Eric Davis and I were back in the States, implementing a stem-to-stern renovation of the Naval Special Warfare (SEAL) sniper course, where I would serve as course master for a few years. And when Nick Irving went deep into Taliban territory in Helmand Province in 2009, I was in the private sector, writing a book about snipers and beginning a career as an analyst and media commentator on military and foreign affairs. Whether from the inside looking out or the outside looking in, for a decade and a half the world of the Special Operations sniper has been my home, my study, and my fascination.

And it is one fascinating world.

Say the word "sniper" and chances are you think of a shadowy figure, so deeply camouflaged he escapes all detection, hiding out for hours or even days on end, waiting for the moment to strike like a snake, delivering the single fatal shot at extreme distances. You might think of Carlos Hathcock, the legendary marine sniper, the one the Vietcong dubbed Lông Trắng: the White Feather, for the feather he wore in his cap. Hathcock famously took three full days to cover a thousand yards before dispatching a Vietnamese general through the heart with a single shot. In 1967 Hathcock set what remained for decades the world record for longest kill shot, delivering death to his target at 2,500 yards.

Or you might think of Vasily Grigoryevich Zaitsev, the Russian shepherd boy turned sniper, made famous (as played by Jude Law) in the film *Enemy at the Gates,* who racked up more than two hundred kills in the defense of Stalingrad in 1942. Or Billy Sing, the celebrated Chinese-Australian sniper, credited with more than two hundred kills (and many suspect it's closer to three hundred), who in the 1915 Battle of Gallipoli put a bullet between the eyes of the Turkish sniper Abdul the Terrible at the same moment the other sniper was also targeting him.

Sometimes, a sniper's mission is exactly like that. But not very often.

That classic Vietnam-era picture is a view of the sniper as the ace of spades. In the reality of twenty-first-century combat, a Spec Ops sniper is more often called upon to serve as the whole deck of cards.

There is a reason for the mystique and fascination that surrounds the military sniper. Sniping is a concrete set of specific skills and training, yet at the same time it is also something more. Elite sniper training aims to develop in this warfighter a set of capabilities that is as close to omniscience and omnipotence as a human being can get. A combat sniper must have an exceptional grasp of every aspect of the field of war, from the overall tactical picture to the finest detail, and be able to function in effect as an entire military operation rolled into a single individual: an army of one.

The modern sniper needs to be a master of close quarters combat, close-range raids, kill/capture, and overwatch/protection of assault teams. He or she must of course also have a complete grasp of long-range marksmanship skills and all that entails. And finally there's the high-risk reconnaissance and surveillance toolbox, because a sniper is first and foremost an intelligence asset. Many of the sniper's most important missions will happen behind enemy lines and without ever firing a shot—though when called upon to do so, he (or she) must be 100 percent prepared, on an instant's notice, to fire that shot and do so with superhuman accuracy, whether at a distance of more than a mile or less than a hundred yards. And mere competence is as good (or rather, as bad) as useless here. The modern sniper needs to possess absolute mastery of all three broad skill sets: advanced assaulter, infallible marksman, and recon operator.

Warrior, assassin, spy.

Over the days and weeks ahead Morrison, Furlong, Delgado, and Irving would play all these roles, sometimes shifting from one to another in a span of minutes. Sometimes in a matter of seconds.

The Somali coast, February 27, 1995

Alex Morrison ate up the minutes by thinking through a range of potential scenarios he might face in the next few days.

He was packing a McMillan M88 .50 cal sniper rifle, a precursor of the big TAC-50 that Rob Furlong would carry into Afghanistan exactly seven years later. The M88, while not quite as large or heavy as the TAC-50, was damn close. Billed as accurate on targets up to two thousand yards, Alex's LRSW (long-range sniper weapon) was shooting a high-explosive Raufoss Mark 211 armor-piercing incendiary round with a muzzle velocity of close to three thousand feet per second.

This was the gun SEALs had used to disable Manuel Noriega's aircraft during the invasion of Panama. It was, in the words of another SEAL who had used it, "a beast."

At the same time, it was a bitch to operate. A single-shot weapon, it was the antithesis of the beautifully efficient semiauto mechanisms we would come to know and love (and rely on) in later years. With the M88, you had to haul out the bolt (that's pull *out,* not just *back,* as in, actually remove it from the rifle), then put in a round, fit the bolt back into the gun and jack it, aim, shoot, then remove the bolt, knock out the spent brass, slip in a new round, and shoot. Not exactly rapid fire—and definitely not as fast as you need it to be when you're in a firefight.

Which shouldn't be a problem, though, right? According to their briefing, no major violence was expected. This was a peaceful withdrawal of troops. Their role was not to fight but to serve as a tactical show of force. A deterrent, in other words: to prevent violence, not to wage it.

Except that this was *Somalia*. The place was stark raving nuts. Alex and every other man sitting on those bench seats in the dark knew that anything could happen, and probably would. *Guess we'll find out soon enough,* he thought. *Meanwhile. . . .*

Nothing drives a SEAL so crazy as being in a position where he cannot act. But for the moment, there wasn't much choice here. Sardines it was.

So they sat in the dark, rocking like bobblehead toys, plowing through the roughening sea state with visions in their heads of something going wrong and the whole goddamn hovercraft sinking, MILVAN and all. SEALs generally are not overly fussed by the prospect of their own imminent death, but Alex couldn't help thinking that drowning in a tin can off the coast of Somalia would be a decidedly UNSAT way to go.

Shahikot Valley, March 4, 2002

Anaconda. The op was named after one of the largest snakes in the world, one that kills its prey by wrapping it in its coils and squeezing it into submission. Which was the general plan here, in what would be the first large-scale offensive in the new war.

Americans had gone into Afghanistan directly after 9/11 to hunt down and kill or capture the masterminds who had perpetrated the attacks. At the same time, we were skittish about going in with too big a presence. We didn't want to do anything that would evoke memories of how the Soviet Union invaded and occupied this land of rocks and poppies in the eighties. At the height of its occupation the Soviet Bear had 120,000 troops on the ground here. We had so far dropped in barely a few hundred Spec Ops guys. We were being very cautious—as many would later point out, a little too cautious.

The attempt to round up Al Qaeda leaders and key Taliban figures at Tora Bora in December had been a dismal failure: the bad guys all slipped through the noose. The solution: build a better noose, one with more armed muscle from the U.S. and its allies. That was Anaconda.

The plan went like this. One group, code name Hammer, would attack the Shahikot Valley, where it was believed some key leaders had gone into hiding, from the northwest, driving the enemy into the waiting arms of a second, larger group, code name Anvil, which would prevent their escape—the anaconda's coils. Hammer was comprised mostly of Afghan troops, supported by U.S. Special Forces "advisors" and supplemented by airpower. Anvil, which would sweep in from the south and northeast and lie in wait in a semicircle ringing the southwestern escape routes, was made up of hundreds of conventional forces, mostly U.S. 101st Airborne and Tenth Mountain Division infantry, supplemented by Australian Special Air Service (SAS), Navy SEALs and Delta Force, unnamed special and covert operators . . . and six Canadian snipers.

Including one who was fresh out of sniper school.

A hunter from the Canadian outback, Furlong is a deceptively ordinary-looking guy. Five-eleven, average build, blond (though these days he wears his head shaved bald), pale blue eyes. Soft-spoken, chooses words with care and speaks in measured tones. Lying on the cool floor of that stillwater pond is a fighter who is as comfortably at home in a brawl as he is in front of a computer console. Not a guy likely to start a fight, perhaps, but sure as hell knows how to finish one. Five years earlier he'd held down a job punching computer keys. Now he was one of his country's top military trigger-pullers.

The Princess Patricia's Canadian Light Infantry, or PPCLI, was about two thousand soldiers strong; Rob's unit, the Third Battalion, was functionally the rough equivalent to the U.S. Army's 75th Ranger Regiment, Nick Irving's unit. The Patricias earned their motto "First in the field" by being the first Canadian unit deployed in 1914 in the Great War. Now, a century later, they were doing it again.

After the events of September 11, some nine hundred Canadian forces had deployed in support of the brand-new War on Terror. Of those nine hundred, just six would be handpicked to be part of the highly secret operation in the Shahikot Valley. On February 1, the ink barely dry on his sniper school certificate, Rob was in Edmonton, Alberta, buying a new home with his wife. The next day he was on a plane to Germany, destination Afghanistan.

"Five minutes out!"

When Rob and his five companions took off for Bagram on March 3, they'd been the only ones on the big C-17. It was an eerie sight: the big ramp coming down, revealing that chasmic interior, and just the six of them walking up, like earthlings entering the spacecraft in *Close Encounters of the Third Kind*. Other than pilot and crew, they were the only ones on the plane.

This was going to be a twenty-four-hour mission; at least, that's what their briefing had told them. Those responsible for planning Operation Anaconda didn't think there were more than a few hundred fighters in the valley (as it turned out, it was more like a few thousand), and did not expect much resistance (wrong again). Expectation was that within two days the insurgents would be negotiating their surrender, reflecting the view at the very top of the command food chain, which was that Afghanistan was by now pretty much a wrap.

As they reached the top of the C-17's ramp and its servomotor ground to life and began raising it again, a Canadian officer ran out onto the tarmac, his arms full of equipment. "Hey!" he shouted out as he ran toward the aircraft. "You guys! You gotta wear helmets!" He reached the plane and stood there, catching his breath. "And—here," he puffed as he held up the mass of gear. "You need—your flak vests."

Rob and the other snipers looked at each other, then back at the officer.

"Yeah," said one of them, "we don't wear that shit."

The ramp closed, leaving officer and gear standing on the tarmac.

Husaybah, April 17, 2004

Jason Delgado is about as opposite a personality from Rob Furlong as you could possibly invent. Five-nine, lean, a coiled spring with 1,000 volts running through it. He doesn't just talk, he shoots strings of profanity-laced Puerto-Rican-accented Bronx patter like a one-man machine gun team doing a turn onstage at the Improv. Listen closer, though, and you'll hear a fine-tuned intelligence behind the words.

Delgado started out in life with a hell of an inner-city Latino chip on his shoulder, but years of hard training in the U.S. Marine Corps obliterated it and honed his volatile temperament to an even-tempered razor edge. This is a guy who knows how to look at anything, anyone, any situation, see past the bullshit of appearances and into the heart of the matter. That mix of skills and temperament had gotten him to where he was, the leader of his platoon—and it was also what told him that no matter what anyone else said, something evil was brewing in the streets of Husaybah.

Start in Husaybah and follow the Euphrates River as it meanders southeast. After some two hundred miles you'll come to a string of large cities: Ramadi, Fallujah, Baghdad. That was exactly the path taken throughout 2004 by a steady procession of contraband and war-making resources. Like drugs coming in through Miami and working their way up the East Coast to the streets of New York, fighters and weapons and ammo were pouring in over the border from Syria, through Husaybah, and flowing their way along the Euphrates and out to what would become the major flashpoints of the unfolding insurgency for years to come.

But we didn't realize this yet. When Jason Delgado took his M40 to the can to brush his teeth and start his day on April 17, 2004, it was barely a year since Saddam had fallen. The invasion was long over. We'd won. Hell, Delgado had been there in Baghdad's Firdos Square providing security when his commander, Bryan McCoy, threw a rope around Saddam's statue and pulled it down. He had seen with his own eyes the ecstatic citizens of Iraq screaming with joy, throwing the Americans flowers, bringing them baskets of food. It was like being an American GI at the liberation of Paris in 1945. *Ding dong, the dictator's dead.* Or if not quite dead, sure as hell ousted. Now it was just a matter of rebuilding infrastructure, winning hearts and minds, helping the country get back on its feet.

At least, that was the playbook. For close to two months now, Delgado and his boys had been playing border-town cop, trying to keep the peace while the U.S. government provided computers to the local schools and soccer balls for their soccer fields ("they were gonna hug all these people and kill 'em with rainbows," as Jason puts it), still under the impression that the "war" phase of the Iraq operation was well behind us, that our mission there now was purely one of aid and transition to a new civil society.

Delgado had a gut sense that impression was about to change.

Helmand Province, July 9, 2009

Nick Irving is a fairly short guy. "I used to be six foot two," he likes to say, "but jumping out of planes and doing fully loaded ruck marches compressed me down to five seven." As a teen he was so scrawny the other kids dubbed him Stick Figure. But Nick exemplifies the concept of mind over matter. Through years of training he has built his body up to the point that he looks more like Mr. T than Steve Urkel. Mr. T with a well-used sniper rifle. You do not want to mess with this dude.

He is also one of the best shots I've ever seen. He has targets set up all over his house, and dry-fires at them constantly. This guy could shoot in the Olympics, that's how dedicated to the craft he is. The man is a born sniper.

Still, it had taken him years to get where he was now. During his first few deployments he had served in every role from door-kicker and Stryker driver to machine gunner and .50 cal gunner, before going through Ranger school and earning his ranger tab. It was only in the past year that he had finally gone through formal sniper training—months and months of it. Now, in his final deployment, he was the leader of his sniper unit, a warfighter come into his element.

The timing could not have been better, because the situation Nick dropped into in the spring of 2009 was a unique one, and uniquely demanded someone of his skills.

Earlier that year the White House had announced that it planned to send a surge of forces to Afghanistan, maybe as many as seventeen thousand American troops, because the situation there was deteriorating. By the end of that summer the number would exceed twenty thousand.

On July 2, just before dawn, more than four thousand marines poured into the northern portion of Helmand Province in an effort to clear insurgents from the area before the country's forthcoming presidential election. It was the largest offensive airlift of marines since Vietnam. Officially the op was called Operation Khanjar, or Strike of the Sword. In the way these things do, though, it soon acquired a catchier nickname.

"You're going to change the world this summer and it starts this morning," the commander of the Second Battalion, Eighth Marines Regiment told his men as they prepared to board helicopters. "The United States and the world are watching. Their expectations are enormously high during this *summer of decision.*"

Summer of Decision it was.

According to the press, no Western troops had been in this area. As one captain was quoted, "We are kind of forging new ground here. We are going to a place nobody has been before." Dramatic—but not quite accurate. Nick and his fellow rangers had been there for months, taking out as many insurgents and high-value targets as possible, cleaning house and paving the way for the marine sweep of the region. The same day that Operation Khanjar launched, Nick was recruited by a scruffy team of deep-reconnaissance operators to venture out into no-man's-land with them, deep in the province where few if any Westerners had dared to tread, and be their long gun.

Right now he was no more than thirty miles south of the marines' sweep. A half-hour drive, if you had decent roads. Which they didn't.

Nick didn't know anything about this larger strategic context. That was all above his pay grade, and in combat the generals don't tend to spell out the larger picture for the fighters on the ground. All Nick knew was that they were there to kill or capture as many bad guys as they could. And that had proven to be quite a few. He figured his unit had taken out close to a thousand enemy fighters during the months leading up to today. On one operation he and Pemberton had killed six Taliban commanders in a single night, effectively shutting down the Tali operation in Marjah for a week and a half.

Still, nothing he'd done had entirely prepared him for where he was right now.

He was about to get into the fight of his life.

Shahikot Valley, March 4, 2002

"Three minutes out!"

As the Chinook approached their preassigned drop point Rob Furlong heard the front gunner's M240 roar to life, its percussive GA-GA-GA-GA-GA-GA-GA-GA-GA shattering his thoughts. He had just enough time to wonder what the hell the guy was shooting at when he saw a stream of bright green tracers zipping up toward them and past the chopper's little porthole window.

He felt the aircraft veer sharply off to the right. They were taking fire.

They hadn't even reached their LZ yet and the mission was already going wrong.

The war was on.

2
BORN TO SHOOT

As a young'n, I'd go sit in the woods and wait a spell. I'd just wait for the rabbits and squirrels, 'cause sooner or later a squirrel would be in that very tree or a rabbit would be coming by that very log. I just knew it. Don't know why, just did.

—Carlos Hathcock

The U.S. Naval Special Warfare (SEAL) sniper program, the U.S. Marine Scout Sniper Basic Course, the U.S. Army sniper programs, and all the other courses of sniper instruction, both military and civilian, that we'll explore in this book are among the most sophisticated, difficult, and exhaustive training programs in the world. But they don't make a sniper a sniper, not in and of themselves. To a great extent, expert snipers are born more than made.

The Killing School happens in three phases, not all of them necessarily recognized as such. You might think of these as primary school, high school, and grad school. The first, primary school, phase is over and done with by the time you enlist in the armed services.

It's what in ordinary society you'd call "childhood."

The eldest of six kids, Rob Furlong grew up on Fogo Island, Newfoundland, a dot of land off the eastern coast of Canada, a place so remote it has its own time zone. His town (total population: maybe three hundred) was a community of fishermen, men toughened by bitter weather and a difficult life. Rob's dad was a member of the Department of Fisheries and Oceans, or, as they are referred to locally, the fish cops. Law enforcement in a town perched on the outer edge of civilization isn't the easiest job. Rob learned how to use his fists from an early age.

Rob spent the better part of his childhood in the great outdoors, either fishing on the water, hunting moose with his dad out in the woods, or cutting firewood to heat the family home. From the time he could walk he could navigate his way around the wilderness using the stars, plants' direction of growth, and the rest of the expert tracker's lexicon.

He was seven years old when he got his first gun, a pump-action BB gun. To Rob it felt like he'd been given ownership of a Ferrari. He couldn't imagine treasuring anything more than he did that BB gun. Still, it didn't take long to realize how underpowered his pump-action gun was, and by age nine Rob had moved up to a pellet gun. Now his dad started taking the time to school him in proper sight alignment and how to adjust his aim for shooting at greater distances. Rob had never heard the term *marksmanship principles* and would have had no idea what it meant if he did. He just wanted to be able to shoot well and hit birds.

Every day when Rob got home from school, he would take his pellet gun and a can of pellets and go out into their backyard—and in Rob's case "backyard" meant acres and acres of unfenced forest—and practice shooting at birds, wooden targets, or whatever he could find to shoot at. Often his little brother would go with him, bringing his own gun along and shooting alongside Rob. They would catch small tomcods, a North Atlantic fish, and lay them on a piece of wood for target practice. After a while the little fish would attract flies.

One day Rob said to his brother, "Hey, why shoot the fish? Let's try to shoot the flies!"

So they graduated from shooting at the fish to shooting at the flies. Every so often one of them would cry out, "I think I hit one!" and they would run over together to examine the board for a fresh pellet hole and pieces of fly. "Yeah," one would say, "I think that's something right there!" Rob says he has honestly no idea if they ever really hit one of those little buzzing flies or not. But, he adds, they did sometimes find little fly remnants.

As their aim steadily improved they made the targets more and more difficult. Rob started stringing up old oil cans and bottles with pieces of fishing line, and they would try to make the can drop by severing the piece of line with a pellet. Shot after shot, Rob continually worked at refining his accuracy. It might take him up to 150 pellets to successfully hit and break a piece of line, but the sense of achievement and satisfaction he got every time he saw one of those cans suddenly drop made the effort well worth it.

Rob's family was not exactly wealthy—this was a single-income home with six kids to feed on a small-town cop salary—and being given those pellet guns was a big deal for him and his brother. They cherished those guns. (In fact, the guns still sit today in his parents' home in the exact same spot where they always kept them as kids.) When he first took possession of the gun, Rob carefully sanded down the stock, painted it jet black, refinished it, then mounted a few studs onto the stock so he could rig a sling on it. Sometimes a whole bunch of kids would get together, seven or eight of them, and all go out shooting together. But Rob was the only one who ever took the time and care to refinish or refurbish his gun.

Why did he feel compelled to do that?

"I don't know," he says. "I just did. There was a sniper inside me."

While Rob Furlong's primary school was happening in the northern wilderness, Jason Delgado's was taking place in the mean streets of the Bronx. In the eighties, the Bronx was a world controlled principally by crack cocaine, crime, and violence. The landscape of Delgado's youth was littered with junkyards and abandoned buildings. The younger kids called them "clubhouses." To older kids, they were places of business. Stabbings, slashings, and shootings were routine events to Jason and his friends; the available figures to look up to as heroes were typically big-time dope dealers who drove around in mammoth Cadillacs and sported flashy wardrobes pimped out with mink accents.

One day when Jason was five years old, he was sitting on a car with his cousins across the street from his father's auto body garage while his uncle worked on his dad's mint-green Cadillac. A strung-out-looking guy walked up, pulled out a sawed-off shotgun, put it to the back of the uncle's head, and pulled the trigger, then ran off in the direction he'd come from.

Jason's mother grabbed the kids and ushered them into their house a block away, where they sat for a while, crying, hugging, and consoling one another, while the adults scrambled to make sure they were all safe. Which of course they weren't.

Two years later Jason awoke one night to the loud hiss and squawk of a two-way radio. He stumbled sleepy-eyed out into the living room, squinting at the living room lights, and found two police officers hovering over his mother, who was hysterical past the point of coherence. A turf war of some sort had broken out between rival dealers, lighting up the entire block with automatic weapons fire and riddling their home with bullets. One round had entered their house and grazed his mother's head as she lay asleep on the living room couch before lodging itself in the far wall.

Jason's mother and father were good parents, but they had to work constantly just to make ends meet, so the two Delgado boys grew up more or less in the streets, forced to fend for themselves and learn the law of the jungle, urban style.

A life of crime seemed like one of the few career paths open to these kids, and Jason had relatives who walked on the other side of the law. But events like his uncle's murder sparked a sort of generational shift. Something inside them said this wasn't fair, that they didn't want to be victims anymore. They wanted guns, but they wanted to be the ones with the guns who were protecting their mothers and families from the evil shit—not the ones *doing* the evil shit. His two oldest cousins grew up to become police officers, one a sergeant in the NYPD. Jason thought about that, too. But run-ins and hassles with the neighborhood cops left him uneasy with law enforcement.

When Jason was about nine years old, he and a friend, an African American kid his age, were walking home one day from a Boys and Girls Club on Fordham Road when a squad car squealed up and turned sharply onto their sidewalk, cutting them off. Two white officers jumped out, threw them against the wall, and started frisking the two kids. Jason's friend asked the cops why they were being searched, and one of the cops said, "Shut the fuck up, kid."

The friend said, "You can't be doing this shit to us."

The cop spun him around and smacked him across the face. "Watch your mouth, you little shit," he said. They let the two kids go. Jason still remembers walking home, tears running down his face, talking with his friend and trying to make sense out of what had happened.

When Jason was fourteen he joined a cadet organization called Third Recon Battalion, named after a U.S. Marine battalion that fought in Vietnam.

The brainchild of a vet named Sean Godbolt, Third Recon was created to give kids something to do after school. More specifically, something to keep them out of trouble. All the facilitators were Vietnam vets, and the organization was highly structured to duplicate the military with complete accuracy. Jason and his compadres learned how to write five-paragraph orders, plan and conduct missions, go through gear checks, and conduct themselves with military precision. All the acronyms used were the same as in the real military. Not only were they learning the trappings of military behavior, but more importantly, they were instilled with a strong sense of pride and the desire to serve.

The kids would go out to Van Cortlandt Park and camp out for days, plan missions, do reconnaissance on other cadet groups. They would troll for intel throughout the week, listening carefully to anything they could pick up, in the schoolyard or neighborhoods, find out when and where the other kids were going to be doing their patrols so they could ambush them. It was complete guerrilla warfare with paintball guns.

"We would build hide sites out there," says Jason, "and I'd wait out there in my ghillie suit with my scoped-out Tippmann Pro Lite paintball rifle. We would wait for other cadet organizations to come out there to set up camp, and when they got within range, I would scope those guys and let one fly.

"I was being groomed for a career as a military sniper and didn't even realize it."

Godbolt, the program's founder, also served as the first major role model for Jason who wasn't a drug dealer. Charismatic and motivational, he was probably the only clear positive influence in Jason's life during those years, other than his own parents.

"He never looked at us as children," says Jason. "He treated us as young men."

Like Rob Furlong, Nick Irving had his first experiences in shooting early on, when at the age of six his dad took him out into the west Georgia woods to show his boy how to shoot his 20-gauge shotgun. Nick couldn't even lift the damn thing, much less hold or aim it by himself. His father stood behind him, cradled the foregrip, set the buttstock into his son's shoulder pocket, and held it in place while Nick pulled the trigger.

From that first shot, Nick was in love. He was good at it, too. Even in those early years when he was too little to hold the gun up by himself, more times than not he hit what he was aiming at. ("Of course," he points out, "this was birdshot, so we're talking about casting a pretty wide net.")

Before long his dad had given him a .22, and he practiced on it as often as he could—which was not often enough for him. Nick grew up in Maryland, just off Fort Meade Army base where his parents worked, but his family on his mother's side is from deep-country Georgia and they would typically spend their summers there. Nick spent those summer months learning how to hunt, fish, make his way around the woods—and shoot.

During the school year he had to content himself with an awful lot of dry-firing to keep his skills from getting rusty. But every summer, he and the .22 would be inseparable. He would sneak cigarettes from his grandfather, go outside and carefully set them up, then walk back a hundred paces, turn, take aim, and shoot at them. By the time he reached high school he was pretty decent at shooting those cigarettes in half.

In addition to his .22, he continued practicing with the shotgun. His father had gotten that 20-gauge as a present from *his* father, and on Nick's fifteenth birthday it now became the grandson's. Nick was a fairly expert shot by this time, and now his dad taught him how to disassemble the big gun. Every day after school, Nick would take the shotgun apart and then put it back together again, timing himself to see how quickly he could do it and still get it right. Before long he could practically do it in his sleep.

Nick wasn't especially into hunting per se. What he loved was that sense of controlled precision, the mastery and elegant simplicity that came with expert marksmanship. For years he had been watching shows on the History Channel about warfare and military operations, especially Vietnam. Carlos Hathcock, who had redefined the sniper's art in the modern era, became Nick's hero. The young boy watched Hathcock interviews over and over. He made his first ghillie suit in middle school, taping lengths of his mom's sewing yarn onto the back of a black jumpsuit. Now he started making regular trips to the library, devouring every book he could find that might enhance his skill and understanding, including everything from math textbooks to books on Special Operations Forces in Vietnam.

"I wanted to be a sniper," says Nick, "for as long as I can remember."

Unlike these other guys, I didn't shoot guns when I was a kid, and I had no aspiration to become a sniper. Other than shooting clay pigeons off the bow of the dive boat where I worked as a teenager, I'd never really handled a rifle until they thrust one into my hands in the middle of BUD/S.

For me, it was spearguns.

When I started working on the dive boat I was hungry to learn, and I began tagging along with Mike Roach, the captain, and Jim Hralbak, the second captain, shadowing these two, watching them closely as they would stalk and shoot their prey. It took me a while to follow exactly what was going on. We'd be swimming along, and all of a sudden—*whooshhhh, thwap!*—one of them had shot something I hadn't even seen. Where the hell had that *that* come from? But before long, I started picking it up, too.

Spearfishing is physical in a very intuitive way. There's no scope, no crosshairs to peer through. As with traditional bow hunting, you're just using natural point of aim. What's more, you're shooting a relatively thick steel shaft, and since you're in the water, that shaft meets a great deal more resistance from the medium it flies through than a bullet hurtling through air. As a result, you can't shoot out to a range of more than twelve feet. Which means you really have to master the use of stealth, if you want to stalk close enough to your prey to shoot it without spooking it first.

I was barely thirteen when I started. By the time I was fourteen I was a pretty accomplished spearfisherman. The Fish and Game guys gave me a hard time for a while. They didn't believe that all these fish I was pulling in were really all my own catches. Since the law didn't require a fishing license until you turned fifteen, they thought I was covering for what were actually other people's catches. But that didn't last for long. Once they got to know me, they started to believe me when I told them these were all my own.

It takes a certain kind of person to make a top military sniper, and it may not be the kind you'd expect. Furlong, Delgado, and Irving all had a powerful affinity for rifles and shooting from an early age—but that was not what made them born snipers. At least, not entirely. Having a natural feel for long guns was certainly part of it, but not nearly enough. There are plenty of great marksmen in the world, match shooters who can do a kickass job on a rifle range but would be useless in the heat and fog of live-action combat, or incapable of the patience and mental stamina it takes to absorb and process massive amounts of information and observation.

Being a sniper is not the same thing as being a marksman. In today's warfare, a sniper is first and foremost an intelligence asset. Which means that as important as shooting is to a sniper, it's less about how to use a gun, more about how to use your eyes, and even more about how to use your brain.

Every great sniper seems to have some quality, skill, or attribute that has nothing to do with shooting but everything to do with mastering the sniper's craft.

For Nick Irving, it was chess.

Nick still remembers his first game on that sixty-four-square board, which he played with his dad when he was three years old. His parents had both worked in army intelligence during the Cold War era, and his father had a deep love for the game of chess. He told his son that chess was a "brain game" and that playing it would make you smarter. Nick liked the sound of that. So as often as they could, Nick's father would take out his beautiful old German board with its hand-carved oak pieces, and they would play.

In fact, the two still play chess when Nick's father comes to Nick's home on their customary Thanksgiving visit.

"Every Thanksgiving, we play chess," says Nick. "And every Thanksgiving, he beats me. To this day, I still can't beat my dad."

What he could do was absorb the game, and the long-range strategic thinking at its core, into his bones. Like Philip Marlowe, Raymond Chandler's iconic private eye, Nick spent hours studying the games of the masters and playing games with himself. And the more he studied chess, the more it reminded him of the sniper's art. It was all about strategy and planning, he realized. Just like shooting.

In later years, his love of chess informed the way he approached his missions in the field.

"I think the reason I eventually got so much action," he says, "was that I played my mission planning a lot like chess. In chess, you always have to think two steps, three steps, four steps ahead. I'd think, *Okay, say I'm at this spot—if something happened over here, where would I immediately go?*"

Before the firefight even started, he would set himself up with his team where he figured the enemy was *going* to be after it broke out, having worked out ahead of time where he would be if he were the other guy. Nine times out of ten, that would turn out to be right where they were. Nick says he reached close to a 100 percent success rate with that chess-based approach to planning his ops.

For Delgado, it was art.

By the time Jason was in second grade he was constantly doodling, drawing caricatures and cartoon strips. That in itself was no big deal; a lot of kids doodled and drew. But early on Jason realized he had some ability here; he could do things with a set of colored pencils that his classmates couldn't. Soon drawing was absorbing the lion's share of his time and attention at school, which seemed like a good thing to him, because otherwise he was generally bored out of his mind.

In later years, when he took college art courses, he learned more about the technical aspects of art, the interplay of light and shadow, scale and perspective, the hierarchy of primary, secondary, and tertiary colors. But long before he had any formal schooling in it, he was already perfecting his craft.

Drawing taught Delgado how to pay attention to every last detail of a scene. If the girl he was drawing had one hair out of place, he would draw her with that one hair exactly out of place. He learned how to faithfully reproduce exactly what he saw—and how to see with far greater accuracy than most.

That sense of visual detail had a huge impact on how Jason worked on the battlefield.

"I have a range finder in my head," says Jason. "If you point out an object in the distance, I can call it to within yards." This was enormously useful in shooting, of course, but also in reconnaissance. Snipers in the field spend a great deal more time in observation than they do on the gun, and the ability to sketch out a scene accurately is critical. In a sheerly technical sense, Jason was able to knock out field sketches of extremely large areas with almost architectural accuracy.

Beyond that, his art also had a profound impact on how he observed situations overall, how details fit together and what they meant, what made sense and what did not. It gave him an uncanny sense of how to read a complex scene.

A skill that would prove critical in Husaybah.

Rob Furlong didn't draw, and he didn't play chess. For Rob it wasn't anything so specific as an artistic skill. It was more the mix of attributes that came from growing up in such a wild and untamed environment, which produced in him that unique sniper's mind-set: whip-smart, focused like a laser, and cussedly independent.

Snipers come in all stripes. You'll find oversize extrovert personalities like the Luttrell brothers and quiet, still-water-runs-deep guys like Chris Kyle. Politically conservative, politically liberal, and politically I-don't-give-a-shit. Brutally aggressive and surprisingly gentle. But one thing we all seem to share in common: a sort of love-hate thing with authority. That is, a deep respect for truly great leadership, and total intolerance for shitty leadership. SEALs have more of a reputation for being, how to say this politely, resistant to conformity, marine and army Spec Ops less so. But Spec Ops is Spec Ops and snipers are snipers: by definition, we exist to function off the reservation.

And independent: that was Rob.

Aside from being big into sports—hockey, basketball, baseball, whatever came along—his interests were focused. He loved to be outdoors; he loved to fish; he loved to hunt. And growing up in the wilds of Fogo Island, he couldn't have avoided developing a seriously independent nature. (Again, a place with their own freaking time zone, ninety minutes ahead of New York and Toronto!)

In school he leaned toward numbers more than words; math and physics held some fascination, and in his teens he got into computers. That would provide him a job, for a while at least, though not a career. But in numbers themselves, the numbers of windage and elevation, range and terminal ballistics: that's where he would find a calling.

Like me, Alex Morrison never shot a rifle until he was in BUD/S. Also like me, though, Alex grew up on the California coast with a speargun in his hands—except that in Alex's case it was a not speargun but a *polespear,* which is essentially like shooting a spear with a slingshot. When you see someone hunting fish with nothing but a rubber-band-powered spear in his hand, you know you are looking at a man who is dead serious about hunting.

And that's a crucial point. Understand that it's not about shooting. Hunting isn't shooting. Hunting is, more than anything else, the art of the stalk. Hunting fish with a spear means you have to master the skill sets of stealth, invisibility, and empathy.

Empathy? That's right. To get within striking distance of a fish, a primitive creature that is about as perfectly designed to be a danger-detection machine as anything on the planet, it's not enough to be sneaky. You have to have an innate sense of what that fish is sensing and feeling. It verges on the telepathic. A sniper has to know the mind of his prey almost as well as the prey himself. Or better.

And that was Alex's chess, his artwork, his uniquely born-to-shoot quality. As far back as he can remember, he was always driven by a burning desire to be in the great outdoors, to travel, to seek adventure—

and, more than anything else, to hunt. Military snipers are sometimes called the "big-game hunters of the battlefield." Those six words express perfectly what it was that led Alex from the polespear to sniper school.

For Alex, it was always a given that he would join the military. Growing up in a marine household where jarheads were the premier fighting men, he always assumed he'd join the marines and become part of Force Recon, the marines' deep-reconnaissance and direct-action Spec Ops unit. Until one day in 1984, when his parents pointed out that one of his karate instructors served in Vietnam as a SEAL.

"What's a *seal*?" asked Alex, thinking that sounded pretty ridiculous.

"Those are the guys who eat Force Recon marines for breakfast," said his mom.

His dad nodded. "Yup." (Disclaimer to my marine friends: no disrespect intended—I'm just reporting what his parents told him.)

That was that. Alex was fifteen years old at the time; three years later he graduated from high school and went straight into navy boot camp, where he did the SEAL selection.

Unlike Alex, Rob Furlong had absolutely no inkling that he was headed for the military. It just seemed to unfold on its own.

One day in the fall of 1997, Rob found himself kicking around town with no clear destination. He'd been up for twenty-four hours (full day at school followed by the night shift at his security job) and wasn't thinking about much. He was, frankly, a little bored with his life. Going to college, doing some computer programming, working a part-time security gig at a compound down on the waterfront. His twenty-first birthday was coming up and he wasn't that thrilled with where his life seemed to be going. Rob liked computers, had spent a lot of time on them, but it was clear that computer programming just wasn't his thing. Every spare minute he could eke out he spent outside, going hunting when he could. He was looking for something, but didn't know what.

As he ambled down the street he came upon a big sandwich board out on the sidewalk. He stopped and read the board. It sported a recruitment ad for the Canadian Armed Forces.

Rob had grown up shooting, but the thought of joining the army had never occurred to him. The military didn't have much of a presence in rural Newfoundland, and the idea seemed almost foreign. But there it was, staring him in the face. What could it hurt to look?

He walked into the recruiting center. A navy officer asked him why he was there.

"I'm interested," he said.

The guy ushered Rob into a room with a television and VCR, a few chairs, and four or five dozen VHS tapes lying around on tables. Told him he should feel free to pop in whichever tapes interested him and watch the brief introductory clips about each branch and trade within the service. And then walked out, leaving Rob with the cassettes and player.

Rob started popping videos in and out, watching bits and pieces. Some were pretty ho-hum, and a few piqued his interest. One of these showed a bunch of young men in green, running around, shooting and blowing stuff up, and jumping out of planes. *Infantry,* he thought. He didn't know much about the armed forces, but he did know that infantry was the point of entry.

Then, as he sat there watching, an image came on the screen that made him sit up straight. There was a guy dressed in some kind of camouflage outfit with pieces of vegetation stuck to him, crawling along the ground.

The guy was *stalking.*

At this point Rob knew absolutely nothing about snipers, who they were or what they did. He'd never heard the name Carlos Hathcock or the term "ghillie suit." But he knew what hunting was, all right, he knew that as well as he knew his own name, and he felt an instantaneous connection with the image on that television screen.

A few minutes later Rob strolled out of that little viewing room, walked over to the recruitment officer's desk, and tossed his application onto the man's desk, fully filled out.

"Here you go," he said. He walked out and headed home to get some sleep.

A few months later Rob got a call from the recruiting office. "Hey," the guy said, "we have an opening in the infantry. Are you still interested?"

Hell yeah! thought Rob. What he said was, "Sure. Let's do it."

"Okay," the guy said. "You leave in two weeks."

And that was that.

Rob hadn't expected it to happen so fast, or even known whether it would happen at all. He hadn't told anyone he'd applied, not even his family, with whom he was quite close. He knew it would come as a surprise to his folks. There was absolutely no military history in his background; the Furlongs had mostly been seafarers, working as captains or mates on tankers or long-haul boats.

He called his parents and said, "Oh, hey, I'm joining the army."

*   *   *

For Jason Delgado, it was a moment that did it, a moment that happened when he was just nine.

Back in mid-January 1991, when Coalition forces began aerial bombardments of Saddam's forces and Desert Shield turned into Desert Storm, Jason was glued to the television. The first Gulf War was the watershed event that established the kind of round-the-clock live news coverage we've come to see as normal, and Jason would watch for hours. One day he saw a short clip, shot in night vision perspective, that showed tracer rounds going off and smacking a building while a team of soldiers penetrated the structure.

Oh my God, he thought, *this is the real deal.*

Sitting there in his living room, watching that footage, Delgado found himself choked up with emotion. Death was imminent, yet here these guys were, plunging into battle. He was watching bravery in its rawest form. It was the moment he first recognized that he had feelings of patriotism. It dawned on him that no matter what one did in this world, there could be no greater act of bravery than to voluntarily go into a war zone and perform. Not even law enforcement would give him that. Yes, as a police officer there was a possibility he would patrol into seriously shitty situations. But as a soldier, his job would be to go willingly into hell and back.

It stayed with him.

A few years later he joined Godbolt's cadet organization and began the training that would eventually take him straight to Saddam's stronghold in Baghdad.

When he was sixteen Jason dropped out of high school. School had always bored him; it felt slow and monotonous, and nothing there held his attention. When the boredom got to be too much he would cut classes and go to the skate park or hit rails all day. (Like approximately one million other kids in New York, he thought he might go pro someday.) By the time he turned sixteen, the legal age for quitting school in New York, he was ready to go.

He made a deal with his mom: if she would let him drop out, he would get his GED. She agreed. Jason went after that GED with a vengeance, poured himself into the work in a way he'd never done in school. He'd bring home algebra textbooks and shut himself up in his room with them, look up the answers in the back of the book, reverse-engineer them, and work out how he could have gotten there from the original problem. Within a year he took the tests—nailed them the first time.

Then the question was: what now? He enrolled at Eugenio María de Hostos Community College, in the South Bronx, but after one semester there he was ready to move on. When he turned eighteen, he decided it was time to join the military. The army, he figured. Not for any special reason; he'd just always assumed that when he enlisted, he'd be going into the army.

But the army said no.

When he was eleven, Jason had slipped on some ice and blown out some cartilage between two cervical vertebrae. The damage was bad enough that it took surgery to correct, a procedure that involved taking some material from his hip and fusing it to his second cervical vertebra. The neck issue was one problem. Having dropped out of high school was another. Lack of a high school diploma, despite the fact that he'd gotten his GED, counted as a strike against him, and the two strikes together got him rejected. The army didn't want him.

He liked the idea of going into the navy to join the SEALs—but no dice there, either: he couldn't get approved for the Naval Special Warfare physical, and having no diploma was a disadvantage there, too.

The Marine Corps was a different story. For whatever reason, they proved the most lenient branch. Still, it wasn't a shoo-in. Jason had to go through a fairly elaborate process, visiting different specialists to get the signed waivers he needed, and it seemed like it took forever. For a period of months, it didn't look like he was going to get into the service at all.

"The day the Corps told me they were taking me?" he says. "That was the greatest news I ever got."

If you'd bumped into Nick Irving when he was six or seven and asked him what he wanted to be when he grew up, he would have said the same thing most of his male classmates would have said: "An astronaut." By the age of eight, though, he was starting to have a sense that he would someday join the military. Nick's dad was a big Chuck Norris fan and had some friends who were Green Berets and Delta Force; Nick had grown up on the *Delta Force* films. By age ten, all thoughts of being an astronaut behind him, he had decided that when he grew up, he wanted to be a Navy SEAL.

Still, this was a childhood dream more than any concrete plan. It wasn't until Nick was fourteen that the idea crystallized into hard reality, in a moment that came at a few minutes past nine o'clock on a sunny Tuesday morning.

Sitting in his seat in his tenth grade biology class, Nick's eyes were riveted on the television set the teacher had hastily switched on. The roomful of tenth graders all watched in silent horror as the World Trade Center towers came crumbling to the ground.

By the time that first period class was over, the third plane had crashed into the Pentagon. Nick's school was located off the Baltimore-Washington Parkway, close to NSA headquarters, and nobody knew just where the next target might be. There was no second period class that day. All the students were told to get up and leave the school immediately.

Nick knew right then that the U.S. would be going to war—and he knew right then that he was going to be part of it. *Hell, yeah,* he told himself as he and his best friend, Andre, started running the mile to his house, *I'm going to go fight.*

Of course he couldn't enlist yet; he was not quite fifteen at the time and still had to finish high school. But he could train like hell for it. And he did.

That year Nick went through the Naval Sea Cadet program down at Annapolis, and after that a sort of SEAL prep course called Baby SEALs, which involved passing the same physical fitness that actual SEAL candidates go through—five-hundred-yard swim in twelve and a half minutes, one-and-a-half-mile boot run in eleven and a half minutes, all the sit-ups, push-ups, pulls-ups, even its own mini–Hell Week. And even before this intensive training, Nick had poured hundreds of hours into studying the SEALs, watching History Channel documentaries and all the videos he could find, learning all about the men in the SOF community.

At the same time, Nick was also going through combat training of a whole different nature: he was getting into serious fistfights.

Not that he was intentionally instigating them. Far from it. Nick Irving is a quiet guy and would have seemed the unlikeliest full-time fighter. When he started playing peewee football in eighth grade, he was the smallest guy on the team, a spindly little guy whose nickname Stick Figure caught on and stuck. By his freshman year he weighed no more than ninety pounds; even as a high school senior he barely topped 105.

Starting in ninth grade, Nick got picked on. He never knew exactly why. "I didn't interact with the cool kids," he says. "Maybe they thought I had an attitude, that I thought I was better than everyone else. But I just liked keeping to myself." In tenth grade it got worse. By eleventh grade Nick started fighting back, and soon he had a reputation. Which seemed to make him even more of a target. By his senior year the fist-fights were happening every day, and his parents were having to take off from work to come rescue him at the bus stop at least a few times a week. One time a group of nearly fifty kids from the projects nearby gathered at the bus stop, waiting for him after school, some with knives, a few with guns. Nick's dad had to call out some of his friends, heavily armed themselves, to come out and break it up.

When graduation came in the summer of 2004, Nick was more than ready to leave his childhood behind and go become a SEAL. Since he was still seventeen, his parents had to sign a waiver allowing him to enter the service. He didn't even wait for the high school graduation parties. Once his parents signed that waiver, he was out the door.

And then, much like Delgado, he ran into a snag. The navy turned him down.

Turned out, Nick was color-blind.

"I had no idea," he says. "I knew there was some kind of issue with my vision, because I had a hard time telling some colors apart. But I'd always just thought it was that the lighting in our house sucked."

Which would have been the end of Nick's military aspirations right then and there—except that a sympathetic army nurse who heard what had happened must have seen something in Nick. Quietly pulling him to the side, she told him that the army had something similar to the SEALs. It was called, rangers.

Is it hard? the boy asked.

"Yeah," she said. "It's *very* hard."

Do they have snipers?

"Yes, they have snipers."

Good enough for Nick. The nurse surreptitiously guided him through the vision test, risking her job and changing the future fate of untold numbers of American soldiers whose lives would be saved by a sniper they dubbed The Reaper.

"I wish I knew that woman's name," says Nick. "I wish I could meet her, face-to-face, and thank her for going out on a limb for me. If it wasn't for her, I'd have no story to tell."

Two weeks after being handed his high school diploma, he was in Fort Benning, Georgia, starting the U.S. Army's basic training program.

3

HELL

Some of you young men think that war is all glamour and glory, but let me tell you, boys, it is all Hell.

—General William Tecumseh Sherman, addressing
the graduating class of Michigan Military Academy, June 1879

If the goal of military training is to prepare you for the hell of war, then there's really only one way that's going to work. The training is going to have to be hell, too.

Military training is like Dante's *Divine Comedy*: it's built on a progressive series of different levels of hell. These vary from branch to branch, but they follow the same broad pattern. There's basic hell, where whatever sloppiness you bring to the table is squeezed out of you, where you learn how to follow orders and fall into formation. Basic hell is where you start becoming military material. Boot camp, basic, infantry school, battle school—the names and curricula vary, but it all boils down to the same essential task: put you on the hot seat, burn away your civilian trappings, and harden you into a disciplined fighter.

And then there's advanced hell, where they turn up the heat and start tempering the steel inside you—if there is any steel there to temper.

There's nothing quite like going through a Special Operations school or advanced-level military course. It isn't just that you find out firsthand what hell really is, what it's like to go through an experience where seven or eight out of ten don't even make it through to the end of the course. It's that here in advanced hell, you are pushed to your absolute limits and then beyond, to the point where you discover that those limits aren't absolute at all. Where you experience pain so great it makes you pass out, and then you wake up and find out you're still here. And then you go through it all over again. And again. You find out what it is to die and then come back to life again . . . and that's just in order to graduate.

Which, if you do, means you get to go on to more training, which means more hell.

We have an expression: *You train harder than you fight.* And another: *The more you sweat in training, the less you bleed in combat.* Only that one isn't the whole truth. Sometimes you bleed in training, too.

For Rob Furlong, the first few circles of hell weren't so bad; it was more an experience of culture shock than one of real suffering.

Basic training in the Canadian infantry was much like basic military training everywhere: the new recruits were drilled in the fundamentals, including rank structure, conduct, basic formations, and weapons training. But all of that was secondary to the *real* training: being pounded, physically and verbally and emotionally, for days on end without letup. To Rob it was one two-month stretch of being yelled at, an experience he didn't find unpleasant so much as bewildering.

When confronted with a task, Rob is the kind of guy who simply does it, no overanalysis or complaint or pushback. He had always been an extremely pragmatic, goal-oriented person. Now he suddenly had these authority figures in his face, screaming at him, throwing his shit around, breaking things, and freaking out at him no matter what he did. It seemed like irrespective of how well he followed orders or how much effort he put out, the result was always the same.

One day, toward the start of month two, he put this conclusion to the test. That morning the master corporal came in and, as usual, ripped through all Rob's clothes, threw them around the room, and yelled at him to iron and fold it all over again. But Rob didn't do that. Instead, he just picked it all up off the floor, brushed it off, and stuck it all back on his shelf the way it was.

The next morning the master corporal came in, gave Rob's stuff a cursory glance, nodded, and said, "Good job, good work. Coming along," and left.

The screaming and punishment notwithstanding, Rob knew right away that he loved the army life. He finished out basic at the top of his class. When it came to shooting, his strongest competition was an experienced reservist who'd had a lot of time behind the C7, the Canadians' basic service rifle at the time, a carbine (shorter-barreled version) of an M16. That soldier already knew this rifle inside and out. Rob had never seen one before. The reservist took the top spot—but Rob took second.

After basic came six months of battle school, which drilled the ABCs of infantry life: tactics, survival, navigation, section maneuvers, more firearms and basic marksman training, explosives training . . . and physical training. PT: endless PT, endless pounding—like basic all over again only ratcheted up a notch.

"At battle school, you're garbage," recalls Rob. "You're just a piece of shit."

For the first month the instructors did everything they could to break the new guys. More than 50 percent of the class washed out. They brought in another class to fill the ranks, and lost half of those guys, too. Some broke mentally, others couldn't hack the sheer brutality of the endless rucksack marches. The attrition rate was vicious.

Rob was unaffected by any of it. When he got to battle school he was coasting on a flow of adrenaline. He could not wait to sink his teeth into the training. Getting up early in the morning didn't bother him. Being worked late into the night didn't bother him. He embraced it all. He was all business. What little precious free time the new recruits were allowed, Rob poured into more practice—practice loading his magazines, assembling and disassembling his rifle, all his gun drills, anything and everything. He didn't want to simply get through the course; he wanted to conquer it, master it, do it to the very limits of his ability. He was hungry for excellence.

This time no reservist was going to best him. In his battle school class, Rob took top shot. The trophy, a six-foot musket with his name inscribed on it, remains one of his most prized possessions.

From battle school Rob was posted to Third Battalion and immediately put onto the Canadian shooting team, where his shooting earned him first place for Western Canada and second place overall for "top tyro" (highest-scoring newcomer). From there he went on deployment, a tour in Bosnia for peacekeeping duty, which wasn't terribly exciting. This was 1999 and the world was mostly at peace, which for an aspiring military sniper meant it was pretty boring.

While he was in Bosnia, command pulled him off-tour for a month to compete for Team Canada again, this time in a competition in Australia.

Rob loved competition shooting. He loved the purity of it, the stretching of perfection. He also enjoyed rubbing shoulders with such accomplished, high-level shooters, comparing notes and sharing tricks of the trade. He noticed, for example, some competitors laying their ammunition out in the sun for a while before shooting, in order to warm it up. Made sense: when using ammunition with a heat-sensitive propellant, heating up the round will accelerate the burn, causing greater chamber pressure and muzzle velocity.

Rob made a mental note to himself. Perhaps this would come in handy later on.

By the end of his first week he was in first place for his division. Things were going phenomenally well. There was nothing Rob wanted to do more than shoot, and this was shooting at an awfully rarefied level. And then he bumped into the downside of rubbing shoulders with competitors. Literally.

One day the contestants were working their way through an event that incorporated an obstacle course. As Rob crawled underneath an obstacle, rifle in hand, another shooter directly behind him accidentally slammed into the back of his shoulder. A bolt of pain tore through Rob's shoulder, the kind of neural impulse that goes screaming up to the brain with the message, *Red alert—we're screwed!* It was a hard hit, and it popped Rob's shoulder out, dislocating his arm.

For him, the competition was over.

Rob was devastated. He spent the next three weeks sitting around in Australia, disconsolate, watching everyone else shoot. Those three weeks were nearly unendurable—far worse than any hell even the most devious instructor could have possibly dished out.

For the rest of '99 and into 2000 Rob's sole mission in life was to recoup his shoulder and get back in shape so he could move on with his grand plan—a plan he'd had from the start. When he entered the military, Rob had formulated a concrete list of goals, which he'd mapped out carefully and written down. The list went something like this:

get through basic
get through battle school
join battalion
get through jump course
qualify for airborne unit
get through recce course
qualify for recce platoon
take the prize

Nobody knew about this list but Rob. He had not shared his plan with another living soul. Each level of the plan raised the bar higher and would be tougher to achieve. Right now his total focus (aside from shooting, always shooting) was on the next item, getting through a jump course. Making that would qualify him for Alpha Company, Third Battalion's airborne unit. Which, if all went well at Alpha, might lead to his getting accepted into PPCLI's recce course.

Recce (pronounced *reck*-ee), the British version of what Americans would call recon, was the quintessential Spec Ops training program, a hellacious mix of land navigation, reconnaissance, assault ops, and sheer survival skills. Few ever made it to the recce course. A lot fewer made it all the way through. If Rob got to be one of those rare individuals, the resulting recce qual could be—*could* be—Rob's ticket to shoot for a coveted spot on the Third Battalion's recce platoon. Passing recce in and of itself was far from a guarantee that he'd then make it onto the platoon, which accepted only the elite of the elite. But narrow as it was, that was the doorway he needed to pass through to get where he meant to go.

The truth was, none of these goals was really important to him, in and of itself. They were all simply stepping-stones toward *the* goal, that final step. *The prize.* He hadn't forgotten the images on that television screen in the recruitment office in Newfoundland.

He was going to be one of Canada's top snipers.

While Furlong was nursing his shooting arm back into shape in Australia, Jason Delgado was riding a bus from Manhattan to Parris Island, South Carolina. The bus ride took about twelve hours, plenty of time for Delgado to think about what he was getting himself into. Although he was pretty sure he already knew. Marine basic training is the longest and toughest of any of the armed services, and by most accounts the most brutal.

"You know what makes marines so good at what they do?" says Jason. "I'll tell you; one word: *misery*." He laughs. "Pure hell and misery."

As he got off the bus he saw a long phalanx of yellow footprints painted onto the asphalt in rows of four pairs. "Stand . . . *to!*" The recruits all placed their feet on the yellow footprints, which had the effect of forcing them all to stand in the correct posture.

That's the marines, right there. The Marine Corps is legendary for its exactitude. In the marines, everything is done by the numbers, micromanaged to the nth degree. And it pays off. They are the epitome of consistent, dependable excellence. When our SEAL platoon went deep into the enemy stronghold in the caves of Zhawar Kili, a unit of about twenty marines came in with us to act as security, and I was damn glad of it. If I were back in hostile territory tomorrow, there's no force on earth I'd rather have guarding my ass than a unit of marines.

Just as you've probably seen in the movies, the first event on arrival at marine boot camp was the ritual shaving of heads, only it was not so antiseptic an experience as it looks in the movies. Quite a few emerged with good-sized nicks in their heads. "It was pretty savage," says Jason. "Blood was drawn."

Next they were given their standard issue: boots, PT gear, and the rest. Except that they weren't allowed to actually wear their boots. Not yet. They had to earn them. In marine boot camp, they had to earn *everything*—their name tapes, their eagle-globe-and-anchor insignia, their boots, everything. What they got to drink was water—if they wanted juice, they had to earn it. Want to place a phone call home? Fine: earn it. They were being taught from day one to appreciate every last thing they had.

How did they earn these privileges? Mainly through being aggressive. Jason quickly learned that the more aggressive you were, the more you were seen as a leader; the more you stood out, the more privileges you got. He soon scored a number of phone calls home, courtesy of a few (tacitly encouraged) fistfights.

One morning Jason arrived at the chow hall, sat down with his food, took one bite, and the sergeant made him spit it out before he could swallow. Everyone had to get up and leave, right then. No breakfast that day. That happened frequently. If you wanted to get to the chow hall in time to eat, you quickly learned the fundamentals of time management.

It seemed like random cruelty—but it was more about breaking down the young men's sloppy habits and preparing them for a life of efficiency. A lot didn't make sense at first, but after a few years in the Corps, and especially once on deployment, the young marines would start understanding why things were done the way they were in boot camp. With his "Third Recon" cadet corps experience, Jason already had a pretty good idea.

"From day one, they were stripping us of our pride and individualism," he says, "and showing us that it's not about you, it's about the mission. Priority one is the mission, priority two is troop welfare. Mission first. Even if you die, you have to accomplish the mission."

The drill instructors had free rein with their recruits. At any moment, if they decided they didn't like what they were seeing, everyone stopped what they were doing and hit the ground for push-ups.

One night Jason's drill instructor (called a "heavy"), Sergeant

Jones, burst into their barracks, flipped over all the bunks, smashed bottles of Aqua Velva on the walls, threw their clothes all over the place, then ordered the men to have it all clean and flawless by the following morning. It was exactly like Rob Furlong's experience, only Sergeant Jones added a unique twist.

Before leaving, he made the men all line up, then ordered them each to drink two canteens full of water before going to bed. After drinking each canteen they had to hold their canteens upside-down over their heads, to prove they'd drunk it all. Those few who tried to slip by were betrayed by water pouring down on their heads. Sergeant Jones made sure everyone drank their full quota of two canteens' worth, and then gave a standing order: "Anyone gets up out of his rack to go use the bathroom is on firewatch for the rest of the night." (Firewatch is so painfully boring that it's typically manned in one-hour shifts; being forced to stay awake and look at nothing for hours, especially when you're already exhausted, is excruciating.) He then opened every window in the squad bay, so the boys would have a nice cold breeze all night, making the urge to pee even worse.

All night long, Jason heard his teammates moaning. Some peed into their canteens. Jason knew that was a bad idea: Sergeant Jones would have thought of that. He needed a different tactic. He quietly got out of bed, slipped into his full cammies, strapped on his pistol belt and flashlight, went out into the halls, and pretended *he* was on firewatch. He walked up and down the squad bay a few times, ducked into the bathroom to piss, walked up and down the squad bay a few more times, then slipped back into bed. All those months of sneaking around in Van Cortlandt Park with his paintball rifle and scope now paid off. Nobody saw him. A sniper in the making.

The next morning, some of the guys had pissed their beds, others pissed their pants. But the worst off, as Jason had figured correctly, were the guys who pissed in their canteens. Sergeant Jones stomped in and gave them their first order of the day: drink another canteen of water. Those who'd used their canteens as urinals tried to fake their way through, putting their piss-filled canteens to their lips and pretending to drink. But they weren't thinking about what came next.

"Okay, now hold your canteens up over your heads!"

A few marines got golden showers that morning. Delgado kept a straight face, but inside he was laughing so hard he almost peed in his pants himself.

In fact, he found everything about boot camp hilariously funny—at first. As far as he was concerned, he'd already done a lot of this stuff, or things much like it, in his cadet corps in the Bronx. And he was just so jazzed to be there, becoming an honest-to-God, real-live member of the U.S. armed forces, a *marine,* for shit's sake. Every time he got yelled at, far from beating him into a corner, it would have the opposite effect. He'd soak it up, enjoy every screaming word of it.

It took an adjustment for him to start taking it all seriously. That adjustment happened pretty fast. It didn't take long to realize that this was not a game. These guys were there to whip him and all the others into shape by any means necessary. Boot camp in the Corps is longer than in the other branches of the U.S. armed services. Longer, and tougher. The PT baseline requirements included running a mile and a half in under fifteen minutes, forty-five crunches or more in two minutes, and fifteen pull-ups (for males). The punishment went up from there.

The three months of training was punctuated throughout by a steadily escalating series of humps (hikes with fully loaded rucksack): a two-mile hump, four-mile hump, seven-miler, and so on. The last one came during the final portion of basic, dubbed the Crucible: a fifty-four-hour-long series of tests including obstacle course, war-gaming, problem-solving, and teamwork-testing, interspersed among the endless drills and dozens of miles of marching. At one point Jason found himself trying to figure out how to drag a heavy ammo can under a net of low-lying barbed wire for several hundred yards. At another, he had to get his entire team across an obstacle course, consisting of huge pegs sticking out of the ground, using just a single plank of wood, like a huge game of human Tetris. One impossible task after another, with no sleep and little food, all blurred together into one endless mass of misery. And Jason totally loved it.

That is, he hated it—but in a good way. He could feel it carving him into the man he wanted to be.

There's one more key element that distinguishes USMC boot camp from basic in the other branches: these guys get extensive marksmanship training. Every new marine coming out of basic is at least a decent shot. The Marine Corps is proud of its slogan, "Every Marine is a rifleman." It's absolutely true, and it starts in boot camp.

When Jason and his classmates got out on the range they started at three hundred yards, standing rapid fire, then kneeling rapid fire at three hundred yards, then went out to four hundred yards, both sitting and prone, and then all the way out to five hundred yards, prone.

Five football fields: that's a very respectable distance, something no other basic training would attempt. And back in 2000, when Jason was going through the course, this was all iron sights, that is, no advanced optics, just sighting down the barrel through the little metal notched sighting device that comes with the gun, which is pretty damn primitive.

But all that range time was still ahead of them, coming in week two. During his first week on the M16, Jason didn't fire a single shot. In classic anal marine fashion, the first week of marksmanship phase was all classroom work, fundamentals of weapon handling, and dry-firing, dry run after dry run. They practiced snapping on barrels, trigger pull, seeing whether their sights were getting jiggled or stationary. It was a week of endless tedium, sitting on the grass for hours at a time, staring at spray-painted echo silhouettes (from the waist up) on a series of 55-gallon drums. Jason and dozens of other "boots" lying on the ground in a huge circle, aiming and "firing" their weapons at the targets.

The M16 is a semiautomatic, its mechanism operated by a gas piston. When you fire a round, the exploding gases from that round work the machinery to rack the next round into place. Which means that if you don't actually fire a round, there's no explosion, and you have to manually rack the thing every time you squeeze the trigger and drop the firing pin. Doing that once? Twice, ten times? No big deal. A hundred times? A few thousand times? It's not only tedious, it's draining. Just lying there, squeezing the trigger, racking, aiming, snapping, racking, aiming, snapping, and racking, for hours on end, day after day, all week long.

And it was hot; South Carolina springtime hot.

The first day, Delgado lay down on the ground, got positioned, and started in: aim, snap, rack. Aim, snap, rack. After a few minutes he felt something tickling his ear. Then the tickle turned to an itch. He told himself to ignore it. Aim, snap, rack. The itch got worse. Sand fleas, biting him in the ears. *Leave it alone, Delgado. Doan do it, dawg.* Aim, snap, rack—now it was awful. He longed to rip his hand off the rifle and start scrabbling at his right ear. But he knew it wasn't allowed, that he had to lie there and take it.

"Yeahhhhh," came a voice above him, mocking, sneering. The sergeant had seen it in Delgado's face: that look of cringing discomfort. "Yeahhh," he continued, "let 'em eat. They need to eat, too . . . my little marines." The shooting instructors knew all about the sand fleas. They called them "our little drill instructors."

Delgado kept on dry-firing, and the little drill instructors kept on chewing on his ears.

Between the little drill instructors and the big ones, that first week was when Jason began acquiring the kind of discipline and self-control that would serve him well in the future. That would, in fact, save his life, and other lives, too.

When Nick Irving entered the army under his Option 40 Ranger contract, he was still a fairly skinny dude, topping out at barely 105 pounds. He wasn't used to eating three square meals a day. As a teenager he would typically eat one solid meal, then snack on candy or other fast calories. He just never ate that much—until he hit the army chow hall. Over the ten weeks of basic Nick packed on close to forty additional pounds, most of it muscle.

Which, as it turned out, only exacerbated the suffering of his personal brand of hell.

Nick had planned to be a SEAL, so he had focused his effort the past few years building himself up as a swimmer. He hadn't trained up for the kind of weight-bearing exertion it takes to be an army grunt. Now he found himself running up and down concrete tracks with eighty to a hundred twenty pounds of ruck on his back. He soon developed a massive case of shin splints that developed further into an extensive series of tiny fractures in the bones of his legs.

The additional forty pounds turned Nick from Stick Figure into a formidable dude—but it also added even more stress onto his injured legs. Every morning, he woke up to a pair of legs that were badly swollen and in severe pain. Finally the pain got to be too much. Nick placed a phone call to his parents and told them what was happening.

"Hey," he said, "I don't know if I can do this."

"Listen, Nick," his father told him. "This has been your dream since you were in elementary school. Suck it up, drive on—and if it gets too bad and your legs fall off, *then* you can quit."

Nick listened. He decided the only way he was going to quit would be if his legs *did* fall off. Or if he ended up dying. *Man,* he recalls thinking at times during those dark days, *I really do hope I die.*

Once out of basic Nick was supposed to go right on to airborne school, but his condition forced him to postpone. The doctors told him he needed to allow six months to a year for the stress fractures to heal. "Screw that," said Nick. "I don't have six months to a year. I'll take a month, and however much they heal at that point, that's how healed they'll be. If my legs snap off, they snap off."

True to his word, he took just one month off and then went into rigger (parachute) school, where he found himself running up to six or eight miles a day in addition to the actual jumping. The shin splints returned, along with the fractures, swelling, and pain—plus one additional element in his arsenal of suffering: fear.

He could push through the pain in his legs. After a while they just got numb. But the jumping itself? That was something else.

The truth was, Nick was absolutely terrified of heights. Just crawling out onto the roof to repair a shingle would make him feel like he was about to pass out. Anything above ten feet freaked him out. And he was about to go a lot farther up than ten feet.

Before doing any actual jumping, the students climbed up into a mock-up of an AC-130 transport plane to simulate free fall. This was only forty feet off the ground, and they were buckled into a harness the whole time. Still, Nick shook so hard he could barely make it through the exercise.

Before long he was up in a real AC-130 at 1,500 feet, traveling about 200 mph, feeling seriously weak in the knees. Knowing how terrified of heights he was, one of the instructors pulled him out of the line. "Hey, recruit, guess what?" she said. "You're gonna be the first guy out."

Nick sat on the plane's bench with the other students, at the head of the line. Then came the dreaded words: "Jumpers, stand by. Stand up. Hook up." They were hooking to a static line, which meant their chutes would be opened for them automatically; they wouldn't need to worry about pulling rip cords and counting or any of the other mechanics of the process. All they had to do was keep a decent form: knees together, tuck in, chin to chest, so when the risers popped out they wouldn't get riser burn.

They stood up and hooked on to the line. The instructor opened the 130's big side doors and propped Nick up there, the tips of his boots hanging out over the edge.

"Don't look down," a voice told him. "Look at the horizon. Do *not* look down."

Nick looked down.

Everything looked so small down there. Nick just had time to think, *This is insane!* when the green light went on, the instructor behind him gave him a smack in the ass, and he jumped. Everything he'd learned, everything he'd been told to do, went clean out of his mind. He dropped like deadweight, had terrible form and a lousy landing. Still, he made it to the ground, conscious and in one piece. It was far from his worst jump.

That was still ahead of him.

* * *

So many levels of hell, so little time.

After airborne came a monthlong selection course called Ranger In-
doctrination Program (or RIP, later renamed Ranger Assessment and
Selection Program, or RASP), designed to weed out weaker candidates.
They didn't learn all that much—basic map-reading, some weapons-
handling, all pretty basic. Essentially it was thirty-days-plus of brutal
PTs. The first day they had a half-mile run carrying a hundred pounds
of gear. The class started out with some eighty-five guys; sixty didn't
make it to day two.

Indoc is to ranger candidates what BUD/S is to aspiring SEALs.
About midway through Indoc comes the part everyone dreads, a phase
called Cole Range, which is the rangers' version of what the SEALs call
Hell Week.

Cole Range itself is a remote training area off of Fort Benning. They
don't drive you out there. You ruck out.

Nick and his compadres packed up everything they'd need to last a
week out there, and got going. They had to be at the compound within
three hours or be automatically kicked out. It was a little over twelve
miles.

It was hot that day, close to 100 degrees Fahrenheit. A little past
halfway to the range, one guy started muttering; no one had any idea
what he was saying. A minute later, he was screaming. Then he fainted,
hit the dirt, came to, and started begging, "Please, someone, stick a
thermometer in my ass."

They took his boots off and discovered that his feet were soaked in
sweat. He hadn't wanted his feet to get wet, so he'd wrapped them in
plastic wraps.

Seriously? thought Nick. *Bad idea, dude.*

They put a thermometer in his ass, all right; his core temp was over
105. They hauled him off to a hospital and kicked him out of the military.

When the group reached the range they were all so dehydrated that
Nick's muscles started locking up worse than he had ever experienced,
before or since. He got them unlocked fast. As soon as they arrived they
had PT: push-ups, sit-ups, running, and more running—buddy runs,
pick up and carry the biggest guy you can find, carry him for two miles,
run back, more push-ups, more sit-ups, more running. Every time they
thought they were finished, it kept going. It went on for eight hours.

Finally it was time to sleep. Only they were not permitted to lie down, or even to sit down. The only option was to sleep standing up. And they had just fifteen minutes to do that, after which it was—guess what?—time for more PTs.

It was a never-ending cycle, and it lasted for nearly a week.

At one point the training cadre brought out some hot pizza, along with coffee and hot chocolate, and damn, it smelled *so* good. All they'd had to eat at this point was a small portion of MREs: Meals Ready to Eat, the standard military ration. (I've lived on MREs for months at a time while being on a compound with servicemen of multiple branches and nationalities, and here's what I learned: you can't trade that crap. You can't even *give* it away.)

"Hey, guys," one of the instructors said. "You want some pizza? It's right here. Just have one guy come out here, and he can grab some for the rest of you."

Nick knew damn well that if you fell for that one and got out of formation, BOOM, you were out, gone, kicked out of the class. You *never* break formation. That pizza was not there for them to eat. It was there to torture them.

One day, they finally gathered up those students who hadn't yet dropped out and said, "All right, guys, it's over. You made it through Cole Range. We're going back to the base so you can clean your weapons, get some real chow, and then go on with the rest of your training."

They all clambered into the back of a big deuce-and-a-half and it took off. The exhausted candidates were all high-fiving each other even as they collapsed in the bed of the truck. "Yeah! We made it!"

Half an hour later, the truck jerked to a stop. The tarp covering the back lifted, and light poured into the bed of the truck. The men spilled out and looked around.

They were at Cole Range.

It wasn't over at all. They were right back where they'd started; they'd been driven in a big circle. Their instructors were just messing with them.

"I can't do this," Nick heard one of his classmates moan. "I'm fuckin' outta here." His spirit was broken.

They lost quite a few guys that day.

A few days later they were taken outside in the rain and set up to practice doing field emergency trauma work. There they were: exhausted, hadn't slept in days, trying to put IVs into each other and sticking nasalpharyngeal airway tubes (NPAs) down each other's noses. Getting it all wrong. It was ugly.

A lot of guys quit that day, too.

Nick's ranger indoc class started out with just over eighty rangers. When he graduated, there were only himself and six others left.

Advanced military training doesn't just beat on you, it examines you, explores your every weakness, hunts for your greatest vulnerability, and then attacks you right there in that soft spot.

For some, guys who are already in tremendous physical shape when they start, things like Hell Week and Cole Range are no big deal—they just kind of go on autopilot and tough it through—but they freak out when it comes to the pool competence testing. You're sitting there at the pool's edge with your back turned, listening to your classmates basically being drowned. It washes a lot of guys out. For me, pool comp was no big deal; I grew up in the water. But I didn't have a lot of firearms experience growing up and was clearly one of the shittier shots in my class, a defect that nearly crushed me, until I made the conscious decision to be the one who crushed *it*.

Everyone has his soft spot.

For Nick Irving it was heights.

Making it through Indoc meant Nick had earned his ranger scroll and was now put on active duty as a ranger and into rotation for a six-month training workup. Within days after being assigned to Charlie Company at Fort Benning, Nick participated in an airfield seizure exercise. This is one of the rangers' specialties. When war breaks out, the rangers jump in and capture an airfield, paving the way for other troops to enter, supply lines to flow, and all the rest of what it takes to mount a full-fledged military operation.

They were scheduled for a night jump. Nick was serving as a 240 gunner. The M240 is a serious weapon (the same machine gun the front door gunner on Rob Furlong's Chinook manned back in 2002), almost as tall as Nick himself, and weighs about twenty-five pounds, not including ammo. With the gun, all the equipment he would need on the op, assault packs attached to his shins with a thousand rounds packed into them, his usual kit stuffed inside his gun case, helmet, night vision, and parachute on his back, Nick was carrying a good hundred pounds or more of extra weight.

As the C-17 climbed Nick told himself, *Hey, toughen up, it's your first big jump with battalion.* They got the green light to jump. He turned to the open doorway to jump out and saw nothing but a wall of blackness. He tried his best not to think about the fact that they were traveling at over five hundred miles an hour and that he was high above the earth.

This was a lot higher than the roof on his house, that was for damn sure.

He jumped.

Feeling the wind smash against his face, he began his count:

One thousand . . . two thousand . . . three thousand . . .

By *four thousand* his chute was supposed to open. Right on cue, he felt the jolt of something release and shoot up behind him.

Everything's cool, he told himself. He should be able to steer now. But that wasn't happening.

Five thousand . . .

Man, he was still hearing an awful lot of wind.

He realized he was also hearing his teammates shouting at him over his comm: "Pull your reserve! *Reserve, reserve!*" He looked up and saw not a big wide-open canopy but something that looked like a cigarette roll. A cloth cigar. His parachute hadn't opened. There was nothing up there but a long roll of fabric fluttering uselessly in the wind.

Oh, shit.

He reached down and pulled his reserve parachute—and everything went into super-slow-motion as

he saw a spring pop out—

and the parachute slip down to the level of his legs—

and then unbutton itself—

and then rise and unfurl above his head—

Except that the risers, those strings that attach to the actual fabric of the parachute, had somehow gotten wrapped *under* his left leg and his weapons case, so as they shot upward they also yanked Nick's left leg upward. Now he was barreling toward the ground while doing a full split, his right leg dangling straight down and his left leg pulled up so far that he could kiss his left knee. He couldn't even begin to steer, let alone prepare for a proper landing. And damn, did that leg hurt, felt like it was being pulled right off.

Nick looked down ("Don't look down!") and saw an expanse of concrete runway leaping up to meet him. He saw a few F-16s parked nearby, shrouded in the semidark. And a *lot* of concrete.

He thought: *This is going to be really bad.*

He thought: *I'm gonna break my leg, I know this for a fact.*

Reserve parachutes are not designed to steer like the primary, but Nick kept struggling anyway, desperate to shift his trajectory off that concrete target, trying his damnedest to pull on that reserve and get some horizontal movement.

No dice.

He tried to bend his right leg a little, to help absorb the impending impact. It didn't move. Now he was at hundred feet . . . then seventy-five feet . . . Nick flashed on his mom, who had always said she thought his job was too dangerous. *You're too young for this, Nick,* she'd said, *you're going to get hurt.*

At fifty feet he said out loud, "Oh, man, my mom's gonna kill me—"

And then he heard a loud POP!

That was my knee, he thought. *So much for that leg.*

The reserve chute, still aggressively doing its job of grabbing at the wind, now began to drag Nick down the runway, shredding his clothes and rubbing the soles of his boots against the tarmac so hard that they heated to the melting point. Nick struggled to disconnect the chute, but the way it was wrapped around him made it impossible to pop the straps, and it continued scraping him down the airfield. He tried to reach for a knife he had, but it was connected to his boot, which was still stuck inside one of the risers.

He was terrified. There was nothing he could do but go along for the ride. He visualized the headline: ON FIRST DAY AS ARMY RANGER, NICK IRVING PRONOUNCED DEAD.

Finally he ground to a halt.

Men from his unit came running over to him, utterly freaked out. "Ohmigod, dude, are you okay?"

Nick lay prone, a sharp pain knifing through his back. His team circled him and one started examining his knee. Miraculously, it wasn't broken. That POP! he'd heard was not his knee going after all, it was the sound of his boots smacking into the concrete. From his waistline down, his clothes were split open and in tatters. He was covered in black skid marks from being dragged down the runway. The soles of his boots had melted and were peeling off. He was a mess—but nothing was broken.

They said, "Are you good?"

He figured he had a choice.

He could say, "Fuck this, that's it, I'm never doing another jump! Sorry, guys—I'm outta here!" Or he could suck it up.

Which, when you put it that way, was no choice at all.

"Yeah," he said as casually as he could. "I'm good." He pulled himself up onto his feet, collected his scattered kit and scattered wits, and limped over to rejoin the rest of the group. Alive, and changed forever.

* * *

Returning from Australia with his useless shoulder, Rob Furlong finished up his tour in Bosnia, then went back to Canada, where he kept up a rigorous schedule of physical therapy. As soon as his arm healed enough to shoot, he was back on the range. He sailed through his three-week jump course and went on to Alpha Company, Third Battalion's airborne unit, where everyone immediately hated him because he was a new guy. He kept his mouth shut, swept floors, maintained equipment, and did his best to remain invisible. When the timing seemed right, he expressed an interest in going into the reconnaissance training program. Command said yes.

Recce is a two-month course, heavily steeped in ambush and raids. It embraced land navigation (much like BUD/S) and survival, airborne ops, water insertions, and more. The washout rate was high.

This is the point where the training goes beyond difficult and starts reaching into your bone marrow. For SEALs, it's BUD/S and the advanced SEAL training that follows. For rangers, it's Ranger School (still ahead for Nick). For Rob it was recce school. While it lasted for only two months, the pace was nonstop—no easing up on weekends, no resting up at night, no classroom academics to vary the pace. It was one constant, unbroken test of performance. No food or sleep for five days at a time (water only), loaded backpacks, and complex, exacting missions that brooked no margin of error. Recce was the first time Rob ever fell asleep while walking. He describes those two months as the most physically demanding thing he has ever experienced.

Rob's recce school took place in Fort Lewis, Washington, supported by a cadre of Green Berets. It was October 2000, and in Fort Lewis in October all it does is rain. The men were drenched the entire time. At one point the Green Berets gathered them all into a bivouac deep in the woods. The guys were all soaking wet, freezing cold, and miserable. Right in the midst of the bivouac they had a big fire going, all the instructors standing around taking it easy.

Hang on, thought Rob, *something's wrong with this picture.* Not only were their torturers not in their usual pissed-off mood, they seem to be kind of joking around and enjoying themselves. And why were they giving the students a chance to take the chill out of their bones?

"Hey," said one of the instructors, "we brought some lunch in for you guys."

Nobody said a word. True? A ray of sunshine in the gloom? Or a trick?

The instructor turned to one of Rob's teammates and said, "Hey,

Hagland, there's a blue glow stick there, just down the path. That's where your lunch is. Run down and grab it."

Hagland disappeared down the path. A moment later the others heard him exclaim, "What the *fuck*?" Then they heard some thrashing around, followed by a sound nobody expected: panicked clucking. Which then stopped as abruptly as it had started.

A minute later Hagland came tromping back up the path, looking pissed off as a thundercloud. In one hand he held what looked like a rock but turned out to be a potato. In the other, the warm, limp chicken whose neck he'd just broken. That was their dinner. Each man got a raw potato and a live chicken. That was it for the next four days.

It was very realistic training, and it taught them serious escape-and-evasion tactics. How are you to survive? When you're out in the wild, on your own in hostile territory, a chicken and a potato would be a damn good meal. In fact, in those circumstances you'd be lucky to have such luxuries—as Rob would later learn firsthand.

Of all his experiences in military training, Rob says that recce course was the worst.

"You're sitting there hating life," he says. "It's exciting to be learning all these crazy survival tactics, but at the same time you're saying, 'Why the fuck am I doing this to myself?'"

The misery notwithstanding, Rob did quite well on this course, and when he got back to Alpha Company in Canada he found the other men now had a whole new level of respect for him. Still a fairly junior guy, he'd done well in his shooting career, gone to an airborne company and done well there, got sent on to the recce course and excelled there, too.

Still, for Rob passing recce was just another stepping-stone.

Next stop: recce platoon.

The PPCLI's recce platoon operates on its own, supporting the battalion in whatever capacity they need. If one of the battalion's companies, for example, is planning an airborne or water insertion and needs reconnaissance done beforehand, they call on recce.

The recce platoon breaks down into three teams.

There's a long-range patrol team, which specializes in patrol for extended durations. These are the guys who do the quintessential reconnaissance missions, slipping in behind enemy lines and staying there lengthy periods of time. They specialize in stealth, observation, and survival skills.

Then there are the pathfinders, extremely highly trained forces schooled in doing beachheads and water insertions, airborne and helo ops, sub insertions, everything—similar to our SEALs.

And then there are the snipers.

Even within the recce platoon, the snipers are a breed unto themselves. You don't just come out of the recce course and head right into the sniper cell. Typically you have to go through additional sniper training before you are even considered as having a shot at it. For that matter, most recce course graduates don't even go into the recce platoon at all. Making it through the recce course simply makes you recce-*qualified*. It doesn't guarantee that you'll go anywhere after that. And Rob wasn't about to make his ambitions public. He knew what the deal was: stay quiet, be professional, do your job, and wait for your chance, because there are other guys ahead of you. He knew if he was seen as acting like he was trying to jump ahead over other people in his unit, all that would get him would be a bad name. He had to quietly prove himself and wait for his opportunity.

What Rob didn't know, however, was that people high up in the system had been watching him for some time. Word had gotten around that this kid could shoot, and that he was made of pretty solid stuff.

In 1999, when he did his Bosnia tour, he'd been invited to participate in a two-week concentration course with a wide range of snipers, including Canadians, Brits, and Czechs. He went with another Canadian, neither of them sniper-qualified at that point, and while they did not exactly kick the shit out of the more experienced Brits and Czechs, they held their own. Evidently that had been a sort of litmus test to see if they might be sniper material down the road. Rob didn't learn this until he'd already made it through the recce course, but these higher-ups had already decided that if he made it through recce, they were going to pull him into the sniper cell and start his on-the-job training right away.

When he heard the news, Rob was elated, ecstatic, on top of the world. Yet at the same time, he knew that making it through recce and being inducted into the sniper cell was only the beginning. It was like finishing BUD/S: sure, it's hard, and yes, it's amazing when you make it through, but it's really only an entrance exam. One seriously sadistic entrance exam, but still, just the beginning.

Once you're through it, that's when the *real* training starts.

Like Rob Furlong, Jason Delgado already knew exactly where he was aiming the day he walked into boot camp. After basic came School of Infantry (SOI), seven weeks of living the marine life, more battle tactics and weapons training and all the rest, and of course, more brutal

PTs. All of this, Delgado ate up with a spoon and couldn't wait to get through. He had an endgame in mind.

The Corps is renowned for its scout sniper program; the marines have been at the forefront of the U.S. military sniper experience since Vietnam. Jason may have landed in the marines more or less by accident, after the doors to both the army and the SEALs were closed to him, but it was turning out to be the perfect path.

When you first start your marine sniper training you're considered a PIG—a Professionally Instructed Gunman. It's only when you graduate sniper school that you become a HOG—a Hunter of Gunmen. When Jason was going through his training pipeline, young PIGs went through an indoc for the sniper program that was organic to their particular battalion. Some indocs lasted one day, some two or three; it depended on the individual unit. While the indocs were short, they were hellacious. Of the eighteen or twenty aspiring PIGs who might try out, typically three or four would make it through, with all the rest being DOR (drop on request).

Jason had no problem with the physical demands, but he tripped over his own personality. A HOG named Rose was counting off Jason's pull-ups. At one point, Rose called out the same number twice in a row, and then again, and then again—pull-up after pull-up, he was counting out the same damn number. Delgado thought the guy was trying to disqualify him because he was Hispanic. He lost his cool and started trash-talking the instructor.

Of course, it had nothing to do with his ethnicity. That was just Delgado's own bullshit that the instructor was triggering—and not by accident, either. Instructor Rose was probing, pushing, looking for a chink in the PIG's armor. He found it.

They have a saying in the Corps: *Nothing is sacred.* Nothing and no one. That was part of the training—anything could be taken from you, including your pride, your self-esteem, your composure, and still you had to perform. They would make jokes about anything and everything: mothers, wives, girlfriends, kids—and it would get raunchy. You couldn't get upset or react at all. The young marines did this to each other over and over, to the point where they couldn't tell if they were making you mad or not, because you would just laugh and play along. It taught them equanimity under pressure, tolerance, and the invaluable life skill of not taking oneself too seriously. More importantly, it taught them to be able to perform in any situation, no matter what.

"It forced me to lose that chip on my shoulder," says Delgado. "I learned that it gets you nowhere. Do we get that racist shit thrown at us? Of course. We get it a lot. But the ones who succeed in the military are the ones who are able to let it roll off their shoulder."

It was a valuable lesson. It also got Jason flushed from indoc.

Getting a "no" vote from the indoc board was one of the most painful things that ever happened to Jason. It was also one of the best things that ever happened to him.

He went back to his platoon and spent the next year proving himself. He took over as fire team leader and went on to be selected to become a MOUT (military operations in urban terrain) instructor. MOUT was a fairly new thing, a Corps-wide program incorporating close quarters battle (CQB) and all kinds of urban-focused raid techniques, from isolating targets to using grappling ladders, as well as teaching infrastructure management skills in areas like sewage, plumbing, and water purification. It was a hell of a leadership role, especially for someone so young, and Jason earned a lot of people's respect.

He also never lost sight of his goal. He wanted to be a sniper.

One of his buddies had made it through indoc and gotten into the sniper platoon, and through him Jason ended up befriending a few of the senior snipers. As MOUT instructor, he had by this time taught a number of snipers. He'd built a résumé and a reputation. Most importantly, he'd worked on getting that chip off his shoulder.

Finally the day came: he went back in for a second indoc, this one lasting two days. At the end, when it came time for the indoc board to vote on who got through, Jason got voted down once again. Only this time the platoon's chief sniper, Jack Coughlin, overrode their vote. "Look," said Jack, "this is the kid's second time through. He's worked his ass off to get here, and humbled himself enough to come back and try again. He's got heart."

By the skin of his teeth and on the strength of his effort, Jason had made it through on his second try—but it wasn't over.

That second indoc didn't produce enough PIGs to fill out their sniper platoon, so command decided they would hold one more indoc. And they weren't going to have Jason and the other PIGs sitting around doing nothing while these new guys were going through the mill, so even though he'd already passed, Jason would now be going through yet one more indoc. Only this one was different. The platoon, as it happened, was going on deployment to Okinawa, Jason's first tour of active duty. This next indoc would take place over there. And it wouldn't last one day, or two days, or even three days.

This one lasted *six months*.

They would go out into the jungle for five days, six days at a time, come back to the marine base for a day, clean up, go out into town and mess around for a while, then go back out and do it all over again. They practically lived in the jungle.

Each morning began with a ruck run for three, four, five miles or whatever the instructor felt like that morning. In each man's rucksack went a PIG egg: a sandbag filled to capacity and wrapped in duct tape. Purpose? None; just extra deadweight. Everywhere you went, a PIG egg went with you. If you happened to be the one carrying radio equipment, if you were the one bringing extra water, didn't matter: you also had to carry this frigging forty-pound PIG egg. And the humidity level in Okinawa was insane. They would come back looking like they'd run through the ocean.

The classes showed the other side of marine training: brutality mixed with an obsessive insistence on perfection. They had classes back to back, every day, sometimes the same class they'd already had before. Sniper school itself was only twelve weeks long, but this indoc was six full months, so they learned everything three or four times over, to the point where they could recite the class material verbatim. In fact, that was one of their requirements. They couldn't mess up an "is," or an "as," or a "the." Everything had to be in place, even when reciting multiple paragraphs at a time.

And they were tested, constantly and mercilessly. They'd be out driving somewhere in the city and one of the senior HOGs would suddenly say, "We just passed seven cars—give me the make and model of each one, and who was driving." Their brains were in constant training as much as their bodies. It was like full-fledged sniper school, only without *being* sniper school.

When it came time to go to the actual sniper school, Delgado would be way more than ready. At least, that's what he thought.

By the time Nick Irving joined his battalion in late 2005, the Iraq War was in full engagement. After that six-month training workup (with that terrible jump), Nick deployed to Iraq for three months as a gunner and Stryker driver, then returned to the States for six more months of training, then back to Iraq for a second deployment, and then back stateside again. That cycle—six months training rotating with three or four months deployment—repeated itself until 2008, when he got the news that on returning home from this deployment (his fourth), he was going to Ranger School.

Shit, was his first and only thought.

Irving had his scroll, but not yet that coveted RANGER tab on his uniform, the one that says you've been through Ranger School and are now a full-fledged ranger. Still, nobody exactly looks *forward* to Ranger School.

If ranger indoc was hell, the sixty-two-day Ranger School was that experience all over again only at a deeper level. Averaging fifteen to thirty minutes of sleep a night (and some nights none at all), Nick soon lost all the weight he'd picked up back in basic.

The low point came while they were in mountain phase, probably the toughest phase of the three (land phase, mountain phase, desert phase). He was carrying around 120 pounds' worth of gear, up and down the mountains. It was bitter cold. By this time he was mostly in a semi-conscious state, something like sleepwalking. They were walking up a mountain slope and finally reached a resting spot. Then it was Nick's turn to pull security. He stood up, sleepwalked over to their perimeter, and stood guard. He was dimly aware of a thought going through his mind: *I'm so . . . fucking . . . tired.*

Nick looked down, and blinked. At least he thought he'd blinked. In reality, the moment he shut his eyes he was fast asleep, and was able to grab several fractions of a second of deep, satisfying repose until he abruptly woke up when his face was six inches from hitting the ground. And then, BLAM, it *did* hit the ground.

Damn, he thought. *I just fell asleep.*

He started getting up, but by the time he had one foot under him he already knew he was going to fall asleep again. To shorten the distance, he stayed right there, pulling security on one knee, rather than going all the way up to a standing position.

And sure enough, fell asleep again.

This time, after waking up as he hit the ground, he thought, *Screw it, I'm just going to lie down.* He figured, if the instructors saw him, maybe it would look like he was lying prone and aiming his weapon at something.

He got down on the ground, doing his best to assume an aiming-my-weapon-at-something pose, and looked up at a nearby bush—and right before his eyes, the bush started to move! In the semidarkness, the vague shape was resolving into a figure . . . and then all at once he realized, it *wasn't* a bush. It was George Foreman, crouched down on one knee!

Holy shit, thought Nick. *It's George Foreman!*

He looked around. Was anyone else seeing this? And what the hell was George Foreman doing out there?

Then he realized, George Foreman was a well-known motivational speaker. Maybe they'd sent him out here onto the mountain to give them a motivational talk. Help them keep going.

Maybe they'd sent him out here to give them some food.

And then the figure began to speak.

"Hey, man," it said. "Listen here—you want to get yourself one of these George Foreman grills."

"Fuck, yeah," croaked Nick. He looked at where George was pointing and saw that he was holding a big, juicy steak in his hand. Then Foreman opened up that George Foreman grill and tossed the steak on there, where it immediately began to sizzle. It looked just amazing, and smelled even more so. Nick licked his lips. He was practically drooling.

No, not *practically* drooling. He *was* drooling. No doubt about it. He just could not wait to bite into that steak.

And then the figure started fading away. A moment later, it was just a bush.

Nick felt so sad he practically cried.

On his first day home after graduating from Ranger School and earning his ranger tab, the first thing Nick did was go to Walmart, buy himself a $29.99 George Foreman grill, and make himself a big juicy steak on that motherfucker. He still has that grill.

Nick wasn't the only one who hallucinated his way through Ranger School. Another day during that mountain phase he was walking along a ridgeline when the guy he was with suddenly took off, sprinting full out along the cliff. For a moment Nick thought he was going to jump off, that he meant to kill himself. Then he was sure of it, because as the guy approached the cliff's edge he actually accelerated.

But he wasn't suicidal, he was a football player, and he'd just seen his quarterback throw him a long pass (as he later told Nick). He was going to win the game.

The pass flew off the side of the mountain, and the wide receiver lunged after it. Hurling his body off the side of the mountain and spreading out his arms, he caught the ball. And took a hell of a fall. Fortunately, he wasn't hurt too badly. He fell asleep halfway through the fall, so his body stayed loose, and when he eventually hit the slope he just rolled.

During mountain phase Nick began picking up a bad stench of something, an ammonia smell. He realized what he was smelling was himself: his body eating away at its own muscle. At one point, desperate for some water, he drank from a mountain stream without first purifying the wilderness water with the mandatory iodine tablets. Oops. Back in camp he discovered he'd contracted a bad infection and parasites.

Having by now lost some forty pounds, he found to his horror that he couldn't absorb anything from his food. Everything ran right through him, even water. One of the guys managed to sneak some pizza into their camp one day and they each had about a half a slice. As soon as Nick ate his share it came right back out the other end virtually intact.

Uh-oh, he thought. *This is not good.*

Medics gave him three or four IVs back to back and shot him full of penicillin, and he was back out in the field within a few hours, but he still couldn't eat a thing, and he was still hurting. The average adult male needs a minimum intake of about 1,800 calories per day. They were getting about half that, along with an insane level of physical stress, and no sleep, sometimes for two days straight. If you needed sleep, you had to figure out how to sleep—you guessed it—standing up. Nick heard quite a few bodies hit the ground.

One classmate lost so much muscle in his neck that he could no longer support the weight of his head. He had to walk around holding his head up with his hand, and if he wanted to look at something, he had to literally take his head with his hands and move it in that direction. He ended up washing out and being sent home.

After graduating from Ranger School, Nick didn't have any feeling in his toes. He didn't get that feeling back until five or six years later, long after he'd been out of the military altogether.

After getting out of the service he went in to the VA for an exam. When the doctor looked at his X-rays and tests he said, "My God, you look like an eighty-year-old man!" He told Nick that in his experience, Ranger School takes an average of about seven years off a person's expected life span.

A lot of people don't grasp this. They think you go through BUD/S or Ranger School or Delta training, and you just tough it through and come out the other end stronger than ever. It doesn't work that way. You don't simply survive it; it beats you up.

It is, in a word, hell. And you do it, because that's what it takes to prepare you for what you'll face in the field, when you go into battle to fight for your country. It's a trade-off we all make willingly: you become a highly skilled warrior, but at the same time it also damages you. And that damage is permanent.

Naval Special Warfare has its own legendary brand of hell. Basic Underwater Demolition/SEAL training, or BUD/S, is a seven-month

marathon of physical and mental punishment, carried out under maximum stress and in every conceivable environment, designed to weed out
every single soul not driven enough, fanatical enough, and downright
crazy enough to push himself all the way through it and out the other
end. Its attrition rate is legendary. Actual death is rare—but it has
happened. It nearly happened to Alex Morrison in '88.

During the land navigation portion of the training, Alex's class was
taken out to San Clemente Island, aka "the Rock," a godforsaken place
some eighty miles off the coast of San Diego where SEAL students are
taken to be trained. (And by "trained" I mean stretched to human limits and beyond.) I remember our first day out at the Rock with my own
BUD/S class in 1998, exactly one decade later. One of our instructors
lined us up and said, "Hey, guys, I want you to remember this: out here,
no one can hear you scream." He wasn't kidding. It was brutal enough
when I was out there. I can't even imagine how tough it was ten years
earlier, in an era of significantly less oversight.

One morning they did an eight- or ten-mile run before breakfast
(standard operating procedure). Alex didn't eat much when they got
back. From there they went out to the demolition range to practice the
fine art of blowing things up. (Don't forget, the D in BUD/S stands for
demolition.) While on the demo range, Alex committed the unpardon-
able sin of briefly kneeling.

Punishment time. His instructor took him out to Frog Hill, a small
mountain in the middle of the Rock, and directed him to perform a
"flight." This consisted of carrying an aircraft pallet up Frog Hill and
back down in X amount of time. Only this instructor also had Alex
strap onto his back a 180-pound dummy they fondly referred to as the
Chaplain.

Already fairly well spent from the run and lack of food, Alex carried the Chaplain up the hill, but as he reached the top the dummy
slipped and he dropped it.

"Do it again," called out the instructor.

He dragged the Chaplain down to the bottom of the hill, strapped
him on tight again, then headed back up the hill. By this time he was
thoroughly exhausted, and so, naturally, he dropped the Chaplain once
more. The instructor didn't have to call out the command; Alex heard
it in his head. *Do it again.*

"You need to quit, Morrison," the instructor yelled up the hill, as Alex
began dragging his burdens back down for another try. *"You need to
quit. Why don't you just quit?"*

"Fuck you," Alex managed to croak. "I'm going to die here."

At this point he was crawling with the dummy on his back, and probably starting to slip into some degree of insulin shock.

Finally, the instructor realized he wasn't going to get Alex to quit, so he stopped him. "You're done," he said, and left him to crawl his way back to base.

When Alex reached his barracks, he crawled up onto his cot and lay there in the fetal position. After a while their class corpsman came over and said, "Hey, man, what's up with you?" Alex didn't answer; he didn't need to. His pupils were dilated, his temperature was dropping, and he was close to unresponsive. The corpsman didn't need a map to see where this was going. They ended up medevacking Alex out of there for emergency medical care. If they hadn't, he would have been gone within hours.

As they bundled him onto a stretcher for transport, one of his teammates got down close to one ear and said, "Hey, Alex. Alex! Are you quitting?"

"No!" Alex gasped. "No, no, no, no, no . . ."

Over the next few hours, Alex was given several IVs and then, when he had recovered enough to manage it, some food. A brief rest.

And then he was back in the air, headed back to the Rock.

At the start of his training, Alex found the runs excruciatingly difficult. He was in every goon squad, the guy at the back of the class who was always being punished with extra flutter kicks in the cold surf while everyone else was sent off to eat lunch. By the end of BUD/S he was near the top of his class.

He says his most satisfying moment was completing a timed run up at the front of the class, having not only finished at the top, but having finished at the top and still not feeling completely crushed by it.

"That sense of absolute confidence, that *I can do anything, bring it on!* feeling," he says. "That was one the most exhilarating feelings I've ever had."

That is the purpose of all the hell: discovering that you have what it takes to come out the other side.

You've probably read training stories like this before, or perhaps you've seen boot camp sequences in movies, and it probably seems insane, as if the instructors are being sadistic sons of bitches, pushing their victims beyond the point of exhaustion out of pure meanness, actually trying to flunk them out. It sure as hell felt like that to each of us, as we were going through it.

It all feels different later on, once you are actually in combat.

Looking back, after coming out on the other side and going on to active duty, you realize that those instructors aren't being sadistic at all. They're not trying to kill you. They're not even trying to hurt you.

They're doing two things.

First, they're there to find out what you're made of. Because if you'll buckle under the pressure of brutal PTs back in some safe training camp in America, you are without question going to buckle in combat in some other part of the world where people are shooting at you, setting off explosives at you, and doing their level best to kill you. The hell of training is nothing compared to the actual hell of combat.

And second, they're there to help *you* find out what you're made of.

We all learned a great deal in our various training programs, both basic and advanced. A massive amount of subject matter, ten thousand detailed and exacting behavior patterns, a ton of mechanical knowledge and technical skills. But the most important thing we learned was something about ourselves: no matter what they did to us, *we were still here*.

Yes, the physical punishment is brutal, but that isn't where the hell resides. Your physical body can go way further than you've come to believe. The boundaries that Spec Ops training pushes up against are not limits of the body, but limits of the mind.

The decision to become part of the most elite fighting force on the earth is not a decision that happens once. It's a decision you make over and over again, every day, sometimes dozens of times a day. In the process, you become more than simply a highly trained warfighter. You become a force of nature.

II.
THE CRAFT

You will be expected to exhibit a complete mastery of multiple weapons systems in impossible conditions. You will be put under greater pressure and more exacting mental demands by far than you've ever been under before, and with zero tolerance given for error.

We will push the limits of your performance to such high levels that even when you are rusty, tired, or unpracticed you will still outperform the enemy. You will be expected to deliver at a level of excellence that will at first seem unrealistic, unfair, and unreasonable. You will come to know perfection as your new normal. And you'll be expected to deliver at that level of perfection day after grinding day without misstep. . . .

4

SNIPER SCHOOL

We do not rise to the level of our expectations. We fall to the level of our training.

—Archilochus, ancient Greek soldier and poet

Rob Furlong was pumped. Finally, after all the years of training and advancement through the system, he had been accepted into the Canadian Armed Forces sniper course and was getting ready to leave for the two-month program.

Early one morning he went to the basement of the quarters where he and his wife were living to retrieve some kit. Equipment in hand, he then headed back to the battalion area and made his way toward the desk where the battalion orderly sergeant and duty corporals hung their hats. As he neared the big stainless steel desk, Rob grew puzzled. Normally there'd be hardly anyone there at this hour, but today there was a crowd, maybe a hundred guys gathered there. It was barely six in the morning. *What the hell's going on?* he thought.

Everyone was watching a television set stuck on the desk. Rob crowded in close to look. On the screen, he saw a skyscraper in flames, smoke billowing up into the sky.

He recognized the building: it was one of the World Trade Center towers in New York.

"This is crazy," Rob heard someone say. "It looks like a passenger plane hit one of the towers there in the U.S."

"That makes no sense at all," said Rob. "What kind of idiot would be flying that low?"

As they stood watching a second plane crashed into the South Tower, and in that instant they all knew exactly what was happening.

We were under attack. If this was happening in New York, it could just as well be happening there in Canada.

Reaction was instantaneous. The Canadian government started locking down the bases. The training workup scheduled for Rob's battalion was immediately accelerated and shifted in content toward a focus on dealing with terrorist operations. By the time Rob checked in at sniper school, the whole concept of becoming a military sniper had assumed new meaning and implications.

This wasn't going to be about marking time at a peacekeeping mission in Bosnia. There was a war on.

When 9/11 happened, Jason Delgado was on the other side of the world, suffering through his six-month Okinawan jungle pre-sniper indoc. Nine o'clock in the morning New York time is 2200 hours (10:00 p.m.) Okinawa time, and that evening they happened to be in typhoon Condition 3 readiness, so when news of the attacks came they were already in lockdown and confined to barracks. As Rob quietly walked back to his station in Alberta that Tuesday morning, the young marines in Jason's unit were running up and down the halls in Okinawa, guns drawn, screaming their brains out.

"Imagine two hundred drunk nineteen-year-old marines watching this shit going down on live television." Jason shakes his head. "It was barely controlled chaos, man. Everyone wanted into the action, right now, immediately."

At that moment Nick Irving was jogging home from high school in Maryland, images of the collapsing towers replaying in his racing mind, the urge to enlist screaming in his blood, his sniper training still seven years in the future.

Alex Morrison was lying in bed, listening to the radio, when he heard the news. He instantly got up, dressed in seconds, and was in the car driving in to work. A SEAL for over a decade by now, he'd been a sniper for seven years and been through multiple tours of duty. He knew he'd be doing more soon.

As for me, I was in Coronado, California, already packing my gear. I'd been through sniper school by this time and had deployed as a sniper in the Far East and Middle East in 2000, and was about to deploy once again. Our platoon happened to be next in rotation to go overseas, and would be among the first to put boots on the ground in Afghanistan.

Each of us went through a different sniper course, in a different branch of the armed services, at a different point in history. Each of those experiences and courses of instruction was distinct, and we'll talk about some of those differences. But fundamentally, they were all the same. They were all sniper school. And sniper school was the most difficult, stressful training experience any of us had ever encountered.

Not physically; it's the constant grueling intensity of mental concentration it demands that pushes you to the edge. In BUD/S you can commit yourself to going all out, make the decision that you're not going to quit no matter what, and that will take you through it. It's a kind of brute force of mind and body. It doesn't work that way in sniper school. If you miss your target, you can't just "dig deep and commit." You can't stay invisible and escape detection on a stalk simply by "giving it your all." You have to get it right—not mostly right, not 99.9 percent right, but *exactly right,* or you're out.

Through basic and advanced training you are forged and hammered into high-grade steel. In sniper school, that steel is milled into a precision instrument.

In sniper school the tolerances are all much tighter, the margin for error shrunk to an infinitesimal scale. Sniper school is not about being strong; it's about being preternaturally precise. You have to focus all your attention into a tiny circle, a laserlike state of concentration we call *front sight focus.* Yet at the same time, you have to remain fully aware of everything and all conditions happening around you, called *total situational awareness.* It's like using your brain as a scalpel and a broadsword at the same time.

Here's an example of what this experience is like.

For me, possibly the single most stressful aspect of sniper school was something they called *cold bore:* the single shot we had to do first thing upon waking up every morning. The point of cold bore was to simulate conditions in the field, where you won't have time to warm up or the luxury of taking practice shots. *One shot, one kill.* Like the old Bic pen commercial: first time, every time.

How murderously difficult is this?

Let me count the ways.

First, there's you. No matter how good shape you're in, you are not operating at your peak when you first wake up in the morning. Compound that with the fact that you're still stressed out and exhausted from the days that came before. Your fingers, your reflexes, your sense perceptions and judgment are all compromised. And it's not as if it will help any to wake yourself up an hour earlier so you can get all limbered up and awake, because that would mean just one less hour of sleep, making you even more sleep-deprived than you already are.

Then there's your rifle. Like you, it's just waking up, too.

When you shoot a bullet through the barrel of a rifle, you're sending a blast of extremely hot gases exploding out through the metal barrel along with the round. That metal heats up fast, and as it does it
expands, which means the interior bore through which the bullet travels gets more constricted, which in turn creates more friction and spits
the round out the other end with slightly greater velocity. Which affects
the shape of the arc it will travel and its range. All of which affects your
accuracy.

Throughout the rest of the day you'll be shooting through a barrel
that is well warmed up. But not that first shot of the day. First thing
in the morning, you're shooting through the bore of a stone-cold barrel.
And the nights would get damn cold out there in our tents in the California high desert, when I went through the NSW course in 2000.

We would get up at six o'clock or so; some guys had coffee, but coffee
can mess with your nerves, so some of us would have just water and
head right out onto the range. Whatever your morning routine was, the
important thing was not to alter it. Consistency in performance makes
a big difference. For me, coffee could wait. *Everything* could wait. All I
could think about was that solitary bullet, that single target that lay
out there waiting for me. Picture a man-sized silhouette, roughly the
shape of a bowling pin, the top of the pin being his head and the body
of the pin covering his vital organs. There's a small ring at the center:
the 10 ring. The rest of the bowling-pin silhouette is an 8. Anything
outside of that is a zero.

Three zeroes and you're gone from the course.

I couldn't change the temperature of the rifle (since it was locked
overnight in a storage container), but I sure as hell could control the
temperature of the round, and that was factor number three. Because
even the bullet itself being cold makes a difference. If you take a bullet
that's been left out in the cold all night, chamber it, and shoot it as your
first shot in the morning, its temperature affects chamber pressure, too.
As Rob Furlong saw at that competition in Australia, heating a round
will affect its performance—not a lot, maybe just a fraction of a fraction of a degree, but that could be the edge that makes the difference.

So I would sleep with that fucking bullet every night, snuggle up to
it and keep it warm like my life depended on it. On the battlefield, it
damn well could.

The first day of shooting phase, I missed my cold bore shot. For the
rest of the day that zero hung over my head like the first trumpet of
the apocalypse. I thought about almost nothing else all day. Which of

course isn't true, because sniper school is sniper school, which means that you have to think about a million different things every second, all day long. But that single dark thought kept running in the back of my mind like a tape loop: *I missed—tomorrow morning I have to nail it.*

The second morning, I missed again. Nerves. Damn.

Two zeroes. My stomach was in knots the whole day. Now I had to get an 8 or higher, not only on the third day but for the next ten days straight, every single day—or I would be flushed from the course and sent home.

I woke up every morning in a cold sweat. The thought of that cold bore sat on my back all day like a five-thousand-pound ruck.

The third day, I hit the target. An 80. I was safe, at least until the next morning. And the next. And the next after that. It was torture.

And that right there, that's the essence of sniper school: the torture of constant maximum focus. As my sniper school training partner, Eric Davis, says, you can't *try* the bullet into the bull's-eye. You have to turn your brain and all your nerves and muscles into a computer-controlled laser beam and *place* the round in the bull's-eye, again, and again, and again.

In Dante's *Inferno* the final circle of hell is especially interesting: its victims are not thrown into some lake of fire but trapped in progressively deeper layers of ice. Nicely put, Dante. If the torture of boot camp and BUD/S were trials by fire, sniper school was being immobilized in a torture of ice.

On Monday, September 24, 2001, Rob Furlong and one of his PPCLI teammates landed in Wainwright, Alberta, where they and thirteen other Canadians met their sniper instructors—an encounter that went absolutely nothing like the way Rob expected it to.

"Hey, guys," the instructors said. "How are you doing? Congratulations on being here. We want to tell you, you've accomplished a lot just to make it this far."

Rob nearly did the classic drop-jaw dumb-face stare. *How are you doing? Congratulations on being here? What planet did you guys beam down from?*

Up to that point, every military course Rob had ever taken was not only physically demanding but over-the-top stressful in the way it was conducted. The instructors were invariably loud, often borderline abusive, and there was always a constant, pervasive sense of being pushed, pushed, pushed to one's very limits, of being pushed to the breaking point and beyond. But the way these instructors were behaving? This was a novel experience. To Rob it felt surreal, as if he'd landed in some other universe. These guys were talking to their incoming students like they were human beings. Like they were *adults*.

What Rob was experiencing is what we call a "gentleman's course." There was no yelling or screaming, none of the typical wearing-you-to-a-pulp games and endless PTs, no piling on of extra stress.

"We do not have to stress you out," the instructors explained. "You'll be under so much pressure in this course, you'll stress yourselves out. We don't have to do anything to push you out. In fact, we're going to do whatever we can to keep you in. And even then, many of you will fail the course."

They were right, of course. At the time, the Canadian sniper program had about a 95 percent attrition rate. Rob was determined to be among the 5 percent.

True to their word, the instructors actually went out of their way to help the students—another first in Rob's military training experience. They would come out to the candidates' shacks at night after training was finished for the day and say, "Okay, guys, who needs help with this? Let's go over what you did today." And one by one they'd work with each guy there, helping them improve in whatever area was giving them trouble.

When my best friend, Glen Doherty, and I went through the NSW course a year earlier, we saw more than our share of assholes and abuse. Not Furlong. These guys weren't just top sniper instructors, they were also *Canadians,* a people known for their general decency and good manners. The positive reinforcement was constant, and Rob never once witnessed an instructor being a jerk to any of the students or putting anybody down. On the contrary, they did everything in their power to mentor and teach their charges.

One instructor in particular stood out, a guy named Tim McMeekin. Tall (standing about six-two) and very physically fit, McMeekin was also very likable and easygoing. Rob liked him right away—a bond that would prove valuable in the very near future.

Rob's two months of sniper school started with two weeks of classroom work: equipment, ballistics, and field craft, along with admin and logistic issues such as how rank structure and deployment works within sniper cells and within brigades, and more: a massive nonstop fourteen-day information download. They then moved on to the field phase, which lasted the full remaining six weeks of the program and started with practical instruction not in how to shoot but in how to *see*.

If you're scanning hundreds of meters of landscape looking for a single well-hidden target, what do you look for? What makes something visible? Out of the dozen or so key visual attributes, including shape, size, contrast, color, silhouette, and others, the most significant is *movement*. Which is why all animals of prey in the natural world have the uncanny ability to stand stock-still for long minutes at a time: they know it is their movement, far more than their shape, size, position, or any other visual attribute, that will give them away. This had enormous implications to the sniper students, both as predator and as potential prey. As hunters, they began training themselves to force the attribute of movement to the top of their natural hierarchy of visual attention. As potentially the hunted, they knew they, too, would need to develop that capacity for complete stillness.

Next came techniques in how to conduct a visual search. Looking directly at an object is not necessarily the best way to see it. Because of the structure of the human retina, the nature and dispersal of its rods and cones, you may be better off looking to the left or to the right of that object, because you may see it more clearly with your peripheral vision. Peripheral vision is not as acute with detail. It's difficult to read a page of text with peripheral vision, which is why you scan a page with your focal vision. But peripheral vision is much more sensitive to picking up movement and has a more acute sense of color (which is the second most important attribute, after movement).

A major part of being able to shoot something at extreme distances is being able to accurately quantify its exact range. Judging distance to target, or *ranging,* was another critical skill the students were taught. And they weren't allowed to use laser range finders, or GPS, or any kind of advanced equipment. Instead, they learned to gauge an object's range using the reticle of their weapon's scope. (More on this in chapter 8.)

They learned how to build a ghillie suit, how to properly use camouflage, how to properly use depth, and how to move properly in ways to best avoid detection.

And then the stalks began.

That morning they got their orders: "Deployed in this area is an enemy OP [observation post] we think is roughly in this grid square," an area of one square kilometer, or nearly 250 acres. The students were taken out in the back of a transport truck and dropped at the edge of the grid. On their maps, arcs were marked off that described a safe corridor, five hundred meters to the left and five hundred meters to the right. If they stepped outside that corridor, it was an instant fail. The actual corridor was also marked off with small bits of orange tape.

Now it was up to them to stalk through that lane to within shooting distance of their prey, without being seen.

And what was their prey? Two Canadian master snipers, extremely experienced guys, sitting backward in a pair of chairs and facing the direction the students were coming, their elbows resting on the backs of the chairs, their high-powered binoculars up, scouring the ground for any sign of approach.

Understand, these were master snipers, gods of their craft. They knew where the students were being dropped off. They knew where that one-kilometer corridor was. They knew exactly where the students were coming from, and they were sitting dead center, watching and waiting. The students had to stalk up to within one hundred to three hundred meters from their targets, fire two shots at them (blanks, of course), and then stalk back out again—and do all that without these two master snipers ever catching sight of them.

Rob disembarked from the back of the truck, hit the ground, and thought, *Before I do anything else, I have to identify that OP.* How could he stalk against something if he didn't know where it was? A few of his fellow students took a more direct approach: without having any clue where those instructors were, they started sticking their heads up like periscopes ("turkey-necking," they call it), in an effort to spot their targets.

"Freeze!" a voice yelled out. They'd barely gotten started, and one of the master snipers had seen something. The students all had to freeze in their tracks and wait for the walkers.

The walkers were four additional instructors who roamed the area dressed in orange marker vests, each with a radio on his back sporting a ten-foot antenna with a flag on the end. They were the hands of the master snipers at the OP; the stalk had now become a deadly game of tag, and the walkers were the hands that would do the tagging.

The master sniper who'd seen movement was now on his radio to one of the walkers, telling him what direction to walk. The walkers were not allowed to use any initiative of their own; they functioned purely as drones, extensions of the master snipers' observations.

Following his instructions, the walker began plodding straight toward one of the students who'd been turkey-necking.

Meanwhile, Rob and everyone else stayed frozen in place. Once a *Freeze!* command was issued, if you continued moving, tried to slip lower to the ground, or did anything at all, and a walker saw you do it, that was an instant fail.

The walker continued on. The master sniper walked him straight up to the poor student, who crouched there paralyzed, unable to do anything but watch as his doom approached. The walker touched him.

Fail.

Now the rest of the students were free to move again. Rob continued. Crawling on his face, he eventually made his way to a location within three hundred meters from the OP. Poking his rifle and scope slowly through the foliage, he peered through the reticle at the master sniper's head, took his measurement and made his calculation, hoping—no, *trusting*—that he was within 5 percent. He dialed the data into his elevation turret, adjusted for wind, took a breath, and spoke out loud.

"Sniper ready to fire."

The closest walker heard him and walked over to within about twenty-five meters of where Rob lay prone, then repeated the line over his radio.

"Sniper ready to fire."

Now the master sniper knew there was a sniper out there somewhere who had him in his sights. Rob knew that from this point on, he had to move with extreme precision.

The walker said, "Stand by for exposure."

The master sniper raised a head-shaped sign with the single letter painted on it. They called this a "hunt's head." It would be either white-on-black or black-on-white, and feature one of the six letters S-N-I-P-E-R. In this case, it was the letter S, painted white on black.

He held up the hunt's head for one, two, thr—and it was already down. A two-and-a-half-second exposure. If Rob didn't see it clearly during that brief window, he would be unable to take the next step.

Which would be a fail.

"Sniper identifies sierra," he said out loud.

"Sniper declares sierra," the walker spoke over his radio.

After the briefest of pauses, the master sniper's reply came back. "Roger that. Sierra. Have him fire his first shot."

The walker nodded in Rob's direction. "Okay, fire your first shot."

A feeling of exultation began to rise, and Rob quickly tamped it down. This was no time to get self-congratulatory. In fact, this was exactly where things got difficult. Because with every new step in the process, the odds that the master sniper would finally be able to spot him increased. And in the next few seconds, they would increase astronomically.

Rob was about to give himself away—possibly.

Crack!

He fired his blank. The master snipers—both of them now—peered intently through their binos, looking for the slightest movement of a leaf, a twig, anything that would betray the unintended slight movement of a rifle barrel. Looking for a muzzle flash. Looking for the inadvertent movement of a stray foot or other body part, anything the student sniper may have neglected to keep in his full control as he squeezed the trigger.

They saw nothing.

"Okay," came the voice over the radio, "move within seven."

The walker now walked closer, coming to a stop just seven meters from where Rob lay.

"Indicate direction."

The walker raised his arm and pointed directly toward Rob.

Meanwhile, Rob was unloading the casing from his first round, pocketing it (leaving a casing behind is an automatic fail) and easing a second round into the chamber, the whole time thinking about the fact that of all the visual clues the eye picks up, the most telltale is *movement,* and hoping—no, *trusting*—that the master sniper would not be able to detect any movement from him.

A lengthy pause. Then:

"Walker, move away. Have him fire a second shot."

The walker backed away, then said, "Sniper, fire your second round."

Rob fired his second round.

Another pause.

"Okay, walker, move to within three and indicate."

You've gotta be fucking kidding me, thought Rob, even though he knew full well that this was what came next. *How is he not going to see me?* he added—and then immediately shut down that line of thought. No room for self-doubt. To pull off a successful stalk requires the patience of a sequoia and the unshakable confidence of a boulder.

The walker stepped to within three meters and again pointed toward where Rob lay—not directly down at the ground, but just in that compass direction, in a straight horizontal.

But the master snipers still could not see him. So they went to the next step: they turned around in their chairs and faced the other direction.

"Sniper is not under observation."

Now the walker (who was also master sniper–qualified) came over and hunkered down to where Rob was. "Okay, what distance are you at?"

"I range at 220," replied Rob.

The walker stood up, took out his laser range finder, lased the chairs, and nodded. "Okay, you're good at 220." He then got down behind the gun and checked the elevation and windage Rob had set. Both were good.

Now, as Rob rolled away to give him room, the walker got down behind the gun, pulled out the bolt, and peered through the barrel to ensure that there were no obstructions and that Rob had set himself up with a clear window to shoot through. If he saw a twig, branch, leaf, or other obstruction in the bullet's path, that would be an automatic fail.

There were no obstructions.

He rolled out, gave Rob his bolt back to reinstall, and got back on his radio. "Everything is good here. Sniper has passed up to this point."

Up to this point, he thought. *Right.*

Now came the hard part. Now he had to stalk all the way back out again. Undetected. Which was far tougher, because now the master sniper knew *exactly* where he was starting from. On top of that, he knew they would check his slug trail, that is, what he left behind, if anything. If he lost track of a piece of equipment, left a compass behind, a set of cutters, some stray pieces of camouflage, an empty casing, anything at all: fail. There were some thirteen specific steps to the stalk, thirteen distinct points where messing up would mean a fail.

They had eight graded stalk scenarios throughout the next few weeks. And they were black-and-white, pass-or-fail: you had to pass every single stage of those stalks flawlessly, or you failed the entire thing completely.

As he started crawling backward on his belly, maneuvering his way toward turning around without being caught, Rob flashed back on what the instructors had said on their first day at the course. *We don't have to stress you out—you'll stress yourselves out.*

One of Rob's classmates, who had earned the nickname Mil Dot because he wore his hair so close-cropped, nearly buckled under the pressure. As the stalking phase stretched on, entire patches of Mil Dot's hair began falling out from the stress. Mil Dot would not make it through the course. Neither would quite a few others.

In fact, stalking is where most people fail in sniper school—every sniper school, no matter what branch or what country. Stalking is the essence of the sniper experience; it's the *spy* in *warrior/assassin/spy,* the ability to slip undetected through terrain and conditions where no human being should be able to pass without notice, to move like a whisper and evaporate like mist. It is, more than any other aspect, the skill that distinguishes an expert sniper from a mere expert marksman.

And stalking is a bitch.

Stalking is a lot like flying. You can climb into a car and drive off without paying all that much attention to what you're doing. Not so in a plane. When you fly, there are a hundred things you have to check before you leave the runway, a constellation of data you have to be aware of and keep track of. The instrument panel of even a fairly simple plane is vastly more complex than the dashboard of your car, and for good reason.

That's what it's like to stalk. Constant, total, detailed situational awareness.

In stalking we talk about having a strategic checklist, very much like what you use as a pilot. As you start out you ask yourself, which way is the sun shining? Before you move, you make sure you're not getting shadows on your face. Which way are the leaves reflecting? Where's the target in relation to you and your shadow? You make sure your background matches, your foreground matches. You make sure you're moving forward, directly toward the target, and not laterally, which is much easier to detect. You check to see if your next movement is going to be silent, or cause any sound. You need to be thinking about dead space, cover versus concealment, and contingency, that is, how the hell you're getting out of there if it all goes to shit. Just like a pilot about to take off, you run that checklist just before you move—only on a stalk, you run it *every time* you move.

You never know when someone might be staring straight in your direction, so you have to assume he is *always* staring straight in your direction. In the case of the stalks in training, he is.

This takes enormous concentration, and you can't let that concentration waver, not even for a single move. If you don't have the discipline and mental fortitude to be continually going over your checklist and holding all the items in your head, you'll fail. The moment you say, "Shit, I just need to move"—that's the moment you get busted.

The truth about stalking is that in order to be able to successfully execute a complete stalk, get in, take the shot, and get out undetected, you have to go through the entire stalk—in minute detail, with not a single detail omitted or neglected—in your head.

And that's the bottom line of stalking: you fail, or pass, *in your mind*.

As Alex Morrison learned, the hard way, when he went through the SEAL sniper course back in 1991.

Still being fairly new to shooting firearms, Alex struggled with the marksmanship portion of the course. Shooting did *not* click for him, at least not right away, and he had to pour himself onto it, listening and watching with the greatest concentration possible as the instructors demonstrated, absorbing every minute detail he could, and putting in dozens of extra hours on the range.

The good thing about the NSW course, even in those early days, was that he *could* pour in those dozens of hours. The SEAL course is resourced like no other; they plow all the time and money, ammo and opportunity it takes to turn you into an expert shooter. The students spent five weeks on the range, and all they did was shoot, shoot, shoot. Some of their instructors were civilians, national match shooters who donated their time, purely out of patriotism and the fun of having such dedicated students. By the time the marksmanship phase was over, Alex could shoot.

While shooting did not come naturally to him, stalking did. All those years hunting fish with a polespear were burned into his bones and muscles, and hunting men on the ground wasn't really all that different.

Ironically, though, it was the stalking that did him in. It was, in fact, what did in most of his class. Those early stalks were so insanely difficult, and the quality of teaching so poor, that out of a class of sixteen, that cadre of instructors succeeded in graduating only four snipers, a dismal pass rate.

It was summer when Alex went through the program, and he remembers the stalks as ordeals of absolute misery. Lying out on the forest floor, sweating like a sow in a sauna, he soon discovered he had become very attractive to the local insect population. During one stalk he crawled across an anthill: red harvester ants. Those little fuckers are often mistaken for fire ants, and it's not hard to see why. Their bites are painful, and they feel like they last forever. Alex became harvester ant food. But there was nothing to do but be still, stay focused, and keep pushing slowly forward, dragging his body over the hill and on toward the target. At the end of the exercise, he was blanketed in bites.

Still, the misery would have been fine if he'd passed. He didn't.

After that first course Alex spent the next few years schooling himself, analyzing where he'd gone wrong and what he needed to do different next time. The stalks were essentially just like hunting fish with a polespear—but the details *were* different, and those details were what he needed to master.

He realized that he'd been relying way too much on his ghillie suit.

Now he started working more with the natural vegetation he encountered in his stalk. He learned to sit tight at the start of the stalk and not move a muscle until he'd located that OP, then—and only then—pick out the exact route he'd take.

Typically, once he arrived at his destination and built his final firing position, he would pull plants from around him and stick them into the rubber bands that covered his bipod, turning his gun into a giant veg fan. But as he came to understand how to work with the ambient light, he realized that this wasn't always the way to go. If the sun happened to be behind him, that tactic wouldn't cut it: the instructor could still see him silhouetted against the veg fan. When he found himself in that situation, he knew he needed to get something behind him to prevent silhouetting. If he was facing into the sun, on the other hand, then he'd use a bunch of light-colored veg in front of him to reflect light back toward the OP, so the instructor's view would be compromised.

Bit by bit, he assembled his skill set, until he knew he could make it all work.

In 1994, three years after his first shot at it, Alex went back and redid the course, and this time he was ready. He was the first one to finish on every stalk and came through the scout phase of the course with a perfect score.

Earlier I said the stress of sniper school isn't primarily physical, and that's generally true. For example, it's true of the Canadian Armed Forces course, and the Naval Special Warfare course, and the Army Special Operations Target Interdiction Course (SOTIC).

Then there's the Marine Corps: the exception that proves the rule.

Unlike Rob's experience at Wainwright, the school Jason Delgado encountered when he arrived at Pendleton in late 2002 was no gentleman's course. In terms of how it dished out stress and abuse, it was less like the SEAL sniper program and more like BUD/S. It even had its own Hell Week. In Okinawa Jason had been so thoroughly prepared that by the time he showed up for the Scout Sniper Basic Course (SSBC), he figured he was more than ready. Maybe so, but that didn't make the experience any easier. For Jason, sniper school turned out to be just one more stop on his guided tour through hell.

The marines ran their school more like a selection program, so in addition to all the instruction and sniper-skill-set training, there were also the push-ups and PTs and shouting and being kept up late at night and constant harassment and all the rest of what in the military they call "fuck-fuck games." As Jason learned his first day there.

The first thing he noticed was that they couldn't *walk* anywhere; everywhere they went, they ran. You want to go get a drink of water? You run. Time for chow? You run. And when you finish, you run back. His old nighttime training companion was there: good old sleep deprivation. And when they picked on you, it was not like a schoolyard kind of picking on you, it was, "Hey, grab your 210-pound partner with his sixty-or-seventy-pound ruck, put him on your motherfucking shoulder, with *your* ruck on, and go run four or five hundred yards and then run back here—and hurry up!" And some days the temperature soared to more than 100 degrees.

The first day started with a basic physical exam, not so different from first days he'd experienced before—except that this one went at a blinding pace, everything happening so fast it was like they'd been swept up in a whirlwind. One minute he was going through a PFT (pulmonary function test) and having a drink of water, the next moment he was stripped down to PT gear, out on a field doing crunches, then pull-ups, then a three-mile run (a *fast* run) and then back to the class-room—

Where they already had a list of classmates who were cut.

What? Yes: cut. Gone. Barely a few hours had passed, and already six guys were out of the course. Jason's sniper class started out with thirty-four men. They lost half a dozen that day and eight more by the end of week one.

To Jason, this was all business as usual. His view was, hey, if the instructors weren't going to be hard on them, they wouldn't respect the course and it wouldn't be worth going through it.

"It's that marine mentality," he says. "We love punishment. We get kicked in the ass and say, 'Thank you, sir, may we please have another?'"

If punishment was what Jason expected, the marine course did not disappoint.

The twelve solid weeks of SSBC (recently scaled back to ten) was broken down into phases: academics, field craft, marksmanship, stalking, tactical operations without troops (or TOWOTs, pronounced *toots*; more on those shortly), Hell Week, a mission/field week, and a concluding PIG party followed by graduation—for those who were still left standing.

The Corps being the Corps, the academics were incredibly rigorous. The classes covered the math of milliradians (mil dot calculations) and range estimation, elevation and windage, scope theory, fundamentals of a solid shooting position, ballistics, weapon systems, history, classroom instructions on observation techniques, sniper missions, radio operations, and the format for calling for fire, close air support, or nine-line medevac (so-called because there are nine distinct lines of information to the call: location; radio call sign; number of patients by priority of urgency; special equipment required; number of patients as ambulatory or not; description of enemy troops in the area; how the pickup site will be marked; how many patients are U.S. or non-, military or non-, or prisoner of war; and description of terrain, including whether or not there is nuclear, biological, or chemical weapons contamination in the area).

Whatever they learned one day, they would be tested first thing the next morning, for a pass-or-fail grade. Which meant that before the day's classes began, the students had to rip through exhaustive testing on everything from the day before. If you had four classes on Tuesday, then you'd have four exams Wednesday morning before the day's classes started.

Field craft consisted of the usual observation techniques, KIMS (keep in memory systems) games, concealment, field sketches, and so forth. In the stalking phase, they were graded on ten separate stalks, similar to Rob's eight stalks, and just as with the Canadian course, it was the toughest phase of the school.

Finally it came time for the shooting portion—and on his first day on the range, Delgado had what he describes as the worst experience of his military training. To which he adds: "And it was my own damn fault."

He and his partner for the day, Aaron Winterle, were shooting string after string of fire on the M40A1 bolt-action sniper rifle. Jason had just gotten finished with one string and started getting up from his firing position to prepare for what came next. Their lead instructor, Gunnery Sergeant Healy, asked Jason if he had cleared his weapon.

Duh, is what Jason thought. What he said was, "Yessir, Sergeant Healy!"

"Just clear it agin," said Healy, in his deceptively relaxed Southern drawl. "For mah sake."

From the deadly calm of his voice, Jason should have known right then that he was screwed. But he was still too green to get that. Without a second thought, he obliged. He racked the bolt on the M40 to the rear to demonstrate that the chamber was empty—and to his horror, a bright, shiny round catapulted out of the gun. *Pingggggg!*

In all the excitement of finally getting onto the range and firing this weapon system, he'd forgotten to clear his weapon. He *thought* he'd done it. He was *sure* he'd done it. Except that he hadn't. And of course Healy had known.

It felt to Jason like it took five minutes for that damn round to pinwheel gently through the air and finally arc to the ground between him and Sergeant Healy. Jason stared at the fallen round.

Without turning Healy softly said, "Sergeant Wright?" Wright, their PT instructor—yes, they had drill sergeants even in sniper school—had materialized instantly behind Healy like a sadistic genie called up from hell's magic lamp. "Take Del-ga-do here and his shootin' partner. They need . . . encouragement."

The round of PT Jason and Aaron went through at the hands of Sergeant Wright that afternoon was the worst PT Jason ever experienced, before or since. After close to two hours straight in the 112 degree humidity, they both went down for heat injuries.

Jason never again forgot to clear his weapon.

The lowest point came with the aptly named Hell Week. These days it's mandatory that the students get at least one meal a day, but when Jason went through it he didn't eat for five days straight. Or sleep, either.

Hell Week started out with something physical, of course: five-mile ruck run, PIG egg run, and more, on into the night. When they got back to the squad bay, they had to work up a TOWOT—an 89- to 150-page op order, spelling out every last thing in detail. What shoelaces they were bringing, what kind of ammunition they were bringing, where they were keeping their dog tags, where they were keeping the first-aid kits, with a diagram drawn up of the marine's body detailing where each thing would be kept, actions on the objective . . . it was an enormous amount of detail, covering every aspect of a mission one could possibly think of.

The marines were already sleep-deprived and had spent hours becoming physically exhausted. Now they had to stay awake all night sitting at desks, focusing on this maddeningly detailed report, making sure they got every piece in and every piece right. And the sergeants kept playing distracting shit over the sound system in the background, a soundtrack of someone speaking in Arabic, interspersed with bits of English translation. It was intensely hot and stuffy in the room. People were getting delusional. Jason recalls at one point writing something about blue balloons and a lobster, and then something about monkeys grabbing his gear. It seemed to make sense at the time. But hallucinating or not, he kept writing. Most of the class failed that one.

The next day, they did something else physical—a fifty-pound ruck run for a couple miles, stretcher carries, and whatever else the instructors had dreamed up for them that day—and when they got back, nicely exhausted, they had to do terrain models for an upcoming mission. These models needed to be as detailed and realistic as possible. They got elaborate with these things, using yarn for the gridlines and carefully spray-painting everything to make it all look as real as possible. By the time they were finished with them, these creations were going to be little works of art.

At this point they had gone without sleep for three days.

As they worked, the instructors stopped them and said, "Hey, what does this mean—" and they said something in Arabic. Jason recognized it as one of the phrases they'd played the night before while they were trying to distract the students from writing their TOWOTs. For some reason, Jason had retained it. Nobody else had a clue. He raised his hand.

"Delgado?" demanded an instructor.

"It means, 'Hey, could you please speak a little more slowly?'"

"Congratulations, Delgado!" the guy said. "You got yourself a reward coming."

Jason's reward was better than cash, better than food, better than anything else he could have dreamed up: it was a big, steaming cup of hot coffee. After three days of no sleep? Pure heaven. He sat there downing his hot coffee, thinking, *Ohhh yeahhhh, I'm the man.* . . . As he drank he felt a crazy surge of energy coursing through his veins. It was the most glorious feeling he could remember ever having. He was on cloud nine, ready to take on the world.

He got up, walked back over to resume work on his terrain models.

"Okay, everybody, stop working," the instructor called out. "Break time. You've got thirty minutes to take a nap."

Jason fell from cloud nine, back to earth—and below.

Everyone else in the class gave an audible, collective sigh of relief and hit the floor. In seconds they were all asleep. For the next thirty minutes Jason lay on his back, staring at the ceiling, cursing under his breath. It was the first time in Hell Week they'd been given a chance to sleep. It was also the last time in Hell Week they were given the chance to sleep. And Jason went through it stone-cold awake.

But he completed Hell Week, and every other aspect of the course.

After that terrible first day on the range, Jason had had a rough time of the shooting portion. He and his shooting partner, Jesse Davenport, were both crack shots, but they were not experienced spotters. The first week of the shooting phase they ran three qualifications and took the best score out of three. Jason flunked the first two outright and squeaked by on the third. But if the first day on the range was his worst training experience ever, the last day of sniper school was his best, when he was awarded the top-of-class position of High Shooter.

Of the original thirty-four who started the class, just twelve were left at graduation. Three were Navy SEALs and two were Marine Corps officers and seven plain marines, including Jason and Jesse. Shortly after graduating, the two friends were on their way to Iraq with Third Battalion, Fourth Marines, as part of the push north into Baghdad.

Within weeks after buying himself a George Foreman grill and eating that steak he had hallucinated during Ranger School, Nick Irving was off to train again. For the next seven months, he was at home with his wife for a total of no more than three or four weeks. The rest of that time he was steeped in a steady procession of sniper course after sniper course.

This wasn't 2000, when I went through the SEAL course, or '01 or '02, when Furlong and Delgado took their versions of the course. And it sure wasn't 1991, when Alex took his first shot at the program. It was 2008, and the United States was seven years deep into protracted war on multiple fronts. The rangers were operating at an insanely high op tempo and spread thin over two theaters. They needed qualified snipers, and they needed them fast.

The quick-and-dirty, five-week basic army course Nick would attend was not an advanced Spec Ops course, and it didn't have a reputation for producing the best snipers. But Nick had a powerful advantage: he was a ranger, and the 75th Ranger Regiment had their own training pipeline, which included a whole range of schools, some of them put on by specialized civilian operations that had been teaching everyone from Tier 1 Spec Ops groups to FBI/HRT (hostage rescue team) and Secret Service snipers for decades. Even better, they had their own in-house "school" of instruction, a sort of pre–sniper school prep reminiscent of Delgado's six-month Okinawa indoc, only this was a two-week intensive crash course in street-smart veteran sniper fundamentals, taught by guys who'd been at the craft for decades.

Before starting, the group of about twenty students had to pass a physical fitness test—two-mile runs with full kit, obstacle course, the usual—followed by a battery of psychological testing, which included a lengthy series of what seemed to Irving like the strangest questions.

"Who do you love more, your mom or your dad?" Nick wondered what the best answer was to *that*.

"Do you like flowers more than you like cake?" *If I say flowers,* he thought, *I'm going to sound gay, but if I say cake, then that makes me seem like I'm stuck in a child's mentality.*

On and on they went, nearly six hours of questions like that, Nick second-guessing himself the whole way through. What the hell. He just threw down answers and hoped for the best. After the battery of questions he had to talk with a psychiatrist for a while. A few of the aspiring snipers did not make it through this part of the process.

After psychological evaluations came grilling by the board. Nick was ushered into a room where he sat at one end of a long table, facing about ten senior snipers at the other end. These guys had absolute power to say yea or nay. You could pass every other qual, be outstanding in every way, but if they didn't want you in the section, if they didn't think you were a guy who could carry on the ranger sniper tradition, they could just say no, and that was that. They said yes.

Then the training began. They were issued all kinds of equipment, some Nick had never seen before, some he had no idea what it was used for. Weird-looking rucksacks. A snowsuit. A ghillie suit for woodland environments. An urban setup. Different poles and sticks and ladders. A ladder you could fit into a cargo pocket but use to scale up onto a fourteen-foot roof.

And their sniper rifles.

Nick was given a Barrett M82 .50 cal sniper rifle, an absolute monster; an MC24 .30 cal sniper rifle, which was a brand-new configuration of the M24 and pretty serious boom stick itself; and an SR-25. Nick shot them all, learned them all, and became proficient on them all. But the moment they put that SR-25 in his hands, it was love at first touch.

That night Nick thought back to an experience he'd had in Mosul the previous year, when he was still a Stryker driver and machine gunner. Nick's unit had walked into an ambush and found themselves in a major firefight. One of his team leaders plugged an iPod into the internal speakers of Nick's Stryker, and they fought their way through that ambush with Michael Jackson's hit single "Dirty Diana" playing at full volume.

Nick had grown up listening to Michael Jackson and couldn't imagine a better name.

Dirty Diana it was.

He spent the next two weeks on the range, every day, six to eight hours straight, shooting the M24 and Dirty Diana. At the same time, the senior snipers did their best to teach them everything they knew— the math of long-range shooting, tricks of the trade in stalking and concealment, the salient points of internal ballistics and external ballistics and terminal ballistics—even as they kept feeding them more rounds to shoot, an endless, unlimited all-you-can-eat ammunition buffet. By the time Nick left his unit and headed off to the army basic sniper course, he was *schooled*.

Once they got to the actual sniper course, though, it wasn't the shooting that killed them. Nick rates the army sniper course as being the single most difficult experience of his entire military training, and the difficulty had nothing to do with marksmanship. It was the field craft and stalking that washed out some 70 percent of the class. For a while, Nick thought he might be among the casualties.

One of their first topics was target detection, which involved being able to spot small items in a large field of vision that were out of place. To Nick this was absolutely baffling. His first day out on the course, he wasn't able to locate a single one of the objects they'd hidden out there.

The instructor then went out onto the course and, while the students watched, he walked around and touched each item, one by one. Nick thought, *Holy shit—there's no way I'll ever train my eye to see things like that!*

Nick knew he could shoot, and he thought he would be pretty good at the stalking part. But he worried about his vision. He'd barely managed to get into the service in the first place despite his color blindness. Would his eyes finally betray him? Would that be his fatal weakness, the thing that kept him from doing what he'd always wanted to do and sent him back to the regiment as a machine gunner or assaulter?

He thought, *Maybe I'm just not cut out to be a sniper.*

But as the course progressed, he started to get a sense of how it worked. Exactly as in Rob Furlong's course in Canada, they were taught how to see differently, to look for key distinguishing elements such as color, shine, shadow, and line. Hard lines rarely occur in nature. Certain shadows just don't make sense in a natural setting. During one practice session the instructor called time, walked out onto the course, and put his hand on a little toothbrush head, tucked halfway in behind a rock and partially covered with leaves.

"How do you guys *not* see this toothbrush head?"

"Man," said someone, "it's the size of a pinky! And it's covered with leaves!"

"Yeah," said the instructor, "but look at this. See this straight line, and how it contrasts with the curved edges of the leaves?"

And all at once, Nick could see exactly what he meant. It wasn't about simply having good eyesight. It was about using your eyes— really, about using your *mind*—to single out small things that just didn't fit into the larger picture. A few days later he was acing the tests.

One morning for PT they did a five-mile run. When they got back from the run, they ran through a series of push-ups and sit-ups, and just as muscle fatigue was starting to set in the instructors pulled them into the classroom, sat them down, gave them each a pen and a piece of paper, and said: "Along that route you ran this morning there were twenty military items. You have one minute to write them all down."

They had placed twenty random objects out there all over that course—on the road, in the trees, on road signs, back in the woods—and they were all either very small or otherwise visually obscured: a bullet taped to the pole of a STOP sign; a ghillie suit hanging up in a tree deep in the forest, maybe thirty yards off the route they were running. And all without letting their students know ahead of time that this was anything but an ordinary morning run. The instructors were devious.

Nick and the others sat there staring at their pieces of paper, trying their best to pull up details of memories they didn't even know they had. Meanwhile the instructors put on loud rock 'n' roll music, started flashing the lights on and off and banging on trash cans. They even flipped over a few empty desks—anything to compound the distraction. The students had one minute to finish.

And, amazingly, they did. It seemed almost like magic to Nick, but both his capacity to see and his power of visual recall were building, just as his physique and physical stamina had been built up in basic training years earlier.

Finally, it was time for the stalking itself, where (exactly as in the marine course) they had to pass at least seven out of their ten graded stalks. A lot of the students didn't have the patience to do what it took to outwit their instructor, a former marine Spec Ops who'd served in Vietnam and could pick out a sniper in full ghillie at a thousand yards with the naked eye. Under that guy's eagle gaze it could take thirty minutes to an hour to move just five feet.

Nick reached down deep in his memory banks, recalling every detail he'd ever read or watched about snipers, and did his best to channel

Carlos Hathcock. *An inch at a time, Irv,* he told himself, *just one inch at a time.* Out of the ten graded stalks, he didn't fail a single one.

After successfully graduating the army sniper course, Nick plunged into a rapid-fire sequence of specialized training programs all over the United States, ping-ponging around the country for program after program.

First up was a privately run, two-week extreme-range precision shooting course, put on by an outfit down in South Texas called Rifles Only. The guys at Rifles Only trained snipers from SWAT teams, FBI, ATF, SEALs, SAS, DEVGRU, you name it, anybody and everybody who specialized in long-range precision. And of course, Army Rangers.

There was no stalking in this course, no field craft, nothing but ballistics and high-precision marksmanship at extreme ranges.

They taught their students a lot of math and techniques to be very, very precise with the gun. There were high winds at this place, which was ideal, because on those long-range shots, the wind is typically what will mess up the shot.

It was very high-paced and very long hours, starting off at seven in the morning and ending typically around six at night. Sometimes they shot at night with thermals. The course went for two weeks straight without a single break.

Irving was in the class with seven other rangers. Over their two weeks there they shot so many thousands of rounds Nick couldn't even estimate the number. It took an eighteen-wheeler flatbed truck to bring in all the ammo they used, just for the eight of them. By the end of that course, the whole right side of his chest was purple with bruises.

In sniper school they'd trained on a twenty-inch-by-forty-inch target, standard for military snipers. In Texas they were set up with circular targets that were three inches in diameter. *Dude,* thought Nick, *there's no way I'm going to hit a three-inch target at three hundred yards!* None of them thought they could do it. But they did. Next they were given targets the size and shape of a human head—at a thousand yards. They didn't think they could make that, either. And of course they did.

Back from the precision course, Nick had time to clean his guns, kiss his wife, and check in with command—and then he was out to the West Coast, to another course being run by Rifles Only, only this time in the high mountains of California.

Talk about a change in terrain and climate. Nick spent the next three weeks hiking up and down mountains thousands of feet high in the bitter cold. The place did a very credible job of simulating the environment of northern and eastern Afghanistan.

This was another high-precision shooting school, only the focus was on extreme long distances—1,800 yards, 2,000 yards, distances of more than a mile—and on high-angle shooting, which requires a whole different math than straight-line shooting. They were shooting very long distances at extreme angles, from the top of the mountain down to the base. They learned to use the Pythagorean theorem to compensate for shooting up or down an extreme slope; they called it "slope dope." (More on this later.) The wind was vicious up there and often unpredictable, and Nick also learned a good deal about the different qualities of wind beyond the basic speed and direction. He also got to experience the impact of altitude on a shot. The higher you get, the colder it gets, but at the same time, as the air is thinner the bullet travels farther and faster.

Once again, it was long hours of nonstop shooting, tens of thousands of rounds. All the while, Nick was keenly aware that this present luxury, having an unlimited supply of ammunition to shoot, was something he would *not* have in the field. In the field, ammunition was liable to be in very short supply. The time would come when he would need to make every round count. His life, and other lives, would depend on it.

There was more. Nick went through an urban sniper course, being schooled in the art of the urban hide—exact same principles as a jungle or desert hide, only in a theater of buildings and busy streets. He went through the 75th Regiment's Designated Marksman course run by the U.S. Army Marksmanship Unit (AMU), the best shooters in the world. These guys go on to compete in the Olympics; they are just phenomenal to watch. He was supposed to go on to the army's elite Spec Ops course, SOTIC—but there just wasn't time. We were neck-deep in war and he was needed overseas.

After more than a half year of nearly continuous sniper training, Nick had a two-week break before boarding a big C-17 transport plane. Next stop: Helmand Province, Afghanistan.

A little more than seven years earlier, as our combat experience in Afghanistan was just getting started, Rob Furlong was entering the last few days of his sniper school experience, starting with their final training exercise (FTX), a two-day mock mission. The course brought in members of the police force, who tracked the students with dogs and dog handlers. Rob had to evade both humans and dogs, reach his target, and take it out. When he successfully got within killing range and set up his final firing position (FFP), he looked through his scope and saw something that quite eloquently expressed the mood of the day: over the target the instructors had pasted a life-sized picture of Osama bin Laden.

Rob got a kick out of placing a round square through bin Laden's head.

But the final ex was not quite final. Still to come were the final stalks, the most difficult of the course. At the conclusion of these two stalks, once a student had successfully reached his FFP without detection, the instructors removed themselves from the OP and steel targets were positioned in their place. Now the students had to end their stalk by firing live rounds at the targets to ensure that, yes, they had indeed established the proper windows for clean passage of their rounds, and done everything they needed to do to complete the mission successfully.

Rob still vividly remembers the sound of his round striking steel in his final shot on that sniper course. It was a huge relief, the most memorable moment in all of his military training.

They held their graduation right then and there, out on the course, immediately after they'd all fired their last shots. The commanding officer of the training facility, a colonel, came out onto the field, carrying the five certificates with him, his presence at the event an indication of how important this particular course was regarded.

The students stood in a knot, still in their ghillies and cam paint, as the colonel presented each with their hog's tooth and certificate right there in the field.

"Congratulations," he told the group. "What you've achieved here, very few have done. Now go wash up and turn in your kit—and then you're going to go have a few drinks together. You've earned it."

As the others started heading back to their quarters, the colonel turned to Rob and addressed him quietly.

"Unfortunately, Furlong," he said, "you won't be joining the others in the evening's festivities."

Oh shit, thought Rob. *What's going on?*

"You need to report back to Edmonton," added the commander. "Now."

The Canadian sniper course normally had an extremely high attrition rate; 95 percent was not uncommon. But this class had been anything but normal. The caliber (pun clearly intended) was exceptionally high, and so was the pass rate. Out of a class of fifteen who started in the course, a full one third made it to graduation. Of those five graduates, one had been selected to go straight to deployment.

Rob shook all his classmates' hands, went back to his barracks, packed up his gear, and made the drive back to Edmonton.

Time to go to war.

5

THE PLATINUM STANDARD

If you want to achieve excellence, you can get there today—as of this second, quit doing less-than-excellent work.

—Thomas Watson, founder of IBM

Throughout the months I spent in Afghanistan following 9/11, I was focused on two things. First, making it back to the States without getting my nuts shot off or brains blown out so I could meet my son, who'd been born while I was gone. And second, if I did make it back, what the hell I was going to do next. The plan I came up with was simple: I would become a BUD/S instructor and finish my college education.

For an active-duty SEAL, going to BUD/S is like taking a break. You work maybe three days a week, yell at some students, get them to wash your car on the weekend, and have a chance to decompress. I could do BUD/S, spend my days off with my family, and finish up my degree in my downtime. All in all, a pretty cushy situation. I liked it.

Didn't happen.

Instead, my BUD/S teammate Eric Davis and I were handed the challenge of a lifetime. "Hey you two," we were told. "We want you to help design, build, and implement the most modernized, effective sniper training program on the planet."

Being invited to take on this task reminded me of the day a few years earlier, in 2000, when a few slots opened up and our platoon chief, Dan Goulart, tapped my best friend, Glen Doherty, and me to enroll in NSW sniper school. We were terrified, because we were new guys—that is, SEALs who had not yet done a deployment and were very much still on probation. New guys were rarely given the chance to go to sniper school. They sent us off with these words of encouragement:

"Don't fuck up."

And now here I was, barely three years later, being tapped not to attend sniper school, not even to teach it, but to reinvent it.

I thought about my BUD/S plan—quality time with my family, completing my degree, moving on with the rest of my life. It was a great plan. But how could I possibly say no to what they were offering? It was an incredibly exciting honor.

Also a ridiculously daunting one. We were, in essence, being given responsibility for an entire generation of snipers. As I heard myself agreeing to take on the job, I silently reassured myself with these words of encouragement:

Don't fuck up.

The strange thing about it was, the whole sniper thing had happened more or less by accident. It certainly wasn't something I went looking for.

Plenty of top snipers already knew their way around guns long before they ever entered the military. Rob Furlong, Jason Delgado, and Nick Irving were handling rifles before they could shave. Marcus and Morgan Luttrell were born shooters who grew up in Texas hunting for food. Chris Kyle probably came down the birth canal with a rifle in his hands.

Not me. Before I entered the service, I'd hardly ever even fired a gun. I didn't grow up wanting to shoot; I grew up wanting to *fly*. As a kid, Nick Irving went hunting for every book and video he could find on Carlos Hathcock and Navy SEALs. The movie that pushed my hot buttons was *Top Gun*. I was a *Star Wars* fanatic. Anything that had to do with flying had my attention. Stick me in a pilot's seat, baby, put me twelve thousand feet above the earth, let me fly the *Millennium Falcon*! (Still true, by the way: there's nothing I love more than taking a friend up and over the Manhattan skyline, or bopping up and down the West Coast at a few thousand feet—even better upside down.)

In my SEAL training I started out as a neophyte on the gun, and not a very good one. Somehow, as happened with Alex Morrison, my years of hunting fish had stuck to me, and that eventually translated into an ability to stalk, spot, and shoot. But you'd never have guessed that if you'd seen my crappy performance on the range during BUD/S.

And then there was Eric.

Like me, Eric is a Californian, grew up in the Bay Area. His father was a sheriff in San Mateo County; his father's father was an FBI special agent, and *his* father was a lawman, too. Being the guy who keeps order with a gun in his hand was more or less in his blood, and his reason for joining the SEALs couldn't have been simpler: to protect and defend those who couldn't protect and defend themselves.

Despite that background, though, Eric was no more brought up with guns than I was, and before SEAL training he had zero experience shooting. (Not even spearguns.) In fact, he didn't even like to shoot all that much. What he loved was the challenge of figuring out how it all worked—how to reverse-engineer and then teach that complex skill set. He's been a student of human performance all his life, and he has a passion for it. But the actual shooting? Let's just say, the dude is never going hunting in his spare time.

So, yeah: the task of helping to create the finest sniper program on the planet was entrusted to two guys who couldn't shoot worth shit when they joined the navy.

That was ironic enough. Here's what made it even more ironic: that this was happening within the navy in the first place. Because, the dirty little secret of the SEAL sniper program? For most of its brief existence, it frankly hadn't been all that good. Yes, the standards were high, insanely high. But the quality of instruction wasn't great, and the attrition rate was atrocious. (Both problems, as we would soon find, could be dramatically reversed.)

Think about this for a moment: SEALs are part of the navy. Not the army, not the marines. The SEALs trace their history back to the UDT (underwater demolition team) warriors of World War II, men whose specialty was swimming underwater and blowing things up. Even today we call ourselves *frogmen.* Just as the air force is all about being in the air, the navy is all about being out on, in, or under the water—not exactly the ideal environment for sharpshooting on an MK13 .30 cal sniper rifle. (Would you expect the air force to be charged with developing a top sniper program?) And while SEALs don't exactly think of themselves as "sailors" or even really as part of the navy, it *is* Naval Special Warfare. We aren't rangers; we aren't Force Recon. We're SEALs.

Basic training in the army gives you a good working familiarity with shooting. Marine boot camp gives you extensive rifle training. In navy boot camp, they teach you how to draw a pistol from a holster without shooting yourself.

You see the subtle difference there?

And those distinctions had historically carried over into the different branches' sniper programs.

The Marine Corps stood up the first genuine military sniper training program in the U.S. during the World War II years, and the USMC sniper course has been a solid course of instruction ever since. It's no accident that Carlos Hathcock was a marine. Marine snipers are legendary, and getting the SSBC qual is a badge of honor in the military. Even today, there's something about marines that nobody else can touch: they get solid training in marksmanship and riflery from day one. The Marine Corps produces some of the finest riflemen in the world. (In fact, a friend of mine who runs the advanced sniper courses for the SEAL program today tells me he recently hired a former marine to teach.)

While the marine course was the gold standard, the army had some pretty damn fine training, too. The basic sniper course Nick Irving went through, while nowhere near as complete as the Corps' program, still provided strong training in all the essentials, and the army's advanced program was first-rate.

Then there was the SEAL course.

The SEALs had been in existence since the days of Vietnam, yet throughout the sixties, seventies, and eighties there was no in-house NSW sniper training program. In those days, any SEALs who wanted to train as snipers were sent to the place where American military snipers were born: the marines. It wasn't until the late eighties that NSW started putting together its own sniper course, and even once it was up and running, it remained the kid nobody wanted to pick for the ball team. *SEAL Team Six* author Howard Wasdin and his teammate Homer Nearpass, decorated snipers who both won Silver Stars for their part in the Battle of Mogadishu (in Wasdin's case, also a Purple Heart), recall being offered the choice of training up with the SEAL school, the USMC program, or the army's SOTIC course.

"When I talked to my SEAL buddies who had been to sniper school," says Wasdin, "every single one of them had chosen to go to Marine Corps sniper school."

He and Nearpass did the same.

When Alex Morrison went through the course in 1991 it was over-the-top difficult, and it was just as insanely difficult when I went through it a decade later. But just because it was hugely difficult didn't mean it was hugely effective. Yes, some excellent snipers emerged from the course, but in some ways that was *despite* the training as much as *because of* the training.

The NSW course was, especially at first, not that well organized. It was taught by guys who had done a lot of match shooting and were superb marksmen, but few had real combat experience. The curriculum was modeled after the marine course program in its general outline—observation training, keep-in-memory games, sketching, brutally difficult stalks, and the rest—but when it came to the specifics of day-to-day instruction, a lot of these instructors more or less made it up themselves.

Throughout the nineties it gradually became more formalized and systematic, improving as it went. Even so, by the time I went through it in 2000 it was still essentially the same course Alex had gone through a decade earlier—and the same course Wasdin and Nearpass and dozens of other top candidates had skipped over in favor of other programs.

When Eric went through it in 1999, he says, the hardest thing about sniper school was getting clear on just what the hell it was they were supposed to be learning.

"The material wasn't at all well organized in those days," says Eric. "Whether it was ballistics, shooting, stalking, or any other piece of it, the instructors dumped a lot of information on us—but it wasn't clear how it all fit together. There was a ton that we just had to figure out on our own."

In its origins, the NSW course had been something of a Wild West show, formed in the days when the ink was barely dry on Dick "Rogue Warrior" Marcinko's retirement papers. It had improved a good deal in the decade-plus since then—but it still bore that DNA.

Our task was to transform *that* into an extremely professional operation of the highest possible standards.

And don't fuck up.

Fortunately, we had a few things going for us. First and foremost of these were the two guys who brought us in and would become our bosses: Senior Chief Bob Nielsen, who was then running the NSW program for the West Coast, and Master Chief Jay Manty, his counterpart on the East Coast.

To give credit where credit's due, a significant amount of the core curriculum had already been significantly reworked by Chief Nielsen and Chief Manty by the time Eric and I arrived on the scene. These two were brilliant, decorated, top-tier snipers who had an incredibly far-sighted vision of where the course needed to go. They hadn't simply hired the two of us to do all the work; they had also done a serious chunk of the work themselves.

The second hugely valuable thing we had going for us was Eric himself. I could not have asked for a better training partner. Eric is a brilliant instructor. No matter what he was teaching, I found I could sit there for any amount of time and listen, riveted—and *learn*. The man is a born teacher. More than that, he has a unique gift. Eric has a fascination with how things work and an uncanny ability to reverse-engineer any process, no matter how complex, breaking it down into its hundreds of component parts and putting it back together on a whole new level, like a Swiss watch disassembled and then rebuilt as a James Bond weapons system.

Plus, the two of us were already good friends. Eric was in my BUD/S class and we were both in Team Three; he went through the SEAL sniper course in '99, two sessions before me. When my platoon went off to the Middle East in the fall of 2000 and ended up on the stricken USS *Cole* off the coast of Yemen, his deployed to the Middle East and worked out of Bahrain, were he participated in a few dozen noncompliant ship boardings. "The pirate stuff," as he puts it. When 9/11 happened, Eric's platoon had just returned and was on post-deployment leave. My platoon shipped out to Afghanistan immediately; his deployed the following January and ended up at the TOC (tactical operations center) in Kandahar while I was out in the field. For Eric and me, the chance to work together, let alone on something as insanely exciting as this, was a gift.

The third thing going for us was history and timing.

Historically, sniper programs in the U.S. have almost invariably been neglected, abandoned, and forgotten during protracted times of peace. In the years after World War II the United States let our military sniper programs more or less slide into dormancy. (The Soviets did not make the same mistake.) It was only once we were drawn into the Korean conflict, and even then only once a marine officer's binoculars were smashed (and his head nearly blown off) by an enemy sniper's bullet, that we figured maybe it was time to pull the program from the mothballs and get cracking again. After the armistice of 1953, military sniper training was nearly shelved, had it not been for the fierce advocacy of two marine officers, Second Lieutenant Jim Land (Carlos Hathcock's mentor) and Warrant Officer Arthur Terry, who kept the flame burning. Before long Vietnam was in full force, and so was American military sniper training.

After Vietnam the Marine Corps' excellent sniper program did not go away, nor did the army's, but little urgency was attached to them. The same thing applied to the fledgling SEAL program throughout the nineties. "Little urgency" means scant attention, which means scant budgetary or logistic support from central command. It costs money to train snipers, and it costs a *lot* of money to train snipers to the highest possible levels of proficiency and effectiveness. The money just wasn't there.

After 9/11 that all changed. By the time Eric and I were onboard, NSW was ready to give the program all the support it needed. We were now a nation at war.

When Eric and I started redesigning the course, it was a hairy time. Not only were we at war, but we were at war in a new and complex environment. This wasn't Desert Storm, where we could rout the enemy by bombing the crap out of them. This was complicated street-level combat on multiple fronts, often with multiple factions having ambiguous loyalties, in shifting and confusing circumstances. Special Operations, classically employed only peripherally and for special situations (hence the term "special"), had suddenly become a central tactical element.

In this new wartime environment, Spec Ops snipers had become the tip of the spear. Our job was to sharpen that tip to the deadliest point possible.

We decided to toss out any idea of training to create *competence*. Screw competence. Good truly is the enemy of great. We were not interested in above average. We were interested in performance that wasn't even in the same universe as average, performance that would blow "good" out of the water. What we were after was *perfection*—or as close to perfection as human beings were capable. For decades the USMC course had served as the gold standard of military sniper programs. Our objective was to build on that success and go further: to create a standard of perfection—a *platinum standard*.

One of our fundamental changes, we knew, had to come not in *what* we taught, but *how*. The quality of the teaching itself had to improve.

At that point, the course had about a 30 percent failure rate. Now, that doesn't sound too bad. You think about the enormous washout rate in programs like BUD/S or Ranger School, and it makes sense. If you're trying to produce an elite force of the best of the best, obviously you need to weed out those recruits who just don't make the grade.

But put that in context. Sniper school isn't like BUD/S, where you expect a major crop of inductees to wash out—where you actually *want* them to wash out. By the time a guy is admitted into the NSW sniper course he is already a serious performer. These were accomplished SEALs coming into the course, men who had already trained to the point where they could do virtually anything required of them, under virtually any circumstances—and we were *still* losing 30 percent of them. When I went through the course in 2000, we started out with twenty-six students. Every one of those twenty-six was a fine warrior with plenty of sniper potential. Yet we finished with just twelve. That's a flunk rate of more than 50 percent.

Eric and I didn't see the high attrition in our course as a badge of honor or symbol of excellence. We saw it as a failure. Not of the students: of the teaching. We wanted to take that attrition rate down—not by lowering the standards but by raising them, that is, by raising the bar on the quality of instruction so that our students would learn more and learn it better. The way to lower attrition, we believed, was to raise the level of excellence.

The year before, when I first got back from Afghanistan in the middle of 2002, I had myself put through the navy's Instructor Training Course, a four-week program that all BUD/S instructors went through. It was a phenomenal experience. They videotaped us as we stood in front of the class teaching, then showed us the tapes. Until you actually see yourself on video replay, you would not believe what you look and sound like, all the *Uhs* and *Ums* and *Y'knows* that slip in, the amount of cursing you do without realizing it. I've seen guys sit there scratching their balls while they teach and refuse to believe it when they're told what they've been doing—until they see it on videotape. It's worse than sobering. It's brutal. And invaluable. To this day I use the skills I learned in that course whenever I'm called on to do live television interviews or paid speaking engagements.

The Instructor Training Course taught us not only how to teach, but how to teach *well*—how to interact with students in such a way that encourages them to really learn, and not just throw information at them.

That experience had also crystallized some thoughts I'd been having about the importance of quality instruction. When I went through BUD/S and the rest of my SEAL training, BUD/S instructors were the *only* ones who went through that course. I thought that was part of the problem with our sniper program. The teachers might be fantastic shots, they might know their shit when it came to stalking and other skills—but that didn't mean they were good teachers. As teachers, in fact, many of them were downright crappy. We decided that in the new course, we would send all our instructors through instructor school to become well-trained and highly professional *educators*.

Then there was the question of *what* we taught. One of the first determinations we made was that the course needed to get its shit together, by which I mean, we needed to make this thing more organized, coherent, and consistent.

The SEAL course was originally run by a chief, along with his cadre of two or three full-time guys, which he would supplement with snipers he pulled from the different teams. While the course was based loosely on the Marine Corps program's curriculum, it ended up being kind of cobbled together, everyone more or less running the course according to his own style and experience.

What's more, while this was happening on the West Coast, the same thing was going on, separately and completely independently, on the East Coast. Naval Special Warfare has always been organized in two main divisions, NSW Group 1, on the West Coast, and NSW Group 2, on the East, and each ran its own program. There was plenty of good stuff happening in these courses. But they weren't reliably on the same page, which meant the students weren't necessarily all learning the same things or being taught in the same ways. Which meant it was all kind of a mess.

And this was a problem.

This is exactly why military pilots have the NATOPS (Naval Air Training and Operating Procedures Standardization) manual and its standardized training. The way they talk to their crews is the same, no matter where they come from. You can take a pilot from the East Coast, throw him onto a West Coast helo flight crew, and he can fly that bird and talk to the crew in an instant in a way that they will all understand exactly what he is saying. Everyone is on the same page.

After 9/11, when we started rapidly deploying our platoons in real-world combat situations, we started realizing, "Holy shit, our snipers are talking different languages." They'd be saying to each other, "Wait a minute—why are you giving me a minute hold? You mean you call your shots in minutes? We call them in mils."

We had to take a good-old-boy course that had grown up without any clear planning, standardize it, and turn it into a professional course.

(Note: While this problem has since been addressed throughout the military, standardization is still a big problem today across the landscape of American law enforcement. With the emerging threats of terrorism and active-shooter situations, we need to standardize the best training and operational practices across all civilian units, too.)

On top of the four-week instructor training course, I also went through a three-month course to get my master training specialist (MTS) certification. The program teaches you how to develop a curriculum from scratch, identifying both learning objectives (what you want to make sure your course *teaches*) and performance objectives (what you want to make sure your students can actually go out and apply practically), and then writing a complete lesson plan that fleshes out and achieves those objectives. They packed an enormous amount of work into those three months, and there's a reason they call it a *master* training specialist. It is, in essence, a concentrated graduate degree course.

I was determined that we were going to erase any hint of that sort of seat-of-your-pants style and raise the quality of the sniper course curriculum to a standard on a par with the best higher-education programs anywhere.

We started in August 2003 and worked like hell for three months, solidifying and putting on a pilot program. At the end of those three months, we were done. Or at least we thought so.

Almost immediately, we were pulled back in. Chief Nielsen wanted us to go further—to keep developing the course, keep pushing the envelope, keep raising the bar and seeing just how far we could take it. And he wanted us not just to redesign it, but to *teach* it. I didn't foresee this at the time (having just been meritoriously promoted to petty officer first class), but within the next year I would end up being promoted to chief myself and made course manager for the entire program, with Eric being put in charge of the critically important Scout (mental performance skills, stalking, stealth and concealment) portion of the course.

Eric and I spent that next year innovating, experimenting, trying things out, and learning what worked and what didn't. We surveyed the best sniper programs in the U.S., adopting or adapting best practices whenever and wherever we found them. We also looked to our counterparts overseas. When we were stationed with Task Force K-Bar in Afghanistan, we'd gotten to know Special Ops guys from Australia, Canada, Denmark, Germany, New Zealand, Norway, and Turkey. Now we started leveraging those relationships. We took a hard look at what the British SAS, the German Kommando Spezialkräfte (KSK), and the Polish GROM were doing, along with a few other Coalition partners and their sniper training programs.

We looked at outstanding achievers in professional sports, then went to explore the Olympic arena, where we focused on gold medal champions. We didn't spend a moment looking at silver or bronze medalists' experience. We didn't care about that. We wanted to know one thing and one thing only: what were the gold medalists doing?

It was an incredibly creative time. Brainstorming, trying things out, adding new courses, totally renovating old ones. Moving things around, changing the order. Bringing in new technologies. We tested tons of ideas, many of which we were not sufficiently happy with and ended up not incorporating into the course. A select handful, we let stick.

During that year, we changed *everything*.

For starters, we added an entirely new program at the front of the course: a full two weeks spent giving our students a thorough training in the postmodern intelligence arts of digital photography and communications, called PIC (photographic intelligence course). We wanted to bring things into the twenty-first century in our use of science and technology—and that started on the first day.

Why place this portion first? Because, again, a sniper's primary task has nothing to do with shooting a rifle. *A sniper is first and foremost an intelligence asset.* Snipers are a field element's forward eyes and ears. Reconnaissance and surveillance is the bedrock of our skill set.

At the time, snipers were still being taught to look through their binos and sketch out on paper what they saw. A great skill set to have, for sure. (Delgado's skills would serve him well in Husaybah.) But we wanted to give our guys a technological edge. We stepped out of the paper-and-pencil era and put top-of-the-line camera kits in our students' hands. During that two-week course, we taught them how to camouflage a camera, shoot photos without being detected, use proprietary software to crop, adjust, and enhance the photos for maximum clarity, then compress them, encrypt them, and send them back to command over radio or satellite uplinks.

Which meant this also had to be a full-bore communications technology course. What do you do when you're in the field, with a bunch of critically important photos you need to send back to TOC, and your radio antenna craps out? You improvise. You tap into your inner Mac-Gyver and build a replacement from whatever you have on hand, and you do it *fast*. This course taught them how to do that.

We also had the most amazing setting for teaching this course, something that looked and felt like it came right out of a James Bond flick. Right on the coast of San Diego, there was an old underground armory that hardly anyone knew about. Bob Nielsen had managed to take it over and convert it into a training facility for our course. Our own secret underground bunker.

This place was seriously badass. You entered the place, went through a set of double doors, and there was our amazing teaching space: high exposed ceilings, high-quality tables for up to fifty students with the sort of standing-height chairs you see with drafting tables; a big podium with a computer server that let you control the digital projector and all the lighting; everything you could wish for in the perfect twenty-first-century classroom. We had our own armory. We had an indoor high-powered pellet gun range. I could open the door to the back, a secure locker area where we kept our ammo and equipment, and get a nice ocean breeze coming in. Students had big, individual walk-in steel cages where they could store their guns and ammo—and their top-of-the-line equipment for PIC. (These cameras were amazing, $25,000 pieces of precision equipment, the absolute best we could get our hands on. Eric would take one of these cameras to the zoo with his family, and people would assume he was there on assignment for *National Geographic*.)

And when I say "secret," I'm not kidding. Nobody else really knew what was going on in there. Other SEALs would come in to Coronado to do some training and see us emerging with our satellite antennas and amazing photographic equipment and say, "What the fuck are you guys doing down there?" We didn't tell them.

With its high-tech, precision science, and professional standards, PIC set the stage for the rest of the course.

In the old course, students would be handed their weapons and sent out onto the range fairly early on, and move on to the scout/stalk portion only after they'd gone through the marksmanship phase. But that didn't make sense to us. Shooting doesn't happen before stalking; it's the other way around. Unless you can make your way undetected to a spot within shooting distance of your target, you're never going to have the chance to take a shot. Marksmanship won't do you much good if you can't stalk.

So we reversed the sequence.

We figured, let's have our students learn all the field skills they need and build up that essential foundation, then integrate those skills into actual field stalking, and *then* let the whole program culminate in the shooting phase, just as an actual stalk culminates in the shot. And it flowed much better. It duplicated field experience, and that was the goal. We weren't trying to make great match shooters. We were grooming silent killers who could function flawlessly as the big-game hunters of the field of combat. This wasn't the shooting school. It was the Killing School. And killing starts with stalking.

Thus, immediately after PIC came the scout portion of the course, which began with KIMS.

There are two different theories as to where the term KIM comes from. Some say it derived from Rudyard Kipling's classic novel *Kim,* the story of an Irish orphan who grew up in India. As a youth, Kim was trained for government intelligence work; his training involved being shown a tray of stones and gems, or coins, or photographs, and then, once the tray was covered, required to describe as precisely as possible what he had seen. Thus, "Kim's game." Nice story. Maybe there's even some truth to it. As far as I know, though, it's simply an acronym for Keep In Memory: thus, *keep in memory systems.* (Who knows, maybe Kipling already knew the acronym, and that's where the kid's name came from.)

Wherever the name comes from, KIMS games have been around since the earliest days of sniper training. But we didn't want to just replicate the usual program. We wanted to raise the bar—and Eric was uniquely qualified to do exactly that. As I said, Eric's specialty is taking a complex process, identifying all the dozens (or hundreds, or thousands) of individual components and steps to it, and then teaching that in a sequence that makes sense. Nowhere was that skill better put to use than in KIMS.

"Memory is like everything else you develop in sniper school," said Eric. "It's not about brute force or sheer effort, it's about concentration, accuracy, and precision. You can try to force yourself to improve your memory by brute mental effort. But rote memory goes only so far."

Eric had learned how to take it a lot further.

Years earlier, before 9/11, Eric was hanging around in Kuwait on his first deployment. Things were pretty slow, and one day he was browsing through books at the PX when one title caught his eye: *The Memory Book,* by Harry Lorayne and Jerry Lucas.

What the hell, he thought. He bought the book and started reading. By the following day, he had memorized the names and dates of all the U.S. presidents, in sequence; a shuffled deck of cards, in order; and the periodic table of the elements. And he had pretty much nailed the technique of memorizing long lists of *anything.*

For Eric, that became not much more than a party trick, something he could impress people with but which didn't really have any useful application.

Until we were tapped to revamp the NSW sniper course.

On the first day of KIMS, Eric stood up in front of a class of two to three dozen men, people he had never met or talked to before, pointed to one of them at random and asked the guy his name. When the student said who he was, Eric rattled off his phone number and address. And his Social Security number.

And then proceeded to do the same with *everyone else in the class*.

I was watching their faces when Eric did this, and I got the biggest kick out of it. It takes a lot to impress a SEAL. These guys were absolutely floored. So was I. It was pretty freaking scary.

The funny thing about it is, Eric's memory is no better than anyone else's. Eric is one of the most devoted dads I know, but he says he has trouble remembering his kids' birthdays—and I'm not sure he's joking. But he had taught himself specific techniques of association and visualization, where you take the raw data you need to remember and weave a context for it, so that the data goes from being random bits to being a meaningful array of points stuck in a multilayered mental spiderweb.

"People don't forget things," says Eric. "They just fail to remember them properly."

Eric started by issuing Lorayne and Lucas's classic text to every student, then taught classes that reinforced the techniques in the book—and expanded on them.

The students quickly mastered the techniques, and in no time at all the traditional sniper KIMS games were no longer any challenge. So we started looking for ways to make them harder.

First, we ramped up the volume on distractions. We started slamming trash can lids and banging shit around during the brief time window they had to glance at their items. We started shooting off flashbangs and live gunfire. We started showing X-rated movies with the volume turned up. *Ooohh! Ahhh! Yeah, like that . . . more, more, deeper, deeper!*

No dice: they still aced every test.

Then we got fiendish. We started showing them items and then waiting for days before testing them. Then weeks. They were still unstoppable.

This was a seminal experience for us: it showed Eric that you can not only master a seemingly impossible skill, but also transfer that seemingly impossible skill to a large group of others. This was critical for the overall development of the course, because it gave us the confidence to continue pushing the boundaries of training in every domain.

* * *

For field stalking, we took our students about an hour's drive inland to the La Posta Mountain training facility (since renamed the Michael Monsoor Mountain Warfare Training Center), which covers about a thousand square miles of high mountain terrain. We've used this place a lot for SEAL training; appropriately enough, it was at this spot, during my own SEAL training, where I first got my shit together and went from being a crappy shot to an expert shooter.

Our stalking exercises were essentially the same as any sniper stalk class—but with a twist. We had our students start out by stalking not with rifles but with *cameras*. They would have to sneak up within two hundred yards of the instructors and take an identifiable picture of their faces, or take a clearly legible photo of an instructor holding up a piece of paper with a sequence of numbers written on it (similar to the hunt's head in Rob Furlong's course). Then the walker would point out their exact location—and they had to be so invisible that, even then, the instructors couldn't see them.

This was even harder than stalking with a gun. You can poke your rifle barrel and scope out in front of you, through all the sticks and bushes you're hiding behind. You need a clear bullet path, but a bullet is only so many millimeters wide. And while your scope needs to give you a clear view of the target, it doesn't have to be a *great* view of the target.

None of that applies with a camera. You can't poke a camera three feet out ahead of you. You need to get that thing right out with a wide-open, unobstructed photo path—and do all that without letting the sunlight catch a glint off the lens that might flash light in your target's direction. And you can't let any dust or dirt get on your lens, or it will ruin the shot. It's insanely difficult.

Our typical shot distance, whether with camera or rifle, would be anywhere from 180 to 200 yards. And they were going up against two trained instructors, like Eric and me, with thousands of hours of experience, sitting comfortably in the shade, looking straight toward them with high-powered binoculars, in a field that we set up in the first place, so we not only knew what direction they were coming from, we also knew every piece of terrain on the way. And this wasn't some lush jungle forest with tons of foliage for cover. The bulk of the stalks were in high desert terrain.

Then we replaced the camera with a rifle, and it became the traditional stalk course: hunting instructors with a rifle, taking shots with blanks, and by the end of the phase, with live rounds. Stalking is typically where the majority of fails occur. By the time our students were hunting us with rifles in their hands, though, they were already skilled stalkers, and we didn't lose many.

After the scout phase we came back down to the bunker for some classroom time before going out to the range to shoot. First we taught them classes in the physics of ballistics—internal (what happens inside the barrel), external (what happens while the bullet is in flight), and terminal (what happens when the bullet reaches its target). We wanted to make them ballistics experts, and not just skillful gunslingers. We also trained them in the use of ballistic software, a technology that was just then coming into its own and becoming truly useful on the battlefield.

There was a very practical reason for all this scientific instruction. The existing training was great at turning its students into experts at the first shot. But the first shot doesn't always find its target. We needed them to be experts at the second and third shot.

This was my baby. While Eric was primarily responsible for the scout portion of the course, the shooting phase was my area, and there was a fundamental change here that I was anxious to implement.

Classic sniper training taught that working with a good spotter is critical to a successful op. Your spotter watches where the bullet goes and then feeds you the necessary adjustments for your second shot. When you're on the gun, you're thinking about your fundamentals: breathing, posture, trigger pull, follow-through; you're focused on making the shot. You need somebody else worrying about the mechanics of what's happening out there—the distance and elevation, the wind, the behavior of the target. The two of you are like pilot and navigator: you're the one flying the plane, but you need the navigator to tell you exactly where you're going. If you want to be an effective sniper, you have to be completely loyal to your spotter: don't argue, don't question, just do what he says.

At least, that's the traditional view. To Eric and me, it was the sacred cow of sniper training—and it was a cow that needed to go.

We had both worked in the Gulf as sniper overwatch from helicopters. I'd seen a lot of our guys serve as sniper overwatch for an assault element going into a village; I'd done it myself. In these situations, you can't rely on your spotter for the simple reason that you don't *have* a spotter. You have to self-spot. So why weren't we training them in how to do that?

The reality of the battlefield is that you don't always have the luxury—no, strike that: you *rarely* have the luxury—of having a guy on a spotting scope next to you saying, "Hey, man, you're six minutes high" or "We've got crazy gusts out there, hold three right for wind." I mean, it's great when you do. But what if you don't? Once you've made the shot and missed, now what are you going to do? You need to be able to know exactly why you missed, what factors are off and by how much, so you can make those corrections pretty damn fast and take a second shot. If your own life doesn't depend on it, someone else's probably does.

The traditional two-man team is great as far as it goes—but in real conditions of war the ability to function that way often goes right out the window once the first shot is fired. We needed our graduates to be able to serve as solo operators, fully capable of serving as shooter *and* spotter at the same time. (It was this solo training that would soon make Chris Kyle and a lot of other SEAL snipers so deadly on the muggy streets of urban Iraq.)

A lot of this shift had to do with the nature of the mission itself, since snipers were being used routinely as ad hoc overwatch for conventional units in dangerous locations. But it also had to do with advances in technology. Not only had the nature of war changed: so had the nature of the warrior's tools.

For example, semiautomatic weapons had taken great leaps in efficiency and dependability, leading to greatly improved performance in the field. Back in the nineties, bolt-action guns were by far the superior sniper weapon. Semiautos just weren't reliable enough, too prone to jamming or other malfunction. Not anymore. By the time my platoon landed in Afghanistan in late 2001 the technology of semiautomatics had become easily as reliable as that of any other gun. And using a semiauto meant you didn't have to mess with the whole business of operating the bolt action—unlock, eject shell, slam home, relock—which eliminates a whole sequence of mechanical movement, accelerates shot output, and increases a sniper's kill count.

Or, another example: laser range finders. Technology had made the process of ranging your target far simpler and quicker, something that in many circumstances a shooter could do himself without detracting significantly from his attention on the shot.

Increasingly, technology was enabling our guys to do it all themselves, rather than having to always pair with a partner—and having two snipers operating independently meant you could now cover a larger kill zone.

We also changed how we tested and graded them.

When I went through the course the first time, I saw guys who could shoot but didn't understand the fundamentals of ballistics, and because of that were shitty spotters. The way the grading system worked when I went through the course was the same as in the marine and army courses: shooter and spotter were viewed as a single functional unit, and therefore they shared a grade. Which meant that a good shooter could be dragged down by having a bad spotter and flunk out because he was getting shitty input. I saw it happen.

In fact, it almost happened to Jason Delgado. As I mentioned earlier, he flunked the first two of a series of three qualifying sessions in his sniper course. And he didn't fail by a slight margin; he wasn't even close. On the third day, his instructors took him aside and pointed out that if he didn't make it through this third and last round, he was going home.

They offered to let him change his spotter. At the time Jason's spotter was Jesse Davenport, his friend and soon-to-be shooting partner in Iraq, where they were about to deploy. Jason figured, if he and Jesse were going to work together, they'd better get the kinks out now. The problem was, as I said earlier, while they were both excellent shots, neither was yet an experienced spotter. Jesse's calls were taking Jason down.

Stubbornly, Jason said he didn't want to change.

"You are about the dumbest motherfucker on this earth," his instructor told him. "We suggest you change your spotter."

A Navy SEAL who was also going through the course happened to be standing nearby. "Hey," said the SEAL, "I'll spot for you."

Fuck it, thought Jason, *why not?* So he did. On his last qualifying round, Jason made every shot.

Now, just look at that for a second. Here's Jason Delgado, an excellent marine who turned out to be a superstar sniper who saved a lot of lives in Iraq (as you'll soon see)—and we almost lost him right then and there . . . *because his spotter wasn't giving him good calls.*

Which made no sense to me. Being an effective sniper is so much more than simply being able to break a clean shot. You can repeat the mantra *one shot one kill* to yourself until you're aquamarine in the face, but it often just doesn't work out that way. If the first shot goes wrong, as it so often will, then you need to be able to figure it out, by yourself, on the spot, under maximum stress, and do it *right*. That's one reason—only one, but a big one—that being a solid sniper is *not* the same thing as being a great match shooter.

I designed and implemented a spotting test so that nobody could slip by without having that skill set totally nailed down. It was fiendishly difficult, but fiendish with a purpose.

We'd test them on the spotting scope, then test them on the gun by themselves. Then we'd mess with their gun and have them shoot again. For example, we might have a student shoot a target at five hundred meters. Boom: center of the target. Fine. Then we'd say, "Okay, get off your weapon." We would take his gun, reset the windage and elevation knobs, up or down, left or right, to within maybe 10 minutes of angle, without telling him exactly what we'd done, then hand his gun back and say, "Here's three bullets. Solve the problem with two shots—and the third better be a kill shot."

Now he'd have to adjust and get back on center target within three shots. The only way he could do that is if he truly understood ballistics. If he could do that, then we knew without a doubt that he could self-correct—and that was exactly the kind of shooter we wanted to put out the door.

Earlier I mentioned that the course Rob Furlong went through in Canada was what we call a gentleman's course, one where the students were treated with respect, like adults, almost like colleagues. When Eric and I went through the NSW course in '99 and 2000, it was pretty much the opposite of that. They berated us constantly, some instructors more than others.

We didn't think that was effective or productive.

It's not that we had thin skins or didn't appreciate the value of tough love. Far from it. Hell, we'd both been through BUD/S and come out the other end, better men for it. But this wasn't BUD/S, and these weren't recruits. These were seasoned warriors. These were SEALs, for Chrissakes. We didn't need to treat them like assholes in their first weeks of boot camp.

So we stopped yelling at them and beating them up. Instead, we tightened the screws on performance. We didn't *reduce* the stress, we changed the *nature* of the stress. Instead of yelling at them, we tightened the tolerances and raised the level of expectation.

We also changed the fundamental nature of the relationship between instructor and student.

In the old class, that relationship varied somewhat depending on the particular character of each instructor, some being more assholes than others, and some being more decent guys. But the relationship itself was unsympathetic to the point of being adversarial. It was like they were *trying* to flunk us out. Again, I supposed this was modeled after the way it is in BUD/S—which works for BUD/S. But not for sniper school.

Instead, we divided the class into pairs and assigned one instructor to each pair, to serve as their personal mentor.

The mentoring idea was brilliant, and I can't take credit for it. I'm pretty sure it was Master Chief Manty's brainchild, but wherever it came from it was already there as a part of the new course's structure when Eric and I arrived.

I immediately saw how smart, how effective, and how powerful this was. Throughout my training, both in the navy in general and especially as part of the SEAL teams, I'd seen plenty of examples of both great leadership and terrible leadership. I'd managed to make my way through and keep going regardless, which is what most guys do. But it was clear to me that where I'd really made tremendous progress was in those times and those situations where I'd had a great mentor. Nothing trains a skill like the apprenticeship model, and that's exactly what a mentor provides, whether it's explicitly structured that way or more informal, based purely on the character of the mentor.

In this case, though, it was structural, hardwired into the program, which meant it was not personality-dependent. Every single student who went through that program was going to have the benefit of a personal mentor, a skilled and highly trained professional instructor who was personally invested in seeing him succeed.

This was an incredibly valuable innovation. It provided a system of accountability that ensured nobody got left in the dark. Every day, we'd be watching out for our four guys. (Typically each instructor was assigned two pairs.) We kept student folders with detailed documentation of everything they did. We made performance notes and kept all their test scores in there. We would work with them one-on-one, coach them if they needed it, do whatever it took. Their success became our responsibility.

Every Friday we would meet with our personals to go over the week's instruction, take a look at whatever they might be having issues with, whatever they felt they needed help with, or what we'd observed they needed help with. We'd review their records and make notes of what we talked about.

If necessary, we'd spend extra time with them over the weekend, which was typically reserved for practice and remedial work.

The following Monday we'd have a meeting where we'd check in with the course manager (which at this point was me), going around the room to each instructor. "Yeah, I checked in with my guys, here's what's going on, Student A was having trouble here, Student B needs help there." Then the instructors on the line with those guys during the day would know which student needed extra work on spotting, or trigger pull, or whatever.

This also introduced a competitive element among the staff, and it was competition of the healthiest kind. We were each determined to make sure *our* guys were the best, which meant there was a constant effort to support them to the maximum of our ability. You did *not* want to show up Monday morning to go down the roster and have your guys at the bottom of the list. We would do anything we could to make sure our guys were keeping up and doing well.

When Glen and I went through the course in 2000, we had instructors who frankly didn't give a shit whether we passed or not. At least one made an active effort to get us to fail. Now we'd turned that dynamic on its head, and built into the program an intrinsic motivation for every instructor to be working with students that he strongly wanted to succeed.

In my three years with the program, seeing more than three hundred students go through it, I only had one of my personals fail, and that was Marcus Luttrell (author of *Lone Survivor*), who went right back through the course again and passed with honors his second time through. All the others passed—because I'd be damned if *my* guys were going to fail!

By the end of that year, from late 2003 to late 2004, Eric and I had worked nonstop to achieve the platinum standard we were shooting for. Through a combination of:

- raising the professional level of instruction;
- systematizing and standardizing the curriculum;
- integrating advanced science and technology into the coursework;
- lengthening, restructuring, and enhancing all the course content;
- focusing on training our students in how to function as solo operators;
- and instituting a targeted mentorship program . . .

we had radically transformed the SEAL sniper school.

Yet for all that, there was yet one more change we built into the course—and for me, that one additional change would have more impact on our outcomes in the field of battle than any of the others. This change had nothing to do directly with training our students in how to shoot or how to stalk.

It had to do with training them how to think.

6

ZEN MIND, LETHAL MIND

There is no hunting like the hunting of man, and those who have hunted armed men long enough and liked it, never care for anything else thereafter.

—Ernest Hemingway, "On the Blue Water"

"In words of three syllables or less, will you please tell me what on God's green earth is going on out there? What kind of voodoo are you gentlemen up to?"

His voice was coming from Fort Benning, Georgia, more than two thousand miles away from where I sat in my subterranean office on the San Diego coast, but it nearly melted the phone in my hand. This army major was a man who knew exactly what he wanted and was accustomed to getting it.

I said nothing, just waited for him to go on. I had a feeling I knew what was coming next. Sure enough, after a pause, he said one more thing.

"Because whatever it is, Chief Webb, whatever craft beer your guys are drinking, I am calling to say, *we want some.*"

It was 2005, war was raging in Iraq, and our graduates were killing it in the field. Word had gotten out. Our guys were making a difference over there, and we were starting to hear from officers in other branches who wanted to know exactly what we were doing with our students that was making such a pronounced difference on the battlefield.

So, what was our secret sauce? It was everything you read in the last chapter . . . plus one more thing. For me, that *one more thing*, that X factor, was the most important change we introduced into the course, the one innovation, more than any other, that transformed the quality of snipers we were producing.

* * *

I have to admit, I was completely resistant to it at first, in part because of who it was that first pushed us in this new direction.

One day, soon after Eric and I had started working on the course, Bob Nielsen called us in to his office and told us he was retiring. This was devastating news; Bob was one of the best mentors I'd ever had and I hated the idea of losing him. As bad as that was, though, it got even worse with his next sentence: he told us who his replacement was going to be.

In my memoir *The Red Circle,* I wrote about Harvey Clayton and about what a nightmare it became to work under him for the next year. A master chief, Harvey was a solid match shooter but not a battle-tested sniper—exactly like the men who ran the course back when Alex Morrison went through it. (As a matter of fact, when Alex went through the course his second time in 1994, Harvey himself *was* the master chief in charge.)

Yet for all the grief I've given Harvey in print, it's time to set the record straight in one regard. To his credit, he did introduce me to the man who would prove to be the single greatest influence on my contribution to the SEAL sniper course.

In early 2004, Harvey told us he'd arranged for us to go out to Scottsdale, Arizona, for a few days to meet with an Olympic shooter he knew who was an expert on mental management.

Oh great, I thought. Here we were, trying to get our guys ready for war, and Harvey was sending us off to waste precious days sitting through some kind of Tony Robbins bullshit? As the Brits say: *Bloody hell.* One look at Eric's face, and I was pretty sure he was thinking the same thing. (He was.)

A few days later Harvey, Eric, and I were on a plane to Scottsdale, where we met up with Master Chief Manty and a few other guys from the East Coast course. Everyone there was an E-7 (chief) or higher, with the exception of Eric and myself. (My promotion was still a year away.) As the most junior members of the group, we didn't think it was our place to voice our opinions too loudly. But we sure *thought* them loudly enough.

We checked into some crappy discount chain hotel, the kind with the same crappy paintings on every wall and same threadbare sheets on every crappy bed. I don't mean to sound like a travel snob, but I hate these places; if we can't go first class, I'd just as soon stay at a cheap B&B (or these days, an Airbnb).

Our meetings were taking place in a crappy little conference room. It felt like I was about to get a pitch for a third-rate timeshare.

This was not building my confidence.

SEALs are always looking for a competitive advantage, so we tend to be early adopters and aggressive innovators. At the same time, we're also huge skeptics and ready to tear apart anything or anyone if we perceive them as not up to snuff. I'd recently been sent out to the East Coast to sit on a board reviewing proposed equipment upgrades for a new Special Operations "peculiar weapons modification kit"— SOPMOD—for SOCOM. One vendor came in and started giving his pitch, and I could see within seconds that it was full of holes. This guy had never been in the field, had probably never even shot a gun. He tried to field my objections, but he didn't have a chance. He exposed his soft underbelly, and I eviscerated him. My point is, we're a tough crowd.

We walked into the crappy little hotel's crappy little conference room, sat down, and waited, prepared to eviscerate.

And then Lanny Bassham showed up.

The first thing that struck me about Lanny was what a humble, affable guy he was. No big ego, no swagger, no strutting—and he had plenty to strut about if he'd wanted to. This guy was the real deal. A shooting prodigy, Lanny had been assigned as a kid to the AMU (Army Marksmanship Unit), whose ranks include the best match shooters in the world. When he went to shoot in the 1972 Olympics in Munich at age twenty-five, he was already the youngest world champion in the sport and odds-on favorite to take the gold.

Those high expectations, however, proved to be his undoing.

One day in Munich he happened to overhear a few Russian competitors talking about him, musing about how much pressure he must be under. Their comments got into his head. He choked—and came away with a silver medal instead of the expected gold.

Lanny was devastated. Objectively, he knew that winning a silver medal in the Olympics was a fantastic achievement. (Hell, just competing in the Olympics is damn impressive!) Yet he couldn't shake the bitterly disappointing sense of failure. He started dreading the moment when a new acquaintance would learn that he had been to the Olympics, because he knew how the conversation would go from there:

Acquaintance: "Oh wow, you were in the *Olympics*?"
Lanny: "Yup."
Acquaintance: "That's amazing. How did you do?"
Lanny: "I took silver."
Acquaintance: "Wow. So who won the gold that year?"

Lanny says his definition of silver medal became "the very best you can possibly do and still lose."

"Who remembers the silver medalist?" he says. "Or the first runner-up to Miss America, or the finalist in the World Series or Super Bowl? The only ones who remember are the runners-up themselves—and they can never forget."

His words were especially meaningful to Eric and me, because we weren't any more interested in second place than Lanny was. In the arena of Special Operations, being second-best doesn't mean you go home with a silver medal. It means you go home in a wooden box.

Lanny suffered with his disappointment for a few years. Then, in 1974, he met a man who changed his life. He recounts the story in parable form in his book *Freedom Flight,* where he calls the man "Jack Sands." (His real name was Jack Fellowes, but I'll follow Lanny's parable here and call him Sands.)

A captain in the navy (later promoted to commander), Sands was shot down over Vietnam and spent more than six years as a prisoner of war at the infamous POW camp known as the Hanoi Hilton. Six-plus years later he was finally released and flown back to San Diego, where they put him in an ambulance to get him over to Balboa Hospital to get checked out. The guy weighed barely a hundred pounds; after all, he had been in prison camp, under awful conditions, for over six years.

As they headed to the hospital, they drove past the golf course by the back gate of Naval Air Station North Island. Suddenly Sands called out, "Wait—stop the ambulance!"

What the hell? The ambulance driver pulled over, alarmed. Was the guy dying or something?

"Let me out for a bit," said Sands. "I've got to play some golf."

The driver looked at him like he was crazy. But Sands insisted. Hey, he was the returning hero. The driver reluctantly let him out of the ambulance and took him over to the golf course clubhouse, where the club members at first refused to let him play and tried to throw him out.

He explained who he was, that he'd been holed up in the worst imaginable prison in North Vietnam for more than six years, and that he really, really wanted to get out on the green and play a round of golf.

Most of these guys were vets themselves. They took pity on him and brought him around to the pro shop to get outfitted, meanwhile shooting each other nervous looks behind the commander's back. This guy was in absolutely terrible shape, not much more than skin and bones, could barely walk on his own. He was on his way to the hospital, for crying out loud. Would he even be able to swing the damn club without falling over?

The commander went out onto the green and shot par on the first hole. And the second. And the third. His drives went ripping down the fairway, every time. His putts were perfect. He shot par on all eighteen holes.

The club regulars all stared at him like he was from outer space. This guy hadn't been on a golf course in years. Hell, he hadn't even seen *grass* in years. He'd been wasting away in a tiny cell, with no exercise. What he'd just done simply wasn't possible. Yet they'd just watched him do it.

"Pardon me for asking, Commander," said one of the clubbers, "but how the hell did you *do* that?"

And he said, "Gents, I've played thousands of rounds of golf in my head over the past six years, and let me tell you, it's been a long, long time since I've missed a putt."

That was how the man had kept himself sane during his long stretch as a POW. He would sit in his tiny cell, build pictures in his head of all his favorite courses, and walk through them, playing round after round of golf. Every day, for six years. He hadn't physically been on a golf course for ages—but he had mentally rehearsed his game to the point of perfection, and done it so thoroughly that his all muscles and articulations knew exactly what to do.

Commander Sands's experience was not unique; quite a few POWs in Vietnam embarked on such massive feats of visualization in order to keep their sanity. One, Commander Howard Rutledge, filled his seven years in captivity by building five complete houses in his imagination, starting with locating the land and negotiating its purchase, then personally clearing the ground and digging the foundation, on through every detail of construction and concluding with landscaping and furnishing the place, putting it on sale and selling it for a profit before turning his attention to the next project and starting the whole process over again. Another, Commander William Lawrence, started combing back through his memory to see how many names he could remember from among his first-grade classmates, and ended up reliving his entire life to date in detail—three times over.

What these men all had in common, of course, was that they were prisoners of war and had virtually no physical freedom. But then, as Sands pointed out, Lanny was imprisoned, too, only in a prison of his own making: he was stuck in a box of frustration, regret, and self-limitation over his inability to take that gold medal.

Because it wasn't really the bald fact that he had come in second that had so bothered Lanny. It was that he had the ability to come in first—but he had allowed his environment, in the form of the Russian competitors' words, to control him and knock him off his game. Those overheard comments had put him in prison, and on some level he knew it.

What Sands told him that changed the course of his life boiled down to this: If your environment and circumstances control your attitude, you're in prison. If you are in control of your thoughts and your attitude, then you're free.

This was a revelation for me. This "mental management" we'd been flown to Scottsdale to hear about in a crappy hotel conference room wasn't just some technique or tactic for mastering a particular skill set. It was a philosophy, one that resonated with me and with the core nature of everything we were up to.

The point of our course wasn't to have our students become expert shooters.

The point of our course was to have our students become masters of their fate.

Which was exactly what Lanny went out and did. After meeting Jack Sands in 1974, he spent the next two years interviewing close to a hundred Olympic gold medalists and their coaches and, much like the way Eric reverse-engineers, he took note of everything they said and analyzed exactly how they trained. Those mental management core principles lay at the heart of it all. In 1976 he returned to the Olympics in Montreal—and this time, he took gold. He went on to dominate the field for years, winning twenty-two world individual and team titles and setting four world records. He also codified everything he'd learned into a system that he had now been teaching to coaches and athletes from all over the world.

Lanny talked with us throughout that day. The army major had it exactly right. We walked out of that little conference room completely drinking the Kool-Aid. I've been drinking it ever since.

We implemented our new mental management philosophy in three prime areas. The first was to establish a fundamentally positive approach to teaching, starting with a bedrock principle that Sands told Lanny he had absorbed while in captivity: "Focus only on the solution to the problem—never on the problem itself."

This idea was familiar to me, and would have been to any SEAL. We are taught from day one never to bring up a problem without having a solution. Spec Ops warfighters are extremely solution-oriented, both by training and by nature. We are the entrepreneurs of the military, not the good employees who follow orders and act along preestablished paths. We go into impossible situations and accomplish the objective anyway.

Still, with all that action-oriented solution bias, I realized, *we weren't teaching that way.* We were teaching the way most of us had learned by example, since we were kids, the way most people teach, which is to *focus on the problem.*

I used to coach Little League, and it always blew my mind how some of the other coaches would talk to the kids. I heard one coach tell a kid, just as he was about to go to bat, "Hey, Billy, whatever you do, don't strike out!"

What the hell did he think that poor kid was thinking about as he stepped up to the plate? He was thinking about striking out. That's *all* he could think about. And when he did in fact strike out (which of course he did), it wasn't his fault, even though he thought it was. As far as I could see, it was the coach's fault, 100 percent.

Here's an example closer to home: remember that pithy little mantra of encouragement Glen and I received as we packed for sniper school, which I was still repeating to myself three years later as Eric and I prepared for our new assignment?

Don't fuck up.

If someone tells you a hundred times, "Don't fuck up" (or you tell yourself a hundred times), then what are you thinking about? Fucking up, of course. And because what you focus on is what you get, guess what happens? You fuck up. It works that way with seven-year-old kids trying to hit a baseball—and it works exactly the same way with grown men seeking to become the best military marksmen in the world.

When I heard Lanny, I instantly clicked with what he was saying, and knew we had to shift our core instructional methodology from "Don't do it that way" to "Do it this way."

Focus only on the solution to the problem—never on the problem itself.

If our new curriculum was the constitution of our new course, those thirteen words became its declaration of independence.

We started by writing down every single aspect of shooting that we saw as important—the classic Eric reverse-engineering tactic. When we were finished, we'd come up with about a hundred distinct points. Then we started a process of sorting and sifting, prioritizing them into hierarchies of importance, and eventually whittled our list down to seven core fundamentals of marksmanship. In the interests of not disclosing sensitive TTPs (tactics, techniques, and procedures), we're not going to spell out that list of seven fundamentals here, but I'll use the example of *smooth trigger pull*.

For a sniper, smooth trigger pull is exactly analogous to the golfer's swing or the quarterback's pass. For a public speaker, it's that first sentence you speak after the introduction is over, the applause has stopped, and the hall has gone silent. It's the keystone of the arch, the pivotal point where the rubber meets the road. The make-or-break moment.

There's a difference, though. For a match shooter, pulling the trigger is like a pro golfer's swing in this all-important way: you do it when you're ready. The crowd is silent. You've done all your prep. You've lined up your shot. You've waited as long as you feel you needed to wait until the moment is just right. And then you go.

In war, a sniper doesn't have that luxury. You're not shooting on a range, you're shooting in the confusing, noisy mess of battle. Which is why we all do our best to place our students in the midst of as much stress and distraction as possible, simulating as best we can the kinds of environmental sabotage they will have to fight through.

What the student does *not* need is the instructor sabotaging his thought process.

You see a lot of negative reinforcement in boot camp and other basic military training programs. (If I had a dollar for every time I heard an instructor say, "You are a worthless piece of shit, Webb!" my immediate peer group would include Mark Zuckerberg, Bill Gates, and Warren Buffett.) This was equally true in the NSW sniper course, which had modeled its teaching style on the negative-reinforcement approach of the marine course.

But I didn't think that was working at sniper school. When they would screw up, we didn't need to rub it in. They would do that all by themselves. Typically when a student missed a shot he would immediately get down on himself. He didn't need *us* to tell him he'd fucked up. He had that territory covered.

The problem with negative reinforcement is that you are essentially programming your student to fail. I wanted to program them to be successful—no matter what.

So once we had identified those seven fundamentals as the focus of our marksmanship teaching on the range, I told all the staff, "Okay, guys, this is what we're going to do. Here's how were going to teach. If you see your student doing something wrong, you give him a positive correction. Not a negative correction. Instead of telling him *not* to do what he's doing wrong, identify the fundamental he needs to be implementing, and remind him to do *that*."

Imagine you're on the gun for the first time, at five hundred yards, and I'm standing over you. I walk you through sighting in the target and you squeeze the trigger. Let's say there's a malfunction, and I notice that when the click comes from the firing pin hitting the bullet but the bullet doesn't go off, you flinch.

I could say, "Hey, next time *don't flinch*."

Now what are you thinking about? Flinching, of course. It's all you can think about. I just programmed you with a negative.

Or, I could take you back over the essentials of smooth trigger pull, and then say, "Look, this was a great learning experience for next time. You know what you need to do differently, right? Good." Instead of pushing your face into what you've done wrong, I've just gotten you squarely focused on how much better you will do next time, and exactly why.

In either scenario, I'm telling you what to do, except in the first case I'm telling you to repeat the mistake, and in the second case I'm reinforcing the positive habit.

So simple. So powerful.

Focus on the solution to the problem—never on the problem itself.

I use that exact same approach today in business, when I talk to my team or I'm training up a new employee. I carefully watch how I'm talking to them, what words and phrases I'm using. I do the same thing with my children. It works.

The second area where we implemented mental management was to begin teaching our students how to hone and perfect their skills through *mental rehearsal,* exactly as in the story of Jack Sands's perfect golf game.

This was something Lanny had observed in all the interviews he conducted with Olympic gold medalists between 1974 and 1976: they all tapped the power of visualization, taking the time and care to fully think through the entire process of whatever their particular sport and event was, visualizing it fully in great detail and mentally practicing it to perfection.

I wrote up a two-hour course on mental management and its application to marksmanship and incorporated that into our Fundamentals of Marksmanship curriculum. It came first thing, right at the start of the first class of the marksmanship portion of the course. And while that was just a two-hour class, we revisited and reinforced the material again and again, so they were relearning it throughout the course.

I started out by telling Lanny's story: his background, his Olympic credentials and history, and how he developed his approach. I explained the core principles of our mental management philosophy. And then taught them how to practice to perfection through mental rehearsal.

In one course I had two personals, Brant and Liebermann, who I knew had great potential. Like everyone in the SEAL community, they knew the course's reputation and its outrageous level of difficulty. At the start of the marksmanship phase, they came to me and said, "Realistically, Chief, what are you expecting out of us on this first shooting test?"

I told them, "I expect you to shoot perfect scores."

Which of course was crazy; nobody shot perfect scores. But that's what I told them. And you know why? *Because it was what I expected from them.*

I had also given them one of Lanny's books, *Freedom Flight,* on CD (with Lanny himself doing the reading), and told them to listen to it, every word, start to finish. The only CD player they had access to was the one in their rental car. So every night, they would climb into the car and sit there, listening to the CD.

The other guys started making fun of them, saying they were going to their car at night to make out, shit like that. Usual SEAL stuff. They ignored the taunts. By the time I was telling them I expected their perfect scores, they had listened to the whole thing through, twice.

Just to give you an idea of the standards: in that first test we had them shooting a .308 semiauto back to one thousand meters, which was at the outer edge of the gun's performance limitations. (Exceed your gun's inherent factory-established capacity and even absolutely perfect shots can go bad.)

We gave them a snaps and movers test, hitting multiple targets that are suddenly snapped upright (snaps) and others that are moving left and right at irregular, unpredictable intervals (movers), shooting out to 200, 400, 600, 800, and 1,000 yards. Then they had to shoot an unknown distance (UKD) test, where they had to view a target, quickly assess the distance by ranging it with their scope—no laser range finders or other technology allowed—and then shoot it accurately. On top of all these variables, plus whatever the wind was doing, they had to contend with unpredictable human variables. The guy who happens to be out there today snapping your targets up may have had too much to drink the night before and start snapping them up a little crooked. (A not unlikely scenario, by the way.)

They would each go through the test twice, first as shooter and then as spotter, and we graded shooter and spotter separately in both cases, so no one could ride on someone else's coattails. They all had to have both skill sets down cold. This meant they would rack up a total of four scores for the pair of them.

When it got around that I'd told those two I expected perfect scores, even the other instructors looked at me sideways.

The next day was the day of the test. Brant and Liebermann shot through and came out with the following scores:

100
100
 95
100

That's missing one shot out of *eighty*. About as damn close to perfection as a mortal can get.

The next day there was a line outside their barracks room: guys who wanted to get hold of those CDs and go sit in *their* rental cars.

We also taught them to use this practice for rehearsing contingencies.

If you think of ten things that could go wrong on the battlefield, you can design contingency plans for each one, then rehearse each of those circumstances along with the execution of your contingency and have the potential problem already addressed, so that when it does happen—*if* it happens—you've already rehearsed this ten times and you can deal with it almost without thinking.

At the time, I was just getting my pilot's license, and I applied the same approach to my pilot training. What would happen, I asked myself, if I were airborne and suddenly faced with an engine fire? Or an engine went out on takeoff? I rehearsed those and other scenarios in my head, going through the entire emergency procedure over and over so that if it ever did happen for real, I knew I could handle the situation with total confidence. It was like working in a simulator, only instead of being physically strapped into an expensive facility, I simply built the simulator in my head.

* * *

Our third mental management area was the application of a positive teaching style to what we called *self-coaching*. This was a huge departure from the negative style of teaching we were accustomed to, and it focused not only on how we talked to our students, but especially on *how they talked to themselves*.

There is no one who has as strong an influence over you as you yourself. Others can talk to you for limited amounts of time, but you talk to yourself constantly, twenty-four hours a day. Not out loud (usually), and most of the time often not even consciously aware that you're doing it. But you're doing it, all right. We all are. And what you say to yourself—about what you're doing, how you're doing, and what you believe you can or can't do—has an incalculably powerful impact on your behavior.

If I hadn't learned this on some level myself, I'd never have made it to sniper school in the first place.

Despite how inexperienced I was with guns, I managed to survive the shooting portion of BUD/S back in 1997. It was when I got to our advanced SEAL training, where we started learning how to actually be SEALs and apply all the skills we'd learned, that I really struggled. We were out at La Posta doing our expert shooting qual on the range, and I was getting a lot of "What's *your* problem?" looks from the other guys. Clearly, I was the worst shot in the class.

Here's how the thoughts in my head sounded:

Oh my God, I suck at this! How am I going to make it through? I'm fucked!

At that point I had a breakthrough. I realized what I was thinking and how much those thoughts were crippling me, how much they were sabotaging any chance I might have of improving. I was burying myself with my own bullshit.

Dude, I told myself, *let's just stop and reset. You have all the skills to be a good shot. You're totally capable. Now let's just smoke this thing.*

In that instant, I changed the way I was thinking about myself and the language I used in how I talked to myself. Progress was slow at first, but it picked up speed. Before long I went from being the worst shot in the class to one of the best in my platoon.

Now it was a few years later, and I was course master for the entire program.

In Lanny's book *With Winning in Mind* he lays out a detailed self-coaching plan. When he explained the essence of it to us that day in

Scottsdale, I immediately recognized the power of what he was talking about and knew we *had* to incorporate it into the course.

In our initial two-hour class I explained what self-coaching was and how it worked. I taught the students how to coach themselves, so if they caught themselves speaking to themselves a certain way, they could correct it on the spot and start changing their own habits of thought.

"Self-talk is not some airy-fairy seminar concept, gentlemen," I told them. "It's as real as blood and bullets. More than all the teaching and coaching we can provide, the most important thing is to make sure you know how to coach yourselves effectively. Because we are all our own best coaches or worst coaches—and typically it's worst, not best."

Even today, working in the worlds of business and media, I'm struck by how often I hear people say, "Oh, I'm not very good at this," or, "Man, I'm having a hard time with that." Yeah? Well keep on telling yourself that, and it will keep on being true. Because you're actually *practicing being bad* at whatever it is you're talking about.

It's amazing how deeply ingrained most people are in their negative self-talk. You can teach people about positive self-coaching and explain it all thoroughly, but it really takes practice—a *lot* of practice—to uproot those deep habits of thought.

On the other hand, these were SEALs we were dealing with. Compared to the average citizen, our students were already tremendously disciplined, not only physically but also mentally. They caught on quickly and started correcting their own thought habits until it became second nature.

Of course, the real teaching happened not in that two-hour lecture, sitting in our little secret bunker, but out on the range in the weeks and weeks of sixteen-hour days that followed. Because it's seductively easy to revert to old habits of thought and self-talk when you're placed under the kinds of stresses we put our students through.

And we would actively look for scenarios to put them in to create maximum stress and adversity, in order to see how they'd deal with it. Better there than in Afghanistan or Iraq, right?

At one point I had two students taking a test, and they started complaining that the head snaps were coming up slightly crooked instead of perfectly straight up and down.

Really? I thought. *What are you going to do on the battlefield? Ask the enemy to please stand up straight while you shoot them?* Jesus.

"Look," I told them, "it doesn't matter if they're straight or not. The target's still there. It's not like they're exposing any less of the target. Just shoot the damned thing."

But they kept complaining. They couldn't let it go.

So I radioed down to the students who were operating the targets on that lane and told them to make it even worse. "Snap it up at a forty-five-degree angle," I said. And then we all watched these two students implode. They completely lost it, screaming and stamping. They couldn't recover their composure. They couldn't deal with the stress.

This is not what you want when you are walking down a rubble-strewn street in Ramadi or storming a compound in Jalalabad. You want a guy watching your back who says, "Hey, I don't give a shit where my target is or how it's positioned, I'll shoot and move on."

I used it as a lesson. Those two failed miserably, and it was purely because of the quality of their own self-coaching. It wasn't the target's fault. The target wasn't any harder to hit, just because it wasn't straight. It was the fact that something went wrong, and they let it get to them.

It wasn't the target. It was *what they were telling themselves about the target*.

It's really interesting to me how different those two attitudes are, and I see it all the time, even in my civilian life today. In the real world, things don't always go well. In fact, they most often *don't* go well. There's a reason "Shit happens" became such a hit as a bumper sticker. But here's the difference: when something goes wrong, the ordinary person gets rattled, stressed, or pissed off. The champion embraces the adversity, even welcomes it as a gift, as an opportunity to say, "Look what I can do! Even given this shit situation I'm in, I'm *still* going to win!"

The exact same circumstances, yet one attitude produces failure while the other creates triumph. That, as Lanny told us, is the mind-set of the gold medalist.

As we implemented all these changes something interesting happened. Our standards went up. Yet our attrition rate went *down*. We had created something like a Wharton MBA equivalent for snipers, multiplying the amount of material to be absorbed and raising the level of difficulty—yet we were graduating more students, not fewer.

Before we redid the course, the NSW sniper school had an average attrition rate of about 30 percent. By the time we had gone through the bulk of our overhaul, it had plummeted to *one percent*. The kinds of unbelievable scores Brant and Liebermann shot on that first test soon became the norm, rather than the exception.

Eric and I started working on the course in the middle of '03 and began teaching it full-time the following January. I continued there until I left the military in July of '06. In those three years I saw a dozen classes go through the course, comprised of more than three hundred students. What I witnessed in these guys was phenomenal almost beyond the point of description. When they emerged from the NSW course, they weren't the same people they were when they started. There was an internal transformation so complete, so bone-deep that you could see it in the way they walked into the room. They didn't just get good. They went beyond what they thought was possible and rose to a level of potential that surprised even them.

These few years also became a sort of who's who of SEAL snipers, as some of our students went out onto the battlefield, distinguished themselves, and then went on to write about their experiences—or, in some cases, to be written about by others. That roster included, among others, Chris Kyle (who went through the course in the spring of '04), Morgan Luttrell (summer '04), Matt Axelson (summer '04), Marcus Luttrell (fall '04 and again that winter), Adam Brown (spring '05), and JT Tumilson (summer '05).

Writing about his sniper school experiences in *Lone Survivor,* Marcus Luttrell refers to me (though his editors spell my name *Brendan Webb*) as having standards "so high they would have made an Apache scout gasp." Later on, recounting what went through his mind as he prepared for a mission to take out a Taliban HVT, he says: "Chances were I'd get only one shot at Sharmak [their HVT], just one time when I could trap him in the crosshairs and squeeze that trigger, probably from hundreds of yards away. I knew only one thing: I better not miss, because the apparitions of Webb and Davis, not to mention every other serving SEAL, would surely rise up and tear my ass off."

Marcus went through the course in the fall of 2004 but failed to pass the stalk phase. He got the hang of it partway through, but by then it was too late; he couldn't quite catch up. Like any good SEAL, though, he did not know the meaning of the term "quit." He turned around and did the whole damn course again, start to finish, and sailed through his second time, in early 2005, with flying colors.

Years after we were both out of the navy, Marcus gave me a tearful embrace aboard the USS *Midway* in San Diego at a charity event and credited his training, especially the stalking portion, with saving his life in Afghanistan.

"Your training saved my life," he said. "I wouldn't be standing here today without it. And I want to thank you for it." It was a proud moment for me as an instructor, and it made the long hours of hard work put into the course and away from my own family all worthwhile.

Because of *Lone Survivor,* Marcus is the Luttrell the whole world knows about. But his twin brother, Morgan, is as outsize a character as his brother. Maybe more. Marcus says he's been jailed four times for Morgan's unpaid speeding tickets. I'm not entirely sure if that's true or a Texas tall tale, but it definitely gives you a sense of their relationship. Even if I didn't know which one was born first, I'd have bet any money it was Morgan. (It was, by seven minutes.) The two are also as devoted to each other as only identical twins can be. "Hey," Morgan would say when he did the course in the summer of '04, "make sure you take care of my brother when he comes through." Morgan was a new guy and hadn't done a platoon yet (unlike Marcus, who had). But he had no problems whatsoever and crushed the course.

For the Luttrell brothers, being SEALs has been a backbreaking experience—literally. Marcus broke his back during his escape in Operation Red Wings (which will come as no surprise to you if you've seen the 2013 Peter Berg film). Four years later, Morgan broke his during a training exercise, when the Black Hawk he was in clipped a cable and crashed into the boat they were about to board. Like Marcus, he defied doctor's predictions, healed up faster than anyone would have expected, and went back out. Morgan eventually left the service after nine tours of combat to pursue a doctorate degree in applied cognition to help in his work with the victims of traumatic brain injuries.

Matt Axelson was Morgan's best friend, and the two were paired up in their run through the course in the summer of '04. Of the three-hundred-plus students I saw come through, Axelson was one of the best. In my book *Among Heroes* I wrote a whole chapter about him. He was also one of the four SEALs, along with Marcus, sent on Operation Red Wings in the summer of '05; he and Marcus were the team's two snipers. Unlike Marcus, Axe did not survive the mission. He is sorely missed by many.

As is JT Tumilson, who was also one of my personals. JT played a special role in the course when he came through in the summer of '05. For each class we appointed one exceptional student as class leader. For that class, it was Tumilson—and he was the best damned class leader I had the whole time. JT was also a close friend of both Marcus's and Morgan's and part of their platoon at Team Five. JT perished in August 2011, along with thirty-seven others, when their Chinook was shot down by Taliban forces in the Tangi Valley, west of Kabul. I wrote about JT, too, in *Among Heroes*.

Like Alex Morrison and Marcus Luttrell, Adam Brown (subject of the bestselling book *Fearless*) failed the stalking phase his first time through the course in 2002. Like those other two exceptional men, he also turned around and did it again, nailing it on his second time through.

When Adam took his second shot at the course in the first few months of 2005, it was the last time we ran the East Coast and West Coast courses completely separately; that summer we merged the shooting phase into one national program (though we continued doing PIC and stalk on separate coasts). For that session I was on the West Coast with Marcus's class and was not an instructor for Adam's course, so I didn't know him well, but I met him briefly out at the East Coast training facility, and by that time I had heard all about him. The guy was already legendary in NSW circles because he'd done something that was over the edge of crazy, even for a SEAL.

Nearly two years earlier, in the summer of 2003, Adam was participating in a CQB exercise when one of those fluke training accidents happened. He took a round in the eye from a sim round (real bullets with liquid, paint-filled tips). The eye was a total loss—and it was his right eye. A natural righty, Brown retrained himself to become left-eye-dominant and to shoot left-handed before going through the course a second time. Just getting through the SEAL sniper course was already one hell of an achievement. This crazy bastard put himself through it with one eye, shooting lefty.

Talk about a testament to the power of thought.

And then there was Chris Kyle, aka the Legend.

Chris's story is so well known by now there'd be little point in my repeating it here. Suffice it to say that even back when he came through the course in the spring of 2004, when he wasn't "the Legend" yet, had no record of 160-plus kills overseas yet, had not been labeled Shaitan al-Ramadi ("the devil of Ramadi") by Iraqi insurgents yet, or had an $80,000 bounty slapped on his head—back when none of that had happened and he was just another sniper student from Texas, it was already clear that he was someone to keep our eyes on.

Unlike Marcus, Morgan, Axelson, and JT, Chris was not my personal (he was Eric's), but apparently I made an impression on him. To put it more accurately, I said *one word* that made an impression on him.

As our outstanding graduates began rotating back stateside from the field—from Iraq, Afghanistan, Africa, and other hot spots—Eric and I started a regular practice of inviting them over to the schoolhouse to sit and talk, debrief about what they'd seen and experienced over there. Were there things we should change, things we should do better, new things we should be teaching? We would incorporate what we learned from them into our regular course reviews, and if it seemed important enough, we'd integrate the change into the course within weeks.

Chris came down to the bunker one day after returning from Iraq. Things were hopping in the office, and just as he started debriefing us on some details about the urban hide sites they were using over there, the phone rang.

I raised one finger to tell Chris I'd make this quick, and picked up.

It was a Special Boat Team guy, calling with a question about quals for sniper school. Really. Quals for *sniper school*? This guy wasn't even a SEAL.

Back then, students who quit or failed out of BUD/S would sometimes get a shot at going to the special boat squadron, or SWCC (special warfare combatant-craft crewman). It created a strange, uneasy dynamic. You'd be out on a boat and suddenly realize that this guy who was driving you was the same guy who quit your BUD/S class a few years ago. It was weird. We just didn't trust these guys. (Point of clarification: these were *not* the same as the SDV or SEAL delivery vehicle teams, like the one Marcus and Axelson were attached to. Not even in the same solar system.) Command soon realized this wasn't working, and since that time they've done a stellar job of making it into an excellent program. But at the time, there was still a stigma about it.

I put the boat guy on speakerphone.

"Hey, this is Petty Officer So-and-So," the voice said, all excited, "I'm from Special Boat Team XYZ, and I wanted to find out what the requirements are for sniper school!"

I looked at Chris.

"BUD/S," I said, and disconnected the call.

Chris totally lost it. He cracked up, couldn't stop laughing about it.

Years later, long after we were both out of the service, when we met up again in the context of being authors, he reminded me about this episode. I'd completely forgotten. He was still laughing.

That roll call—Kyle, Luttrell, Luttrell, Axelson, Brown, Tumilson— gives you a sense of the caliber of platinum-level snipers coming out of the program. And they are only the names you've heard of. For each of them there were dozens of others, and they were having a tangible impact, changing the way the enemy behaved. When the enemy has to worry, "Am I being watched by one of their snipers right now?" it denies them their freedom of movement. It shifts the equation on the battlefield.

Word started getting back to us about how thankful the marine and army forces were to have the SEAL snipers with them. You've probably seen the movie *American Sniper* (or read the book), and might remember the scenes where Chris Kyle is moving around Iraq with a unit of marines who are clearing building to building. Knowing that Kyle was up there somewhere—on a rooftop, at a window, wherever he happened to hide himself that day—made those troops feel safer, which in turn ratcheted up their effectiveness. Having him up there gave our conventional forces more room to move around without getting shot at or blown up. Chris was making it more dangerous for the other guys—and safer for our guys.

Now, multiply that effect by a hundred—because there were dozens and dozens of other guys just like Chris, with the same training and same level of skill and lethality, watching over our guys and laying down the enemy by the hundreds. Guys who never wrote books, were never interviewed on CNN, and whose names you'll never hear, but who changed the face of combat for thousands of men and women in our conventional units.

Over the decade-plus that the putative War on Terror has been waged in the Middle East and Africa we've lost a lot of Americans, and a lot of Coalition brothers and sisters, too. But without the Kyles, Luttrells, and Tumilsons—and the Furlongs, Delgados, and Irvings—we would have lost an awful lot more.

At thirteen weeks, the new course was almost twice as long as the U.S. Army sniper school and longer by weeks than either the army's advanced SOTIC course or the USMC scout sniper basic course. But even that wasn't the whole of it. We also ran advanced classes beyond the basic course, a sort of continuing education for snipers that extended the reach of our curriculum even further.

For one of these, our rural program, we would take our students out into the wilds of the Northwest, up by the Canadian border, for a weeklong hunting trip to stalk elk and whitetail deer. Some of these guys had hunted before; many had not. This was their chance to go out, stalk, shoot, and stop a beating heart.

It was literally a Killing School.

We would start out before sunrise, in the dark, and be on the hunt by the time the sun was warming the frost off the tips of branches. We would hunt for a few hours, then come back to the lodge for breakfast. Toward dusk we would go out a second time, hunting well past dark, then come back to dress out whatever we caught. This wasn't some recreational junket where guys pulled triggers and then slapped each other on the back and went out for beers. We stalked, shot, skinned and gutted, cleaned, cooked, and ate every animal we killed.

In the full daylight hours in between, we ran advanced classes in long-distance shooting and real-world stalking.

These stalk sessions were like nothing else these guys had ever experienced before. In the classic course you stalk through an established sector and you know where your left and right boundaries are. Here we put our students into a very dynamic 360-degree environment with live fire. And while they were working for hours to get close enough to their targets to take a clean shot, we set countersnipers after them with radios to do their best to bust them. It was the same essential concept as the regular stalking course—just far more realistic.

As I said, I grew up spearfishing, but I'd never done any land hunting before. On one of our rural courses I shot my first deer. At the time, we were just starting to use ballistic software. Sitting in Southern California beforehand, I took a brand-new gun, zeroed it at one hundred yards, then took it with us up to the Canadian border. I did not zero the gun again; in fact, I didn't shoot a single round out of it in this new environment, just applied the data the software gave me. Out in the wild, I lased a deer with my range finder, plugged in my elevation adjustments, aimed, and fired. The gun's first shot in an entirely different environment, different elevation, different climate, shooting at 437 yards, on an upward 20 degree incline—and that first shot took the animal up off its feet. One shot, one kill.

There were some in the circle of command higher-ups who tried to snuff the program. Just a bunch of SEALs out on a nice boondoggle; that was their view of it. Fortunately more sensible heads prevailed. This was no boondoggle; it was a level of essential training that we couldn't achieve in any other way. We were conditioning our students for the kill.

If you can track and hunt deer successfully then you are well trained for the battlefield, because humans are actually much easier prey than the animals we were hunting. Humans tend to be lazy, their situational awareness blunted by the comfort and security of domesticated living. Animals in the wild have razor-sharp instincts, and they know how to listen to them. Their senses are preternaturally keen. To sneak up on an elk in the Great North, you need to be part wild animal yourself.

There were students coming through the course who had grown up hunting, the Chris Kyles and Marcus and Morgan Luttrells. But there were also plenty who'd hardly ever touched a gun before SEAL training—

people like Eric and me. For these people, this was the first time in their lives that they had ever stopped a beating heart with a lead slug. This gave them the chance to find out if they could do it.

More importantly, it gave *us* that chance.

Because not everyone could. And that's something you need to know about someone you're sending into the field of battle. He may be a tremendous guy, full of courage and loyalty and dedication and all kinds of great qualities. But if he cannot stare at a living being in his scope and pull the trigger without hesitation, he is not the guy you want on sniper overwatch as your unit enters a compound overflowing with lethal threats.

You want a guy who will not hesitate to kill, if killing is what's called for.

Still, with all the improvements we made in the core NSW course, and even with advanced training like our rural course, we never lost sight of one unassailable fact: *it still wasn't reality.* Not the reality of pointing a weapon at a human being, in the midst of the chaos of war, and shooting him. There really isn't any way to train for that, no matter what sort of program you create.

The only way to truly train for the reality of war is to go to war.

Which is the third and final phase of the Killing School.

7
THE REALITY OF WAR

The essence of war is violence, and moderation in war is imbecility.

—**Admiral John "Jacky" Fisher**

Training is one thing; the reality of landing in an alien world, of being in the presence of dead bodies, of having people shooting at you with the intention of killing you and shooting back at them with the intention of killing them first, is quite another. It's only once you're in the field that you go through the final phase of the Killing School, the graduate and postgraduate phase.

My first experience of the reality of war hit about a year before the 9/11 attacks, when the destroyer USS *Cole* was struck off the coast of Yemen by a pair of suicide bombers in a speedboat.

A corpsman friend of mine in our platoon, Clint Emerson, was flown out there a little ahead of the rest of us to help deal with the dead and wounded as quickly as possible. Clint describes the scene as one of the worst things he ever saw, and as a combat medic, he's seen some ugly things. He got to the ship, made his way down to the keel area where the bomb had hit and where more than a dozen bodies had been sitting now for hours, bloating in the hot pools of water. He reached down and took an arm to haul the body up, and the arm gave way and came off in his hands. Clint says it felt like the body was made of Jell-O.

Seventeen crew had died in the attack. There were seventeen of us SEALs there to cover it, so whenever we had a chance to grab any rack time, we slept in those dead guys' racks. It was eerie.

As sobering as the *Cole* was, it was an experience shared by only a few. The world at large was still mostly asleep to what was brewing. Nobody was really paying much attention to a bombing off the coast of some Middle Eastern country that few could locate on a map, or say for sure whether it rhymed with *lemon* or *semen*. Ten months later that all changed, when two commercial jetliners crashed into the tallest buildings in New York City and the reality of war came knocking on our door.

My platoon was one of the first units of SEALs on the ground in the new war, which so far was being waged in a cautious, surgical way, with selected Spec Ops forces supporting Afghan military and American ground troops being used only in small units for very concise operations. We were more than eager to get into the fight; everyone was. Along with our Echo Platoon patches, which I'd designed and featured a white devil with the slogan "Embrace the Hate," we also had NYFD patches sewn onto our uniforms. We spent October and November running interdiction ops in the Gulf and staging in Kuwait and Oman. Finally, in mid-December, we boarded a dark C-130 and a few hours later were walking down its ramp in Kandahar.

It was surreal. Storming Kandahar International Airport was one of the first things the Soviets did when they invaded in December 1979. Now it was exactly twenty-two years later, and whaddya know, here we were doing exactly the same thing. A decade of duking it out with the Soviets had ruined the place; when the Taliban took it over as one of their key strongholds, upkeep and repair was not at the top of their to-do list. And when a company of U.S. Marines landed and wrested it away from the Talis just a few days before we arrived, the place had taken one hell of a beating. There was broken glass everywhere, bloodstains on the floor, wreckage strewn here and there. We slept in the main terminal that night. It looked like the movie set for a postapocalyptic film.

The *Cole* had been an incident. This was war.

A few weeks later we would go up to northeastern Afghanistan and spend time in the mountains, near the Pakistan border. The area up there had a completely different feel, with its beautiful and terrifying countryside, its small farm communities surrounded by immense, jagged, snow-capped mountains. You knew there was some bad stuff going on up there, but it was still in a setting of some sort of normalcy, a fabric of culture and heritage.

Not Kandahar. Kandahar was a hellhole, just flat, hard desert and ugly urban sprawl, and you could tell bad shit was going down everywhere. It was like one gigantic seedy arms bazaar, and there was a sense that any minute someone was going to pull out an AK-47 and start shooting.

Kandahar has a distinct odor, a smell those who've never traveled outside the corridors of developed Western nations have never encountered—untreated sewage combined with the constant stink of open fires, of stoves burning wood and whatever else people could find to use for fuel to keep their bellies full. You could blindfold me, stick me on a plane, drop me there without telling me where we were, and I'd sniff it out in a heartbeat.

The most striking thing about Kandahar was its strangeness, its weird otherness. There was nothing in the U.S., or Canada, or Europe, or anywhere else I'd traveled to (at least in the West) that compared to it.

Years later I spent time in Iraq working as a private contractor. One day I was driving down the road in an Iraqi city when I noticed a kid in a cage sitting by the side of the street, right out in front of a busy market. A boy, maybe five or six years old, crammed into the kind of little wire box you'd set up for hamsters or guinea pigs. A kid. In a cage. What was *that* about? But I knew what it was about. The kid had been put there as some form of punishment, a public shaming. He looked miserable, but completely acquiescent, accepting of his fate. His posture said, *This sucks, but I deserve it*. Made me shudder.

I saw a lot of terrible things on the battlefield—people living in the worst of conditions and under crushing oppression, fields strewn with body parts, people reduced to a smear. But happening upon that little boy sitting in his cage ranks as the weirdest, strangest thing I saw, and in many ways the most disturbing.

That was what Kandahar felt like. An alien world. That was the world Rob Furlong landed in a few weeks later.

On February 2, 2002, Rob and his teammates bused out onto the tarmac at Edmonton International Airport to board a massive Lockheed Galaxy C-5. Rob had never seen anything like it. The C-5 is massive, one of the largest military transport planes ever built. (It also has a nickname among Galaxy flight crew: FRED, short for Fucking Ridiculous Economic Disaster.)

The U.S. was clearly serious about going to war.

The six Canadians got out of their bus and headed for the giant craft. The flight crew were all Americans and all smiles, obviously quite happy that the Canadians were joining them.

When the warning order came from the Canadian government that the PPCLI were being deployed to Afghanistan, they decided they would take their own snipers with them, deployed in two teams of three each: one on the big McMillan TAC-50, one serving as spotter (the team leader), one as security. At that point there were five men in the PPCLI's sniper cell; they needed a sixth. Tim McMeekin, the instructor Rob had gotten along with so well through sniper school, came onboard as leader of 63 Bravo and would be pairing up with Rob as shooter. The other team, 63 Alpha, was led by Graham "Rags" Ragsdale, who had also been an instructor at the course. The phrase "cream of the crop" was never more aptly applied as it was to these six men. They were Canada's best.

The group flew from Edmonton to Germany, then Germany to UAE, where they boarded a C-17 bound for Afghanistan. Landing on the tarmac at Kandahar, they walked down that big ramp and witnessed much the same thing I'd seen when our SEAL platoon landed there about seven weeks earlier, except that by then we'd cleaned it up somewhat and there was a hell of a lot of activity going on, personnel in dozens of different uniforms buzzing around the place.

Rob describes the scene with exactly the same word that came to me when I first walked down our C-130's ramp: *surreal*. A blown-out old concrete airport, with hulks of ancient Russian planes and fighter jets lying around. They started settling in and unpacking their equipment. Before long they had to take cover in shelters because of incoming rocket attacks. That got their adrenaline going.

Still, they didn't feel they were in much danger. They were in that weird purgatorial place: in an environment of war, on the edge of war, but not yet really within the gritty reality of war.

They were tasked into two-man sniper teams and sent off to deploy along with a team of U.S. scouts and some local Afghani fighters to man some old Russian-built guard towers about two kilometers outside the camp, to serve as an OP (observation post) and early warning system.

For the next two weeks they lived out there with these locals. Rob spent most of that time up in his little perch on top of the guard tower with his .50 cal and a spotting scope. They interacted quite a bit with some of the local warlords, and did actually catch a few bad guys as they tried to slip through their perimeter and get closer to the Coalition base at the airport. To Rob, this was not exactly what you'd call "action," it was like making an arrest on any urban street back home. These guys would roll up in their vehicles or dirt bikes, the locals would start chatting with them, and suddenly there'd be raised voices and signs of a commotion. The locals would haul a guy out of his vehicle, identify him to the Americans and Canadians as Taliban, Rob and his colleagues would bag 'em and tag 'em, call over an MP, and that was that. The dude was on his way to Guantánamo, and Rob was back up on his tower.

One day, after about two weeks of this glorified guard duty, Rob saw an American Humvee come bumping out in their direction. They were scheduled for resupply every Tuesday. This wasn't a Tuesday. The Humvee rolled to a stop and the front passenger window rolled down.

"You two," said the guy inside, referring to Rob and one of his fellow snipers, "pack up your shit. You're coming into camp. The CO wants to see you."

Back at the camp Rob and his buddy joined up with the other Canadian snipers of 63 Alpha and 63 Bravo, and the six of them were ushered into a command tent, where they found themselves face-to-face with Lieutenant Colonel Pat Stogran, commanding officer of the PPCLI battle group. Next to Colonel Stogran sat an American commander, accompanied by a few attachés.

The colonel looked at the six men and said, "I've been asked by the American commander here," and he nodded in the direction of the man to his right, "that you guys support an operation."

"Sure, whatever you need, sir," replied Ragsdale.

Colonel Stogran leaned in slightly. "Okay, guys, here's the deal. It's a Special Operations thing that's going to be happening. I don't have a lot of information, nor would I probably be allowed to tell you anyway."

Rob knew full well that was about as much information as they were going to get, whether now or later. He also knew what it meant: they were going to be sent into the middle of a war zone to seek people out and kill them.

"But you're going to be quarantined for a while first," the CO continued. "You'll probably fly out tomorrow. Take some time; get your kit ready. If you need anything, just let us know."

A few American MPs appeared at their sides to escort them out. They turned to leave the room, and just as they reached the door Colonel Stogran spoke up once more.

"By the way," he said, "I haven't been able to get hold of the Canadian government yet, to run this by them. I'll be pacing like a waiting father."

In other words, he was acting without permission.

"Don't worry, sir," replied Ragsdale, "we won't disappoint."

Colonel Stogran would remember those words.

The MPs took the six of them out to a fenced-in compound set apart from the rest of the base and left them in there. They were not allowed to have any contact with anyone—not their parents, not their spouses, not other Canadian teammates, not a soul. To the rest of the world, they simply vanished.

Rob Furlong in full camo. *(Courtesy of Rob Furlong)*

BELOW: Rob working with students in ghillie suits. *(Courtesy of Rob Furlong)*

BOTTOM: Can you see Rob's rifle barrel? (Hint: It's pointing straight at you.) *(Courtesy of Rob Furlong)*

Jason Delgado at four years old. *(Courtesy of Jason Delgado)*

Jason, age nineteen (second from left), as a new PIG in his first deployment, in Okinawa. Far left is Geof Lancaster, the HOG who worked most with Jason. Third from left, Doug Carrington, who was one of the snipers across the street from Jason throughout that terrible firefight at the Diyala River Bridge in 2003. *(Courtesy of Jason Delgado)*

Jason with his sniper platoon at Camp Husaybah, Iraq 2004. Top left to right: Matt Thompson, Brandon Delfiorentino, Josh Mavica; bottom left to right: Lucas Munds, Steve Reifel (Sierra Four team leader), Greg Slamka, Jesse Cheon, Jason Delgado (Sierra Three team leader). You can see the tower in the background. *(Courtesy of Jason Delgado)*

Jason in full regalia as a member of the Marine Reserves, fitted out for 2010 Marine Corps ball. (Photo taken inside Jason's first tattoo shop in NYC.) *(Courtesy of Jason Delgado)*

Jason with his Reserve platoon on the range at Fort Dix, getting behind the gun to check something out for one of his students. *(Courtesy of Jason Delgado)*

Jason at work as a private contractor in Erbil (northern Iraq), 2013. *(Courtesy of Jason Delgado)*

Nick Irving at age five. *(Courtesy of Nick Irving)*

Stick Figure in training, after putting on some major muscle. *(Courtesy of Nick Irving)*

Nick and his platoon, ready to rock. *(Courtesy of Nick Irving)*

The Reaper taking aim. *(Courtesy of Eric Davis)*

Nick and Mike Pemberton moments after making their dash to the "Alamo" safe house, deep in Taliban country, Helmand Province, after some eight hours of sustained combat. *(Courtesy of Nick Irving)*

Me and Eric Davis during BUD/S, getting ready to jump out of a perfectly good plane. *(Courtesy of Brandon Webb)*

Me commandeering a sweep of the town in Kandahar in the fall of 2001. *(Courtesy of Brandon Webb)*

TOP LEFT: Me instructing a sniper school class on the basics of stealth and concealment. *(Courtesy of Brandon Webb)*

TOP RIGHT: Sniper students about to begin a stalk in the stalking-and-concealment phase of training. *(Courtesy of Brandon Webb)*

BOTTOM LEFT: A sniper student camouflaged in a tree. *(Courtesy of Brandon Webb)*

BOTTOM RIGHT: A sniper student at our SEAL sniper school, setting up for a shot in his FFP (final firing position) at two hundred yards from his target. In the distance, Eric and I are watching for him. *(Courtesy of Brandon Webb)*

Eric about to provide sniper overwatch for a VBSS (vehicle boarding search and seizure) operation in the Persian Gulf, not long before 9/11. *(Courtesy of Eric Davis)*

Eric working with one of our sniper students at the NSW course. *(Courtesy of Eric Davis)*

On the receiving end of a student at his FFP. *(Courtesy of Eric Davis)*

For the following two weeks they lived in that small compound, training and waiting. It was a weird existence. They prepped their gear, kept up their PTs, went through the motions of maintaining their Spartan surroundings . . . but underneath the veneer of keeping busy they were really doing absolutely nothing but spinning their wheels. *Okay, we're here; now what?*

At one point a warrant officer came in and briefed them on the nature of high-altitude operations. He put them on acetazolamide, a med to help offset the effects of extreme altitude, and asked them if there was any special equipment they needed or wanted. They could ask for pretty much anything, he said. "That's okay," they replied. They had everything they needed. He left.

And they waited.

A big part of war is waiting. In some ways—in many ways—the waiting is worse than the combat. You've prepared for this for years. You want to be in action. You don't want to be sitting around in some shithole, watching while the war machine slowly grinds into motion. But that is generally the way it works. The skill of war depends upon the warfighter's capacity for boredom and inactivity, laced with tension and nervous apprehension.

Finally one evening an officer came in and said, "All right, guys, thirty-minute warning. Get your shit ready. We're heading out."

They got their gear ready—which took no effort at all, since they'd been ready for days—and a half hour later some men came in and walked them out to a waiting C-17. They walked up the ramp to find the big beast's cavernous interior completely empty. They were the only passengers.

As the ramp began to close a Canadian officer ran out onto the tarmac, his arms full of equipment. "Hey!" he shouted. "You guys, you gotta wear helmets!" He held up a mass of gear: six sets of flak vests and helmets.

Rob and the other snipers looked at each other, then back at the officer. "Yeah," said one, "we don't wear that shit."

The ramp closed, leaving officer and gear standing on the tarmac.

For Rob the war was about to get real in the Shahikot Valley.

For Jason Delgado it all got real a year later, in the spring of 2003, when his unit, the Third Battalion, Fourth Marines, went driving up through the belly of Iraq, heading for the capital city to pull down Saddam's statue. It was about 350 miles from the southeastern tip of Iraq northwest to Baghdad, and for most of that push Jason and his sniper partner Jesse missed out on what little resistance the battalion met.

Until they reached the Diyala River.

On April 6 the marines arrived at the small urban town of Jisr Diyala, just across the Diyala River (a tributary of the Euphrates) from the southeastern tip of Baghdad. They were meched up—that is, traveling on military motorized vehicles, convoy style—and in motion. Nobody had any intention of stopping at that town. The plan was to drive through, cross the bridge, hold up on the other side, and wait for permission from regiment to push on past the Al Rasheed Air Base and into Baghdad.

But the sequence didn't go that way.

Jason and Jesse pulled into the town in their amphibious assault vehicle (AAV), also called an Amtrac, short for *am*phibious *trac*tor. Following their standard sequence, they stopped the vehicle and got out so they could find a good location from which to serve as sniper overwatch for the moving column of India Company, the unit they were supporting. Quickly locating a small bell tower, they judged it to be adequate for their purposes and climbed up with a few other members of the platoon. On an upper floor they gained access to an empty room with four panel windows, one looking out in each direction of the compass. Perfect.

Jason had his M16 out, Jesse was on the M40; another sniper, Alex Cordova, was on the .50 cal SASR (special applications scoped rifle, pronounced *sasser*). India Company starting moving through the area and toward the bridge.

At that moment Jason noticed a figure huddled on a nearby rooftop with a long tube resting horizontally on his shoulder. The tube was pointed directly at one of India's AAVs. Jason just had time to register the thought—*That cocksucker is firing on our guys with an RPG!*—when he heard the explosion and simultaneously saw the plume of gray smoke billow out the back of the tube. A fraction of a second later the grenade slammed into the side of the AAV.

Incredibly, it did not explode. The AAV wore a layer of false armor, a hollow layer on the outside with the actual steel armor underneath protecting the troops inside the vehicle. The grenade had pierced the hollow outer shell and lodged there. No one was hurt—but the company reacted immediately, and reacted hard. A few days earlier they had taken their first casualty, when a young PIG named Mark Evnin had died from a gunshot wound sustained in a skirmish at Al Kut, some one hundred miles southeast of Diyala. The day before that, a hastily assembled Iraqi truck bomb had crashed into an Abrams tank—an *Abrams!*—and blown it to hell. The marines were now on a hair trigger and in no mood to be casual.

In seconds Cordova had his SASR up on the ledge pointed toward that other rooftop, and let a round go. The sound of that SASR round going off was so loud that for a moment, Jason thought *they* had been hit with an RPG. Everyone in the room grabbed their heads, hands over the ears.

"Oh my freaking God," yelled Jason, "what are you *doing,* man?"

Meanwhile everyone on the ground was scrambling. None of them knew where the RPG had come from. Jason and Jesse, who had clearly seen the shooter and the smoke plume, were frantically trying to get through on their comms to tell the guys on the ground. But no one was listening. They were immersed in the fog of war. The radio channels were full of voices shouting, "We got hit!" "Contact left! Contact left!" "No, it's contact right!" and everyone was opening up fire.

Unable to get through on comms, they bounded down the stairs and outside, where they saw a platoon running by across the street. It happened to be the India Company platoon Jason had belonged to before becoming a sniper. They recognized him, and he called out, "Follow me!" He and Jesse started running for a nearby alley, headed toward the building where the guy had launched the RPG, the other platoon now following their lead. They tore through the alley, and the moment Jason reached the end and poked his head around the corner, sure enough, there was the guy slipping out of the building in a black tracksuit.

The man hadn't seen him. He turned, glanced briefly in Jason's general direction—just long enough that Jason could see his face—then turned away again and started walking casually down the street in the other direction.

No way was Jason letting this guy get away. He took two steps out from the alleyway, brought his weapon up, took careful aim, and let a shot go.

Nothing happened.

The guy heard the shot and started running without even turning to look.

Shit! thought Delgado. *Maybe I was a little jittery and not steady enough on the rifle.*

It should not have been that difficult a shot. The guy was running away from him in more or less a straight line, which meant that he still presented a dead-on target. Jason embraced his M16, sighted in once more, steadied his breathing, and squeezed the trigger, as calmly as he could.

And once more: nothing. The guy kept running.

What the fuck is going on? thought Jason. He'd now missed his target twice. The guy knew he was being shot at and was running away. There was no point just shooting a third time; he'd already done his best to aim correctly and missed, twice.

What the hell was he supposed to do now?

Delgado had been through U.S. Marine Corps training, some of the best on the planet, and a brutally thorough six-month-long "indoc" that was for all practical purposes a six-month full-bore sniper school, plus the Corps' sniper school itself. He was as trained as it gets.

But no matter how thoroughly you train, it's still not the same as the real thing.

You take someone who has gone to Tae Kwon Do classes faithfully for ten years, gotten his zillionth-degree black belt, and throw him into a bar fight in a bad section of town where he suddenly finds himself grappling on the floor with some mean drunk motherfucker who's doing his best to tear this guy's eyes out, and what's going to happen? The mean drunk motherfucker is going to tear his eyes out.

Classes are classes. Real is real.

When it's real, there's so much going on internally. Your heart is racing, you're anxious, adrenaline's flowing, random thoughts are zipping unbidden through your mind, and you're trying to ignore the absolutely unignorable voice in your mind going *Shit, this is actually happening!*

The military did its best to train for that. Coming out of the Vietnam experience, especially, and then from other more minor combat experiences since then, they had developed a science-based sort of approach, looking at what went on in a person's physiology when they were engaging in combat and attempting to replicate that in training. They knew that in the thick of war, when you're downrange and entering a firefight, your heart rate goes up. So they got their people's heart rates up in training. They would have their trainees do extensive PT and then jump straight onto the range to shoot.

But the reality is nowhere near that simple. There's a lot more going on than an accelerated heart rate. You can do a few push-ups and run a few hundred yards, then grab your gun, and, yeah, it gets you breathing hard while you're trying to shoot. *But you still know you're in train-*

ing. You know what you're being tested on. You've been on this range before. You know what's coming. No matter how hard they bust your balls, no matter how hard the hell is, it's ultimately not that big a deal. It's not combat.

In combat there are so many unknown factors, and no one can really train you for that feeling.

By the time Jason went through his training, the military had become more sophisticated in their efforts. Now when marine instructors trained their snipers they had flashbangs going off, sporadic automatic weapons fire, or maybe rock music blaring at ear-splitting volume and lights flashing on and off at random intervals, anything to overload and overwhelm the senses. Because if a sniper can operate when his circuits are being overloaded, that's your guy for the battlefield.

But still. It's not combat.

Jason took a breath and tried to clear his head. He had missed twice and the seconds were ticking. He knew he'd get only one more chance. He was about to experience the art of self-correction.

You'd think that when you miss a shot, your tendency would be to overcompensate on your second try. That jibes with our normal experience. Imagine you're driving along, not paying attention, and you suddenly realize you're drifting left into the oncoming traffic's lane. What do you do? Most people will jerk the wheel to the right—usually a little too far to the right, perhaps even hitting the guy in the next lane over. That's how a lot of highway accidents happen: not from the original drift but from the overcorrection.

Curiously, though, that's not what tends to happen on the range. When a student marksman misses, his tendency will be to *undercorrect*. When I went through the SEAL course in 2000 I remember the instructors saying, "Make bold corrections."

Which is not bad advice, to some extent. Better to act boldly than timidly. But it's really not that helpful. Eric Davis says that whenever he heard an instructor say that, he would think, *What the hell is "bold" supposed to mean?*

A few years later, when we were teaching the course ourselves, I had to laugh every time I heard what Eric would say to our students: "Don't make bold corrections—make *correct* corrections."

Because it isn't about being bold. It isn't about having a different attitude. It's about precision. It's about a number. This speaks to that point about accuracy and the demands of being laser focused, the whole reason sniper school is so murderously difficult. Telling you to make "bold corrections" is like telling you to try harder, or to be more inspired.

But you can't try, or bluff, or attitude-adjust that round onto your target. You have to surgically *place* it there.

And that's what needed to happen now. Delgado had to make a *correct* correction. And he had to do it right now, immediately.

Delgado felt his weapon, its butt stock pressed against his shoulder, his 203 grenade launcher attached underneath the barrel, making the M16 feel heavy and cumbersome. He looked down at his sighting mechanism—and it dawned on him. He had his rear sight aperture set to six hundred yards. The guy was at probably two hundred yards or so.

Jason was shooting for a six-hundred-yard shot, which meant he was way over-shooting his target.

There was no time to reset the elevation on his gun. He had to run a seat-of-the-pants calculation and compensate on the fly. He brought his M16 back up level, put his front sight close on the running guy's butt cheek, and squeezed the trigger—

This all happened in the space of a few seconds, but in Jason's mind it stretched out over minutes, like a long, slow sequence, each step happening with great deliberateness, as if he were crossing a river, stepping carefully from rock to rock and placing each foot so he wouldn't slip and fall in . . .

First shot—
Observe—
Missed! What happened?—
Contemplating—
Don't know—
Steady up, aim—
Second shot—
Observe—
Missed again!—
Now the guy was moving faster—
Shit, he knows I'm on to him—
Contemplating—
What's going on? Why am I missing?—
Looks down at his gun—
Light dawns: it's set on six hundred yards—
No time to reset sight—
Nod: *I know what to do*—
Aim back in, lower the M16 just a hair to place the center of the sight square on the guy's buttocks as he runs—

Jesse is now swinging his rifle up into position, too, to take a shot—
But by this time Jason is already squeezing the trigger—
He lets go with a third round—
Observe—
Boom! . . . sssssssmack!
—and the third round hit the man square in the back.

That's the surreality of combat. In situations like this your brain operates so fast, there's so much adrenaline flooding your system, that everything around you goes into extreme slow motion. To Jason, it might as well have taken an hour for the whole sequence to elapse. It was timeless.

And then the surreality of it all became even more so. As Jason watched what happened when the round hit the man, it seemed to him the weirdest thing he'd ever seen. He was waiting for that Hollywood scene—the one where the guy takes a shot, flips over like a bowling pin, and lies there dead. Ominous chords in low brass fade on the soundtrack. But that wasn't what happened. This guy grabbed his stomach.

What? Jason had shot him in the back. So that was already confusing. Jason had the half thought, *Wait, did I shoot him, or did someone else shoot him from the front?* But no, he'd shot him all right. But the guy grabbed his *stomach.*

Then he took a few steps forward, like he was walking over to do something. And then he sat down on the ground, very calm.

Then lay down and died.

As the war ground on Jason saw this again and again: he would shoot someone, and know he'd hit him, but would see some reaction that seemed so completely out of character for what he was expecting that he would doubt for a moment whether he'd made the shot at all. Or, no visible reaction at all: the guy would just take a few more steps, then sit down, perhaps light a cigarette, and then, after lighting his cigarette, lie down, cross his legs, and die.

Just like this man. There was something about it that was so unexpected, so peculiar, that it seemed way worse to Jason than if the man had just done the movie stuntman thing and flipped over onto his back.

But Jason didn't have time to think about it, or even to react to it. Because on the heels of his first combat kill, he was about to have another first-time battlefield experience.

The unexpected RPG shot, and the response that it elicited, seemed to have touched off a fair amount of chaos there at the river's edge. A firefight was erupting. Jason and Jesse scrambled back up to a second-story vantage point and were soon running from rooftop to rooftop, looking to secure the best positions from which to see the action and provide their compatriots protective fire. As they stood for a moment on one rooftop, Jason suddenly heard the damnedest thing: a swarm of angry bees started buzzing right past their heads.

What the hell? he thought. *Bees? On a rooftop in Iraq, in the middle of a firefight?*

It took them both a moment to realize what it was they were actually hearing. It wasn't a swarm of angry bees at all. It was a swarm of angry bullets.

They were being shot at.

We're a long way from Van Cortlandt Park, Delgado.

They had both fired tens of thousands of rounds themselves, and been around other guys firing tens of thousands of rounds. But actually being shot at, having live rounds fired directly toward you, is one thing that never happens in training. This was the first time either of them had ever been targeted by focused enemy fire like that.

And it was *targeted* fire, all right. Jason didn't want to think it was sniper fire per se, but it sure as hell seemed like that's what it was. Those shots were being aimed right at them, and they were high-speed rounds. Jason had thought "angry bees" because that was exactly what the rounds sounded like as they flew past: Eeeee*thup*! Eeeeee*thup*! Eeeeee*thup*!

They both reacted simultaneously, melting into the base of the roof and slipping down behind the slight rampart. For the next few minutes they were pinned down.

Damn! thought Jason. They had an enemy sniper homed in on them and they couldn't even pick up their heads to try to see exactly where he was. It was frustrating.

Jason looked at his M16 again, with its damned clunky 203 attachment. That thing pissed him off. It was so cumbersome, and whenever he broke into a run it would continually smack against the back of his knee. It really was a pain in the ass.

Then it occurred to him: he had a load of twelve 203 grenades with him.

He smiled.

Kaboom! Kaboom! Kaboom! Jason turned into a one-man mortar team, letting off those 203s in the direction he guessed the gunfire was coming from, slightly changing his angle of fire with each one. *Kaboom! Kaboom! Kaboom! Kaboom!* he wondered exactly where they were landing, and hoped wherever it was, it was helpful.

They waited a moment.

Apparently it was helpful, because when they poked their heads up over the lip of the roof to look around, they didn't see anything happening. And no more angry bees.

They got off that rooftop fast and moved on to an adjacent rooftop to set up in a spot where they hadn't already been targeted.

Jason believes the enemy had not intended to mount an offensive, not right then and there. He believes they had planned to wait and let some of the marines cross the bridge, then blow up the bridge and attack them on both sides with their forces divided. But the scuffle that resulted from that RPG attack went on long enough that the enemy finally said "fuck it" and brought the fight to the marines on the south side of the bridge.

It's impossible to say what would have happened if that one Iraqi hadn't lost his cool and shot off that one RPG, but he did, and it affected the course of the whole mission, with terrible results for all parties involved—as we shall see later on.

In the reality of combat, things don't always go the way they went back in the training exercises. In 2005, Alex Morrison and a few other snipers were working with a conventional army unit in Tamin, right across the river from Ramadi, doing a lot of sniper overwatch to try to force the insurgents to think twice before placing their IEDs (improvised explosive devices). It was exactly the kind of work Chris Kyle had done in Fallujah in '04 and would do again in Ramadi in '06, and it was having an impact. Alex's teammates had already killed a number of insurgents trying to place bombs on the major routes through Ramadi, and the frequency of IED events here was starting to drop off.

There was an intersection by a cab stand that was getting hit with IEDs about once a week, and the army unit asked the SEALs if they could set up an overwatch there. They chose a nearby building on the main thoroughfare there that had one second-story wall facing the intersection.

They went out at night in a few Bradley fighting vehicles and drove around the area, stopping in a few places to do false inserts, then got dropped off within eight hundred meters of the building they'd selected. They slipped into the building, explained to the building's occupants why they were there and secured them for the night, then headed up to the second floor, where they popped a few loopholes in the wall and set up to wait.

And waited.

Nothing happened that night. Alex was on watch first thing in the morning, and saw a series of shifty-looking characters pass through, but no actionable behavior. About two in the afternoon, now off his shift, Alex was sitting up against a wall, trying to catch a quick catnap. Another sniper who'd been stationed at one of their loopholes for a while stood up to stretch, and happened to glance out the window.

"Holy shit!" he exclaimed. "There's a guy right there!"

Alex lurched to his feet and took a look. Sure enough, there was a guy barely forty yards away, digging into the street.

"It was like sitting for hours in a deer stand," says Alex, "then getting up to take a piss, and suddenly realizing there's a giant buck standing right behind you."

The thing was, they were set up to shoot toward the intersection, but not out in this direction at the street. They couldn't just shoot through glass, and the window was a thick, solid piece with bars over it. And they didn't want to spook the guy and lose him before they could get a clean shot.

"Listen," Alex told his sniper friend. "I'll sledge out the window, then you can pop out the glass and shoot him." They would have to pull off the move in perfect sync, and quickly.

Alex grabbed their sledge, swung it behind him, and—CRASH!—smashed out the window.

At which point the sledge was caught fast in the bars. Alex tried to yank it out. It didn't budge.

The insurgent stopped dead in his tracks and looked up at the building. Out of the corner of his eye, Alex could see him staring right toward them. He looked very much like he was thinking, *Wait a minute—why did that window just break?* but he didn't move a muscle. Which was fortunate for Alex, because he was still trying to wrestle the damn sledge out of the wreckage.

Meanwhile the other sniper got his SR-25 up there and managed to poke it out through the shattered window just as Alex hauled the sledge free.

BOOM!

The man was still staring at the window when the SR-25's slug caught him in the chest and threw him to the ground.

Nick Irving plunged into the reality of war when his ranger unit hit the ground in Tikrit in the middle of 2006. For the next three years, his life would career from one firefight to the next. At one point his unit conducted 120 missions in ninety days. The op tempo was unreal. Still, the first handful of firefights he was in were all essentially one-sided, with no real organized return fire.

One night they were on a mission going after a very well-known high-value target (HVT), one of the top figures in the shadowy Al Qaeda network at the time. They had walked for what seemed like forever. Nick then weighed about 150 pounds, and with all the ammo he brought he was carrying probably another 150. Nick's legs never did get used to the business of endless marching while carrying a massive load. Neither did the rest of him.

Finally they reached their objective. As a machine gunner, Nick pulled security duty and was stationed standing up on a big brick wall at the back of the site, responsible for making sure no one slipped out the back.

He stood and waited for the mission to go down. And waited. Suddenly he heard a weird noise:

Sssssnap! Sssssnap! Ssssssnap!

Oh shoot, he thought. His earpiece was going out. He started tapping on the thing. It seemed okay. So what the hell was that snapping sound—

He was still in the middle of the thought when his team leader grabbed him, shoved him on the ground, and put his knee in Nick's back. "Get the fuck down!" he said. "We're getting shot at!"

The enemy snipers on the roof of the next building over were shooting at them with suppressed rifles, so there was no loud *bang* coming from the shot itself. The only noise they made was the sound of tiny sonic booms as the supersonic rounds zipped past his head and impacted on the wall behind him.

That was what he'd been hearing.

Training had taught Nick how to clear rooms, how to bait explosive breaches and blow open doors, how to conduct hand-to-hand combat. It had prepared him for the suck and stress of endless marches, no sleep, and impossible circumstances. It had even taught him how to shoot and kill people. But being shot at himself? And still do all those things he'd trained for while being shot at? That was graduate-course work.

The thought flashed through Nick's mind: *I'm still a young guy!* He could really, no shit, *die,* right here, right now.

But he didn't die. Ranger snipers started returning fire, and then the assault team made their way up onto that other rooftop. One intense firefight later it was the enemy snipers who were dead.

The night wasn't over.

While the immediate danger of the enemy sniper team was neutralized, activity all around them was exploding, and they were in danger of becoming surrounded by hostiles. Nick and the rest of his machine gun team began moving out to secure the perimeter and make sure no one came in. As he moved, he glanced over his right shoulder—and spotted an MH-6 Little Bird helo in the distance flying dangerously low. At that moment Nick heard a loud BOOM. Smoke started pouring out of the top of the chopper and it started spinning. For a moment Nick thought it had been hit by an RPG; then he realized the pilot had hit a power line.

The bird went down about a mile from where Irving stood, watching it all happen. *Shit,* he thought, *this is looking just like* Black Hawk Down.

A platoon sergeant strode over to where Nick and a few other guys were standing and barked at Nick, "Hey, we've got a Little Bird down, we need you and your guys over there to go secure this pilot."

They took off running, a mile-long dead sprint with hundreds of pounds of gear, Nick's internal commentary running the whole time. *I'm eighteen years old, and I'm going with a couple of teenagers to secure a freaking downed helicopter surrounded by hostiles.* When they reached the Little Bird they climbed up on a berm and found the pilot cradled behind a bush, holding a little MP5 Heckler & Koch machine pistol. The poor guy was freaking out.

One of Nick's squad members picked up a Mark 48, the same weapon Nick was packing (and a more substantial machine gun than the MP5) and started laying down lead. Some guy had been coming toward them with an AK-47. It seemed to Nick that the entire village was rolling in behind this guy, *all* of them with AK-47s. It was indeed starting to look like a scene from Somalia.

And then it got worse.

Nick glanced over to his right and was stunned to see a tank grinding its way in their general direction. *Holy shit!* he thought. *These guys have tanks?*

He swung to his right and aimed, centering his weapon's infrared laser directly on the small sensor that sits on a little turret toward the front, where he figured the driver would be. If he made the shot, he knew he would at the very least halt the tank's progress. If he was lucky, he'd kill the driver and maybe additional personnel in there to boot.

He flipped his Mark 48 off SAFE and slipped his finger inside the trigger guard, then felt the metal of the trigger press against his index finger as he began to squeeze.

A fraction of a second before the trigger engaged and the Mark 48 burst into life, the tank came to an abrupt halt, swiveled its big cannon, and pointed it right at Nick. Time seemed to come to a complete halt, too, as he gazed down that long, black hole. Well this sure was going to be an education. Less than an hour ago he'd been shot at by snipers, and now he was going to find out what it was like to be shot at with a 120mm tank round. That's a "bullet" with a diameter bigger than his arm.

Oh shit, he thought. *This is going to be very bad.*

"Hey," said a voice by his shoulder. It was their team leader. "Hey," he repeated, "that's *our* guys."

It was an Abrams M1. Nick had been about to shoot a U.S. tank.

He slowly lowered his weapon, backed away from the tank, and went over to help secure the pilot.

His unit killed close to thirty insurgents that night, but their HVT had already moved on to another location. Didn't matter. The pilot was safe, and their work was done for that night.

Nick never forgot the feeling of looking down the black tunnel of that tank's gun.

Being in combat doesn't always mean being shot at. Sometimes the threat of lethal violence simmers just beneath the surface of unfolding events and never quite erupts. Sometimes the tension of an uncertain standoff (are they bluffing or are they going to shoot?) or civilian interrogation (are they *really* just innocent civilians?) is so thick you could cut it into blocks and use it as high explosive. The reality of war encompasses a huge range of situations. But whether you're facing off with armed insurgents in an urban ambush, or conducting sniper overwatch on a raid, or doing a room-to-room sweep in the dead of night and taking prisoners, missions are missions, war is war: you're thrust into a situation where there are armed hostiles whose mission is to kill you, and no matter how well it was been planned it's essentially a powder keg with a match tossed into the middle.

This is the central reality of war that's impossible to convey in training: every op is semi-organized and highly lethal insanity. There's no such thing as a safe mission. And even when that reality makes itself stark and clear, you have to jump in and perform anyway.

Every mission feels something like skydiving. There is an edge of anticipation, a fractional nervousness, but as soon as you jump off the ramp and you're in the air, the nerves and anxiety and misgivings all disappear, blown off by the wind velocity of the reality you've plunged into. It all goes away, and you're in the zone. You don't think about anything or care about anything but the deadly game in which you're engaged and doing whatever it takes to make sure your teammates come out of it alive, and if possible, that you do, too.

Which is an interesting distinction.

For some, access to that zone is denied. There are guys whose immediate and total response, when plunged into the boiling water of armed conflict, is to do everything they can to scramble back out again. There's no room in their brain for concern over their teammates' safety. It's not that they don't care about their teammates, it's just that the scream of survival instinct is at such a deafening pitch, it drowns out everything else. I've seen it happen. So has everyone who's ever gone into combat.

Nick saw it happen in Mosul in 2007, on his second deployment. His unit was already deep into an especially long and bitter firefight, when an RPG skipped off the front end of his Stryker and landed on the ground right in front of them.

One of the guys in Nick's unit saw that unexploded grenade sitting there—and he just folded. Lay down and curled into the fetal position. And that was the end of that. He wasn't moving.

Nick jumped up on the Stryker hatch and started laying down suppressive fire, dumping all seven mags into his M4, killing every enemy fighter within the immediate perimeter. The grenade never went off. And the whole time, this guy just lay there curled up on the round. After the mission wrapped, he was shipped directly home.

Rob Furlong saw it happen in Anaconda, when one of his team simply shut down, much like the guy in Nick's unit.

In one particularly hairy mission my unit engaged in, we had just landed at our drop point in Afghanistan's mountain country, when one of our guys suddenly said his ankle hurt. He turned around and climbed back on the chopper.

Okay, I and everyone else in our platoon thought, *I know I don't want to be next to* him *in a firefight.*

I don't judge these folks as lesser human beings or in some way morally flawed. It's no indictment on their character. It's simply this: they don't belong in combat. The rigors and hell of military training do everything possible to weed these folks out beforehand, but no system is foolproof. Cowards leak through.

And the truth is, you don't really know for sure about yourself, you *can't* know for sure about yourself, until you are standing there in the smoke and clamor and adrenaline of war. Everyone *thinks* they're going to be able to perform the job. But you just don't know, until you know. When you go into combat for the first time there are the inevitable questions hovering in the back of your mind. *Will I get shot? Killed?*—those are back there, yes, but they're not first and foremost. The bigger question is, *Will I measure up?* This is the question that most strongly stalks you as you approach your LZ: *Do I have what it takes to go to war and perform, and not be a wuss?*

That's perhaps the most critical piece of information you gain in the first days of the Killing School's graduate program, that you cannot get any earlier or anywhere else: this gut sense, once you've been out on a couple of missions, that you know who's got it and who doesn't. It's a good feeling, to know: *I have what it takes; I will not wimp out. I've got my brother's back.*

A few weeks before Rob Furlong arrived in Afghanistan, my platoon went on its first major mission, a search-and-destroy drop into the training compound in the caves of Zhawar Kili, planned for twelve hours, that would turn out to be an extended one-week operation. That first night, we staged in an abandoned village we found on top of the mountain there.

Just before dawn the next morning, a small team of us went out to conduct a BDA (battle damage assessment) on an area that had been bombed the night before, looking for the body of one particular KIA. We humped out for a while, maybe twelve to fifteen klicks, or kilometers (seven and a half to nine miles), reached the spot, and set up a perimeter. The sun was just starting to come up. Two guys went off searching for the body we were supposed to find; the rest of us sat tight.

A few minutes later we heard a group of men emerge from a nearby cave. While not close enough for them to notice us, they were close enough that we could see they were armed: RPGs, machine guns, AK-47s. This presented a problem. They significantly outnumbered us. Our lieutenant, who was part of the group, told me we had a nearby B-52 on comms that would drop a guided thousand-pound bomb called JDAM (joint direct attack munition). He needed me to give the range.

The problem: we had no range finder. Worse, I didn't have my sniper scope, either, and no sniper rifle (this was supposed to be a twelve-hour op, remember), nothing but an M4, basically a lighter, smaller version of an M16 with a little ACOG mini scope. Nothing that would do us any good here. I was going to have to guesstimate the distance.

The reality of war.

Okay, guesstimate it would have to be. Not much margin of error here; if I was off the wrong way by a little, the bomb would kill *us* just as easily as the other guys. *Hey, no pressure,* I thought. I worked out the range—about five hundred yards, danger close—and gave coordinates to the LT, who relayed them to our guy on comms, who fed them to the B-52. By this time the enemy fighters had either seen us or heard us and were firing in our direction. The LT gave us permission and we started firing back, knowing a bomb was on its way. Toward them, hopefully.

The first bomb dropped wide. I'd hedged our bets and given coordinates about a hundred yards long. Better too far than too close. I gave adjusted coordinates to the LT. The second bomb was a direct hit—on them.

As the smoke cleared we walked over to do our BDA, not on the bomb drop from the night before but on the bomb drop we'd just called in. The graphite smell of the blast, mixed with the stench of burnt flesh, hovered over everything. There were no body parts, or at least not anything you'd recognize as such. Nothing that large. More like a vague foul-smelling smear. A thousand pounds of explosive dropped directly on top of you will do that.

It was a strange thing, to realize that there had been more than a dozen people standing here moments earlier, and now they were gone. Evaporated.

Later we all got an award for the action. It looks heroic on an award. This kind of thing looks heroic in a movie. When it's happening, it doesn't feel like heroism. It's just the truth of the moment. You're about to be killed. Or, you're about to kill.

That's the reality of war.

8

THE ART AND SCIENCE OF THE SHOT

They wouldn't hit an elephant at this distance.

—Union General John Sedgwick, moments before being fatally shot in the face by a Confederate sniper at eight hundred yards

Jason Delgado and his sniper partner, Jesse Davenport, crouched on the rooftop under the hot Iraqi sun, scouting for potential targets. As the sporadic firefight triggered by a lone RPG continued to sputter, they were providing security overwatch for India Company and the rest of the battalion as it continued moving toward the Diyala River Bridge, the last gateway before Baghdad.

In the far distance they noticed a figure popping up over a rooftop parapet, shooting toward them at irregular intervals with what looked to be an AK-47. The guy would take a shot, duck down behind the short wall, then bob back up again and take either another look or another shot.

Of all the friends Delgado had gone through marine training with, Davenport was the only one who hung in all the way through sniper school. They'd been through so much together that they'd begun to have the kind of immediate, automatic rapport in battle that makes words all but unnecessary. They'd also both been through that initial test of combat, where the sense of *How am I gonna do?* is replaced by *Okay, we got this.* They had started relaxing into the flow of combat, shooting, moving, and communicating smoothly together.

The two friends rotated on the M40A1 sniper rifle, taking turns as shooter and spotter. Today Jesse happened to be on the long gun, Jason spotting for him.

Jesse nodded in the direction of the distant rooftop and said, "See that guy?"

"Yeah," said Jason. No need to speak in sentences; they each knew what the other meant. Delgado pulled out his range finder and lased the building. It stood at eight hundred yards distant.

"Yo," he said, "eight hundred." *He's at eight hundred yards.*

From a distance of eight hundred yards the guy wasn't doing any damage at this point, but both snipers knew that once their element on the ground got closer, he was going to be a problem. They had to take him out.

Jesse set his BDC (bullet drop compensator) on 8. The M40 was equipped with an Unertl scope, which was a pretty basic piece of equipment and lacked the fine-tuned adjustment capacity of the kind of sniper scopes we were using in the SEAL teams. A bullet drop compensator offers a degree of adjustment, but there's still a good amount of seat-of-the-pants involved.

Jesse sighted in and murmured, "Wind?" *What have we got for wind?*

Jason had already observed their surroundings and calculated direction and wind speed. On nearby rooftops he could see clothes hanging out to dry on lines, fabric coverings over open windows, even a flag or two here and there flapping in the breeze. Plenty enough visual clues to tell him that a mild wind was coming from the left. Before Jesse even asked the question, Jason had already determined that he needed to compensate for that breeze by adjusting his aim slightly to the left, that is, positioning the guy slightly to the right of his center of aim. So when Jesse said, "Wind?" Jason simply licked his finger, held it up, cocked his head thoughtfully, as if he were running through some arcane calculations based on exactly how the saliva on his finger dried, and said, "Uh, yeah, that'll be one and a half right."

In his best impression of an elegant British gentleman, Jesse replied, "Roger, one and a half right."

Sometimes humor is the most efficient way to keep your cool in the midst of combat.

Jesse dialed one and a half right on the scope for windage. "On target."

"On scope"—replied Jason—"fire when ready."

This was the very definition of an implausible, if not impossible, shot.

Experienced snipers never go for a head shot if they can help it. For one thing, it's way too easy to miss; the head doesn't give you nearly the target acreage that a torso does. And besides, it isn't necessary. Hit a person with a metal slug traveling at a velocity at or near the speed of sound, and you're not going to "just wing him," you're going to do terminal damage. So no, snipers don't aim for the head; they'll aim for center mass, middle of the torso, every time. If possible.

Which, for Jesse, it wasn't. The man's body was tucked down behind the parapet. Worse, not only could Jesse see nothing but the man's head, but he had only a brief sliver of the man's face in view as he bobbed up to peek over the rim and ducked down again.

And he was shooting out to eight hundred yards, right at the upper limits of the gun's maximum effective range. Eight football fields. That was a hell of a distance to nail some guy's erratically bobbing head. Not a snowball's chance in hell.

He took the shot.

Boom.

Nine tenths of a second later the guy lurched, grabbing his face as if he'd been smacked with a two-by-four, and flew backward.

"Holy *shit!*" Delgado murmured. It was Jesse's first kill shot, and it was the craziest shot Jason had ever witnessed. Before long he'd see crazier.

I know I've repeatedly pointed out that stalking is the toughest part of sniper school, and that shooting occupies a relatively small portion of the sniper's time in the field. But make no mistake: you also have to be an exceptional shooter.

You know how people have the expression, "Hey, it's not rocket science." Well, being a Spec Ops sniper *is* rocket science. Every round you fire is in essence a miniature rocket ship, launched on its own unique journey, and that journey is no more a simple straight line than a NASA mission to Mars. Understanding all the factors that affect that bullet's flight and how to adjust to compensate for any variation in circumstances, no matter how slight or how great, is what separates the professional sniper from the aspiring one.

We've talked about dialing in adjustments and used the terms *elevation* and *windage* without really explaining what those things are. So let's hit PAUSE for a moment, for a quick primer on how this all works, starting with those two terms and how a sniper uses them.

ELEVATION

Just because you look through your scope at a target in the distance and see a clear, unobstructed pathway between you and it for your bullet to travel, doesn't mean there *is* a clear pathway. There may in fact be a branch or overhead wire or some other obstruction in the way. You just don't see it. Why don't you see it? Because the bullet isn't going to go where you're looking right now.

You *think* you're looking at the bullet's path. But you're not.

Your bullet is not going to travel along a nice, neat, linear path defined by your line of sight. To reach your eye, light from the distant target travels a straight line. Actually, it doesn't, not literally, because light itself curves—but at the distances we're talking about that curvature is so minuscule that for all practical purposes you can ignore that and say your line of sight travels a perfectly straight line.

Your bullet doesn't.

When you pitch a bullet toward a distant object it's exactly like throwing a baseball: to get from here to there it has to travel in an arc—up, over, and down. The moment the bullet leaves the barrel it's being slowed down by air resistance and tugged toward the ground by gravity. If you point your barrel directly at your target the bullet will never get there, because by the time it reaches its intended destination gravity will have pulled it down so that it flies below the target. Or, depending on how far you're shooting and how high the target is, it may even plow into the ground before getting that far.

To compensate, you have to aim the barrel at a point above the target. How far above? That depends on a lot of factors, including the physical particulars of the weapon and ammo you're using. Determining exactly how high above the target you have to aim is what we mean when we say "adjusting for elevation."

By the way, this also means you cannot simply look down your line of sight when plotting your shot; you also need to be aware of the overhead space. In making a shot of any significant distance (say, three hundred yards or more), it's not unusual to have your bullet knocked completely off course when it collides with an overhanging branch or other obstacle that you completely failed to notice, because it was placed far above your line of sight—but right smack in the bullet's actual arc of travel.

WINDAGE

If you let go of a balloon on a windy day, what happens? The wind carries it away. Your bullet weighs more than a balloon and is hurled out of the barrel with considerable velocity, but that wind will still carry the damn thing away, or at least far enough off course so that there's a decent chance it'll miss your target even if your aim was dead-on perfect.

Which was why Jesse was relying on Jason to tell him exactly which way the wind was blowing, and how hard. Or more specifically, to tell him exactly how many degrees in which direction he needed to adjust his aim to compensate.

There are other factors, too. For example, there is *spin drift,* which is a bullet's natural tendency to peel off clockwise, to the right, at a certain point in its trajectory, typically when it slows from supersonic to transonic speeds. If you've ever played with a toy top, you know that when it slows down to a certain point it starts to *precess,* that is, to wobble, and then spin out into a wider arc and fall. A high-speed bullet, which is spinning like a top, will do the same thing.

But spin drift only becomes a factor in very long shots, those going out to a thousand yards or further. Ditto the Coriolis effect, the impact of the earth's rotation on the transit of the bullet in the air relative to what's happening on the ground. We'll come back to these and other more arcane considerations in a later chapter. For most of the shots we're looking at here, elevation and windage are the central factors, the X and Y axis of making the shot.

So there you have it: point your rifle directly at your target, with perfect aim, and you'll miss. Gravity and friction will pull your bullet down, and the wind will push it to one side or the other. Theoretically perfect aim would work in deep outer space, where there's no wind and no significant gravitational pull. Here on earth, it'll get you killed.

The art of the shot is not about perfect aim. It is the art of crafting the perfect *imperfect* aim—an aim with precisely the right set of imperfections such that gravity, wind, and other environmental forces will corrupt your imperfect shot and cancel out its imperfections, resulting in . . . perfection.

You have to aim *wrong*—just right.

To do that, you have two adjustable knobs, or turrets, located at about the midpoint of the scope: an elevation turret on top, and a windage turret on the right. The elevation turret is calibrated to adjust your scope to compensate for specific distances, and the windage turret for left-right adjustments to compensate for wind; they are both calibrated in minutes of angle (MOA), a minute being one sixtieth of a degree, or more typically in fractions of MOA. (Typically there is also a third knob on the left for focusing, which functions like a focus adjustment on any optics, like binoculars or a telescope. Most scopes these days also have a zoom control toward the front that lets you zoom from 10x up to 22x. But these two knobs don't actually adjust the point of aim, only the clarity of the visual image.)

These turrets make a pronounced click you can clearly feel in your fingers, like the rings and knobs on a good camera, so you can make an accurate adjustment without taking your eye from the scope, purely by the feel of the clicks.

But here's the thing: in most situations you *leave those knobs alone,* especially windage. Instead of fussing with the knobs and readjusting the scope for each shot, in most cases you're going to compensate manually by correcting in your reticle.

CORRECTING IN YOUR RETICLE

Before going into the field you will have "zeroed" your rifle, which means you've got your scope adjustments all set perfectly for your rifle, ammunition, and a given range, say, a hundred yards. With a properly zeroed sniper rifle, if you sight a target at three hundred yards, you're good to go.

And if it's further, or, for that matter, closer? And there's wind involved? Typically, you make adjustments in your reticle.

The reticle is a high-precision version of scope crosshairs that features a series of tiny markings, called mil dots, that run vertically and horizontally through the field of vision, providing a precise scale of measurement. Mil stands for milliradian, which is a thousandth of a radian, a measure of angle. (Think *degrees*; not the same thing, but close enough to get the general concept.)

Most of the time, when you're making adjustments for a shot, you make the adjustments in your head and then *hold right* or *hold left* a specific number of mil dots to compensate for wind, and *hold over* (farther) or *hold forward* (closer) a specific number of mil dots to compensate for elevation. For example, if you "hold one and a half right for wind" that means you move your rifle slightly to the left, so that the point you're aiming at appears not in the dead center of your crosshairs but at 1.5 mil dots to the right of center. Which was exactly the direction Jason gave Jesse for his eight-hundred-yard shot.

Sometimes you might dial in your elevation, and hold for wind. Often you won't even do that, and simply do all the compensating in the reticle.

At this point you're probably wondering, *Why?* If a sniper's optics are such finely calibrated precision instruments, why not just dial in everything? Why not lase the target for its exact distance, do your best to judge exact wind, and then simply dial it all into your magnificent weapon system for a perfect (that is, perfectly imperfect) shot?

If sniping was all about sitting there with all the time in the world to set up your one perfect shot, and then taking that one perfect shot, then packing up and going home, well, that might work.

But that's not how it is.

Jesse's first kill shot was a classic one-shot/one-kill situation. But that's not always how it goes. In fact, that's most often *not* how it goes. If you can make that hole-in-one shot, then fantastic. That makes you an expert marksman—but not necessarily an expert sniper. In the field of war, it's often the second shot that makes the difference.

You take in an enormous amount of information in sniper school, but no matter how much you absorb and practice on the range, it's never enough, because learning isn't the same as doing. It's only when you are dropped into the reality of war that you go through the final phase of the Killing School. As you engage in battle, your skills move from *learned* to *known*. They sink into your bones and become the stuff of instinct.

By the time the 3/4 Marines entered Baghdad, Jason's and Jesse's skill sets had clearly moved from *learned* to *known*.

I'm not sure exactly what our military planners were expecting to happen when American troops reached Baghdad, but it probably wasn't what actually did happen. Once Saddam was toppled, the constrictive yoke of tyranny was removed, and the initial flush of celebratory relief was gone, the place imploded. A sprawl of looting, confusion, and random civilian violence spread out through the city. In hindsight, those days of post-"liberation" chaos offered strong hints of what was to come in the years ahead. All Jason and Jesse knew was that they had an urban mess on their hands, and they had to do their best to keep order. Days earlier they had been warriors spearheading a successful military campaign. Now they were urban police in an alien city in turmoil.

One day, about a week after Saddam's statue came down, the two of them were standing sentinel over the city from atop a fifteen-story building in the government district. Suddenly they noticed a ruckus unfolding below them. Some idiot had run into the street with an AK-47 and was randomly shooting the thing off. The area was jam-packed. People were about to die—not American soldiers but ordinary Iraqi citizens doing their best to go about normal life. As if anything was "normal" in Iraq in mid-2003.

Jason was spotting that day. He ranged the guy at 180 yards and fed the dope to Jesse, who took him out with a single shot. One shot, one kill. Classic.

A few weeks later, on May 3, Jason and Jesse were once again providing overwatch, this time from the roof of one of the tallest buildings in Baghdad, some fifty-plus stories up. The power was out, and Jason vividly recalls hoofing it up thirty-six flights of stairs, then finding they needed to hoof another seventeen flights after that. Running up fifty stories with full gear, an M40, and ammo, is not for the faint of heart. "So this—is why—we ran around—for months carrying—those fucking PIG eggs," he huffed.

By this time the chaos in Baghdad had deepened. Once again they saw a scene erupt below, this time a small group of men spraying bullets around with their AKs. The one who appeared to be the leader wore a blue tracksuit.

Jason instantly knew what he was looking at. They might be halfway around the world from where he came from, and this might be the center of one of the oldest cultures in the world rather than one of the newest. But the city is the city. Jason grew up in the streets. He knew a gang leader when he saw one. This was not just some random guy terrorizing a neighborhood, and he was no freedom fighter. That was a hood boss down there. And if they didn't stop him, a lot of people were going to die.

This time it was Jesse spotting, Jason on the long gun. Jesse gave him the range: 446 yards. Jason got the ringleader in his sights, and took the shot.

Nothing.

He checked his aim, took another shot.

Nothing.

Had Jesse seen any splash—that is, the telltale puff of dirt or dust kicked up when the bullet hits the ground? He had not. They had no idea where the round had gone.

It occurred to Jason that there was also a very good possibility his zero was off. They'd been jumping in and out of Amtracs that day and had just run up more than fifty flights of stairs. That kind of thing gives your gun a good banging around. He needed to get his bearings—and he needed to do it somewhere away from the crowd.

He yelled over to Jesse, "Let's swing over to the other side of the building. Find me something at 446 yards. I gotta zero my gun."

They ran over to the other side of the roof and Jesse started lasing targets, quickly locating a water tank standing way down below them at about 430 yards. "Got it!" he shouted, and he pointed at the thing.

Delgado set his sight on the center of the water tower and *Boom!* took a shot. *Pinggg!* A flash of dust shot off the top of the structure. It was an enormous target, he'd been aiming dead center, and yet he'd barely nicked the very *top* of the damn thing!

He stared at it for a second. His zero couldn't be *that* far off. And while 446 yards was a good distance, it certainly wasn't far enough away for his shot to go so far afield.

Then he realized: *the angle*. "Holy shit," he murmured.

And he thought about Scott McTigue.

The marines had a specialized high-angle course at the Marine Corps Mountain Warfare Training Center in California, with a curriculum basically identical to the private course Nick Irving would attend in California years later, but that was an advanced course, something Jason wouldn't go through until later in his career. And they had other advanced sniper programs that covered this topic—but there hadn't been time to put Jason through any of that. Iraq was happening, and the Corps needed snipers, so here he was. At that point, sitting up there on his skyscraper perch in the heart of Baghdad's financial district, the only time he'd ever heard anything about the technique involved in high-angle shooting had been in back in Okinawa, when he was still a PIG going through his third indoc.

In a marine sniper platoon, the senior HOG in charge is called the chief scout. The chief scout is responsible for billeting, who goes onto what team, and all training. He spends a lot of his time teaching the younger guys everything he knows and everything he can think of to teach them. This is exactly what Jason himself would be doing in the future, when he became chief scout of his platoon in Husaybah. In Okinawa their chief scout was Scott McTigue.

McTigue had a dusty manual on high-angle shooting, and at one point during those six months he decided to throw that into his classes. It wasn't that in-depth, and even McTigue didn't have a complete

command of it, so the PIGs learned the formula but didn't really understand the physics of it. But Jason's artist's mind could visualize the
whole scene in vivid 3-D. What he was doing was basic trigonometry:
solving for x, the missing factor. As long as he could visualize it, he could
do the calculations. Because this math was no abstraction. It wasn't
simply numbers. That guy on the ground with his AK-47 was about to
kill a bunch of people.

Delgado started breaking down the math.

He was at the top of a tall building, let's round its height to four hundred yards, while his target was at ground level, out from the building
at a distance of about half the building's height, or two hundred yards.
For simplicity's sake, let's call the height of the building 4, and the distance from the base of the building to the target 2.

Shooting from the top of the building down to the level where the
target was located would be a distance of 4, in terms of height. But from
where Delgado stood going out horizontally to the target's location—
that is, from the base of his building out to the target, since Delgado
stood directly above the building's base—was a distance of only 2. So
putting aside how far *down* he was shooting, he was shooting *out* only
to a distance of 2, exactly as it would have been if he were standing at
ground level at the building's base.

That was significant because the horizontal distance from the building out to the target was the distance over which gravity would be af-
fecting the bullet. Since that was the distance he had to mitigate for
the effects of gravity, that was the elevation he needed to dial in on his
scope.

But not for windage. Because the round's actual path of flight from
where he stood down to his target at ground level was not 2 but 4—
actually a little longer than that, because he was really shooting along
the hypotenuse of the triangle, which would be more like 4.46. And
because the wind would be pushing on that bullet from the moment it
left the barrel throughout the entire time it took to traverse that full
distance, *that* was the distance he had to mitigate for wind.

Optically speaking, in other words, his target was about 446 yards
away—that was the distance he needed for windage. But in ballistic
terms, it was more like 200 yards away—that was his value for elevation.

He quickly set his windage, based on the actual distance to target,
at 446 yards, and calculated his elevation (amount to compensate for
gravity) at 200 yards, the distance he gauged from the building to the
target.

Only when I say "he quickly set his windage," that's a gross over-simplification. Their M40A1 was, remember, outfitted with an Unertl scope. The Unertl was the most advanced sniper scope of its time . . . in the sixties. This was essentially the scope Carlos Hathcock used in Vietnam, and the Corps was just about to phase it out (the company that manufactured it would close its doors in 2008) and replace it with the more advanced Schmidt & Bender, a very decent piece of equipment. But that was a few years away. Unertl is what they were still using at the time. As Jason says, "It was the oldest, most brutish, diesel engine of scopes. You had to do a lot of Kentucky windage."

Kentucky windage meaning seat-of-your-pants guesswork.

"None of my shots were particularly glorious," says Jason. "Because that's not what it's about. There's this great mystique around the idea of *one shot, one kill*. But one-shot/one-kills are extremely difficult, very rare, and usually very lucky. Let's talk about reality. Tell me what happened after you missed your first shot, let me know what you do then. Because *that's* what it is to be a sniper. In real combat, that's what we do."

Sniping is problem-solving under pressure. When you've got targets moving downrange and don't have time to sit there and dial in wind, what do you do? You have to become comfortable with the reticle, to be able to translate what's happening out in your battlefield into the world of mil dots on your scope.

To adjust on the fly, in other words, and make it work.

Kentucky windage.

He shot off a few more rounds, enough to pop a few holes in the water tank. Once he saw water spurt out a hole in the center of the tank, he had it.

"Okay," he said to Jesse, "let's go."

They ran back to the other side of the rooftop and, sure enough, that tracksuit-clad dipshit was still over there, terrorizing the neighborhood with his AK, yelling at people and spraying the neighborhood with lead. The AK isn't a terribly accurate gun but its rate of fire on full auto is a hundred rounds per minute, nearly two shots per second. That's a lot of damage, a lot of tragedy, a lot of death.

Jason sighted him and instantly took the shot.

The man went down like a puppet with his strings snapped.

Just as with his first kill shot weeks earlier, in Jisr Diyala, what happened next was so unexpected that Delgado almost didn't believe his eyes were giving him accurate information. A moment after going down, the guy sat up again.

Jason thought, *What the hell is going on?* He knew he'd hit the man. He saw the impact, saw the guy go down, and could see blood pouring out of his back, around the kidneys. So why was he sitting up? And *how* was he sitting up?

Again, Hollywood prepares you for the perfect movie death, the one where you shoot the guy and he just goes down and stays down—but it doesn't always work that way. Death is a strange character. It's not tame, or predictable, or calm, the way you'll often see it portrayed in movies (even the "violent" ones) or television shows (even the "realistic" ones).

Death has its own rules. Death is wild.

So this guy, having been mortally wounded by a 7.62 round to the kidneys, sat up again and then, as Jason stared at him, he gently lay back down again, crossed his legs, then crossed his arms over his chest, and in that mummylike pose, quietly died.

"It was the craziest thing." Delgado shakes his head, thinking about it. "He was already gone the moment I hit him. But he didn't just die—he took the time to get ready to die. And *then* he died."

Of course, you don't *have* to do all the math in your head, strictly speaking. This is the twenty-first century, after all. Every sniper program these days schools its students in how to use sniper software. As Apple used to say, "There's an app for that."

Still, anyone who really knows an art knows that you don't *know* it until you know it in your fingers, flesh, and muscles. Painting by numbers will take you only so far.

Nick Irving is not a big fan of ballistics calculators. "I've seen sharpshooters who act like their sole mission in life is to master this calculator," he comments. "That may be fine for match shooting—but I wouldn't want them watching my back in the field."

He invokes his hero, Carlos Hathcock, pointing out that the White Feather and others like him did what they did using basic mathematics.

"Basic math didn't fail those guys," he says, "it never failed me, and it won't fail the next guy. If you rely on your calculator, what do you do when the battery suddenly runs out?"

Irving had the chance to call on that basic math when he faced a unique ballistic challenge during a deployment in Marjah, in southern Afghanistan.

On a mission one day as he was lying in prone position doing overwatch, he spotted an enemy fighter with a machine gun at a pretty good distance, coming around a corner. Nick estimated the guy's range at about five hundred yards and figured he could drop him fairly easily.

Nick always kept Dirty Diana dialed in at three hundred yards, the average range of his typical kill. If he had to make a shot at less than three hundred, he'd just hold forward; if it was more than that, as in this case, he would just hold over.

He got the man in his scope and held over for an additional two hundred yards, which meant raising his rifle slightly, so his aim was 2 mils high in his scope's reticle.

He took the shot.

Missed. And not by a little. Nick saw the splash and was startled to see that his round had hit more than a full 2 mils low, as well as 1 mil to the left. He scanned the area for clues, and as he did he realized that the urban terrain was not at all level; the fighter stood on higher ground, and the disparity in elevation had affected Nick's depth perception, making the man seem closer than he actually was.

The guy was not five hundred yards away. He was a good half mile away, or more—and there was significant wind involved.

Jack Nicklaus, arguably the greatest golfer of all time, said that 90 percent of the shot is setting it up, and the last 10 percent is actually taking the shot. It's the same thing with marksmanship: 10 percent is execution, being a surgeon with the bullet. The rest of it, the 90 percent, is all surveying the scene, doing the math, and planning.

For Irving, in other words, it was a lot like chess.

The first thing he needed was to find the range to target, so he could either dial it up on his scope or know by how much he needed to hold over.

Nick liked working in meters. Forty inches, which is basically a meter, is the standard measurement from groin to top of the head. To convert inches to millimeters you multiply by 25.4; 40 x 25.4 comes out to 1,016. Then you take that number and divide it by how tall (from groin to top of head) the guy is in your scope. Let's say he shows up on your reticle as 2 mils tall, groin to crown; you would divide 1,016 by 2 to get 508. There's your range in meters.

An old-school ranger had taught him how to simplify that. "You guys want to be fast at this?" he said. "Chop it down."

First of all, it's not practical to do that kind of math on paper. Ninety-nine percent of the time, a sniper is operating at night. And besides, who has time to pull out a piece of paper and a pen?

The old ranger taught him to simplify things by rounding down. They would take the 1,016 down to an even thousand and use that as the constant for height. If the guy showed up as 1 mil tall in his scope, Nick knew he was 1,000 meters away; if he was 2 mils tall, then he was at 500 meters. He might actually be 508 meters away, but that was close enough: you might not hit him in the chest, where you were aiming, but in the gut or sternum. You don't care about finesse here; you just want to put him down.

They had formulas for width and the height of the head, too: five hundred, two hundred. One thousand, five hundred, two hundred: those were their three constants.

Of course Nick wasn't sitting there with pen and paper going through all that math in the moment. He had already been through that math, a thousand times, ten thousand times. Like a concert pianist whose fingers know where to go without conscious thought, or a major league slugger who automatically adjusts his swing to match his instantaneous estimate of the speed of the pitch coming at him, he had trained exhaustively, at every range, every wind condition, every angle, to the point where he could remember setting up a shot so similar to this one that he could say, "Right, I know exactly what to do."

Nick realized that the wind had also fooled him. A small stream ran through the city between his location and his target's location. The stream ran left to right—but the fact that his bullet had impacted at 1 mil to the left of his target told him that the wind was moving from right to left.

He held 1 mil to the right, then cranked upward 2 mils . . . plus a smidgen.

He released the shot.

Meanwhile, the fighter he was shooting at had seen Nick's first bullet hit the ground near him. At the same moment that Nick was watching the little spray of dirt kicking up and parsing through what it meant for his follow-up shot, the guy was staring at it, too, and processing its implications for him. He looked up in Nick's direction and squinted, no doubt trying to see if he could locate where the shot had come from. It was a fatal miscalculation on his part, because he didn't have the luxury of time to determine where the shot had come from. By the time he was raising his head to squint into the distance, Nick's second 7.62mm round was about halfway through its journey in his direction.

Nick caught a glint off the tail end of the bullet an instant before it reached a half mile. *Shit,* he thought, *it's off.* He could clearly see the path it was on, and that path would take it just a short distance off to the man's right. His shot was going to miss.

And then in the last fraction of a second, like a sailboat unfurling its canvas as it reaches the open water, the round caught that right-to-left wind—and an instant later it connected with its target.

The man went down, dead before he hit the ground. He did not sit back up, cross his legs, or light a cigarette.

An excellent example of that kind of from-the-hip calculation happened to Jason one night on his 2004 deployment in western Iraq, when he and his sniper team were out in the city on a quiet LPOP (listening post and observation post) and suddenly heard a large explosion. They had been there only a few weeks, and this was one of the first explosions they heard there. (These were the days when the phenomenon of IEDs was not yet that commonplace.)

They ran downstairs and out onto the street to go see what had happened. As Jason began heading in the direction the sound had come from, he saw a car barreling down the street coming in his direction.

Jason swung his rifle up so he could look through the scope, saw that it was a civilian in the car, and he was heading straight for them. It seemed like a pretty safe bet that this dude was running away from whatever the hell had just happened. There was a curfew in the city and *nobody* was supposed to be out on the streets right now, let alone speeding away from the site of an explosion.

A moment later the guy sped by. Jason had a second sniper team stationed a bit farther down the road and called them on his radio: "Sierra 4! Sierra 4! Sierra 3! I've got some joker coming straight toward you in a vehicle. I want you to run a snap VCP—" A vehicle checkpoint, which meant they would stop the car and check the guy out.

"Roger!" said the other team. Jason stood out in the middle of the street and watched the car disappear over a slight crest in the road about two hundred yards away.

A few seconds passed. Then he heard from the other team on his radio, yelling, "Hey, man, we tried to stop him. He's coming back up your way!"

Evidently the guy had seen the other snipers, done a fast U-turn, and started hauling ass back in Jason's direction. He hadn't seen Jason when he blew past the first time and didn't realize he was there. He didn't realize he was playing chicken with a marine sniper.

Jason raised his rifle, setting the butt onto his shoulder, and waited, standing on the edge of the street like a sheriff in a Western—only this wasn't a six-shooter, this was a forty-four-inch, high-speed bolt-action M40 sniper rifle with an effective firing range of eight hundred meters.

Go ahead, thought Delgado. *Make my day.*

The car came back up over the crest and started screaming toward him.

Jason put a round straight into the car's hood, which seemed like a pretty clear message that said, "I recommend you stop the car."

The man did not stop the car. In fact, Jason heard the engine opening up as the guy accelerated further.

Jason shot back the bolt on the M40, but by the time he had racked in a second round the car was already speeding past him. He whipped his body around in an effort to track with the guy, pulling his rifle around with him.

As the car shot off in the other direction, he fired.

His two spotters, standing at his left and his right with M4s, both fired as well, as the vehicle zoomed away from the three of them.

The car kept going for another two blocks or so, then suddenly decelerated, rolled off to the side of the road, and stopped.

Yeah, thought Delgado, *one of us hit this motherfucker!*

As they came running toward the vehicle, a man opened the driver's-side door and came out with his hands in the air. "Don't shoot!" he said. "Please, don't shoot!" And then he got down on the curb and sat there, his hands still up.

Delgado and the others were still a block away, and he started yelling toward them, "Don't shoot no more! Don't shoot!" Speaking perfect English. They finally reached him, guns trained on him, and stopped. He slowly lowered his hands and lit a cigarette, then started talking.

"I'm sorry! I'm sorry! I didn't do anything, I'm sorry! I have daughters. I have daughters. Please, don't kill me. I have two daughters." He seemed totally sincere.

Shit, thought Jason, *we just lit this guy up for no reason. We're gonna have some explaining to do.*

At least they hadn't actually hit him.

Jason was pissed. A bomb had gone off, their adrenaline had been flowing. Why hadn't the guy stopped his car? What the hell was he doing out past curfew anyway?

Just then the man pointed to his armpit and said, "I'm shot! I'm shot! Please, take me to hospital. I'm shot!"

Jason looked, and sure enough, he was bleeding out of his side. One of the guys with the M4s must have landed a round.

They went over and began inspecting his car. They found a single bullet hole in the hood of the trunk that went right in through the trunk and into the car, through the right rear passenger seat, and into the driver's seat, right by his shoulder. They could see the seat cushion, where it had punched through. It was a hole made by a 7.62 round—later confirmed at the hospital when they dug the slug out of the guy.

It was Jason's round.

When they popped the trunk, they also found a bunch of cell phone parts, SIM cards, wire cutters, and electrical tape. This was the guy who'd set off the IED. They later discovered he had been arrested before by the U.S. military for subversive activities, but eventually let go.

"Okay, asshole," said Jason, "you can turn off the charm now."

After a brief hospital stay, the man was on his way to Guantánamo.

He hadn't expected to actually *hit* the guy with his shot-from-the-hip. It was pure instinct and muscle memory.

As Jason said, "None of my shots was particularly glorious." Maybe not, but this one was pretty damn spectacular.

Alex Morrison had a pretty damn spectacular shot, too, in the late summer of 2009 in an area just north of Kandahar. He and a few dozen other SEALs were there with a FAST (foreign-deployed advisory and support team) from the DEA (Drug Enforcement Administration). These FAST teams are typically manned by former military, many of them ex-SEALs, and they're trained and outfitted like a SEAL platoon because their missions are so freaking dangerous. They were there with Alex and the other SEALs for a classic disruption operation: seize a known enemy compound and sit on it for a day, see how much damage you can do and how much Taliban economic flow you can disrupt.

They inserted at first light. They took two compounds, side by side, right on the river next to a big open area. From the moment they hit the ground they were taking sporadic fire. By noon it was coming at them from every point on the compass.

Alex wasn't packing a sniper rifle on this op; instead, he had a Mark 17, a new assault rifle also called SCAR Heavy, "SCAR" for Special Operations Forces Combat Assault Rifle, and "heavy" meaning it was chambered for 7.62mm rounds rather than the 5.56 rounds fired by the "light" version. He was using a special solid-core bullet made for penetrating surfaces like windows and walls.

SEAL snipers weren't using SRs that much in Afghanistan, because the shots were typically a fairly good distance, and they preferred the carrying power of that big .30 cal boomstick. Typically one sniper would bring his .30 cal, and everyone would rotate on and off that rifle. When they got that first shipment of SCAR Heavies, all the snipers pulled the

NightForce scopes off their SR-25s and mounted them on the SCAR Heavies. With that assault rifle, they were getting kills out to eight hundred yards.

Their ISR (intelligence, surveillance, and reconnaissance, coming in from manned aircraft, Predators, and other sources) told them there was a white minivan driving around, picking up fighters, driving a big circle around the Americans, and then dropping the fighters off again. This van was repositioning the Tali forces to maintain maximum tactical advantage.

In most situations, there's a key pressure point where, if you take care of that point, the rest of the deal starts to come unraveled. Loggers know this. When a logjam happens, there is usually one critical log holding the mess in place, and once they pull it out, the rest of the knot comes apart; they call it the kingpin log.

This minivan was a kingpin log, and Alex meant to yank it out of there.

Word came over the comms: "The van left . . ." And a few minutes later, "Okay, the van's back."

Peering down through an alleyway between two buildings out the other side, he caught a glimpse of a white minivan stopping. It was straight to his north, about 250 yards away, positioned perpendicular to him, so that he was looking at its passenger side.

He spoke into his comms: "Hey, you got eyes on the van?"

The reply came back: "Yeah, it's directly to your north, at about two-fifty."

Bingo. He put his crosshairs on the passenger's shoulder and squeezed off a round—BOOM!—and saw his round hit the side of the vehicle.

As he watched through his scope, he saw a weird scene unfold. At first the passenger started jerking. A split second later, the driver slumped forward over the steering wheel. Then the jerking stopped. Neither man moved.

Alex had pulled out the kingpin log, all right. His shot had taken out both men at once—two guys with one bullet.

Sometimes the most critical calculation a sniper needs to make has nothing to do with the mechanics of the shot itself but with the timing of the shot, and the decision as to whether or not to pull the trigger. As Nick Irving experienced one day in Marjah, not long after his half-mile-plus shot.

Before you can serve as a sniper in the rangers, you have to do years of being an actual ranger, which involves kicking in doors, clearing rooms, close quarters combat, and that sort of thing.

Now that Nick was a sniper, he was working at more distant ranges. His average shot was at about three hundred yards, which is not extremely far, but hardly close-range. On this day, though, he found himself in an unusually close-range situation.

He was out on a mission with the platoon when a guy came walking toward them, slowly, very deliberately, doing the whole "I'm gonna blow you guys up with a suicide vest" walk. Irving had by this time witnessed suicide bombers blow themselves up just like this at least a half a dozen times. He knew what he was seeing.

The other guys in the platoon yelled at the man to stop. He kept walking toward them.

Nick told the rest of the guys to go ahead and move out, continuing on their mission, while he and his spotter stayed in place to keep an eye on this guy. They remained back as the platoon moved on, until the rest of the guys were about a hundred yards away. His spotter stayed a few yards back.

Now it was just Nick and the vest dude, one-on-one, talking.

Nick's unit had already been in close to a dozen firefights that night. Frankly, he was getting pretty tired of being pinned down and shot at, and didn't have much humor for this guy. He got on his radio to call it in.

Most of the shots Nick took on this deployment he didn't bother to call in. He didn't need to. The ROEs (rules of engagement) were fairly liberal for a ranger sniper, at least at this point. If the man had a weapon, Nick was free to use his judgment. However, this guy didn't have a visible weapon. It was pretty obvious to everyone there that he intended grievous bodily harm. Blowing them all up with a suicide vest seemed to qualify as "grievous bodily harm." But still.

"I have a guy at thirty yards walking toward me, ignoring commands to stop, looks like a vest. Permission to shoot."

"Roger that," came the reply. "Take him."

Nick kept calling over to the guy in Pashtun. The dude just continued slowly walking closer, staring at Nick with that fuck-you-I'm-gonna-kill-you glare.

Nick put a red laser dot on his eye. He didn't seem to care.

Nick then put the laser dot on his chest and said, "Dude, I'm gonna do this." The man may or may not have understood English, but he could not possibly have failed to grasp the general meaning. Especially with the red dot sitting on his chest and the Army Ranger twenty-five yards away, pointing a rifle at him.

Nick had decided that if he could persuade the man to stop walking, he wouldn't shoot. If he and his spotter could get the guy to keep his hands free, where they could see them, if they could get him down on the ground with his arms stretched out, they would be able to bag him and tag him.

He just kept coming.

Oh, man, thought Nick, *I really don't want to get blown up.* Nick called out for him to stop a few more times, in Pashtun.

He kept coming.

"Roger that," said Nick. He figured twenty feet was about as close as he wanted it to go. "I was young and cocky," he says. "I thought I could probably survive a blast at twenty feet away. Which of course," he adds, "I probably couldn't have."

When the guy got to the twenty-foot mark Nick shot hit him square in the chest, and he dropped in place, without having the opportunity to detonate the vest.

It was the closest shot Nick ever took.

There was no math involved.

III.
THE STALK

You will be asked to penetrate deep behind enemy lines, move through unsurvivable territory undetected, slip deep into their camp and deep into their minds, and survive to bring back what you see and hear and learn.

You will be expected to see the enemy where others see nothing, to hear the enemy when others are aware of nothing, to understand the enemy's next move even before the enemy understands it himself; to sow fear and confusion among the enemy's ranks while at the same time providing critical intelligence to your own forces. Your circumstances will require you to be invisible, unpredictable, and lethal.

You will find yourself in situations where you do not have the tools necessary to do your job, the resources critical to the success of the enterprise, and will still be expected to adapt, adjust, invent, survive, and prevail. . . .

9

WELCOME TO THE JUNGLE

No battle plan survives contact with the enemy.

—**Field Marshal Helmuth Karl Bernhard Graf von Moltke**

"Three minutes out!" As Rob Furlong's Chinook got close to their drop point the front door gunner suddenly opened up, letting it rip on the big gun. Sitting just behind him, Rob had just enough time to think, *What the hell is he shooting at?* when he saw a stream of tracers arcing back up directly toward them and zipping past their chopper.

In machine gun ammunition, every fifth round is a special round that contains an illuminant that will burn with a bright light, either red or green, as it flies, illuminating the gunner's line of fire to help him stay on aim. That's what Rob was seeing right now.

This is contact, Rob thought. *We're under contact. It's happening, right now.* It was his first time being under live fire.

They hadn't even landed yet and things had already started going wrong.

As the front door gunner's M240 spat rounds into the darkness Rob felt a surge of adrenaline pumping through his body. He felt his grip tighten on the big .50—a futile but irrepressible gesture. It was a weird combination of thrill and frustration, like a super-heightened version of that maddening waiting game. They were under attack. They were being shot at. And there was nothing he could do but grip the nylon netting and wait. He wanted in the worst way to get off that aircraft and down there on the ground, where he could *do* something.

He felt their craft veer off sharply to the right. Of course: their chopper must be breaking off and heading for an alternate LZ. But it didn't take more than a few minutes to realize that wasn't what was happening. Their aircraft was not heading for an alternative LZ. It seemed like they were flying north, heading back the way they'd come.

Wait—they'd been *called off*?

Once they got on the ground back at Bagram they got the update on what had happened. The entire airborne convoy had taken heavier than anticipated enemy fire. Of the eight fully loaded choppers that had left in the predawn darkness, most had turned back. However, a few actually *had* landed. One of those had carried 63 Alpha, the other Canadian team.

Their guys were over there on the ground—and they weren't.

The men of 63 Bravo freaked out. "This is *bullshit*," Rob told the ground crew at Bagram.

"Get us on a fucking aircraft," McMeekin added. "We're going back there, *now*!" Leaving their teammates behind out there in the mountains of Afghanistan, while they sat here on the ground? Abso-fuckinglutely unthinkable. Not happening. Canadians may be a polite people, but Rob and his mates could curse as well as any American sailor when the occasion demanded it.

The occasion demanded it.

It took a few hours, but before long they were loading onto the chopper again, heading back south for their rendezvous with war.

As they boarded the Chinook the second time, a young Delta sniper climbed in with them. They'd met earlier out on the airstrip at Bagram, when they were all sitting around after a debriefing, and Rob had noticed he was carrying an SR-25. They'd struck up a conversation about the merits of different sniper rifles. Now here he was, with his SR, heading out to the Shahikot Valley on the same aircraft Rob was taking.

They started talking about what they were heading into. Some of the Delta guys had already been out there, come back, and were on their way back out again.

"Shit, man," said the young Delta operator. "We're going into a hornet's nest."

War is improvisation. You'd like to think it's different, that everything goes according to plan. Sometimes that happens. But not very often. Here's what normally happens: things start going to hell the moment the shit starts hitting the fan. That is exactly what was happening in Anaconda.

The plan was, go in, provide overwatch while the American forces round up the bad guys, and then get out. The op's planners still had the expectation that enemy forces were small, ill-prepared for a set battle, and would either be killed or voluntarily surrender on short order. Thus, the snipers' task would be a quick in and out: predawn insert one day to exfil the next. A one-day op. Easy.

The check is in the mail. Promises, promises.

Back at Bagram a few hours earlier when they'd been packing their kit, the Americans had told them, "Guys, don't worry about bringing sleeping bags and stoves and Gucci kit—" the term *Gucci kit* referring to equipment you buy personally to add to your unit-supplied kit "—we're only going for twenty-four hours."

In their briefing, Rob and his teammates had not been told exactly how long they were expected to be out on this mission, nor precisely what the mission was. They knew there was quite a bit of secrecy around it, and that something big was happening out there. No one needed to tell them that; they could feel the hum and crackle of excitement. Now their American colleagues were telling them it was going to be an in-and-out run. Not a big deal. That they should pack light. But that went against their training. The minimum they should pack for, they'd been taught, was seventy-two hours, no matter what the mission was. Hope for the best, prepare for the worst. They ignored the Americans' advice and went on with their packing.

As it turned out, even packing for seventy-two hours would not be nearly enough.

When Jason Delgado stepped off the transport plane in the early months of 2004, he found himself in . . . well, he wasn't sure just *what* the hell this place was. It had been nearly a year since he and Jesse Davenport had been part of the column driving up through the center of the country to topple Saddam's regime. *Mission accomplished.* Now, here he was again, this time in the western part of the country with a different unit—Lima Company, Third Battalion, Seventh Marine Regiment—if not exactly to "keep the peace," at least to help *establish* the peace. Help the country put itself back on its feet. Win some hearts and minds.

But *this* place? He could have been standing in the middle of some Dallas suburb. Had he taken a plane to Iraq, or Vegas? Strolling through the base he saw a nightclub, a Carl's Jr., a Burger King, a Pizza Hut, and a KFC. A movie theater. Hell, they had a *Cinnabon*.

Standing roughly halfway between Baghdad and Iraq's western border, the Al Asad Air Base was then the largest U.S. base in western

Iraq, the Anbar Province equivalent of Baghdad's Green Zone, a six-hundred-plus-square-mile oasis of imported Western amenities.

This isn't Iraq, thought Delgado. *This is America in a bubble in Iraq.*

He wasn't there long. The 3/7 Marines were told their main base of operations would be a place about ninety miles to the northwest called Al Qaim, just fifteen miles from Iraq's border with Syria.

When he got to Al Qaim he found a pretty cozy setup. The Americans had commandeered a major railway station for use as a military base, and Jason's accommodations had bunk beds with mattresses, air-conditioning, running water, all the amenities. In the chaos of the invasion the previous spring there'd been times when they would go thirty days without taking a bath. But that was an invasion. Now they were in the occupation/rebuild phase, and by all accounts it was supposed to be a much calmer, more peaceful deployment.

He was looking forward to a little comfort. *The check is in the mail.*

The moment he got to Al Qaim he was tapped to take a few of his PIGs and go head up the sniper platoon at the western forward operating base (FOB) in the nearby border city of Husaybah. He pulled his gear together and got ready for the quick drive out there. He hoped it would be as peaceful and as nice as Al Qaim.

It wasn't.

Husaybah was a funky square mile of urban crawl, population roughly 100,000—think Erie, Pennsylvania, or Flint, Michigan, only in post-invasion Iraq. Situated right at an angular spot where Syria juts into Iraq's western territory, the place was a hotbed of criminal activity, with a long history of serving as the region's capital for trafficking in illegal goods, including the shuffling of arms (and the people to shoot them) back and forth across the border.

When the 3/7 Marines arrived in Husaybah they were taking over from the army's Third Infantry Division. The Third ID was not big on putting their soldiers out on the streets in harm's way. They would drive through the city in small tanks and armored Humvees and then hurry back to their bases. This was something the commanding officer of the 3/7 Marines, Lieutenant Colonel Matthew Lopez, wanted to change. He wanted grunts out on the streets, covering the city with patrols. The departing army unit thought the marines were crazy to walk through the streets. To Colonel Lopez, that was the only way to do this thing right: make sure the good people of Husaybah knew who was in charge here. Driving around in armored vehicles was not the marine way. Show of force: *that* was the marine way.

So the marines hit the streets. By and large, things seemed tolerably quiet. Yes, there were small outbreaks of violence here and there, the occasional roadside bomb or fitful armed skirmish. Yes, every so often someone fired mortar rounds at the marine camp. But it all seemed fairly random, nothing organized. And that was why they were there, right? *Show of force.*

Camp Husaybah, where the U.S. forces were stationed, was set up in a group of abandoned buildings on a little trapezoidal patch of land at the city's northwest corner, butted right up against the desolate fifty-yard-wide strip of no-man's-land that formed the Iraq-Syria border. It had no running water, no working plumbing, no city services, no amenities, nothing. Definitely no Carl's Jr.

Jason and the others walked into the place, noticing the oppressive heat inside, and were just about to ask where they should stash their gear, when they were called up.

"Delgado! Get your section ready. You're out in thirty."

So much for getting settled into their new home. Not only had they not stashed their gear, they hadn't even been told yet *where* to stash it. They dropped all their stuff where they stood, grabbed up their weapons and assorted equipment, and got ready to head back east out of the camp and into downtown Husaybah on their first mission here.

It was supposed to be a routine LPOP (listening post and observation post), watching over the Husaybah police station and reporting on anything that looked suspicious. Something just to give them the feel of the place. A quiet night of nothing but monotony and hourly radio check-in.

Promises, promises.

When Nick Irving boarded his C-17 in early 2009, bound for southern Afghanistan and what would be his last deployment, there were two things on his mind. There was what he hoped to see happen. After more than three years and multiple deployments as a ranger, he'd just spent the last seven or eight months in advanced sniper training. He'd busted down doors and shot machine guns and been part of plenty of fast and furious firefights. He wanted to get down slow and quiet in the dark, and *stalk*. He wanted to go out on a mission that lasted for hours unseen, silently zeroing in on his prey. He wanted to take the long shots.

He wanted to see some Carlos Hathcock action.

And then there was what he expected—which was to spend the next few months being bored out of his mind.

Back home at Fort Benning, rangers who'd just rotated back to the States from Afghanistan told Nick and the others in his platoon that they needed to be prepared for a whole lot of nothing. Reports from Kandahar were that things were very quiet over there. "Better take your Xbox and PlayStation with you, dude," was a comment he'd heard more than once. Some of his teammates loaded up on DVDs of their favorite films before leaving. They figured they'd have a lot of cinema time to catch up on.

He had already deployed once to Afghanistan, up in Bagram and Jalalabad. They'd spent a lot of time in the mountains up there, working as support to other Spec Ops forces already in theater; it had been a lot of walking up and down the mountains in the bone-freezing cold. Not many people lived out there; they'd see a single house and then nothing else for miles. To Nick it seemed like Afghanistan's Appalachia. They'd go hit or capture their HVT, then go back home. They got into a few firefights, but getting fired on was more the exception than the rule in that deployment.

When he arrived at FOB Wilson, just west of Kandahar and about an hour's drive from Helmand Province, he could see things were different. For one thing, it was a hell of a lot hotter. And there were no mountainside villages here; this was a land of mixed desert scrub, flat sprawling towns and cities. And poppy fields. A *lot* of poppy fields.

The other guys started unpacking their Xboxes and PlayStations, DVD players, music and movies. Not Nick. He liked his room simple and sparse. Maybe he'd do some reading. Maybe he'd do a hell of a lot of dry-firing.

Welcome to boredom kingdom.

Except that the boredom didn't last more than five hours before Nick and his spotter, Mike Pemberton, were summoned for their first mission and plunged into a breakneck op tempo more insane than anything Nick had ever seen.

When people asked Alex, "Why did you want to become a SEAL?" he had plenty of answers. "For the thrill of adventure," he'd tell them. A passion for the outdoors. A love of travel. If he knew the person better he might say, out of a desire to be thrust into the chaos and fury of combat, where he would be tested to his core. A desire to find out how he would hold up, whether he did in fact have what it took to stand side by side with his brothers in the face of mortal threat and not waver or buckle.

And all these things were true—but they weren't *the* truth.

The truth was, Alex joined the SEAL teams out of a morbid fascination with the idea of hunting other men. Hunting them honorably, legally, and in pursuit of a just cause . . . but still: hunting them. *That* was why he joined the SEALs.

So far, though, it hadn't worked out that way. The world was not at war when he signed his induction forms in 1987, fresh out of high school. Three years later he was in the middle of a fairly boring peacetime deployment when Saddam Hussein invaded Kuwait. Within months Alex found himself in the Persian Gulf, participating in Desert Storm—but from his vantage point, not much really happened. That action consisted mostly of Americans dropping bombs and Iraqi forces running. For warriors like Alex, sitting on the sidelines even as they were in the midst of it, Desert Storm was like watching a gigantic videogame.

After returning from Kuwait Alex had gone through sniper school, failed the stalk portion, then spent a few uneventful years doing what SEALs do (train, train, and then train some more) before going back through it again in 1994. The second time through he crushed it. Alex was now officially a SEAL sniper, and champing at the bit more than ever.

That October Saddam once again started rattling his sabers, moving his forces toward Kuwait to reach within fifteen miles of its border. An amphibious readiness group (ARG) of the 15th Marine Expeditionary Unit (MEU), led by the USS *Tripoli,* was dispatched in a mission officially named Operation Vigilant Warrior, but which Alex and his mates thought of as Operation Back the Fuck Down.

Saddam backed the fuck down.

As the *Tripoli* ARG made its way back home, it crossed paths with another ARG heading right back out to the Persian Gulf. This second ARG, led by the USS *Essex,* and including elements of the 13th MEU, was preparing for an entirely different mission. For the complex, delicate, and potentially volatile task ahead of them, the operation's joint marine/naval command had assigned a platoon of SEALs to join the marines, knowing that the SEAL snipers had a unique ability, with their .50 cal sniper rifles, to reach out and touch someone in a highly surgical manner, should the need arise.

One of the platoon's two snipers was Alex.

On their Chinook's second approach Rob Furlong's sniper team made it to their LZ without any further contact. The moment the chopper settled itself onto the ground they were out of there, hoofing their way southward and up the slope of the valley's western side. The other team, 63 Alpha, had gone in under the cover of darkness, just as planned. No such luck for Rob's team; the lengthy delay meant it was already bright daylight by the time they were making their way toward high ground.

The Shahikot Valley runs on a diagonal, from southwest to northeast, about five miles long and two and a half miles wide, its eastern ridge defined by a range of soaring mountains and its western ridge by a single long mile-high ridge dubbed the Whale. Rob's chopper entered from the north, passing the Whale on their right, and dropped them at the foot of one of the eastern mountains about three quarters of the way down the valley. The plan was to head immediately for the southernmost mountain, Takur Ghar, which at nearly two miles in height was also the range's tallest mountain, and make their way up toward the presumed crash site of a Chinook that had been shot down up there.

Their mission: secure the crash site so a rescue operation could proceed.

As soon as they were clear of the chopper they tried to raise comms with 63 Alpha, but they couldn't get through to them. They had no idea where their compatriots were or what they were doing. They were on their own.

Rob and his two teammates started moving into the valley, making their way southward and upward. The valley floor of the Shahikot Valley was already about a mile and a half above sea level, but the summit of Takur Ghar loomed above them another half mile, and they had easily a mile to go horizontally.

Partway there, though, they got a call on their radio. The plan had changed. Instead of heading farther south to scale Takur Ghar, the Canadians were to remain at their current latitude and move to high ground, where they would help support a brigade of troops from the U.S. Tenth Mountain Division who were pouring into the valley from the southern end.

They were not told exactly why they were called off, but the abrupt change in plans made Rob suspect that one of two things had happened: either another team had already secured the LZ they'd been heading for, or it was too late for anyone to do any rescue at all. But that was all speculation. Orders were orders, and they had a job to do.

As they moved up the slope, McMeekin got a call from Lieutenant Justin Overbaugh, the commander of the American scout platoon they were attached to. Overbaugh said there was a Toyota pickup sitting in their area, and asked if they could get the vehicle in their sights.

They scoped out the area. Sure enough, they found a Toyota pickup truck, about eight hundred meters away. They radioed back, "Yeah, we have eyes on."

"Can you neutralize the vehicle?"

The truck wasn't moving. In fact, there was nobody in the truck. It was just sitting there. The lieutenant didn't say why he wanted Rob's team to hit the thing. They just got the order to hit it. They figured, either they believed this truck posed some kind of threat, or they just wanted to do something to drum up some chatter on the radio channels, maybe help get a better sense of who was there in the valley.

Rob's team was the logical choice for this task, mainly because of the thunderstick he was hauling around with him.

It takes a particular skill set to handle the .50 cal, maybe even a particular temperament. There are plenty of good snipers who are not great .50 shooters, either because they just aren't uncomfortable with it or because they haven't learned how to mitigate and absorb its massive recoil. It's a very unforgiving weapon if you don't know how to shoot it correctly. It tends to be a black-and-white thing: either you like shooting .50s, or you don't—and there are more in the *don't* category than in the *do*.

When Rob returned from sniper school in late 2001, the Canadian Armed Forces had just received a shipment of McMillan TAC-50s as a trial purchase. He went out on the range with it. It was love at first shot.

One day they were shooting their standard rifles at a steel target at two hundred yards, and just for fun he grabbed the TAC .50 and took a shot. It didn't just hit the target, it took the entire thing and flipped it over. This is a steel plate weighing hundreds of pounds.

Now he would have his first opportunity to put it to the test in the field of battle.

He unfolded and extended the big gun's two bipod legs and settled them firmly into the dusty, granular hardscrabble, then lay down behind it, placed his left cheek against the stock and the butt on his shoulder, and sighted in. Squeezed the trigger.

BOOM!

He took out the entire engine block with one well-placed shot.

It was the first shot they took as part of Anaconda, Rob's first shot ever fired in the commission of war. You could say it was his first kill shot, if you want to look at it that way: they left one dead Toyota on the Afghan mountainside.

They didn't know this until much later, but that shot did in fact generate a ton of chatter. American technicians working the signals intercept detail reported that that they started picking up a burst of back-and-forth immediately after Rob neutralized the Toyota with his big gun. The boom of the .50 also telegraphed their own position to the enemy. It wouldn't be long before they would be under fire themselves.

They continued moving in, climbing as they went. After a while Tim stopped, pointed upward and to the south, and said, "Hey, I can see some guys up there on that ridgeline."

Rob pulled out one of their spotting scopes and started scanning the distant ridgeline near the top of the mountain while McMeekin got on the radio to Lieutenant Overbaugh.

"Sir," Tim said, "we have eyes on possible friendlies." They knew some SEAL scouts had gone somewhere up into that area a few days earlier to provide a crucial reconnaissance element; perhaps a few were still up there.

As they continued scanning the area through his spotting scope, Rob saw a guy crouched up on a distant ridgeline. The man was visible only from about chest-level up, and Rob couldn't tell for sure what division he was from, but he was obviously an American: he could see him just well enough to clearly make out the unmistakable American BDU (battle dress uniform) top, American helmet with its "rhino horn," the top-mounted night vision bracket, and the M4 he was carrying.

Rob told Tim, "Yeah, we've definitely got a friendly at this location," and he gave him the coordinates.

McMeekin relayed the information over comms, then relayed Overbaugh's response back to Rob: "Negative. We do not have friendly forces in that area."

Rob said, "Um, yeah we do—I'm looking right at them. Radio back."

They went back and forth like that for a few moments. Then, as Rob continued watching the guy with the M4, the man stood all the way up—and Rob saw that underneath the American BDU top he was wearing a long cloak of Afghan drab.

In an instant Rob understood for the first time what he was seeing.

That wasn't *his* BDU top. That wasn't *his* rifle. That wasn't *his* helmet. These guys had already killed one of ours—a SEAL, a ranger, Rob didn't know exactly who—and then taken his clothes and weapon.

An electric current of ice-cold fury shot through Rob's body. That was the moment it all became as real as blood.

That piece of shit is up there walking that ridgeline, he thought, *wearing one of OUR boy's things like a fucking trophy.*

Now he knew exactly why they were called off their original approach to the crash site on Takur Ghar. It was because it was too late for a rescue. Our boys were already dead.

In fact, a rescue had been attempted: a Chinook full of rangers had been flown up to the top of Takur Ghar (the same chopper that my SEAL teammates and I were sitting in when those rangers were sent in to replace us) and had been shot down as well. By this time Neil Roberts was gone, and now others had died, too. The chain of command would spend the entire day trying to figure out how to mount another rescue operation to rescue the first rescue operation.

But Rob didn't know any of this at the time. All he knew was that the rescue effort must have gone wrong, and this guy standing on that distant ridgeline had killed one of our guys and was now walking around in his clothes.

Something in Rob ignited. It was this simple: he was going to kill those guys. He didn't care what it took or what he might have to sacrifice. If it took his life to do that, then that's what it would take. Up to that point they'd been following their training, following orders, doing what they'd been schooled to do. It had been, for lack of a better word, a job. Not anymore. In that instant it had become deeply personal.

He stared at the figure in his spotting scope and thought, *You're mine.*

As Jason and his team rode out into Husaybah they got their first tour of the place that would be their home for the next few months.

Husaybah is laid out in a fairly regular grid, about one square mile, bordered by large avenues. The streets running north to south on the eastern and western edges had been dubbed West End Road and East End Road. The southern edge was bounded by a road they called Route Train, for the Iraqi Republic Railroad tracks that ran along a few dozen yards south of the city. Right now they were driving out along the main street that ran along the northern side of town, which the Americans called Market Street.

This was where the police station was located. Their mission: put eyes on the police station and report any suspicious activity there.

After getting a quick orientation of the town, they decided to set up their observation post in the big Baath Party headquarters building, abandoned since Saddam's ouster. This not only was one of the biggest structures in the town but it also happened to sit on the south side of Market Street directly across from the police station. Perfect.

They inserted via combined antiarmor team (CAAT), a sort of rolling artillery unit that groups a half dozen to a dozen guys in a few vehicles with machine guns and heavy artillery, such as grenade launchers and TOW missiles. Jason and his team rode the CAAT across Market Street to within about two blocks of the building, near the northeast corner of the city, then dismounted so they could make a quiet approach. There were five of them: Jason, the two PIGs in his team, Josh Mavica and Brandon DelFiorentino, and two infantry guys along to serve as security.

They crept through the alleyways until they reached the Baath building, then quietly broke in and slipped up to the third floor, where they set up their urban hide by some north-facing windows that gave them a clear view of the police station across the street.

Once they were in, the first thing they did was a radio check.

Nothing.

The way their radio comms worked was by using *freq hop,* a technique of rapidly skipping through different frequencies as they broadcast. If anyone listened in, all they'd hear on any given frequency was a blip. The only way to hear the full transmission was if they had the algorithm that generated the pattern of freq hopping, which they called the radio's *fill.*

Somehow, in the relatively calm fifteen-minute ride from Camp Husaybah through the city, both MBITR (multi-band inter/intra team) radios they'd brought had lost their fill.

Classic, thought Jason. He set DelFiorentino to screw around with the radio while he and Mavica started observing the police station and annotating their observations. An enormous amount of a sniper's time is doing exactly what they were doing now: watching, sketching, and writing.

The minutes ticked by.

They watched.

They sketched.

They wrote.

Until suddenly all hell broke loose.

They'd been there just under an hour when they heard machine guns going off, from what direction they could not immediately discern. Bullets started smacking into the lips of the windows where they'd been sitting, looking out. Some were pinging directly into the room. They all threw themselves down on the floor, "belly and dick to the ground," as Jason puts it.

"No fucking way!" yelled Jason. "How the hell did they see us?" Bullets were flying everywhere, chewing up the room's sparse interior decoration.

Then they heard another sound chip in—similar, but slightly different. Louder. It was *another* machine gun going off, but this one was much closer. From the sounds of it, they were under attack from an assortment of machine guns, perhaps a few blocks away, and now one of their own guys right outside their building was giving them cover fire.

Yes! thought Jason. The cavalry to the rescue.

They started finding cracks where they could peep out. Once they got eyes on the scene, they realized the picture was completely different. The close-by gunfire wasn't covering them at all. It was coming from a machine gunner perched atop the police station—only he was oriented to the north, *away* from them.

They looked way out past the gunner to the north and saw a string of muzzle flashes in a field some distance off. That gunfire wasn't directed at them. Whoever those gunners were—Saddam loyalists? Zarqawi's boys? some organized criminal element with a local beef?—they were firing on the police station itself, and the room they were sitting in was just getting incidental fire and ricochet.

Okay, so the good news was, nobody was shooting *at* them and they hadn't been discovered. The bad news was, plenty of stray rounds from the barrage of machine gun fire were still spraying into their room.

They had no radio anyway, which meant they had no way of finding out what the hell was going on out there. Jason give the signal to initiate extract.

Their extract plan was to ride back out with the CAAT team, which had a react time of three to four minutes. Which meant that if they got into deep shit, they knew that they'd need to hang on for at least four minutes before they could get safe escort out of there. It was also a no-comms plan: instead of calling for help on their radio (which was still not working) they were supposed to signal the call to exfil with a red star cluster, a small aluminum tube with a tiny rocket-propelled package that fires up to a few hundred feet and then bursts into an illuminated five-pointed star.

He grabbed the aluminum tube and ran to the rear window, away from the gunfight, then slammed the device on the windowsill to initiate it. As it went off it smacked the lip of the windowsill. In his haste, Jason had neglected to hold it properly (hand upside down, so you can immediately flip it upright to point into the air), and he nearly launched the damn thing right into the room. Fortunately, he managed to flip it around enough to get it aimed out and up. A few seconds later the CAAT team was seeing Jason's bat signal lighting up this funky Gotham's skyline.

Or at least they hoped so. There was so much gunfire happening, they couldn't assume that anyone would notice their get-us-outta-here fireworks display. Figuring they might need to manage their own E and E (escape and evasion) back through town to the FOB, they started quickly packing up their gear.

Then it got worse. Now they heard yet another gun, a big one, joining in the mix—GA-GA-GA-GA-GA-GA-GA-GA—and it was coming in closer and closer to where they were sitting. Jason ran around to different windows to steal more peeks wherever he could. When he got around to the east-facing side of the building he realized there was now a convoy coming up from the east to join the party. Not from the west, where Camp Husaybah was. These guys, whoever they were, were ripping down the street like something out of a Hollywood movie, coming in from Route Jade, the eastern continuation of Market Street. They must have come from the FOB at Al Qaim. They were coming to rescue Jason and his guys.

Jason ran over to one of the front windows and saw one of the convoy vehicles parked directly in front of the Baath building. A few others drove past and parked in front of the building next door, to the west, which was a large mosque. Marines started piling out of the vehicles, deploying security teams, and quickly aligning themselves in a stack. Jason recognized them: it was a Marine Force Recon element—basically the Corps' version of SEALs or Delta.

"Yo, guys," Jason called back into the room, "it's not CAAT, it's fucking Recon to come get us out!"

Jason knew you don't just go popping out of doorways on these guys. Too easy to get shot that way. He initiated the pre-coordinated signal to ensure friendly fire was not directed their way and started yelling out the window, "Friendly! Friendly!"

The Recon marine standing security in front of their building looked straight up, saw Jason, and shouted up, "Friendly? You American?"

"Yeah," Jason yelled back. "American! We're coming down. We lost comm."

The guy shouted back, "Come on down. It's cool."

They grabbed their gear and ran down the few flights of stairs. When they got outside to where the marine was standing, Jason said, "What's up, bro? Why are you guys rolling up here?"

The guard said, "We came to pick up a sniper team."

Jason said, "Yeah, that's us."

He said, "Wait—that's *you* guys?"

Jason said, "Yeah, dude, it's us. You got us."

"Oh, shit!" said the marine. "We thought you were in *that* building," and he pointed over at the mosque.

"Nah," said Jason, "we were in this building right here." He jerked his thumb back to point behind him.

"Then what's *that* building?"

Jason said, "Man, that's a mosque."

"Oh, shit," the guard said again. "Come on, we might want to tell the lieutenant before they—"

Boom! Boom! Boom!

A string of charges went off. An instant later a truck barreled in from the street, knocking down a big chunk of the mosque's front wall before jerking to a stop. Marines piled out with door-busters and flash-bangs and started clearing room to room, blowing all the locks off the doors. Another stack lined up to go in right behind them.

The young guard went up to the lieutenant and said, "Hey, sir, these are the snipers."

The lieutenant was so hyped up that he didn't fully grasp what the kid said. "Snipers? All right, get in the stack."

The young marine said, "No, sir—*they're* the snipers! The snipers we came to get!"

The lieutenant turned to look at him, and the penny dropped. He looked at Jason and the other snipers. "You guys are not in there?"

Jason said, "No, sir, we're right here."

"Well, then who the hell's in *there*?"

"Nobody, sir."

The young marine added, "That's a mosque, sir."

"Oh, shit!" said the lieutenant. He surveyed the wreckage for a moment and then said, more to himself than anyone else, "They're going to be plenty pissed in the morning."

He called in to his base in Al Qaim to let them know they'd picked up the sniper team, then gave the call sign to load up and pull out. The rest of the unit came streaming out of that building like a waterfall and loaded up on the vehicles in what seemed to Jason like less than a second. Jason and the others jumped on, too, and the marine convoy took off westward to bring the snipers back to Camp Husaybah.

At which point they saw, way down the street ahead of them, a convoy of trucks with guns mounted on their backs rolling toward them. It looked like the ICDC, Iraqi Civil Defense Corps, an armed indigenous security force created by the Coalition's provisional government to help keep order. But wait—they weren't coming to *attack* the marine column, were they? They were on our side, or were supposed to be. But it was hard to tell for sure. The armed elements in Iraq were forming factions and splitting into variously aligned groups faster than the Americans could keep track. It was hard to know who was who and whom you could trust, if anyone.

As the two convoys got closer Jason noticed another pickup truck swing in from a side street and join in ahead of the ICDC column.

"Got some headlights coming our way," called out a marine. "What is that?"

Jason and his guys got on their scopes and peered up the street. There was a DShK (pronounced *dooshka*) mounted on the goddamn truck. The DShK is a heavy, Soviet-made antiaircraft gun. You see a DShK coming toward you, it's a decent bet the guy behind it is not a fan of yours. And this truck was coming in fast.

They conveyed the information. The marines fired at the DShK-laden pickup until it hit an embankment and flipped over. Seconds later they were driving past it and on their way back to the camp.

Welcome to Husaybah, Delgado, thought Jason. It was the most bizarre extract he had ever witnessed.

As they drove west on Market Street, Jason thought about Al Asad, where he'd been just days earlier. Like Baghdad's Green Zone, Al Asad was probably something like what Americans hoped would become the new reality in Iraq: a Western-style democracy with Starbucks and Cinnabons on every street corner. *Dream on.* Al Asad was someone's fantasy of Iraq.

Husaybah was the reality of Iraq.

On Nick Irving's first night in Helmand Province he and his spotter, Pemberton, were sent out to provide overwatch as their unit, Charlie Company, First Platoon, went on a fairly routine mission to capture a maker of suicide vests. A simple snatch-and-grab, just like the missions they'd run in northern Afghanistan.

Within minutes after arriving on site, the assault team had their HVT—but while they all sat awaiting an early exfil, Nick and Pemberton saw three figures with AK-47s, about four hundred yards from their hasty hide site, doing their best to sneak up on the American squad. The two men silently sighted in, let out their breath, and squeezed. Nick dropped one; Pemberton took out a second. The third began to run, but as the classic sniper saying goes, "Don't bother running: you'll only die tired." Nick tracked his motion for a second or two, then nailed him with a single shot. Thirty seconds and three kills between them.

An exciting first night, Nick thought with a trace of regret that it was already over. And that, he figured, was the only action they would be seeing for weeks, maybe for the whole deployment. Boredom kingdom, right?

But the next night they were called out again. Again, the assault team quickly bagged their target, and again, Irving and Pemberton spotted an immediate threat, this time in the form of a lone figure they glimpsed through a canopy of trees running toward a weapons squad with a Russian grenade. Nick's first shot missed; Pemberton's shot nicked a tree branch and was deflected; Nick's second shot burst in through the man's back and pushed his heart clean out of his chest, still pumping blood.

Two nights, two missions. So . . . was *that* all the action they'd be seeing for a while?

Apparently not, because just days later they were called out yet again, and this time things got a little more complicated.

On the way to their objective they were ambushed and pinned down in the middle of a small village by four guys on a rooftop about 150 yards away. Using the lip of the roof as cover, the shooters were peeking over the ledge just enough to survey the scene and take a few more shots. As Nick sighted in, he discovered something interesting: when he shone IR (infrared) light on their eyes, they glowed bright white. He thought, *Hey, that's pretty neat.* Then he shot them. *Bam, Bam, Bam,* like targets in a shooting gallery, the first three went down one after the other. The fourth tried to crawl away. He did not get far.

As they made their way closer to their objective (still a few klicks away) they encountered more firefights. Intel came from an overhead AC-130 gunship that a small group from their main objective had left the building and run into a forested area, maybe four hundred yards from their current position. Evidently they'd heard the ruckus and decided to squirt. The snipers took a squad with them, plus their dog, Bruno, and the dog's handler, to slip out to that area and capture or kill these guys.

Nick and Pemberton stopped to set up overwatch at an irrigation mound about a hundred yards away from the wood line, while the rest of the guys continued to advance. They lay down against the mound, propped their rifles up on top of the berm, and watched the squad's progress through their night vision.

Nick turned on his IR light and started shining his laser into the woods. At first, he couldn't see a thing. Then he noticed something weird: he saw little white dots appear, then disappear, and reappear. Was he seeing things? Were there fireflies in Afghanistan? Nick wasn't sure.

Then he realized what he was seeing: it was the eyes of the squirters lurking in the woods, facing the Americans. They were blinking.

At this point the line squad was maybe twenty-five feet away from the wood line and closing in on these guys fast.

Nick got on his radio. "Hey, are you guys seeing them?"

"Where?" they said back.

"You're walking right up to one, man! There's a dude at your twelve o'clock, twenty feet in front of you!"

"I don't see shit."

Nobody in the squad could see a thing, and they were about to walk right into them. Nick couldn't shoot at them because his guys would be caught right in the middle. He radioed again and told them to stop. As they froze in place and carefully went down on one knee, Nick got one set of blinking eyes in his crosshairs. He slipped off his safety.

"Hey," Nick said to one of them. "Listen, I'm going to drop one of these guys. But I have to shoot right over your shoulder—so you have to stay really, really still."

"Roger that," came the reply. The kneeling ranger stayed really, really still.

Nick's finger tightened on the trigger—and just as he was about to squeeze off a round the squirter moved. Nick saw a long glint and a spark and had just time to think, *Shit, that's a machine gun,* when a burst of gunfire shot out from the tree line.

Everyone in the squad hit the ground, but as they did one of the rangers took a round in the helmet. Another got hit in his night-vision goggles, shattering the device.

Nick immediately started putting down suppressive fire.

Bruno, the ranger dog, took off toward the shooters, took a bullet in the ribs, but kept going, caught up to the guys in the woods and started biting them viciously.

Nick found one target and shot the man directly in the head, then took out a second.

The squad leader got to his feet to drag out one of the men who'd been shot. At the same time he was dragging he was also doing his best to stay low; as he dug in with his back leg he had his front leg extended out at a pretty good distance, halfway to a full split. As Nick watched him he glimpsed one of those sets of blinking white dots appear right through the space between the team leader's legs, maybe twenty feet beyond him.

The man was about one football field away.

Nick took careful aim.

At a hundred yards, that bullet was going to reach its position directly between the squad leader's legs in one tenth of a second or less. Too fast for his friend's legs to change position much.

This should work, Nick thought. *I really hope I don't shoot this guy's balls off.*

He took the shot.

The bullet traveled more or less in a straight line—no arc to speak of in a mere one hundred yards—and screamed between the squad leader's legs without touching him and onward twenty more yards, where it found its target.

The guy's head exploded—came completely off the neck.

Their saving grace was that the enemy did not have night vision, and in the dark they didn't have good visibility, even at twenty-five feet. The rangers managed to keep dragging both shot men back from the tree line.

Nick was so glad he hadn't shot that poor guy's nuts off.

As Nick continued doing his best to acquire targets in the thick of the forest, one of the rangers called in an air strike. They were far too close for five-hundred-pounders, so they opted to call in some 105mm howitzer rounds. Even with the 105s, they were at the absolute minimum possible distance.

The first howitzer strike was way off.

Nick called a better set of coordinates back to their RTO (radio telephone operator), who relayed them to the howitzer. For a few moments, the ground around them turned to jelly as the big explosive shells did their work.

Once it got still again, they got up and advanced toward the tree line. There were fingers on the ground, butt cheeks, thighs, faces. They walked around picking up the pieces to try to patch together who was who. It was such a mess they never were able to determine exactly how many bodies there were out there.

The rangers had lost nobody on the team. The two men who'd been shot in the helmet both suffered only bruises, and Bruno was fine once the canine handler got his ribs wrapped up and gave him some medical care. They all carried on with the rest of the mission, which lasted another four hours. The primary objective was secured, that is, bagged and tagged.

Nothing in Nick's previous deployments had quite prepared him for this. In Iraq he'd seen a fairly heavy op tempo. Still, the firefights there were mostly more one-sided. Typically they would catch their targets off guard and have the advantage of surprise and overwhelming force. It was generally more like being on a SWAT team raid than engaging in an entrenched gun battle.

But this? This was insane. It seemed like everywhere they went there were Taliban taking arms against them. They were receiving contact constantly, and sometimes the other guys would actually own the firefight for a while before the rangers managed to regain fire superiority.

And it kept going like that. They'd be out night after night, sometimes multiple missions per night, then get a break for a day or two, maybe even three—and then be back at it. They traveled all over the province, north, south, east, west, everywhere, rolling up HVTs. On one op Nick and Pemberton killed five or six Taliban commanders in a single night.

If it wasn't exactly the Carlos Hathcock kind of work he'd always dreamed of doing, it certainly was more action, and crazier action, than Nick had ever seen before.

For three months, from December 1994 through February 1995, Alex Morrison's platoon ambled around the Persian Gulf on their amphibious warship (otherwise known as a "gator freighter") as part of the *Essex* ARG. There wasn't much to do; there never is. Being part of an ARG is typically as boring as an all-week C-SPAN marathon.

Still, every chance they got, every time they put in to port and could get off the ship for any length of time, Alex and the platoon's other sniper would head ashore to go off and find somewhere they could practice. They wanted to keep their shooting skills honed to a razor's edge, since as near as they could tell they'd soon be needed, or so they assumed. They hadn't actually been told anything about why they were there or exactly what was the point of treading water in the Gulf for weeks on end. But they didn't have to be told; they could connect the dots.

Somalia had been a shit storm. In October '93, less than a year after Operation Hopeless began, everything had gone to hell in a battle that left eighteen American Spec Ops warriors dead and the United States deeply traumatized. Within weeks of the Battle of Mogadishu, the U.S. had washed its hands of the whole operation and turned it over to the U.N., who gave up on it after another year of trying. The decision to pull the plug had already been announced. Everyone knew the Americans would have to lead the final evacuation. *That* was why Alex and his teammates were there.

And now here they were, anchored four miles off the southern Somalia coast, all briefed up and ready to go.

They knew that Operation United Shield (or Operation Abandon Hope, as one wag had dubbed it) was supposed to be a peaceful withdrawal. They also knew this was one seriously funky neighborhood. The odds that the locals would let it go without making some kind of play were ridiculously low.

For the past few days, Alex and his fellow SEALs had been busy doing hydrographic surveys, a throwback to the World War II days when underwater demolition teams (UDT, the precursors of SEALs) would swim in close to shore, gather as much data as they could, and then put it into a hand-drawn map for the landing crews to use in navigating a landing. Or to blow the crap out of whatever they needed to blow up. Hydrographic surveys are an exacting, time-consuming, tedious process. They used to make us do them during BUD/S as a way to wear us down. Alex could do them in his sleep. (That's often exactly how it felt back in BUD/S.)

But the surveys were over now; the months of floating round the Gulf were over; the years of training were over.

It was time to go on the hunt.

You're mine, Rob had thought as he gazed through his spotting scope at the Taliban fighter with the dead American's BDU and helmet.

But that wasn't going to happen, at least not right then, not in those circumstances. While Rob could clearly see these Taliban fighters on his scope, they were well out of any conceivable range. What's more, they were standing at above ten thousand feet, while Rob and his buddies were not much above eight thousand feet, so in addition to being an impractical range it was also quite a height difference. There was no possibility of engaging them, and he couldn't exactly start running toward them, as much as he felt the urge to do exactly that.

Sixty-three Bravo still had a mission to run. They had to get in place so they could provide cover for our guys moving into the valley.

Discipline.

They relayed the information to Lieutenant Overbaugh at command, annotated it, and moved on. But Rob would never forget what he saw.

Soon dusk started cutting in. They had reached about halfway up the ridgeline, high enough to qualify as high ground. This was where they would set up their observation point. As the American scout platoon started digging foxholes, getting some chow into them, changing their socks, and setting up for nightfall, the Canadians covered them.

They began their routine.

First they searched out a patch of ground that would provide them the biggest field of view while also giving maximum natural cover. They found a slight depression in the ground wide enough for their purposes.

Extending the big gun's bipods and getting it settled onto a level spot, McMeekin climbed in behind it (he and Rob would trade off shooter and spotter roles throughout their time in Anaconda) and started laying out his ammo. Rob, meanwhile, pulled out his range finder and began building his range card, that is, a detailed mapping of the area of fire. He did a quick sketch of the valley itself, then began methodically identifying every significant visual element in the valley below them, so that if they suddenly started acquiring targets they would already have ready reference points with all their ranges worked out.

Large mud compound at twelve o'clock, that's at 1,800 meters.

Large cliff base, 2,200 meters.

He worked quickly; there wasn't much light left, and what there was wouldn't last long.

AK-AK-AK-AK-AK-AK-AK-AK!

Suddenly they were being hammered by machine gun fire.

Everyone scrambled.

Rob realized that these guys had probably had eyes on them from the moment of that first shot they fired at the Toyota pickup, and they had probably been followed all the way to this position. Although the Americans and Canadians were fairly far up the mountain at this point, the other guys still had high ground, and they had held off opening up on them until dusk fell. Typical military move: wait until last light.

It sounded like a DShK antiaircraft gun. These guys were not supposed to have DShKs up here. This was most definitely not going according to plan. They were supposed to be there to prevent the bad guys from escaping. But it looked like escaping was the last thing the bad guys had in mind. Now the Americans and Canadians were being heavily engaged by machine gun fire. Guys were scattering everywhere, scrambling for cover.

Tim and Rob started shouting back and forth, "You see where the fire's coming from?" as they both scanned the valley looking for a source, Rob on spotting scope and Tim on the gun's optics.

Suddenly Tim shouted out, "I've got a guy! I've got a guy!"

There was a shooter positioned behind a piece of corrugated steel. They ranged him: just short of 1,500 meters. Tim sighted in and put a round downrange.

BOOM!

The big Hornady BMG .50 round caught the guy and threw him backward like a rag doll. One shot, one kill—from 1,500 meters. Not bad. But that wasn't the guy who was putting out the heavy machine gun fire. The Canadians and Americans were still taking direct fire.

Then the mortar rockets started.

Wait—*What?* Mortar fire was *definitely* not something the Anaconda planners had been expecting. But there they were.

The first few rockets came whistling in and struck the ground just meters in front the snipers' position. They could both hear the fins rotating as they flew.

Rob and Tim both dove for cover behind some small rocks, scarcely big enough to provide cover for a muskrat, but it was all they had. *You know what?* thought Rob. *Maybe we should have brought those helmets and flak vests*—and just then another mortar shell hit the ground, this time directly behind them.

Here's a piece of field wisdom they had all learned about mortars: if one hits in front of you, and the next one hits behind you, that means the other guys have got your position bracketed—and the next one will land *on* you.

No one had to say a thing: they all knew their position had been bracketed. They jumped up, grabbed their kit, and ran out of there. Seconds later, the position they'd just vacated was blasted to rubble by another mortar round.

They pushed back to where the American platoon had dug in, Tim carrying the .50 and Rob the spotting scope. The scouts had dropped their rucks there, grabbed just their day packs, M4s, and ammo, and boogied. As the two snipers followed back into the mountain, Rob came face-to-face with an eager young American sniper he'd met before they all left Bagram. Great kid, brand-new sniper, pumped to be going on this mission. He was carrying an M40—nice gun, but not much help at the distances he'd be shooting. He took one look at Rob and thrust the rifle in his hands, then handed him a small pile of ammo.

"Here," he said, "you can use this better than I can."

Rob looked at him, and thought, *Why not?* The kid would still have his M4. "Sure," said Rob. "Thanks." He stuck the rounds in his pocket, grabbed the sniper rifle, and got down behind some cover.

They stayed back in that position, under heavy direct fire, until it got dark enough to start moving around again. Once it finally quieted down, they set up their .50 in an overwatch position again and talked about what to do next.

They couldn't move back to the spot where they'd been hit. The enemy knew that position; it was tainted. They'd all left a lot of kit back there, though, and they were reluctant to simply abandon it. And some of the Americans, the ones who'd been in the middle of changing their socks, had left weapons back there, too. They needed to slip back out there and secure their stuff.

The Canadians had one advantage: they had night vision. The Taliban—and Uzbeks, and Arabs, and whoever the hell else was out there—presumably did not.

Tim and Rob started taking turns leading teams back to their mortar-blasted former position to start retrieving equipment under cover of night, using their night vision scopes to help them, one taking a team back out while the other caught a little rack time. They did that throughout the night, staying in that position until the break of daylight.

One thing was clear: this was not going to be a twenty-four-hour operation.

The truth was, they would not emerge from the wilds of the Shahikot for well more than a week.

10

OUTSIDE THE BOX

Always listen to experts. They'll tell you what can't be done and why. Then
do it.

—Robert Heinlein

There is the mission, there is the plan—and then there's what actually happens. Nothing ever goes according to plan, *ever*. It's the first
rule of combat. Which means simple reaction is rarely an effective
tactic. The essence of effective Spec Ops is the ability to respond and
adapt, to be instantly creative and inventive. In other words, to think
and execute outside the box. By definition, as I said earlier, we exist
to function off the reservation.

Alex Morrison, Rob Furlong, Jason Delgado, and Nick Irving were
all about to go off the reservation.

Alex was mulling over thoughts about death and water as he felt their
craft heave and plunge in the midnight African sea swell a few miles
off the Somali coast.

He thought about the forces arrayed in a several-mile radius around
him, picturing how it would all play out. The landing force consisted of
about 1,800 U.S. Marines, an Italian marine battalion of 350, and a
handful of "supporting forces." Like Alex and the other SEALs packed
into this tin can.

He looked around, craning his eyes in the dark. There were about
forty of them, probably all going through the same thoughts he was.
Running the mission, sifting through the variables, assessing the unexpected, and weighing the imponderables.

About half the landing party were heading up to Mogadishu's harbor, New Port, a mile or two up the coast, in large landing crafts. Hundreds more were rolling in on the AAVs (amphibious assault vehicles) the marines had used to such stellar effect in Grenada and Desert Storm. Some personnel were flying in on transport choppers. Not Alex and his team. They were going in in true SEAL fashion: shuttling in on an amphibious hovercraft, known as an LCAC, for landing craft air cushion—essentially an oversize Zodiac raft outfitted with a bunch of monster window fans. You can't ride on the deck of an LCAC; if you tried, you'd be blown off by the hovercraft propellers. Hence the MILVAN.

The plan was straightforward, if not exactly simple. Of a U.N. force of nearly thirty thousand less than a tenth remained, mostly Bangladeshi and Pakistani military plus assorted admin and HQ staff, all housed on and around the airport grounds or up at New Port. The landing force was to go ashore, set up a narrow secure perimeter running parallel to the shoreline, between the airport's main runway and the ocean, from the airport clear up to the harbor. From there, they would oversee the withdrawal of the U.N. contingent of 2,500 to within the perimeter and then onto outgoing ships. Once the op was concluded, they would pull back to the beach, climb back on the amphibs, and head back out to sea.

From Alex's vantage point, it was a classic SEAL operation: approach from the sea, support from the sea, withdraw to the sea.

In the rolling dark, Alex thought about the briefings they'd received—both what was said and what could be inferred from what was said.

They were evidently caught between two contradictory imperatives, reflecting two currents of paranoia at the highest command levels. On the one hand, people in Washington were terrified that the action might spark off another powder keg like the Battle of Mogadishu sixteen months earlier. Yes, the local warlord had promised a hands-off policy for the evacuation, but you couldn't trust that bastard Aidid. If any violence should begin to erupt, it had to be contained at all costs.

On the other hand, command was also extremely skittish about the use of lethal force. The disaster of the *Black Hawk Down* episode had so spooked U.S. policymakers that the entire U.S. military had sat on its hands during the genocide in Rwanda the previous summer. During the briefings their current hyper-conservative rules of engagement had been drilled into them. "And if you screw up," the briefers added, "they *will* prosecute you." Oh boy.

Operation Hopeless had left our military planners gun-shy.

Gun-shy. Haha. That was the right term, all right. To bring the point home, some of the marines had been armed with various "nonlethal technologies"—pepper sprays, flashbangs, and guns that shot a sticky foam in place of actual bullets—"to fill the gap between verbal warnings and deadly force," went the official reasoning.

The heave and roll slowed, then ceased, and Alex could feel their craft sliding over the shallows, then bump to a stop. They had arrived at Green Beach: Somali soil. He grabbed his big .50 cal—the Beast—and got to his feet.

If things got ugly, he sure as shit would not be shooting foam or pepper spray.

When morning broke on March 5 after their first night in the Shahikot Valley, Furlong and McMeekin had a problem to solve. Tenth Mountain Division troops were pinned down by machine gun and mortar fire and needed assistance. This was not how things were supposed to go; Coalition forces were supposed to be hemming in the enemy forces, not the other way around. But there it was.

This presented Rob and Tim with a clear agenda: shut these guys down. They needed to do what they could to take out the mortars and machine guns that had the American forces boxed in. But that presented a tactical problem: they were at a disadvantage. The day before, they'd managed to get partway up the ridge, but not that far. This close to the valley floor, they were somewhat boxed in themselves. They needed to secure one of the most basic and time-honored military advantages: high ground.

They had been given a designated area within which they were supposed to operate, a set of coordinates that defined a "safety box." They were not to go outside those coordinates. But if they stayed within them, they couldn't do what they needed to do. They needed to get outside that box, to gain the high ground so they could lay down a serious leadstorm and dislodge the forces who had their boys pinned down. To do that, they had to go up higher.

The problem was, according to the air force, anything outside that box would be considered enemy. If they went up there, they would run the risk of being fired upon by their own guys. That risk was quite real. (In fact, although Rob and Tim didn't know this at the time, Operation Anaconda had launched two days earlier with a devastating "blue-on-blue" incident, when an AC-130 had mistakenly fired upon a joint Afghan-American convoy of four vehicles, killing the convoy commander and wounding quite a few others. I was there when they brought those poor bastards in for emergency care.)

This was the dilemma: to do their job they needed some elevation, but if they moved up the mountain outside the parameters of that safety box they could become targets themselves.

Rob and Tim looked at each other and shrugged.

"We can die here, sitting at eight thousand feet," said Tim, "or we can die up at ten thousand. Right?"

Rob flashed back on the feeling he'd had the day before, staring at that Taliban fighter wearing American BDUs, and realized he'd rather die up on the mountain being effective than sit on his hands back inside the safety box, watching their guys being pinned down and shot at. If they got killed, they got killed. At least they'd be making a difference.

"Let's do this," he replied.

They didn't consult with anyone or phone it in, and they didn't take anyone with them for security. They just moved out, the two of them, and started heading up the mountain.

As they pushed up toward higher ground, they passed an American team dug into the mountainside. "Hey, where are you guys going?" the Americans asked. "You guys know you're about to move outside the box?"

"Yeah." McMeekin nodded as they kept walking. "We know."

"You guys are fucking crazy," replied the Americans. "You go up there, you're gonna get engaged."

"Don't worry, it's okay," said Rob. "We got this."

Leaving the Americans behind, they kept walking.

It took them a while to get up into position. There was scattered snow the whole way up, but once they broke nine thousand feet the ground was covered with snow. Snow on the ground meant footprints, and sure enough, within minutes after pushing above the nine-thousand-foot mark, they found several sets of footprints. There were no other friendly forces up there at this altitude, not now. Nobody up here but the two of them, and the bad guys. And those footprints were fresh.

Rob felt his skin crawl. This was where they had spotted movement the day before, where he'd seen that Tali, wearing his purloined American BDU top. They were standing exactly where the enemy had stood.

Tim and Rob looked at each other without a word.

We're sure as shit up in the hornet's nest now, thought Rob.

* * *

About a week after Jason Delgado arrived in Husaybah, his team was given a mission to go observe an area they called the 440.

The 440 was Husaybah's version of a high-end gated community: a large, squared-off cluster of houses set within a fenced perimeter, down on the southwest corner of the city, a stone's throw from the Syrian border. The people who lived here were Saddam loyalists, Baath Party people who'd been rewarded for their fealty with a relatively cushy place to live. As far as command was concerned, Baath Party people were still considered the core of resistance, Saddam holdovers, and were the prime suspects for whatever level of instigation might be happening here in Husaybah. The snipers were directed to go observe this area to see if they could detect any suspicious activity.

Jason didn't want any vehicle signature, so he decided to head down there on foot with his team, which included Mavica, DelFiorentino, and himself, plus the four snipers of the other team stationed there. Camp Husaybah had just one entry-and-exit point, facing the city, and Jason didn't want to use that. He didn't particularly want anyone in the city to know he and his men were out there. He got someone to open up a hatch for them in back of the complex, just enough for the seven men to squeeze out, and they left the FOB from the rear.

He didn't trust Husaybah, not one thing about it. This was only his second or third mission there, and he and his team were just getting a feel for the place. So far, they didn't much like what they felt.

Despite his bizarre first night in Husaybah with its police station shoot-out, Jason had at first been optimistic about what he and his team could accomplish there. The larger mission, according to policymakers at the top, was to help bring peace and stability to post-Saddam Iraq. They could call it that, if they wanted to; in Jason's more pragmatic view, they were there to bring law and order. It hadn't taken long to figure out what this place was. He'd understood where they were that first night as they rode in their Marine Recon convoy back to base after that crazy firefight.

This is the fucking Wild West, he thought. *And we're the new sheriff in town.*

"Listen, guys," he'd told his snipers the next day. "This is going to slow up once we start locking down the place. Let's just get out into the city and show 'em there are marines here. Once we flex our muscles a few times, let them know we're not playing around, these guys will stand down."

That's what he thought. Or at least, that was what he was telling himself. But the reality on the street seemed to be telling another story. His gut said there was more going on here than anyone was seeing or talking about.

After sneaking out the rear of the camp, he and his sniper team started walking, moving southwest, away from the FOB and toward the back side of the 440, the Syrian border side. It was close to a mile's hike in nothing but open desert, but they were used to walking in the desert.

As they got closer to the 440 area, they passed a deep quarry where people were mining quartz or something. It was nearly dusk by this time and nobody was working; machines sat still and deserted. The seven men stopped for a moment to admire the scene; it was huge, like something from a megalithic era.

Suddenly they heard the clatter of gunfire. The sound was coming from farther down the border, away from the city. They sprang into go mode and started running southwest toward the commotion. They ran well over a mile, Jason estimates about four klicks, until they could just see something happening in the distance.

They got down and got on glass.

Jason saw an Iraqi border shanty, a little cement thing, no bigger than a portable toilet.

There was just one official border crossing in the area, up behind Camp Husaybah. But the border itself was nothing but a berm and open desert; no barbed wire, no fence, no anything, really. Even the precise delineation of the exact borderline itself was a matter of debate. For security, a series of little shacks were strung out along the border, essentially no more than observation posts. Anyone could sneak through, pretty much anywhere.

This poor guy sat there on one side of his little observation shack, facing northeast toward Jason and his group, sitting on his ass with an AK-47 propped on the ground between his legs with his head down against it, rocking back and forth like he couldn't believe what was happening to him. His little shed was being shot up—chips of concrete blowing off and dust flying everywhere. The damn thing was being chipped away to nothing by machine gun fire.

The snipers scanned farther off in the direction of the gunfire to try to locate where it was coming from. And there, a ways past the border guard, was a five-man team, the one in the middle hunched over on an RPK, just laying into this poor Iraqi border guard like they were using him for target practice.

Jason called in to the watch commander at the TOC. "This is Sierra 3, we've got a group of five men dressed in black on an RPK, looks like a machine gun team, and they're tormenting the shit out of an Iraqi border agent."

Snipers typically have different rules of engagement from the line company, because they can see what's going on with their own eyes. Normally, they're allowed to make the call themselves, and take the shot. At this point, though, they were not in combat mode. This was, after all, the occupation phase, or peacekeeping phase, or whatever the correct term du jour was. They were supposed to call these shots in before they took them.

The officer on the other end said, "They're shooting at an Iraqi, and he's a border officer?"

"Yes, sir," said Jason. They didn't know exactly where they were; there were no landmarks, nothing around them but open desert and that little cement shed. But he gave the officer their GPS coordinates, then asked for permission to reduce the target.

"That's what we're here for," the officer replied. "Help the poor fucker out."

"Roger that!" said Jason. That was all he needed to hear.

Brandon DelFiorentino was on as Jason's spotter, and he called out distance: 1,015 yards.

One thousand fifteen yards. Almost a full klick, well over half a mile. Jason had his M40A3 sniper rifle with him, but this was outside the maximum effective range even for the M40A3. To make things worse, it's tough to call wind in the open desert where you have no visual cues to gauge by. No fluttering leaves or blowing grasses, let alone the hanging laundry and window curtains that had helped him gauge wind when shooting off a rooftop in the middle of Baghdad.

He sighted in on the RPK shooter, maxed out his elevation turret, said a little sniper's prayer, and took a shot.

Nothing happened. No hit, no dust, no splash. Nothing.

He racked the bolt again, took a second shot.

Nothing.

"You guys see anything?" he asked. Nobody had.

He had six guys lying down on scopes, some on his right, some on his left, as if they were all lined up at a county fair shooting gallery. (Or working the range at sniper school.) All six of these guys were highly trained, and all six were trying to solve this problem. Where the hell were Delgado's rounds going? And no one could see anything.

After the third round Jason said, "All right, stop. This isn't working." He thought for a second, then said, "Find me something to zero on."

The other guys started scanning all around the horizon with their scopes, until someone said, "I've got a berm!"

They looked over where he was pointing. There it was. Barely visible, since it blended in perfectly with the rest of the sand, but there it was.

"All right," said Jason, "I've got the berm. Walk me out to something."

"Okay," said DelFiorentino, "about four fingers to the left of the slope of the berm, you see where it raises up? Three fingers past that, there's a boulder. You see the boulder?"

Jason saw it. "Yeah, Roger that. I see the boulder."

"Take a shot," said DelFiorentino.

Boom . . . splashhhhh. He could see a big splatter of dust kick up, way beyond and to the right of where he'd shot. Perfect. Now he had a reference point in his scope's reticle. He wasted no time.

He swung back over toward the group of five guys, racked another round, and, using that exact same reference point in his scope—what Nick Irving calls the "cut and paste method"—he took a shot. He didn't aim specifically at the guy in the middle. The distance was so insanely far, he just did his best to aim into the middle of the group, center mass, figuring his chance of hitting one of them was high.

The M40A3 has a muzzle velocity of 2,550 fps, or 850 yards per second. Shooting out to 1,015 yards, the round would be airborne for a little over one full second.

Boom! The round burst out of the barrel and took off toward the group—*one thousand, two th*—and the guy on the machine gun flipped over backward.

Jason stared through his scope, hardly believing what he saw. He had scored a *direct hit* on the dude on the machine gun.

The other four guys scattered—ran and hid under a little concrete A-frame structure nearby. Jason and his guys hopped up and down, pumping their fists in the air. The sniper's touchdown dance. Then they began collecting their stuff to leave the area. These other four attackers were hidden, and there was nothing else they could do here. They figured they'd call it in and then go on their way, back to the 440 to carry out their mission for the day.

And then one of the four decided to sneak out from under the little A-frame and go back to where his dead buddy lay. He crept over there to the inert machine gunner and leaned over the machine gun.

"Mother fuck," whispered Jason. "This guy is stupid."

Jason wasn't sure whether the guy was going to lay hold of his dead friend's body to drag him away, or to pull him out of the way so he could grab the RPK himself and start shooting again. All he knew was, this guy was now on the machine gun, and he had to go. They'd seen these five jokers tormenting this poor border guard. They weren't about to let them continue.

Because the guy was now leaning directly into the space where his friend had been stationed, Jason didn't have to make any kind of new adjustment. He already had his gun set up perfectly. He had the guy perfectly in his scope, knew exactly where his reference spot was on his reticle.

He took another shot.

Guy #2 dropped and hit the ground.

The snipers all started our victory dance again.

One of Jason's snipers now got behind the gun and took a look, wanting to see if a third brave soul would give it a try—but at that point they got a radio call to come back to the camp. Like, right away.

Lieutenant Colonel Lopez, the commander of the entire battalion, was there, and wanted to talk to him.

Delgado was in trouble.

As with Jason Delgado, his final deployment would be Nick Irving's first time in a leadership position. As a newly minted E5 (sergeant) and sniper team leader, he would have rank and responsibility for planning some missions. And he wanted to use the latitude that gave him to fulfill his concept of what it meant to be a sniper—even if it meant bending (or breaking) the rules a little. There was still a nine-year-old kid inside Nick wearing that ghillie suit made out of his mom's yarn and shooting his .22. He wanted the chance to color outside the lines, get out there outside the wire, build a hide sight, and stalk his prey like Carlos Hathcock.

He wanted to go outside the box.

"Hey man," he told Pemberton when they first arrived in Afghanistan, "this is my last deployment. I want us to do some cool stuff, kind of do our own thing, and if we get in trouble, I'll take the heat for it."

It was July 2, after a good three months of the insane pace of action in Helmand Province, when the chance to do exactly that finally came. That was the day the U.S. commenced Operation Khanjar, the Summer of Decision offensive that dropped thousands of marines into the middle of Helmand Province in an effort to root out Taliban forces there. None of which had any immediate impact on the rangers of Charlie Company. But that was also the day Nick was approached by a scrungy-looking character with a mountain-man beard and serious need of a bath.

If this had been back home, Nick would probably have taken the guy for a homeless dude bent on panhandling. But this was no derelict, this was a member of a four-man team from the rangers' regimental reconnaissance division, a special unit of recce operators.

These guys were legendary. They operated on their own, often deep behind enemy lines for extended periods of time doing their own who-knew-what ops. They were as Spec Ops as Spec Ops gets.

And they were looking for a good sniper.

They were hunting a particular HVT, a leader quite high up on the terrorist food chain. They had surveilled him for a while, spotted him a few times, at one point gotten close enough to see him getting into a car—but they hadn't had a sniper with them. They didn't have the skill set to guarantee a one-shot/one-kill at ten football fields, and this was the kind of shot they had to be 100 percent sure of making—miss and they'd just spook the guy into deep hiding.

They needed a sniper who could make a crazy-long shot like that, if need be.

"Listen," Scruffy Beard said to Nick, "can you hit a guy in a car moving at a thousand yards or more?"

"With a .30 cal, if he's coming toward me," replied Nick, "I might have a shot at it. But don't quote me on it."

A .30 cal sniper rifle cartridge is packed with significantly more powder and is a significantly more powerful round than the .308s Nick was shooting with his beloved SR-25. Pemberton, in fact, carried a big bolt-action .30 cal, and Nick was quite familiar with it. But he figured, if it came to it, he and Dirty Diana could handle whatever they needed to handle.

"All right," said Scruffy Beard, whose name turned out to be Derek. "We want you to come in with us on this operation." He took Nick to their tent, showed him some maps, and described the type of terrain they'd be operating in, and gave him a quick mission brief.

Irving was completely psyched. It was a classic sniper mission—exactly what he'd always dreamed of doing. He and Pemberton were going to spend days out behind enemy lines, stalk the hell out of this guy, and hopefully take that one perfect kill shot. Nick filled Pemberton in and got clearance from First Platoon's CO. After a few days of packing and preparation, they were ready to go.

The final plan was this: they would go hunt this HVT, and once they got eyes on him, they would call in whatever platoon was nearby and available for support, much the way a city cop will call in backup before venturing into a crime-in-progress scenario.

First, though, they would stop over at a small marine outpost to link up and see what intel on the area they might have.

They loaded onto a Chinook—just the six of them: Nick, Pemberton, and the four recce operators—and flew west for about an hour, deep into Helmand Province: poppy capital, heroin central, the heart of Taliban country. As Nick peered out the chopper's porthole he saw a stretch of tall grass, then scrabbly desert fields with huge intermittent sand dunes, then long swathes of Afghan-style semi-urban sprawl. As they reached their destination and began their approach Nick scanned the terrain below, looking for signs of structures. He didn't see anything but open desert with a little grass. Where were all the marines?

As they dismounted he noticed a series of small craters in the earth. Had they been taking mortar fire here? he wondered. As they got closer he realized there were *people* sleeping in there. A marine came out to greet them in his underwear and flip-flops, smoking a cigar. Nick decided on the spot that he would never again complain about the air-conditioning back at FOB Wilson being too cold, or not cold enough, or the chow not being as hot as it should be.

Man, he thought, *we are outside the freaking box.*

At the back of the compound he found a sort of makeshift hammock made of 550 cord, that slightly stretchy braided nylon all-purpose parachute rope so common in the military. "I claim that one," he said. "That's where I'm sleeping tonight!"

But that didn't happen. First they set up their comms, including the satellite radios and other arcane equipment the recce crew had brought, then spent hours monitoring and following the intel. And then they planned, and planned some more. For hours Nick studied maps and charts, planning out the whole operation, considering contingencies and alternates. He was doing his chess thing: looking at the board, working out in his mind the different plays, what his opponent might do. He went all that night and into the next day.

In fact, he wouldn't be sleeping for days.

Mogadishu Airport butted right up against the ocean, its main runway running diagonally, southwest to northeast, in approximate parallel to the shoreline. Just below the halfway point, time and the elements had carved out a single scallop-shaped bite, forming a small natural seaport.

Green Beach, so named for its rich green tropical sand floor, would be their base of infil and exfil.

Earlier that day there had been a lot of gunfire near the seaport; the day before had seen an intense spate of clan fighting. Mogadishu's version of Hatfields and McCoys, only with heavy artillery. Right now, though, the environment seemed entirely benign. They could see tracer fire in the sky, but that was off in the distance, somewhere in or beyond the western edge of the city. Who was shooting? And at whom? They had no idea. Here at the airport the U.N. forces were still in charge, and everything was calm as could be.

Hundreds of marines had already gone to work, establishing their lines along the two-and-a-half-mile line of beachhead. Nearly eight hundred had come ashore in the first wave, half of those arriving in AAVs here at Green Beach.

The SEALs split into two groups and headed for their predetermined positions. Typically the two snipers would have been working together, in a classic shooter-spotter team, but for this op they were splitting up in order to cover the airport from two positions. Alex and half a dozen others, including the LPO (leading petty officer) and OIC (officer in charge), a comms operator, a corpsman, and another two men for security, would take up position toward the southwest; the other sniper and his team would set up on a hillside by the northeastern tip of the runway, about a mile and a half away. Alex wouldn't see them again until after the op was over.

Alex and his team broke off to the southwest and patrolled to a spot they had already pinpointed from studying satellite imagery that would give them a clear, full view of the southern half of the main runway and all the buildings in the airport's lower half. Reaching the solid cement bunker they had picked out as their base of operations, they climbed in and began setting up. Alex took out his M88 .50 cal, carefully slid the barrel out through the slit in the bunker wall—and found himself staring through his scope at the inside of the bunker's goddamn cement wall.

Shit.

The slit was just big enough for the barrel—*just* the barrel. Not the scope. Somehow the satellite imagery had not told them this. So much for planning.

Time to get outside the box.

Alex stood, gathered his equipment, climbed out of the bunker, and clambered up onto the roof. It looked like he'd be making his "hide" out under the stars.

On the perimeter wall up on top of the bunker, they used sandbags to build a small fighting position that could hold up to four of them at a time. The rest of the guys could stay down in the bunker and swap out positions with those above. Alex would be staying on top for the duration.

He laid out his supplies and got his position set up. A quick survey of the area told him that the .762 he'd brought along would be worthless. Any hostile activity, if it happened, would almost certainly be coming from the other side of the runway, the city side. Unless he was going to be shooting at someone actually coming straight toward them across the runway (unlikely), the very closest shot he could expect to be taking would be at a range of at least five hundred yards, and probably farther.

Alex put the .762 away and got the Beast up on top of the sandbags. And waited.

Now up in the snowy higher elevations of the Shahikot Valley, Rob and Tim found a good location to set up position. While Tim begin surveying the valley floor below and building his range card, Rob planted the big .50 into the snow on its bipod legs. Today Rob would be on the .50, Tim hunkered down on his right, serving as spotter. (Though a natural righty, Rob had trained himself early on to shoot equally well with either hand and preferred to shoot long barrel left-handed, which made the natural position for spotter to his immediate right.)

They knew immediately that the decision had been a sound one. Their position gave them an excellent vantage point from which they could glass the entire range below them. Looking around the valley with the naked eye, everything looked pretty quiet out there. No movement, no signs of life. But the moment they got behind their optics, they started picking out movement everywhere. It shouldn't take too long to begin identifying the mortar pits and machine gun nests that had the Americans pinned down.

They didn't have long to wait. Down at about 1,700 meters they spotted a man wearing a shawl, carrying an AK, walking with his back to them toward a mud hut area. Not a machine gun nest, but certainly an enemy fighter whose presence could spell American deaths if he wasn't eliminated.

Tim fed him elevation and windage. Rob watched for a few moments, to make sure he was tracking the man's progress correctly. There wasn't much to track: he was walking more or less in a straight line away from them, which meant there was no horizontal movement requiring Rob to lead the target. He was, for all practical purposes, a stationary target.

BOOM!

There is nothing quite like the sound of a .50 cal round going off. Even a .300 Win Mag, not a shy sound, doesn't come close. It sounded like the peal of a thunderbolt from the heavens. Which, in a way, is exactly what it was.

The round flew downrange toward the valley floor at a velocity of about 2,640 fps, or half a mile per second, arriving at the man's location in a little under one second.

It missed, passing the man a few feet to his right, and drove into the ground a few feet in front of him.

As Rob made an automatic mental note (*mild wind coming from the left*) he watched the man through his scope and couldn't quite believe what he was seeing. If it were Rob who'd been walking along and had suddenly seen a high-powered round plow into the ground just a few feet away, he knew what he'd be doing right now. He'd be running like crazy and diving for cover. Not this guy. The man stopped, turned, and kind of waved his arm in the air (what did *that* mean?), then turned back around and continued walking in the same direction.

At the same pace.

No dropping for cover, no breaking into a run. Nothing. Clearly he'd seen the splash from Rob's shot.

Rob was floored. Was the man completely stupid, or completely fearless? Or maybe he truly believed that, hey, if it was his time to go, if it was Allah's will, then so be it. Rob didn't really know, and he didn't really care.

He worked the bolt mechanism in a practiced *one-two-three* blur—up and back, spent cartridge ejects, forward and down, slamming home a fresh cartridge—made a quick adjustment for wind, and let the second round go.

He planted this one right in the man's back.

It was Rob's first kill; it certainly would not be his last.

For the rest of the day the two men continued locating, sighting, and engaging targets—including the mortar pit that had held the guys of Tenth Mountain captive.

When darkness fell they headed back down toward the safety box. As they hiked down past the same American team they'd passed on their way up, a few of the guys who'd told them they were crazy for going up there came over and said, "Hey, thanks, man!" Evidently the news had spread about how busy the Canadians had been up there, and how they'd been able to eliminate the mortar position that had Tenth Mountain pinned down. A few of the Americans started applauding.

To Rob and Tim, it felt like a day well spent.

The next morning they climbed back up the mountain to go outside the box again and spend another day taking out whatever targets they could find. Again they watched as the snow cover spread out and became an unbroken blanket at about the nine-thousand-foot mark. Again they had that spine-chilling feeling that went beyond the effects of rarefied air and bitter temperatures. This time, though, the riskiness of what they were doing hit home, in a literal and decidedly uncomfortable way.

They had just pushed outside the box, set up their long gun, and started glassing the valley, when they both heard a loud, piercing *crack-kkk!* like something breaking right between the two of them.

In an instant both men were down on the ground. Though neither one had ever heard that sound before, at least not that up close and personal, they both knew what it was. It was the sound made by a high-speed round cracking the sound barrier.

A single shot. Without question, a sniper round. And it had passed directly between them, inches away from both men. An American sniper had seen them, taken them as enemy combatants, and put a round in their direction with near-fatal accuracy.

Blue on blue.

McMeekin got on the radio and said, "Cease fire! Cease fire!"

Once they'd determined that no more Coalition rounds were coming their way, they got down to the business at hand.

While they'd taken out that particularly troublesome mortar pit the day before, there were still others out there, and they seemed to have an endless supply of rockets.

Down on the valley floor the two snipers noticed a dried-up wadi bed where two or three guys would go back and forth across the valley, from the vicinity of the Whale down to an area below Takur Ghar called Ginger Pass. Walking between them were several donkeys loaded down with some big boxes. It didn't take any inside intelligence to know what was in those boxes. So *that* was how those mortar teams kept being resupplied with fresh rockets.

Tim got one of these donkey runners in his sights. BOOM! Another thunderbolt from the sky. The man went down.

The donkey convoy paused, trying to make out exactly where the shot had come from, but the sniper team was situated at such an extreme distance that they couldn't work it out. They continued on. Before long Rob and Tim had acquired a second target. BOOM!

The men were now confused. They'd lost two of their company and had no idea where the shots were originating from. They got down on their knees, then on their bellies, and started crawling through the wadi, no doubt figuring that this would take them completely out of their invisible assassin's line of fire. As long as they were snaking along on their bellies, they wouldn't present any kind of target, right? But that assumed that the bullets were coming at them from the same elevation where they were. Which of course, they weren't. Rob and Tim were so high up that they could look right down on them. In fact, when the men started crawling they made themselves into easier targets, not more difficult ones.

Before long Rob and Tim had racked up a pretty decent body count. But the donkeys didn't stop. They'd made this trip who knew how many times, and it didn't seem to bother them that their human handlers were now lying dead all around them. By the time Rob and Tim had shot the last man standing, the donkeys had moved out of range, carrying their mortar supplies off to wherever they were headed.

When the donkeys eventually reappeared with new handlers, they took them out, too. Eventually they had to take out the donkeys themselves.

By the end of their second day up there they had completely shut down that resupply line.

And that was a good thing, too, because now they faced a new and different problem.

When they boarded that Chinook at Bagram three days earlier, Rob carried the big .50 with five rounds in its detachable magazine. In addition to his C8 combat rifle and Browning 9mm sidearm, and the rest of his kit, he also carried extra radio batteries and twenty extra .50 cal rounds. McMeekin carried the radio itself and, along with his C8 and Browning 9mm, another ninety .50 cal rounds. The third member of their team, who served the role of security, carried a C7 with 203 grenade launcher plus thirty grenades and extra rounds for their C7 and C8 rifles, but no .50 cal rounds.

Which meant that between them, they set out with a total of 115 rounds for the long gun. All of which they had now shot.

Their packing for seventy-two hours had been spot on. But seventy-two hours had come and gone, with no mission end in sight.

And they had just run out of ammo.

* * *

When Jason Delgado and his team of snipers got back from their aborted 440 mission to base, he learned that he was in some deep shit, all right. Which made no sense to him whatsoever. The leadership of a marine sniper platoon is as follows: first in charge is the platoon commander, usually an intel officer; second in command is the platoon sergeant; then comes the chief scout, who is nominated from within the platoon and is typically the most senior HOG in the platoon. In Husaybah, Jason served as both platoon sergeant *and* chief scout. The platoon commander, Lieutenant Doug French, was a solid guy who trusted Jason and had given him fairly free rein.

So why had he now been recalled back to camp for a scolding?

In a way, Delgado wasn't even supposed to be there. After his marine battalion took Baghdad in 2003, his term of service was over. He was supposed to be back in Brooklyn, getting his degree in media studies and flexing his muscles as an artist and filmmaker. So why was he being called before a battalion commander for shooting people in Husaybah?

It's hard for us now to fully appreciate the general mind-set of 2003, but back then the campaign to liberate Iraq had seemed to a lot of people like pretty much a slam dunk. The Shock and Awe campaign and push into Baghdad was a roaring success. Saddam was out. The good people of Iraq were free. We won, right? As far as the American top brass were concerned, now it was a matter of transitioning from successful campaign to graceful, gradual withdrawal.

You're welcome, Iraq, was the general sense of things.

So when Delgado returned home from that deployment, there was no firm plan to go back into war. Plus, he was itching to get out of that platoon. As much as he loved the marines, the platoon commander on that first deployment had been absolutely terrible. This guy was so weak he couldn't run more than two miles. For early morning PT, he would get the guys into the gym to play basketball. Here was a platoon of men who'd been tortured for two years preparing them for the reality of war, guys who routinely ran five, six, seven miles every morning— and now this dick was getting them together *to play basketball*?

The rest of the battalion leadership was excellent, from Lieutenant Colonel McCoy right down to their platoon sergeant. But a bad CO can ruin an otherwise awesome platoon, and that is precisely what this CO did.

So Jason and his buddies mutinied. As an act of rebellion, when they returned to the States, all eighteen of them left the unit and got themselves moved to Third Battalion, Seventh Marines, intending that to be their transition home and EAS (end of active service). But that wasn't what happened. When they got to Third Battalion, Seventh Marines, they realized the battalion didn't have a single HOG (certified scout/sniper) in their sniper platoon. It was a sniper platoon of PIGs— and they were deploying to Iraq in less than a month. These poor guys had no odds; they were about to go into a meat grinder.

Jason couldn't see letting that happen.

He talked to two buddies from his first platoon, Steve Reynolds and his shooting partner, Jesse Davenport, and the three decided to stay on and help the guys out. And now here they all were, back in Iraq— Steve working a team in Al Qaim, Jesse in another nearby location, and Jason running the platoon here in Husaybah.

In terms of leadership, it felt like this time he'd won the lottery.

Doug French was one of those all-too-rare leaders who not only knew what he knew, but also knew what he didn't know. He focused on intel and deferred to Jason in all matters sniper. "Let me do what the battalion needs me to do, which is be an intel officer," he told Jason. "You run your missions by me, and if I have a problem, I'll just grunt at you."

The CO of Lima Company, Captain Richard Gannon, was an incredibly down-to-earth guy who gave an actual shit about ordinary marines. Jason had never seen a marine officer so beloved by his troops, let alone a company commander. When Gannon gave instructions, Jason would sit and quietly drink it in for the sheer pleasure of listening to someone who so clearly knew what the hell he was talking about. At the same time, Gannon was the kind of officer who knew how to listen to his men, too. Like Lieutenant French, he respected his snipers and encouraged Jason to come up with his own missions.

And Captain Gannon's second in command, First Lieutenant Dominique Neal, was another excellent leader, a guy who wore his feelings on his sleeve and had the respect of his men.

But Jason wasn't here to see Lieutenant French, or First Lieutenant Neal, or Captain Gannon. He was here to see the man himself. And the man himself was not happy.

When Jason and the others got back to the camp, Lieutenant Colonel Lopez was waiting there for him with his legs crossed, his finger on his lip, the very picture of an authority figure about to administer a serious tongue-lashing.

"Do you know what you just did, Sergeant?" he said.

"Yeah," said Jason, "I just pulled some poor border agent out of some shit."

Lieutenant Colonel Lopez drilled Jason with a withering look. "You know you killed two guys across the border, in Syria. Right?"

Aha. So that was what this was about. No wonder he'd been recalled from their mission. Jason had been outside the box, all right. He'd shot his rifle clear outside the border of the country they were stationed in! And kill shots at that.

But Jason did not intimidate easily. *I didn't do shit wrong,* he thought.

"Well," he said, "they were shooting at him, and they were wearing black pajamas. I don't know why Syria would want to start a war with Iraq while we're sitting right here, sir. I didn't know if they were inside or outside the border. All I knew was that they were shooting at this poor guy. I don't know what else I can tell you."

What he thought but didn't say was, *And besides, I called it in first— if anyone's getting burned for this it's the officer who gave me the okay.*

Which was what saved his ass. It was the watch officer's job to plot that location the moment Jason gave him their coordinates, but instead of doing that, he just gave them an immediate thumbs-up. The commander didn't seem very happy about it, but he couldn't do anything to Jason. If anyone was going to get in trouble, it was the officer who cleared the shots, not Jason.

What annoyed Jason was that the line of questioning wasn't, "Hey, Delgado, you're my guy on the front lines, tell me what happened out there," as it would have been with Doug French or Captain Gannon. The tone of it was more like, "Do you realize what you've done? Well, we're going to open up an investigation."

This was the first time one of Jason's shots prompted an investigation—but it sure wasn't the last. In fact, over the next six weeks it would happen again and again, as he kept seeing trouble, taking what he viewed as appropriate action, and then getting called onto the carpet for it.

Delgado was way outside the box, and, at least for now, he was all alone out there.

On their second night at the remote marine outpost in Helmand Province, Nick Irving and his spotter, Pemberton, went out hunting. Time to pull away from all the communications equipment and go stalking their prey.

They left on foot, just five of them: Irving, Pemberton, one of the recce operators, and two marine scout snipers, who knew the lay of the land there better than their guests did. It took them several hours to reach the village where they were headed. It wasn't all that far, but their progress was slow.

As they started moving into a more populated area they slowed to a crawl. They had night vision, and the locals did not, but this just happened to be the night of that month's full moon, which shrank that visual advantage. Though it was after midnight, they could still clearly see the stray person here and there who was up—which meant, of course, that they could also be seen. So they had to use the cover of shadow.

That was Nick's primary job as they moved: keeping everyone in the shadows.

So this is what it feels like to be a ninja, thought Nick, and he suppressed a grin.

Back in sniper school Nick had gone through an exercise called a "fun stalk." It wasn't graded, you didn't have to pass; the idea was to sort of stretch out and see what you could do, probe the outer limits of outrageousness. You didn't have to carry a rifle if you didn't want. You could dress up however you wanted to dress up. A few students wore bright yellow, just to see if they could pull it off and still not be seen.

Nick was partnered with a guy named Chris. They both wore T-shirt, jeans, and baseball cap, and stalked with their sniper rifles.

The instructor with the high-powered binos, the one they were stalking against, was an old-school sniper from the SOTG (the Marine Corps' Special Operations Training Group) who had spotting powers that bordered on the supernatural. Everyone hated this guy. Nick had seen him call out a team of snipers stalking him from a thousand yards away—*without* binoculars. "I see his left shoulder!" he'd called out. And no shit, the walker went to exactly where he directed, and touched the guy's left shoulder. At a thousand yards, with no scope, just his naked eye. And the stalker was wearing a ghillie suit.

So Nick and Chris went up against this guy in their T-shirts and jeans. They set off, moving inch by inch, slowly eating up the yards like twin snakes. When they reached their FFP (final firing position), this fact was relayed back to the watch post.

"Give those guys a fucking pat on the back," said the old HOG, "because I don't see shit."

In all the sniper instruction he went through, every course, every session, Nick had never been caught; not once.

Now it was time to put those skills to work.

Once they reached the outskirts of the little village, they began making their way to the spot Nick had picked out that would give them the best visual and tactical advantage.

Everything Nick had done up to this point in his career as a ranger, even here in Helmand Province, had been extremely fast-paced. Run into an objective, bag the guy and/or shoot everything up, and get out. Tonight there was no running, no shooting, no commotion or chaos. Tonight success was measured in inches and long minutes that oozed past, second by nerve-racking second. It was a total transformation from warrior to spy. They crept along for a few feet, stopped, listened. Did he hear anyone moving? Smell anyone's presence? They began moving again, incredibly slowly. A mime troupe on Valium.

Nick found the place. Felt the door. Found the lock. Picked the lock—quietly, quietly. Opened the door. Slipped silently inside.

"It was so damned scary," says Nick, "being out there by ourselves, completely alone in the middle of this village. It was insane. We were sneaking around in someone's house with sniper rifles."

They laid up there all night long, waiting for their target to come into the area. No one spoke more than a whispered word or two. Finally fingers of light began stealing in from the edge of the village with the silent approach of the sun. All their senses became heightened. If their target appeared Nick would take the shot, then they would immediately break down and get the hell out of there.

Their target did not arrive.

As the sun continued its climb, they slipped out of the house, away from the village, and back to the marine outpost for fresh intel and another round of planning. More chess.

Later that day (it now being Wednesday, July 8), the team got intel from a group of marines from about a half-hour ride away, where evidently a lot of activity was happening. The intel suggested that their HVT might be heading in that direction. They needed to go over there and take a look for themselves.

They made the ride on Amtracs, not the most comfortable ride under the best of conditions, which these sure were not. They bumped along a trail ("Calling it a dirt road would be generous," says Nick) out through the desert scrub. As they drove Nick noticed a series of little red markers marking the path, and asked his marine hosts about them.

"Oh yeah, those are land mines," he said. "We have to stay within those markers." He grinned. "Otherwise, boom."

"Wait a minute," said Nick. "So, if we get in contact, we can't veer off the trail? We have to just *sit* here?"

The marine shook his head. "Not to the right, not to the left, not the slightest bit."

Bullshit, man, Nick thought. He figured he'd rather take his chances with a run through the land mines than just sit there in a rolling coffin and get shot up.

Making the ride in broad daylight was good, in that it allowed their driver to see the red markers, but also bad, in that they were clearly visible to all the people who lived in the areas they traversed. Nick more than half expected some good local citizens to wave to them as they passed, then shoot them in the back. He'd seen it happen in Iraq.

But it didn't happen here. After a tense but uneventful ride, they arrived at their destination, an abandoned schoolhouse that was really no more than a bare structure of concrete and mud. The marines who greeted them had been living out there for six or seven months, in this grimy, sweat-soaked place. Their toilet was a cardboard box that they would use for a while, then ignite with some diesel fuel and burn, then get another cardboard box.

If where they'd just come from was a remote outpost, this place upped the ante.

"Dude," said Irving, "how do you guys *live* out here, man?" They had one satphone, which they used to sneak in a call to family maybe once a month or so. Back at FOB Wilson Nick was used to talking to his family at least once a day.

They were greeted by the base commander, who mentioned that they'd been getting attacked daily for the past few months. It happened every morning at the same time, about five o'clock, just before sunup.

The recce team leader looked at Irving and Pemberton and said, "You guys want to help him out?"

Nick and Pemberton had different ROEs (rules of engagement) than their hosts'. The marines had to wait until they were actually being shot at before they could engage. The ranger snipers could shoot someone if they felt threatened, if they felt someone else was threatened, or if the person had a gun. If Nick saw a guy with an AK-47, he was automatically cleared to shoot. All of which, along with their training as snipers, could put them at a distinct advantage in this situation. This was not their mission, but hey, they were here, right?

"Hell, yeah," said Nick.

He got on the radio and pitched the idea to their chain of command, who were skeptical at first but eventually signed off on it. (Irving admits that if they'd said no, chances were good he would have said "Fuck it—we didn't hear that part" and gone out anyway.)

After hitting the maps and working out the best place to set up their hide site, they readied their ghillie suits and equipment, grabbed an MRE and some water, and got busy waiting for the sun to dip below the horizon.

At this point they had been three days straight without sleep.

11

THE LONG NIGHT

Alone in the dark with nothing but your thoughts . . . time can draw out like a blade.

—Red (Morgan Freeman), *The Shawshank Redemption,*
by Stephen King and Frank Darabont

In Hermann Hesse's classic tale *Siddhartha,* the hero is asked what he has to offer, since he has no possessions. He replies, "I can think, I can wait, I can fast." Later on he amplifies the point: "Being smart is good. Being patient is better." The character of Siddhartha is meant to be an example of the ideal seeker on a spiritual quest.

If you ask me, he also could have made a hell of a sniper.

With all the breathtaking prowess in those long-distance shots, high-angle shots, through-the-legs shots, and from-the-hip shots, it's easy to forget that the sniper's most critical skills don't involve shooting at all. (All together now: *A sniper is first and foremost an intelligence asset.*) Surveillance, route reconnaissance, detailed description, spending time out beyond the front lines, taking pictures and drawing sketches, gathering information, observing where nobody else goes and seeing what nobody else sees—that's the foundation of the sniper's contribution to war. Warrior, absolutely. Assassin, no question. Spy, *quintessentially.*

Put it this way. Yes, a sniper needs to be able to fight like a lion and strike like a snake. But even more critically, he must have the capacity to wait, watch, and see like an eagle.

Alex and his teammates waited for hours, Alex alternately sitting and lying on the cement bunker's roof, the others spelling each other periodically. Every so often another few AAVs emerged from the Somali surf, belching out another few dozen marines, who joined the rest as they worked away at their fortifications.

At nine minutes after 0600, a thin laser line of sunlight poked up over the Indian Ocean at Alex's back. He turned and looked. Four miles out, the mother ship waited. Beyond that, nothing but ocean for twenty-five hundred miles until you'd bump into Sri Lanka.

He turned back to watch some more nothing happen.

By 0800 hours the last few waves of the landing party had come ashore.

At 0830, the U.N.'s forces stationed a few miles to the northeast around New Port began to withdraw. Hour after hour, a steady procession of Bangladeshi troops and their equipment were loaded onto a fleet of ships the Coalition had contracted for the purpose and ferried out to sea. There were more than a thousand of them, along with tons of vehicles, weaponry (most of it on loan from the U.S.), and other equipment. It took all day.

Meanwhile, two and a half miles to the southwest, Alex waited and watched.

The northern operation was the easy part. The tricky part would come the next day, when the Pakistanis would start pulling out from their positions in and around the airport. Once the last elements of the U.N. force abandoned their current positions and pulled inside the landing force's thin coastal perimeter, what would happen then?

As the hours ticked by, the sun slowly climbed.

They were practically sitting on the equator, and it was approaching the hottest part of the year. (Somalia hits its highest temperatures in April.) Still, being on the coast mitigated the climate somewhat, and the heat was not too bad. The flies, though: the flies were horrible. Big black motherfuckers, and aggressive as buzzards. You could shoo them away all you wanted, and they would be right back on you in seconds.

Could you kill a fly with a .50 cal?

And if you did, would the rest take the hint and leave?

Questions, questions.

The hours rolled on, and they kept watching more nothing happen. Finally, at thirteen minutes after 1800, the last orange crest of sun slipped below the western horizon: the Mogadishu skyline, such as it was, chewed to rubble by the ravages of civil anarchy.

The coming of dusk signaled a shift change: the flies left, and the mosquitoes arrived to take up station. If there is one thing worse than the flies in Africa, it's the mosquitoes in Africa.

It was going to be a long night.

* * *

By the end of their third full day out in the Shahikot Valley, Rob and
Tim had used up all their .50 cal ammo. There wasn't much they could
do up there in the crow's nest now, so they pushed back into the position with the American scout teams, there to stay, at least for the
moment.

The scouts had dug some foxholes and set up a command element,
kind of an ad hoc admin area out of which they could operate with rea-
sonable security.

The question was, operate how? And do what? At this point their .50
cal was nothing but deadweight. They couldn't hit the targets they
needed to hit with their other weapons. With a .308, like the one the
American sniper had given Rob, they could shoot effectively out to maybe
a thousand meters, possibly a little more. But these targets were way
out beyond that; they were at two, three, even four kilometers. What
could they really do?

Then they realized, maybe there *was* something they could do. They
were, after all, snipers. Right now they couldn't shoot—but they could
still stalk. And in addition to their Leupold spotting scope they also had
a laser range finder with some technology built into it that could do
something pretty amazing.

The Leica Vectronix allows you to measure the distance between two
lased points with tremendous accuracy. First you lase your target. Then
you take a sounding shot (a shot placed purely for its use in gauging
location, as Jason Delgado did on that rooftop in the middle of Baghdad) or move your view to a spot somewhere relatively near the target—
say, a spot where aircraft has just dropped ordnance. You lase that
reference point, then click and drag over to your target, just as you
would click and drag with a mouse on a computer screen. And *presto!*
The Vectronix gives you the exact distance between those two points.

The Vectronix was fairly new technology at the time, and not very
many had it. Rob and Tim realized they were probably the only guys
on the ground with the type of optics in their possession. Which meant
they were in a unique position to precisely pinpoint multiple targets at
extreme distances—machine gun emplacements, mortar teams, even
howitzers, and others. And the Leica had an effective range of five kilometers, more than three miles. In other words, it could pinpoint targets clear on the other side of Shahikot Valley and up on the side of the
Whale, if need be.

Of course, since they had no more .50 cal ammo, they couldn't shoot those targets, not with their own guns. But they could be the eyes for guns in the air.

Like most other conventional resources, air support had been badly lacking at the outset of Anaconda, but within the first two days the Coalition generals realized how badly they had underestimated the resistance their troops would meet. Soon a raft of airpower joined the party, including U.S. Air Force A-10 Thunderbolt (Warthog) attack planes, marine AH-1 Cobra attack helos, and more than a dozen additional Apaches from the 101st Airborne.

The American scout element Rob and Tim were attached to had set up a ground-to-air asset in their little ad hoc TOC. Which meant that Rob and Tim could lase targets with the Vector and feed precise coordinates to the forces in the sky, and continue raining down death upon the enemy.

They also had communication with some American mortar teams situated a little ways downslope from them, who were loaded with 81mm mortars as well as monster 120mm's.

They started glassing. The scout unit put them into direct communication with the ground-to-air representative, and they started calling in indirect fire right and left on every target they could see—fast air, B-52s, Apaches, Cobras, F-16s, everything they had at their disposal. They located knots of fighters moving in and out of compounds, vehicles transporting them from one position to another, mortar pits and machine gun nests they hadn't been able to reach before—all kinds of targets that they had seen while up in their crow's nest but hadn't been able to engage even with their .50 because of the extreme distances.

They became two lone snipers wielding a "sniper rifle" comprised of an entire fleet of American airpower. Talk about leverage.

At one point they identified a mortar position clear across the valley, high up on the edge of a cliff on the side of the Whale. At nearly four and a half kilometers (2.8 miles) away, it was the farthest mortar position they'd identified. There would have been no way they could ever have gotten to that target before without physically moving down into the valley and walking right through enemy-held territory. Now they called in a Cobra attack helicopter, which flew over and dumped its payload.

Watching those attack choppers raining down destruction, they could see the place being absolutely destroyed. Clearly, there was no one alive left.

Then, as they scanned the area with their scopes, they saw movement.

"Holy shit," Rob murmured. "Those guys are still in there."

They'd been raked with machine gun fire from the Cobra's big guns and bombed with Hellfire missiles—and they were still there. Rob and Tim couldn't tell what caves might be there or how far back they might go; the entire valley, like most strongholds in the eastern Afghanistan mountains, was laced with networks of caves and tunnels. Still, it seemed beyond the limits of physical possibility that these guys could still be alive.

Yet there they were.

Now Rob called in a B-52 bomber run, his first. Soon they saw a tell-tale vapor trail streak across the sky, and moments later the five-hundred-pounder landed with an enormous boom and shock wave they could hear and feel clear across the valley.

After the smoke cleared, they resumed glassing the area.

"And, so help me," says Rob, "we see this fucking guy—*moving.*"

The man slowly pushed something aside, a large blanket, or piece of wood, or some other sort of covering, then stood up and bolted from his position, most likely back into a tunnel.

It's not too often you see someone get up, dust himself off, and run away after a B-52 drop. But this guy? They figured he probably got out of there safely and lived to fight another day. The Afghanis had a knack for doing just that, as the Soviets had learned to their considerable chagrin in the eighties and America was just beginning to experience firsthand.

Hour after hour, Rob and Tim sat in position on their ridgeline, glassing, lasing, clicking-and-dragging, calling it in . . . glassing, lasing, clicking-and-dragging, calling it in. They continued identifying distant targets and calling in air support for the rest of that day, and throughout the next day as well.

Rob estimates that the time he and McMeekin spent lasing targets and calling in ordnance over those two days had even more impact on enemy forces than all the shooting they did the entire time they were in the Shahikot Valley, both before then and afterward. And they did a *lot* of shooting.

It didn't take Jason long after arriving in Husaybah to see the limitations of their unit's patrols.

Marines were going through the city on foot, which was an improvement over the more superficial drive-throughs that came before. When they took the area over from the army's Third ID, the marines instituted a curfew, and that was a big help, too. If anyone was out on the streets at night, by definition the chances were good they were up to no good, and they were fair game for questioning and possibly detaining.

But it was a big city and there was a lot to surveil. Jason could see that normal patrols weren't telling them what was really going on. They needed to do some extended urban hide operations, to insert themselves deep within the tissue of the city.

This, he soon discovered, could take some careful planning and bureaucratic maneuvering. For example, the marines were mandated to take men from the Iraqi police and Civil Defense Corps with them on some patrols ("bullshit politics, bro"). Jason had no clear knowledge as to whether or not they could trust these guys, but he doubted it, and he was careful not to share much information with them. He took them along, got along with them fine, but observed carefully. Before long he noticed that on certain ones of these joint patrols, the Iraqis would at some point quietly shift to the back of the stack. He also noticed that those were the same patrols where bad things would happen—an armed confrontation or attack, or an encounter with a roadside bomb. ("What a fucking coincidence.")

Despite the fact that he was the sniper platoon leader, and even though he had some great commanders in French, Neal, and Gannon, Delgado often found himself chafing at what seemed to him pointless missions.

One of the marines' principal aims in Husaybah was to help guard the border and prevent illegal supplies from leaking into Iraq, which included working with the Iraqi border patrol, teaching them how to use dogs, how to search vehicles, and other border-policing activities. But this felt a bit like trying to bail out a sinking ship with a colander. The border itself was ridiculously porous, and the city's civil authority structure was so shot through with corruption that any real attempt at enforcement was doomed to fail.

One night found Jason ghillied up with his team hiding out in almond groves, trying to catch people smuggling illegal goat milk across the border. He figured this was no doubt at the request of some Iraqi official the Americans were doing their best to get along with ("more bullshit politics"). To Jason it was an egregious waste of time and human resources. Here they were, the only snipers in all of Husaybah, a city of 100,000 with rampant crime and simmering insurgency, and they were lying in wait to intercept a goat milk operation?

But he went along. He knew he had to pick his battles. He could go along quietly with the more asinine missions—if it meant having the freedom to also go out on the missions that mattered.

And those missions revealed a sobering picture.

One day, not long after the episode with the Iraqi border guard and the Syrian shooters, Jason got a whiff of some useful intel that some suspicious activity might be going on in a certain residential neighborhood. That night, Jason took a team out on a reconnaissance op.

This was not a traditional two-man, shooter/spotter operation. Someone had to man the optics; someone had to be on the radio; they would need two people on security, who would also sit with the family of the house they were taking over. And since they were planning to be out for twenty-four hours or more, they needed enough men to rotate out tasks while giving each team member a chance to catch a few hours of rack time. So they went out as a four-man sniper team, augmented by a couple of infantry grunts pulling security, making a six-man element all told.

They inserted at three in the morning, when most everyone in the city was asleep. They slipped through the streets, staying in the shadows, exactly as Nick Irving and Pemberton and their recce colleagues would do five years later in Helmand Province.

On some of these nighttime ops a few of them would wrap themselves in plastic trash bags, then go out and hide in the garbage piles all night to see if anyone tried to bury an IED in trash heaps, inside paper bags, or in dog carcasses, as they sometimes did. But not tonight. Tonight they were taking over a home in that residential neighborhood they wanted to watch.

They reached the address they'd picked for their hide site. The house was surrounded by six-foot walls, typical for the neighborhood, closed by a simple steel gate. Not hard to climb, but that wasn't practical because the moment they did it would start clanging back and forth and wake up the people. And the dog, if they had one. So they scaled over the cement wall at its most solid point.

Now came entry. They couldn't exactly bang on the door. Using a tactic they'd worked out by now, they searched out the window that held the home's air-conditioning unit, then tapped lightly on the glass with a pistol. *Tap-tap-tap.* Experience told them that the whole family would be sleeping here, and someone would always come to the window to see who was tapping on it.

Someone did. Jason made eye contact, got them to open the window a crack, and quietly said, "Efte'elba'ab. Efte'elba'ab." *Open the door.*

They hustled back around to the front door and got into the house without making any noise. Since everyone in the family was already in one room, they kept them all there. Sometimes they would bring an interpreter along with them, but not tonight. Jason picked up one of the family's phones and dialed a local number.

Back at camp, a phone rang in their suite of little bank offices, which the snipers shared with the canine handlers and the HET (human exploitation team) guys. HET maintained a landline there so that whenever an informant in town might want to give them any intel, they could just pick up the phone and call.

"Yo, it's Delgado, whassup," he said when the phone on the other end picked up. "Listen, put the terp on and have him tell this guy what's gonna go down."

As Jason handed the phone to the father of their temporarily captive family, the terp (interpreter) got on the other end. The father spoke a few words into the phone, then listened for a while, as the terp told them that they would be completely safe, what would be happening, what to do and not to do while the snipers were there, and the rest of his instructions, all of which he knew so well he could probably have given them in his sleep. Then the father started speaking. Jason's limited grasp of Arabic didn't let him catch most of the words, but he followed the gist of it. The citizen was giving up some intel, something useful. They usually did. Having six armed marines standing there in the middle of their living room was a little intimidating.

The snipers donned head wraps and dishdashas (man-dresses), so that if someone passing by the window happened to look in and see them, they'd think nothing of it.

While the infantry guys watched the family, Jason and his snipers went through the house looking for a good vantage point. As they went, they unplugged and gathered up whatever phones they found, so no one would try to sneak one, go plug it in, and try to call somebody. A second-floor room offered the best OP; they drew the curtains. They would be observing just through a crack.

This would now be their urban hide and observation post for the next twenty-four hours. Sometimes they would do this for forty-eight or even seventy-two hours, but this time they had planned for a one-day op. From here they could observe everything going on in the neighborhood around them. They would take photographs, draw sketches, and record their observations in detail.

No one in the adjacent buildings knew they were there, so the neighbors would all go about their day, business as usual. If anyone came knocking on the door, they would let them just knock. If they persisted and didn't go away on their own, Jason would eventually open the door and add them to the party. *Congratulations, you're going to be late for dinner.* But this time it didn't happen. They were left alone.

And then they watched. They were there all night. When morning came, they remained.

After a few hours, they saw one of their own foot patrols go by. The marines moved down the street and around a corner. The moment they disappeared, Jason noticed a young boy emerge from a nearby house, run up onto a small hill, and start tapping his leg. Then he ran back down and back inside the house. "What the hell was *that* about?" he murmured to himself. Then it occurred to him: there were six guys in that patrol.

The boy had tapped his leg six times.

Okay. Got it. The kid had just counted how many marines were in the patrol and communicated that to someone elsewhere in the city. Someone was using this kid as an intel asset.

A week or so later he saw this happen again, and then again. Sometimes a kid would jump up and hold out his fingers, visibly counting. And not just troop numbers. Sometimes it was about a patrol's direction of movement, or force of arms, or whether or not there was an officer involved. Whoever was behind this operation, they were scouting out and compiling all kinds of information about how the Americans worked.

Jason noticed that these guys were also using their women as tactical pawns. For example, the task of sitting on weapons caches was evidently being delegated to women in the community.

One day Jason observed a squad of marines approach a house where they had reported seeing a cache of weapons off-loaded. As the marines approached, a woman ran out, yelling at them, trying to grab them and swing on them. It was almost as if she were trying to provoke them. At first Jason didn't understand what the hell she was doing or why she was doing it. Then he caught on. She *was* trying to provoke them, to get them to take a swing at her, or worse. The ones pulling the strings, the ones who were giving her and all the others their marching orders, *wanted* the Americans to hurt them, maybe even kill them. It would make the Americans look bad, which in turn would make them easier targets for an aroused and angered populace.

Of course, it didn't work. The marines weren't about to go in and hurt or kill unarmed civilians. But armed hostiles? No problem there. Those guys, Jason was entirely prepared to hurt or kill.

And he did. Which was what kept getting him in trouble.

* * *

As the afternoon shadows melted into dusk, Nick Irving and Mike Pemberton set out on foot for the location where they would set up their all-night hide to wait for the expected morning attack on their marine hosts.

They walked out single-file, the six of them: Irving and Pemberton; Finnegan, the comms operator from the recce team, plus two marine snipers and one marine with a machine gun, all in ghillie suits. Within a short time the marines' secure area had disappeared behind them. They were alone now, just the six of them, in enemy territory.

The group arrived at the edge of a little village, about a mile and a half from the marine compound, just as night began to fall. From this point on they continued moving very slowly.

They stopped when they reached a spot where there was about a thousand yards of open field. Out to their nine o'clock stood about a mile of open fields, leading off to a little creek. Straight ahead lay another village; this was where all the local Taliban lived. This was where the morning attack would come from, and they planned to have eyes on these guys long before the attack began.

By this time it was dark out, but the moon was still quite full. They moved off at the vector the marines directed at an extremely slow creep. After a short while one of the marines said, in a voice so quiet it was nearly inaudible, "This is where you guys want to be."

They stood before a small, well-built mud home, surrounded by another one of those area-typical big mud walls, with a locked blue metal door in the middle of it. It looked abandoned, but it could have been occupied. They had no way of knowing. Nick sent Finnegan, the comms guy, up first, because he was carrying an M4, a weapon more suited to a quick-reaction QCB situation, if one should happen, than Dirty Diana or Pemberton's big bolt-action .30 cal. Nick put himself second in line, Pemberton on rear guard. They stacked up at the door.

The marines, meanwhile, went back to set up in the open field, to a well-camouflaged hide site they'd already established out there on previous stalks, where they were going to crawl in and wait out the night.

Finnegan cracked the door a bit: a soft breach, no flash bangs, no running, no noise. If anyone was in there, they would have to tie them up and have them wait it out along with them.

Nobody. He slowly pushed the door open. Nick followed him in. They were through the door. They started clearing the place.

To the right was an outdoor kitchen setup with a roof on top. To the left, the actual living quarters. Then there was a small yard in front, with stoves, piles of wood, bunches of clothes, and other signs of active domesticity. But no people. Good.

Nick's first thought was to set up inside the kitchen area, with its little rooftop. They punched a small hole through the wall so they could look out with their rifle scopes and spotting scopes. Nick didn't like the position. It didn't give him the vantage point he wanted. It didn't give enough range. It just didn't feel right.

They continued moving, over to the left.

"Hey, man," Nick said softly to Pemberton, "we need to go up a little higher. I want to get a field of view, everything out to a mile."

If need be, Pemberton could probably make a shot out to 1,300 yards or more. Nick had seen him do it. The longest Nick had pulled off with that rifle was 1,800, but that was at a really high altitude, and on a steel target.

They moved on into a second compound structure that was a little more elevated, dug in their position, and set up their sniper hide and overwatch position.

They radioed back to the marines and told them they were set up and good to go. The marines had just gotten to their position and told Nick exactly where they were. Nick looked off to his left, directly at their location, and didn't see them. He checked the location with them to make sure he'd gotten it right.

"Yeah," they replied, "we're right here. We can see you guys."

Nick was staring right at them and couldn't see a thing.

"Dude," he said, "that's scary."

They hunkered down and waited. No moving. No talking. It was now somewhere between 2100 and 2200, or nine and ten at night. It was going to be a long wait till morning.

Off to his right Nick noticed what looked like a pile of clothes. He was about to push the pile off to the side—but then thought better of it. He decided he didn't want to disturb anything or do anything that might look out of place from the way things usually were. They wanted to leave no trace behind. He left it all exactly as it was.

He told Pemberton to take an hour-long nap. Finnegan was down at the bottom of their position, his back up against the wall. His job was to make sure no one came through the front door. He just sat there with his gun. Nick had no idea how he occupied his mind for all those hours.

I thought sniper hides were cool, he thought. *This is boring as hell.*

Nick thought about all the stakeouts he'd seen in movies. They always seem to have some kind of interesting conversation. No conversation here. Just the conversation in his own head, which he was already bored with.

He ate a little bit. Tried to empty his mind. Found it full again.

After a few hours he thought, *Screw this, man, I'm going to have a cigarette.* He had with him a pack of shitty Afghan cigarettes. He got down and put a hood up over himself, so no one could see the light flashing on the outside. Once the cigarette was lit, he kept the burning end covered. He knew that you can see that cherry-red ember from a cigarette a good mile away. If he were the one seeing that little red cherry in this situation, he'd just aim right at it and shoot. Chances were good, he'd hit the guy in the face. That was, after all, where the "three on a match is unlucky" superstition came from.

And it wasn't just a superstition. First guy: range. Second guy: windage. Third guy: BOOM.

Keeping his ember covered, he took a drag, then exhaled the smoke downward, blowing it onto the rooftop so it would spread out and be absorbed by the dirt and all the crap on the roof. The thing tasted like cardboard. It was the most disgusting cigarette he'd ever had.

Within thirty minutes he'd smoked the entire damn pack.

Now he'd run out of things to do.

He woke up Pemberton and told him they needed to start getting their targets set up and keep their brains moving.

They started by mapping out the pattern of how the wind was moving. Using their night vision scopes, they observed the tops of the grass and the leaves flickering on the trees. They knew there was a very slight wind coming off the creek, and they knew it was moving up toward their position. Good: they had a mild left-to-right wind. Every once in a while, it would change, but at least they knew its general velocity, which was about three to five miles an hour. They notated it.

Then they started mapping out possible targets and where they would come from. *If I were a bad guy out there, where would I be?* Looking at every single position, marking it in his brain, then marking it down on paper. They set up which sector Nick would cover, and which sector Pemberton would cover. "If anything starts happening from here to here, you engage, and anything from over here, I'll engage."

Then he started taking distances of potential targets, using his rifle scope. He knew the size of an average Afghan doorway, the size of an average car tire, and with those and a handful of other solid reference measurements he could work out fairly precise distances.

The distance from them to that building over there was 720 yards; to that one over there, 725; and on throughout the grid.

There were about twenty to twenty-five buildings in his sector; Pemberton had maybe ten in his sector; mainly it was open field. Nick thought, *If I were the bad guys, I would flank us to this open field, up to our nine o'clock.* He smiled. If that happened, Pemberton would just lay those targets right down.

Doing his chess thing.

Nick was no longer bored.

At midnight on the Mogadishu shore the dicier part of Operation United Shield began. Now that the Bangladeshi forces had vacated the Somali seaport to the north, it was time for the other half of the U.N. contingent, the half occupying the airport grounds, to pack their bags and leave, too.

Alex and his team had now been in place for about twenty-four hours, but the next twenty-four hours would likely not be so tame. There was no moon out (the new moon happened to fall on March 1, the following night), and the blackness could not have been blacker, the total lack of ambient light making the SEALs' night vision equipment useless. Whatever happened out there, he would have to rely on whatever illumination the marines created with flares or other spot illumination.

The Pakistani forces now commenced a maneuver known as a "passage of lines," a term that describes the movement of one entire fighting force through another fighting force's active combat position. In this case, the thousand-plus Pakistanis plus admin staff, plus all their equipment, would be withdrawing from the airport grounds, outside the secure perimeter, toward the beach, to positions within the secure perimeter, at which point they would begin the trek up to the seaport and begin the lengthy process of unloading their vehicles and ammunition and preparing everything for boarding, a process that itself would take nearly another twenty-four hours.

Passage of lines is a complex and delicate operation under any conditions. These guys were conducting it during the darkest nighttime hours, and with forces of multiple nationalities, both significant complicating factors. It would also involve not only more than a thousand troops but also seventy tanks and armored personnel carriers. It was enormously complex and would take massive coordination. The marines would be busy.

All through the night, the evacuation proceeded, people filing out of the buildings, boarding their vehicles and driving up to New Port and boarding the ships. As much as the spotty illumination allowed it, Alex watched the entire airport complex being gradually drained of its personnel.

At 0600, tanks rolled up to serve as security at the guard towers and other manned watch positions around the airport, as the last dribble of personnel evacuated their positions and headed northeast to join the exodus. The last to leave were a few dozen civilian U.N. personnel and a dozen logistics staff. Then they were gone, too.

Nine minutes later, a crack of sunlight appeared over the rim of the Indian Ocean. Then, in the flat gray half-light of early dawn, the tanks also began falling back, leapfrogging up from southwest to northeast toward the seaport, maintaining a sort of rolling security as they went.

By 0630, it was done.

Twenty-six months after U.N. troops first landed to commence Operation Restore Hope with great fanfare and high expectations worldwide, the entire two-year effort had packed up and gone home. The airport was now deserted. All that was left was a few square miles of abandoned sand, tarmac, and empty buildings . . . and the landing force, quietly watching.

Now the place was up for grabs.

Every night, as darkness threw a blanket over the day's firefights and temperatures in the Shahikot Valley began to plunge, the men with whom Rob and Tim had dug in turned their attention to an entirely different problem: survival.

Nighttime in the Shahikot was weird. For the men dug in on the side of the mountain, it was their downtime, since the firefights and mortar attacks and such would cease for the night. For the AC-130 Spectres overhead, though, this was office hours, and any sleep the men got was to the background rumble and boom of air strikes.

And of course they had to maintain steady security around the clock. One night a Taliban fighter walked right into their position, clearly not intending to do so. Whoops. They quietly bagged and tagged him. One less guy to shoot—and one less to shoot at them—during the day.

But by and large, it was not enemy forces that threatened them at night, it was the elements. Not the men hiding in the mountains, but the mountains themselves.

These guys were in extremely good shape when they landed in Afghanistan. In the airborne unit where they'd been serving, physical fitness is a huge thing, much like it is with SEALs. A short run was five miles, and doing a fast ten before breakfast was a commonplace thing.

They ran constantly, along with weight training, swimming, and various other kinds of PT. They were one physically fit team.

But those mountains did take their toll. They were doing a good deal of climbing up and down the slopes, in that loose-gravel kind of treacherous desert-mountain soil that can send you skittering on your ass in a heartbeat. And getting around on the mountain ridges was complicated. If they wanted to move one klick to the north to gain access to a different field of targets, they would have to climb up and down five, six, seven klicks just to reposition themselves at that one-klick distance.

Then there was the altitude, which made things worse. Being up at 8,500 feet plays havoc with your energy levels. (The cold and altitude even cut the life of their radio batteries in half.) This was the highest altitude at which either the Americans or Canadians had ever fought.

The big problem, though, was the cold. Severe, unrelenting, bone-chilling cold. The kind of cold that slips in through any available portal and silently steals your life away.

Back at Bagram, when they'd been told not to bother packing for more than twenty-four hours, Rob had gone ahead and packed his trusty little WhisperLite portable gas stove, some extra gas canisters, and enough food and water for seventy-two hours—and also grabbed some cold-weather gear: gloves and toques (wool cap, pronounced *tuke*) and neck warmers, things like that. He did leave his sleeping bag behind, but instead he took a ranger blanket into which he'd had sewn a zipper that would allow him to use it, if necessity called for it, as a lightweight sleeping bag. An American staff sergeant had glanced at this and said, "You know, you're not going to need that." He gave Rob a look that said, *Why the hell are you hauling around all that unnecessary crap?*

Rob rolled up the blanket anyway and tucked it into his waterproof GoreTex bivvy bag, which he stuffed into the top of his valise. Tim was doing likewise. A few Americans kind of laughed at them. "Hey, aren't you guys Canadians?" In other words, *What, you afraid of a little cold? Isn't it supposed to be pretty chilly where you guys live?*

But nobody was prepared for the brutal nights they faced on those mountains. Here in the Afghan mountains it went well below freezing at night, with the considerable wind chill pulling the effective temperatures even lower.

Rob and Tim would take turns, one on the gun and night vision keeping security while the other jammed as deep as possible into that zipped-up ranger blanket to eke out an hour of thin sleep, then trade places. One especially frigid night they huddled up together for a few hours just to achieve something vaguely close to warmth.

In the morning they would see the Americans, huddled four or five guys together, desperately trying to conserve some body heat. They saw the early signs of hypothermia. It was getting serious.

By this time the Canadians had gone well past the seventy-two hours they'd packed for, but the Americans were in even worse shape, since they'd packed for only twenty-four. At several points during those four days attempts had been made to resupply them, but so far it had proved too difficult and too unsafe; the helicopters kept getting engaged by enemy firepower. The Americans had already lost a few choppers and more than half a dozen men in the early days of the op, and command was now supremely skittish about sending any more birds into danger.

Not only had Rob and Tim run out of ammo, they had also run out of food. Rob thought about his recce course back in Fort Lewis, Washington. *A live chicken and a raw potato.* That was sounding pretty damn good right about then. He glanced around at the dismal Afghan landscape. They might as well have been on the moon. No chickens here, and no potatoes, either. *Nobody here but us humans.*

What was worse, they were also running out of water. They knew that soon they'd be in trouble. By the end of day four, that trouble had arrived. At this point they'd been a day with no water at all, and they could feel dehydration setting in. And they knew it was worse for the Americans.

But Rob had an advantage.

If he'd listened to what he was told and packed for twenty-four hours, he wouldn't have brought anything that wasn't absolutely necessary for a short mission. Why load himself down with extra weight for stuff he didn't need? But he didn't listen. Rob didn't grow up in the city, where you can get whatever you need by ducking into a store on the corner. He knew what it meant to improvise, break the rules, and survive in the wilderness. He grew up there.

He had packed for survival.

He had brought that WhisperLite portable stove.

On the morning of day five, after an especially bad night, Rob and Tim gathered up all the empty two-liter water bottles they could find, took a day pack with them, and started climbing, heading up outside the safety zone, bound for the snow line. Before long they were back up there, on their own, up where they'd first seen those Taliban footprints just a few days earlier.

While Tim watched his back, Rob set up the little stove and fired it up. He started melting snow, filling up their empty bottles one at a time, adding iodine tablets they'd brought with them to purify the water. It took quite a while to fill all the bottles they'd brought.

They set off down the mountain again.

Once they were back down at their ad hoc base camp, Rob went rummaging in his rucksack. Along with his other supplies he had also packed a sizable quantity of juice crystals. The Canadians liked this product as an emergency source of instant energy; it served almost like a jolt of caffeine, only less jangling on the nerves. And it took up hardly any space or weight.

He passed some of the packets over to Tim and they both started adding the crystals to the bottles, shaking them up, and passing them around. For some of the guys who had progressed further down the hypothermia road, Rob warmed the juice-flavored water over his portable stove. One by one, the Americans started showing a little more color.

The firefights resumed. Rob and Tim got back on their range finders and continued lasing targets, calling in coordinates, raining down death, until the long night came over the mountain once again.

In the early morning hours of their sixth day in the Shahikot Valley, someone finally managed to get a resupply drop to the unit successfully. When Rob and Tim sorted through the drop, they found not only enough food and water to keep them all going, but also an extremely welcome addition to the cache: more .50 cal ammunition.

Their two-day stalk was over; they were back on the hunt.

It was time to start pulling the trigger again.

From February through mid-April the level of violence in Husaybah continued to simmer as the city baked. There were random mortar attacks on the camp. Roadside bombs went off here and there, causing minor damage but in no discernible pattern. An IED would go off and a marine would get hurt. They would isolate the area, bring the dogs out, try to sniff out where the traces of bomb came from. They'd talk to the locals and HET would run their HUMINT sources. Nothing added up to anything significant.

Squads of marines from the line platoons continued patrolling the streets, but there wasn't a great deal they could do. In a way, the situation was weirdly reminiscent of Vietnam, only instead of melting into rice-paddy villages and tropical wilds, here the perpetrators would slip away into the urban jungle of this border town. A roadside bomb would go off, or shots would be fired, and the source would evaporate into the city landscape before it could be identified. They knew plenty of insurgent activity was going down. They just couldn't quite *see* it.

Except for Delgado and his team, who knew where to look, or more specifically, *when* to look. The line squads continued doing their patrols during the day. For the snipers, most of the important work was happening at night.

They did this for weeks on end, and they learned an enormous amount about how the city operated and what was going on behind the scenes. They saw weapons being transported in and out of trucks, men setting up what was clearly a mortar nest on the bed of a flatbed truck, improvised explosive devices being planted.

Meanwhile, Jason kept getting into trouble. Not intentionally, and not because of any attitude issues or insubordination. That chip on his shoulder that got him tossed out of his first indoc was long gone by now. What kept getting him into trouble was that he was shooting people.

There were times, as when they rescued the beleaguered border guard in Jason's first week there, when he would radio in for permission before he took the shot. But there were also plenty of times (like that amazing hip shot that stopped the bomb-maker speeding away from an IED explosion) when he just didn't have time to call it in. And every time, he got called on the carpet to explain himself. Another shot, another interrogation, and yet another investigation. Over the weeks, Jason got to know just about every lieutenant in Lima Company, because every lieutenant there took a turn being the investigating officer. It got to a point where it was almost funny.

Except that it wasn't.

For Jason this all only added to his increasing frustration. To the lieutenants, each one of these events was an "incident," like a police department investigating an officer who has discharged his weapon. They viewed Jason's sniper team as cops policing the populace in an unruly town that just needed to have civil order preserved.

Jason was seeing an incipient battle zone.

Jason knew one essential fact of life about the city: money drives everything. In struggling cities and neighborhoods where order breaks down and a more dog-eat-dog culture emerges, the crime world thrives. Corruption runs deep. Jason grew up seeing it.

"You're not going to piss on my leg and tell me it's just raining out," as he puts it. "I'm from the streets, I can see what's going on. I can *smell* bad, bro."

And the bad he was smelling was showing a pattern. These guys weren't smuggling goat's milk, they weren't small-time criminals, and they weren't just doing your typical border-town gunrunning. They were systematically moving massive amounts of arms, drugs, and money—bricks and bricks of American cash. Jason had never seen so much money in his life. And not only automatic weapons of all sizes but also tons of munitions: RPGs, mortar shells, 107mm rockets (a popular insurgency missile because it's fairly easy to fire with an improvised launching tube), and more. A full arsenal.

Why? Because they were funding a rebellion. They were funding a war against the Americans and other Coalition forces. From Husaybah the goods would travel along the Euphrates trade route to Ramadi and Fallujah. Husaybah was the gateway to the money and ammunition that was being laid in to make war throughout Iraq.

But Jason was the only one making these shots, because he and his team were the only ones in Husaybah staying out there in the midst of the civilian population, hiding out for days at a time, and getting to see what was actually happening. No one else was seeing the way this situation was developing.

After a while he started feeling like Dirty Harry: the guy out on the street taking down bad guys and pissing off his captain for doing it. It got to the point where he almost started second-guessing himself. Was he going a little *too* aggressive with these people? Was he making bad decisions?

Was he reading more into what he was seeing than what was really there?

Meanwhile, things kept getting worse.

- On April 8 a Lima Company patrol ran into three different roadside bombs on Market Street in the space of an hour. One marine was killed; six others were wounded.
- On April 10 a Lima Company lieutenant, Aaron Awtry, took a piece of shrapnel from an IED on his chin. Later that night another guy took an IED shrapnel wound to his shoulder. That same day a marine from Kilo Company, their sister company stationed over in Al Qaim, was killed by an RPG attack.
- The next day, April 11, three more marines were wounded by shrapnel from IED blasts.

On April 14 the violence intensified further.

That morning a squad set up patrol watch on the roof of a beaten-up three-story building, an abandoned hotel the marines had dubbed the Crack House. As they stood on the roof surveilling the area, a 155mm artillery shell buried in an innocent-looking pile of scrap exploded, injuring one marine in the foot and another in the neck. Someone on a nearby rooftop, no doubt watching for just the right moment, had triggered the explosion, most likely with a cell phone. Gunfire erupted in a firefight that lasted nearly an hour.

A sniper team set up less than half a klick to the northeast, on the eastern edge of the city, heard the explosion and got on optics to see what was happening. One of Jason's snipers, Matt Thompson, stood up to get a better look around—and a single shot rang out. *Crack!* The high-speed round slammed into his left thigh, punched clear through and into his right thigh and exited to smash into his holstered pistol. Thompson went down. Unfortunately for Matt, he was a lefty. Had he been a righty, his pistol would have been slung on the other side of his body, and chances are pretty good it would have taken the bullet. The bullet that penetrated both legs was a 7.62. Definitely a sniper. *Shit.*

It was touch and go there for a while. Thompson was hit on his femoral artery and bleeding badly. They got him safely back to base and medevacked out; he survived, but had to be shipped home.

At about the same time this was all going down, a convoy of vehicles led by Colonel Lopez was ambushed in the Husaybah-Karabilah triangle, off the northeast corner of the city. Lopez was grazed in the back but returned fire, killing a few of the attackers; his translator was injured and had to be medevacked out. A number of others were badly wounded. A squad responding to that attack intercepted a few vehicles near the scene, and in the melee that followed the squad leader, Lance Corporal Jason Dunham, threw himself on a live grenade to protect two buddies. Dunham died of his injuries a week later and posthumously received the Medal of Honor for his actions—the first marine to receive the Medal of Honor since Vietnam.

That was a hell of a lot of contact in a single day.

Jason was upset about the deaths. He was also pissed off that he'd lost one of his snipers, and the son of a bitch who'd hit him was clearly a sniper for the other team.

One more thing. The team at the Crack House had observed men firing on them a few houses away wearing identical black robes with red-and-white head wraps. The sniper element over to the northeast also reported that *they* were fired upon, from a different location, by guys wearing identical black robes with red-and-white head wraps.

That sure as hell didn't sound like spontaneous urban violence or random attacks. There was something coordinated about what they were doing, something intentional. It was like they were probing the Americans' defenses, pushing on them to see exactly how they would respond.

Like it was all preparation for something big.

Dawn finally broke in Helmand Province. Nick Irving sat and waited. For now, at least, the long night was over.

Just then Finnegan called over quietly; he'd just heard from the marines back at their compound. They'd decided they didn't want to wait for yet another morning attack. They wanted to take the fight to the enemy. They were on their way to join the group.

All riiight! was Nick's first thought. They were going to see some serious contact.

At the same time, it seemed kind of bizarre that the marines would make the decision to go in on the very same day that Nick and his team were out there, ready to ambush them. Nick wished they could hang on and wait a bit. He could already see signs of people in the village starting to prepare. He could see the movement, feel the energy in the air, that sense of something bad about to happen. He knew that very soon, the moment these guys presented themselves clearly, he and Pemberton could do some real damage.

The two snipers were perked up and ready. Nick had his spotting scope set up right next to where he sat with Dirty Diana, everything clean and good to go.

Okay, the marines were coming. So be it. Nick would support the overwatch. From his high-ground vantage point, he could see things the marines couldn't and was in a good position to take out danger before it happened, or call it out if he couldn't hit it himself.

Just as the sun began peeking up over the horizon, giving a grayish tint to the scene before him, he heard the approach of a column of Humvees. Then—

Ssssnap! Ssssnap!

Someone was taking sporadic shots at the marines. Nick heard them on the radio asking, "Hey, you guys see where that's coming from?" The marines in the Humvees couldn't see it. The marine snipers in their hide couldn't see it. Nick couldn't see it, either.

Then the whole area in Nick's sector started coming alive, people hustling, running around, clearly getting ready to fight.

Nick called over to Pemberton, "Hey, man, get ready to start dropping guys." But neither of them saw any weapons yet, so neither of them took any shots. So far, it was just a bunch of people running around.

The marines were getting closer.

Nick noticed one guy in his sector who stood out. Something about the way the guy was acting struck him as suspicious.

Gunfire erupted. The marines' column was being fired on. Nick heard their .50 cal gunners return fire. Their guys were in serious contact.

Just then the guy Nick had been watching ducked behind the corner of a small house. A moment later he reappeared bearing an RPG. Nick looked a few degrees to the right. A marine Humvee was approaching, closing in on passing the guy at a distance of maybe fifty meters, at most. For an RPG that's not point-blank range, but damn close.

He looked back at the guy. Sure enough, he dropped down to one knee and took aim. He was tucked into the corner pretty well; the Humvee driver didn't see him. Besides, the Humvees were absorbed in their own firefight, engaging targets mainly in the opposite direction.

From his long night of detailed calculations, Nick already had the kneeling guy's range: 743 yards. He quickly dialed the distance into his scope.

"Watch this guy," he told Pemberton.

"On 'im." Pemberton was already there.

The two didn't need to talk, at least not in sentences. For months they had already been operating together like a single organism, and a word or two was all it took to convey the necessary meaning.

On 'im.

Rog.

Pemberton's job was to watch the target and make sure Irving had hit him, and if not, then to see exactly where the bullet went.

Irving's job was to shoot.

BOOM.

The shot took the man in his upper stomach area. The guy dropped and folded, like a folding chair collapsing.

Up to this point the enemy hadn't suffered any actual casualties. Yes, they were mounting attacks on the marine camp every morning, but they were the type of firefights where both sides shot at each other but no one really hit anybody, it was just a bunch of bullets flying back and forth. (You might be surprised how often this happens in war.)

Now these guys suddenly saw their friend just drop, DOA. And Dirty Diana was wearing her suppressor, so the shot was quiet, too, and probably impossible to hear in the midst of the rest of the gunfire.

It freaked the Taliban forces out. They started shooting like crazy. One Tali fighter stood up a little too brazenly—Pemberton took him out with a single devastating explosion from the Win Mag. Now a barrage of gunfire started pouring onto the site where Nick and Pemberton were holed up. Nick and Pemberton returned fire, joined by their recce mate, joining in with the marines.

The barrage didn't last. After a few minutes the Taliban collected their slain and made a hasty retreat. Nick later learned that after that dawn skirmish, that marine unit never got attacked again for the rest of that deployment. The victory came at a cost, though: during the barrage, the marines had taken one KIA as well.

Just then they got a call from the other recce operators back at the marine base. Rangers from Second Platoon evidently had some intel on where their HVT was now headed and were on their way to rendezvous. Which meant that as soon as Nick and Pemberton could extract themselves from their ambush of the ambush, they had to get back and plan for the next mission—the *real* mission, the reason they'd gone out there in the first place.

When they got back to the marine compound they found four truckloads of men and equipment waiting for them. Second Platoon had arrived. Dress rehearsal was over. Time to plan and move.

While the platoon organized themselves and prepared for their nighttime departure, Nick lay down on the ground by a good-sized rock he'd noticed. Not much of a pillow, but it would have to do. He placed his head on the rock and stretched out his aching limbs. He was hoping to grab a few quick Zs. Aside from a catnap snatched here and there, they had now been up four days straight without sleep. A very long night.

It was about to get a lot longer.

IV.
THE SHOT

There will be no warning; no practice run; no opportunity to warm up or get ready. When the moment comes, the instant of reckoning, you will twitch your finger a fraction of an inch and send a copper-jacketed leaden missile hurtling away from you at velocities greater than the speed of sound, at distances of multiple football fields to a mile and more, through the corrupting forces of wind, air drag, variable barometric pressures, and unpredictable field conditions, to find its target with deadly and machine-predictable accuracy.

Taking a second shot will greatly increase the odds of your detection, and your detection may well mean your destruction, so you will want to make the first shot count. . . .

12
AMBUSH

Let your plans be dark and impenetrable as night, and when you move, fall like a thunderbolt.

—Sun Tzu, *The Art of War*

Mogadishu Airport, March 1, 1995

The last tank rumbled away in the early dawn, its low clatter echoing across the tarmac. Then there was silence. Alex Morrison and his team watched and waited. One senior Pakistani officer had predicted that it would take just fifteen minutes from this moment before the looting began. He was wrong.

It took a little over an hour.

At 0745 Alex spotted a head pop up briefly over the wall that surrounded the runway. A few minutes later, he glimpsed another. Then more, every minute or two, wide-eyed Somali faces appearing just for an instant to scope out the grounds and then ducking down again. He could almost see what was going on behind those eyes. Was the place really vacated? Was everyone really gone?

Then a trickle of people started slipping over the walls. The trickle turned into a stream, and soon they were everywhere, ripping off roofing material, stealing water, food, anything that they could pull up and take off with. In this poverty-ravaged country, anything they could get their hands on was worth something. There was no formation to it, no sign of any warlords or organized factions. Not yet, anyway.

That took just over an hour, too.

By 0900, as the looting continued, the warlords showed up.

First it was just a lone jeep coming in from the west. It headed toward one knot of looters, across the runway to the west, where the airport tower and the buildings of the main complex were located, and then someone in the jeep began shooting into the crowd—*Boom! Boom! Boom! Boom! Boom! Boom!* Civilians scattered everywhere.

Then, about a half mile to the southwest, Alex noticed another group of Somalis taking over an abandoned camp at the southern end of the runway, tearing everything apart.

Oh boy. Warlord Gang B.

At 1000 hours a deuce-and-a-half started gunning it down the runway with a quad antiaircraft gun mounted on the back, manned by a big dude sitting up on a chair. Behind the truck came a series of smaller Toyota trucks, each with 106mm recoilless rifles in the back, and then more jeeps, with Russian .51 cal DShKs mounted on them, and about fifty more guys on foot, running alongside the vehicles. The whole convoy was making a beeline for the site at the southern end that had been taken over by the other gang.

Warlord Gang B, meet Warlord Gang A.

As the convoy reached to within a hundred yards of the southern camp, it suddenly started taking heavy fire—not from Warlord Gang B to the south but from above them, off to the west, from somewhere within the large hillside that rose up beyond the runway, a dense urban area completely covered with buildings and narrow alleyways.

What the hell, thought Alex. Armed militias? Warlord Gang C?

The convoy swiveled to face the hillside and returned fire, launching their recoilless shells up onto the hillside, their quad antiaircraft gun stitching up every compound they could find. Then they did a quick about-face and started heading back up the runway toward the main airport complex to the north.

This was getting crazy. The SEALs were watching some kind of civil war/gang war shoot-out playing out right in front of them.

Still, it was clear that the shooters in the convoy had been very careful the whole time to keep their weapons trained *away* from the Coalition forces, both when they went roaring down the runway and when they went roaring back up again. None of this slugfest was aimed at Alex and his buddies. Not yet, anyway.

That didn't take long, either.

Shahikot Valley, March 9, 2002

When an American helicopter finally managed to get a resupply to the group on their sixth day in the Shahikot Mountains, it was a huge relief to everyone. Food, water, other critical supplies . . . and more ammunition. Finally, the Canadians could go back to what they were there to do: locate dangerous people and shoot them.

Except that the ammo was not what Rob and Tim expected.

They had radioed in and requested more of the ammunition they had deployed with: Hornady A-MAX match grade 750-grain .50 cal. This is a unique, very distinctive-looking round, its multiple colors reflecting the different types of metal used in its manufacture. Rob and Tim naturally expected that they would be resupplied with more of the same.

When they opened the box—surprise. A solid-colored, plain copper-jacketed bullet.

Fuck! This was not the ammo they deployed with, the ammo they had trained with, the ammo they were used to.

You don't just load your long gun with any available ammo. That's not how it works. Every load has its own specs, its own powder, pressure, shape of bullet. Its own personality. Which translates into a unique performance profile. And variability in .50 cal rounds could be particularly dicey. The bulk of military .50 cal ammo was manufactured to be used in big machine guns, which means it's intended to be shot in a general pattern, not necessarily with bull's-eye accuracy.

Hell.

They had no idea what this ammo would do. But, hey, it was ammo. *Whatever,* they thought. If this was what they had to work with, work with it they would. They had a job to do. So they got back to it.

Husaybah, April 17, 2004

When Jason Delgado woke up on the morning of April 17, his first thought was, *Shit.* He sat up on his cot, swiveled around to plant his feet on the floor, and looked over at Mavica and DelFiorentino in the next room, sitting on their bunk beds and shooting each other on their Xboxes. "You guys don't get enough of that shit in your day job?" he called out. They laughed at him and kept shooting.

Delgado was frustrated, and pissed off; worse, he was worried. In just the last few days he'd lost Thompson, one of his snipers; another marine had died; a third was back in the States in a coma; and there were a lot more IED shrapnel wounds going around than usual, even for Husaybah. To Jason, this did not feel like random attacks.

He reached down and grabbed his M40, taking it with him to the john. After brushing his teeth and shaving, he headed over to the COC (combat operations center) to find out what was on the day's agenda. Did anyone want his boys for any ad hoc missions?

Nothing in particular. Just another day in Husaybah.

Suddenly the base erupted in chaos, dozens of men running back and forth, gearing up for some kind of response effort. Delgado caught only snippets of conversation; snippets were all that was happening.

"Where you going?"

"Hey, what are you guys doing?"

"What's happening?"

Obviously something was up in the city. Before long Lima's third rifle platoon, a weapons platoon, a recon platoon, and a CAAT had all saddled up and ridden out into the city. It wasn't at all clear what was going on, but it had the smell of something pretty major.

Bits of intel started trickling in.

There'd been some kind of ambush in the northwestern quadrant. An IED had gone off somewhere in town and killed someone from one of Lima's weapons platoons, a young marine named Gary Van Leuven, from Klamath Falls, Oregon. Others had been wounded, and the platoon was now fighting it out. That's what all the react forces were going out there for. The focus of the fighting had moved toward the northeast, where a group of insurgents were using the old Baath HQ building as a stronghold.

Oh yeah. The Baath building. Where Jason had spent his memorable first night in Husaybah. He knew about that place.

Scattered reports kept coming in to the COC, where Jason and his sniper team stood waiting for orders.

At 8300 hours, Captain Gannon radioed Lieutenant Neal to apprise him of the situation. They'd succeeded in getting some of their wounded onto a bird and evacked. The situation on the street was a mess.

"I'm going off freq for a while to go develop the situation," he said, signing off.

He was, in other words, going in there himself to get eyes on.

"Typical Captain Gannon," says Delgado. "He was the FOB *commander*, for shit's sake, it wasn't his job to go out there and respond to this skirmish in person. But he went anyway."

It was the last time Lieutenant Neal would ever hear from his friend.

When Captain Gannon's react team reached the site of the firefight and dismounted their vehicles, they were immediately hit by an ambush, with a barrage of RPGs and small arms fire pouring at them from the Baath building. A marine named Gibson attempted to storm the building and was shot. Two others from the weapons platoon, Smith and Valdez, ran into the place, grabbed Gibson, dragged him into the courtyard within the building, where they engaged in a fight for their lives. It was not a fight they would win.

Captain Gannon went in after them. None of them came out alive.

That goddamn Baath HQ. As Jason and his team had learned in that first night, the place was not only the biggest building in the immediate area, it was built like a fortress. The marines fired a bunch of antitank rockets in there, but they could not make a dent in the place or shake out the mujahedeen who were hunkered down inside. They even tried smoking them out. No dice. Those sons of bitches were tough.

But marines don't give up, and eventually show of force prevailed. There were nine insurgents inside; they killed them all and were finally able to retrieve the bodies of their four fallen comrades: Gibson, Smith, Valdez, and the commanding officer of Lima Company, Captain Richard Gannon.

First Lieutenant Dominique Neal, Gannon's friend and second in command, was frocked to captain, the first time since Vietnam that a marine officer assumed command of a rifle company due to the combat death of his CO.

The day was just getting started.

Helmand Province, July 9, 2009

Nick Irving stood up, stretched, and yawned. He looked down at where he'd been sleeping: a spit of desert scrub with a small rock serving as his pillow. Not exactly the Hilton. Still, it was sleep. How long had he been out? He glanced at his watch. More than two hours. Amazing. Given that he'd hardly slept for the past ninety-plus hours it didn't exactly make him feel caught up; more like giving a starving man a single oyster cracker.

He bent down and picked up Dirty Diana off the blanket where he had carefully laid her down, then walked over to a knot of marines who were playing poker.

"Hey," said one of them, "we heard where you guys are heading. That's some far-flung shit out there."

Far-flung shit indeed. Operation Khanjar was now exactly one week old, and in those seven days the massive influx of American forces in Helmand Province had stirred up quite a bit of movement among the Taliban, which was probably why they were having such a convoluted time tracking down their HVT. The man now had apparently retreated deep into the Afghan hinterlands, in an area neither rangers nor, as far as they knew, any other American troops had ever ventured into before.

"Watch out for the Chechen," said another.

The Chechen, one of the marines explained, was what they called a sniper who worked with the insurgency in the area. Nobody knew his name, but according to his reputation he went back to the days when the Soviets were the occupying force. Which meant he'd been out there doing his thing for more than twenty years.

"He's good, man," the marine added. "He's racked up a helluva lot of kills."

Yeah, yeah, thought Nick. They made this guy sound like the bogeyman. Nick knew how these stories got exaggerated, and he knew that by now "Chechen" had become American troops' shorthand for "competent foreign fighter." Still, the jihadist fighters of Chechnya did have a well-deserved reputation for being exceptionally disciplined and well trained, and they had a long-standing enmity with Russia, which would have made them prime candidates for Afghanistan's guerrilla warfare against the Soviet Bear. There were Chechen and Uzbek fighters in the Shahikot Valley during Anaconda, way back at the start of this whole mess.

He made a mental note. *Watch out for the Chechen, Irv.*

As soon as night fell they headed out in those incredibly uncomfortable Amtracs. Nick could have groaned out loud. He was used to flying to ops in helicopters, where he could actually grab some decent rack time, but for this op helos were out of the question because they attracted too much attention. In those trucks, sleep was impossible.

The guys in Second Platoon were all pretty jacked up. Not Nick. By this time he was so exhausted that it took a constant effort to stay awake and alert. He found himself almost hoping they *would* get shot at. He figured the shot of adrenaline would wake him up. One look at Pemberton said he felt the same way. So did the four recce operators, and these were guys used to some pretty rugged conditions.

After about an hour of driving, they came to a sudden and unplanned stop. The terrain had gone from a rockier, hard-packed desert to a less rocky, softer surface. He looked out. The trucks' tires had gotten bogged down in the sand.

They were stuck.

Shit. So much for all their planning. Nothing to do but get out and walk, which was exactly what they did. With miles still to go, they began slogging through the sand.

Among its many brutal PT traditions, SEAL training is famous for long runs through the sand in boots. (That city in Southern California that the rest of the world knows as San Diego? To us, it will forever be *Sand* Diego.) That was exactly what Nick and his group were doing now: hoofing, in boots, now carrying on their backs all the gear they'd brought along in the Amtracs, for miles. To Nick it felt like walking through mud, every step sucking at their feet and pulling at their legs.

He reached back to grab some water, and realized he was completely out.

There was something horribly familiar about this.

Oh, yeah. Ranger School. Exhaustion. George Foreman. So this was why they'd trained so hard. For exactly this night.

Save a ribeye for me, George.

Mogadishu Airport, 1995

As the firefight between the different warlord factions petered out, something shifted. Alex would never know exactly what caused it. Did the group camped at the southern end of the runway think the Americans were supporting the guys with the big antiaircraft guns? Or were they just anti-American? Whatever the reason, Alex and the others now started taking fire, too.

At first it was sporadic. Every five minutes or so, they'd hear a few cracks over their heads, someone from down at that southern site taking a couple of pot shots in their direction. It was just harassing fire, really, and nothing very effective—but it was definitely aimed at them. And it was slowly picking up its pace.

Then things got a little more complicated.

Glancing up toward the top of the hillside on the far side of the airport, well more than a thousand yards off, he noticed a truck speeding by along a road with one of those recoilless rifles on back. It zipped behind some buildings in an alleyway and he didn't see it come out again. What was it doing back there? he wondered.

A moment later he got his answer. He saw a large plume of smoke rising from that location and an instant later heard that telltale screeching whistle.

Incoming!

Boom, the shell landed out on the runway in front of them. Not close enough for concern, but still. No one loves having 106mm shells lobbed in their general direction.

Alex spotted the truck moving to another spot, but it was visible for too brief a window to get a good fix on it. A few moments later, they launched again. Screeching whistle. This time, the shell landed in the ocean at the SEALs' backs.

This was followed by a fresh wave of sporadic small arms fire from the hillside, joining that from the southwest.

Then he saw a plume of smoke from an RPG launching at them from the hillside. It, too, went long and exploded over the ocean.

Alex was on the glass now, searching hard, trying his damnedest to pinpoint the guys who were doing the major shooting. But these were no random trigger-happy Somali citizens. They were smart, and they'd been trained. With maybe 150 windows directly visible up there, a guy would pop out of one window and shoot—or launch another RPG—then scoot back in, move to some other location, pop out and shoot (or launch) again, and then move again.

The cat-and-mouse game continued on for an hour, then another, and then into a third, as the sun climbed at the SEALs' backs. The shots still were not getting close enough to their bunker to be a critical threat. But they were getting closer.

Shahikot Valley, 2002

Rob and Tim grabbed up the tools of their trade, including their untested new ammo, and set out to climb again, this time moving to perhaps 8,800 feet, pushing the upper edge of the safety box. Far enough, in other words, to get maximum range but not get shot at by any snipers from their own team.

Once again, they began setting up their position: range card and target reference points, pull out the bipod legs, situate the long gun, lay out their new ammo, go through the sequence.

They located a target. They set up the shot, squeezed. Missed. And not by a little. By a lot.

Did it again.

They quickly realized they were not just off, they were *way* off. All their dope, all the data they had for their usual .50 cal ammo was nothing more than a vague estimation. Whether this was a lighter round or not, whether it had faster-burning propellant or propellant packed under greater pressure, Rob didn't know, but the moment he took his first shot with the new round he could tell it was different. It *felt* different. Different kick.

Adapt and adjust.

Starting with their 1,500-meter dope on, they started logging corrections and adjustments as they shot. Even as they were engaging targets, they were at the same time also collecting as much fresh dope as they could.

By the way, in the years since Anaconda it's been widely reported that the Canadian snipers deployed with Canadian-made ammo, and that this new ammo was an American-made substitute, with statements like "American ammo burns hotter," as if that were a de facto bit of proof of American superiority. Which of course is all utter horseshit. They were *both* American-made. There aren't any Canadian ammunition manufacturers. (Goes to show: don't believe everything you read.)

Whatever it was—the propellant? the bullet's shape or weight, or both?—they were getting a lot longer range from these bullets. In terms of performance, shooting out to 1,600 or 1,700 meters now felt like they were shooting at 1,500.

They kept pushing it out, seeing what the new ammo could do.

According to the manufacturer, the McMillan TAC-50's maximum effective range was 1,800 meters, or 1.12 miles. By now, they already knew they could shoot past that. Before they'd run out of their own Hornady ammo they had already been shooting out to as much as 2,000 meters—nearly a mile and a quarter. Now they found themselves engaging targets effectively at 2,200 meters (1.37 miles) and more.

They were already way past the point where dialing elevation was even an issue. There was no elevation dial that went to numbers like these. Once they broke the 1,800-meter mark, supposedly the outside limit of what this gun was capable of, it was all trial and error. And they weren't hitting targets on the first shot anymore. In some cases it took three, four, even five shots (something a sniper would normally not do, but at this range they were scarcely concerned about giving away their location to the enemy). But they *were hitting* them. They were eliminating targets at unheard-of distances. It was amazing.

The shots were at such extreme ranges that they were the only ones shooting. Most of their guys were packing 7.62s and .223s, and there were really no targets within sight for them. There was a .50 cal machine gun set up back in their ad hoc admin area, and on day two someone had opened up briefly on a few targets, but it wasn't that effective. Other than fast air, there wasn't a lot of gunfire.

Yet these two Canadian snipers were knocking them out there, sending rounds downrange left, right and center—

BOOM. BOOM. BOOM.

After a while they heard an American commander's voice come over their radio saying, "Hey what the *hell* are those guys up there doing? What are they shooting at?"

Rob and Tim were in an overwatch position, which meant in some cases that they were shooting directly over the heads of friendly forces downslope from them. Naturally, these guys wanted to know why bullets were flying over their heads when there weren't any visible targets.

Rob thought back to those first lessons in sniper school on how the human eye sees: shape, contrast, shine, skyline, and the rest. One of the biggest factors is movement. The human eye is keenly sensitive to movement, especially at the periphery of its field of vision. But at distances like these, the naked eye doesn't even pick up movement, unless it's really obvious or there's a shine or a glint or something that attracts your eye to that area. It's just too damn far.

No wonder the commander wanted to know what the shooting was all about. As far as he was concerned, there wasn't anything out there to shoot at.

Rob radioed back, "Sir, we know you can't see it, but this place is crawling with enemy fighters. You can't see them. We can, and we're eliminating those threats."

The reply came back: "Fire away."

They knew they were pushing the envelope. What they didn't know was that they were about to push it further than it had ever been pushed before.

Husaybah, 2004

Jason and his team knew none of the details of what had happened over at Husaybah's former Baath Party headquarters building. In the chaos and confusion of developing events it took a while for the information to reach to command, let alone to filter out to the troops. But they knew two things: their captain had been killed, and the shit was hitting the fan. There is nothing so galvanizing as the death of a commanding officer—especially one so universally beloved as Rick Gannon.

They took to the tower.

There were two sentry towers at Camp Husaybah, one by the entrance, and one they'd built recently out back by the border crossing. Jason and his snipers grabbed their heaviest guns and ran up the tower facing the city to start scanning for anything worrisome. Their first thought was that there might be an organized effort to storm the camp itself.

But once they got up there and looked, they realized it wasn't about a localized attack on the camp. The entire city was going off like a long series of lit fuses. They'd thought the main action was the skirmish that had happened out on the other end of Market Street, by the Baath building. But when they turned their spotting scopes eastward onto the city, they saw men in those telltale black robes practically everywhere they looked. It seemed like every rooftop within a thousand-yard distance had men in black pajamas brandishing AK-47s and RPKs.

"I've got guys over here!" shouted Mavica. "Guys over here!" echoed DelFiorentino, who was looking in a completely different direction. "Black pajamas over here!" "Black pajamas over here!"

They were on rooftops. They were in windows. They were running across the street with AKs and Russian Dragunov SVDs. It was crazy. Something was happening, all right, something on a scale and level of coordination nobody in Husaybah had ever seen before. This wasn't just random trouble in the streets and local dustups and pissed-off Saddam loyalists. This wasn't a series of skirmishes. This was a full-blown military attack.

This shit was organized.

This shit was *war*.

The observation towers were only three stories high, like many of the taller buildings in the city itself, but they gave the snipers a fairly good line of vision down the east–west-running alleyways of Husaybah.

They started sighting, aiming, and squeezing triggers, picking off targets at practically cyclic rate, that is, the maximum speed at which their weapons were capable of firing.

It was about six hundred yards from the edge of Camp Husaybah, where the towers stood, to the western edge of the city, which meant that however far into the city their targets were located, they had to add another six hundred yards just for their rounds to reach the edge of the city itself. Soon they were shooting out to 1,200 yards, 1,300 yards, and farther. On some shots the trajectory was so steeply arced to compensate for the extreme distance that their rounds would hit overhead power lines.

Jason started out on his M40, but soon swapped it out for one of the SASRs. The Barrett M82 is a monster, a .50 cal with a theoretical effective range out to a little over 1,900 yards.

They spotted a knot of fighters at 1,800 yards, way out in the middle of the city. At that distance, they figured the best they could do was make the insurgents stop shooting and keep their heads down. But their SASR was loaded with Raufoss rounds, which have both explosive and incendiary elements, and those rounds were exploding on the ledges and on entry points to the rooftops where these guys were hiding, so even some who kept their heads down were being killed by these 1,800-yard shots.

One of Jason's snipers pointed south (to their right) and yelled, "Truckload of black PJs—just crossed the border by the 440."

Jason swung his SASR around to the right, thudded it down on a south-facing sandbagged wall (the thing weighs thirty pounds empty, more with its ten-round mag attached), and sighted through the scope. There it was, a blue Bongo truck with a shit-load of dudes stacked like rounds in a magazine, all of them with AKs. The cavalry from Syria, coming in to reinforce their boys in the city.

Jason opened up on them with the SASR. The M82 is a recoil-operated semiautomatic and can pump out those .50 cal rounds, one after the other, at quite a rate. The Raufoss .50 cal round is capable of taking out a small aircraft; its explosive-incendiary tip can ignite jet fuel. It isn't gentle with human targets. Jason took all their heads off at the shoulders, shrouding the truck in a spray of pink mist. A strange image flitted through Jason's mind, of a gardener taking a weed whacker to a field of strawberries.

"Hey, snipers!"

He looked down and saw a lieutenant he knew, Aaron Awtry, waving up at them.

"Come with me!"

Awtry was a mustang officer, that is, a former enlisted man who circled back to come in on the commissioned officer track. Mustang officers tended to be especially well respected by their troops, and Awtry was no exception. Jason knew him as a solid guy and an excellent leader.

Stacked up behind Awtry was his platoon, Lima 2, getting ready to head out, along with first platoon from Kilo Company under Lieutenant Neal. They were the last two rifle platoons left in the base; everyone else had already been mobilized into the city to the northeast sector where the attack had happened.

By this time command had gotten a bearing on what was going on and realized that they were dealing with a full-out offensive. Under Lieutenant Colonel Lopez's command, the entire battalion was coming in from Al Qaim, and they wanted all available forces at Camp Husaybah to start squeezing in from the west.

"All available forces" meant Lima 2, under Awtry, Kilo 1, under Neal, plus Jason and his two PIGs, Mavica and DelFiorentino. There was no one else.

Roger that, thought Jason.

The three snipers scrambled down from the tower and headed out with the two platoons.

Helmand Province, 2009

For a while, Nick slept as he walked.

After a while more buildings appeared; they passed a dam and found themselves moving through what looked like the industrial outskirts of a small city. From this point on they had to be extremely quiet and careful. Once again, they were sneaking around the corners of houses and slinking through shadows, heading farther west and deeper into Helmand Province.

Finally, after about three hours of walking, the group reached the point, about a half mile from their objective, where the snipers and recce operators had planned to split off from the main element and set up a blocking position.

Had they been going in just themselves, without the platoon, they would most likely have opted to go straight to the building where their target was holed up, where they would then lay up for a while, just as they'd done the past several days, wait for their HVT to walk outside to make a phone call or something, and then make the hit. *If* he came out. They knew exactly what building he was in, all the way down to which corner of that building.

But it made no sense to wait for hours for this guy to emerge—possibly, maybe—when they were there with a whole platoon and assault team who specialized in exactly this kind of op. They had excellent intelligence: they knew exactly how many other people were with him in that building, exactly where he was, and exactly how to take him down. So the plan was for the door-kickers to blow the gates, barge in, and pull a classic snatch and grab. Nick's little group's job was to provide overwatch and perimeter security. To make sure no one came in or out.

Which was all good, except for one thing. This was supposed to be an in-and-out hit, all done under the cover of night. The fact that Americans had night vision, while the enemy presumably did not, coupled with the element of surprise, made this a slam dunk, or as close to one as any insanely dangerous foray deep into enemy-held territory can be. By the time daybreak came, they would be long gone.

Except that it hadn't gone that way. Once those Amtracs got stuck in the sand and they had to get out and hoof, their timing was shot to hell. Instead of sneaking in under the cover of night, they were arriving right at sunup.

This is not good, thought Nick.

Welcome to the jungle.

While the main element forked left and headed south toward the main objective, Nick's group split off to the right and headed five or six hundred feet to the north-northwest, into a wide open field where they had a clear view in multiple directions.

By this point they had broken out into the open and the sun was poking well up over the horizon, so they were completely visible. They moved very slowly and even more cautiously.

As they walked into their blocking position, standing out in a wide-open field, Nick on point, he noticed there were a number of small craters around, like perhaps mortars had been fired at this location in the past. One of these holes was especially large, maybe two meters wide and about two feet deep. He looked over at Pemberton and quietly said, "Anything happens, let's go back to that hole right there."

Pemberton gave him the thumbs-up.

They moved on another ten or twenty yards, then got down in the grass and set up their position, Pemberton on Nick's left, the recce team spread out to his right, and lay there ready to provide overwatch for as long as it took.

They tried their radios. Nick's had crapped out. So had Pemberton's. So had Derek's. Three for three. Army equipment: when you need it most, it isn't there for you.

So much for planning.

From where he lay, Nick had a view of a village ahead, about three hundred yards to the west, on the other side of a main road that ran roughly north to south; a small city skyline of relatively taller buildings directly to the north; and to their south, the residential area where Second Platoon was right at this moment slowly creeping up on their objective.

"Allahu akbar, allahu akbar . . . ash-hadu an-la ilaha illa allah . . ."

Nick heard the sound of early morning prayers floating in across the field. The little village to the west was waking up.

The sun was now fully above the horizon. Whatever meager advantage of semidarkness they had on their approach was completely gone.

Shit, thought Nick. *This is SO not good.*

Mogadishu Airport, 1995

At about 1300 hours Alex saw a small company of men gathering down at the camp on the southern end of the airport. He counted three carrying RPG tubes and one with a PKM, a big belt-fed machine gun. The others all had AKs. They started patrolling, moving around between the different buildings there. Clearly they were working up some kind of maneuver.

Sitting out on the runway and facing the Americans, another group of men had formed up into a classic C-shaped fighting position, with two lines spread out along forty yards of sandbags, some sort of abandoned checkpoint that airport personnel had been using before the evacuation.

Now these heavily armed guys walked out into the middle of the C formation and started talking with the men there, gesturing and pointing over toward Alex and the other Americans to their north. This was a troubling development. These dudes were not crouching up on a hillside more than a thousand yards off, they were standing on the runway, directly level with Alex's bunker, maybe six hundred yards away. Still at the outer limits of the RPG's effective range, but close enough to be a credible threat, should they start aiming in the SEALs' direction.

Peering through his scope, Alex focused on the man in charge, the one who was doing most of the talking and pointing. He was wearing a gray U.S. Army shirt.

Irony on the battlefield.

At that moment the gesturing stopped. Evidently the time for talking was done, because Mr. Army Shirt now shouldered his RPG, aimed it directly at the Americans, and started tweaking his sight.

He was dialing in their position.

Shahikot Valley, 2002

On their eighth day in the Shahikot Valley, Rob Furlong and Tim Mc-Meekin were once again perched on the crest of the valley, shooting at targets in all directions. Rob, who was on the gun that day, was scanning the area with the TAC-50's 16x scope; Tim was on the 40x Leupold. (They brought a second spotting scope with them, a 60x Leupold, but it was hardly necessary; the 40x offered magnification as powerful as they would possibly need.)

They saw movement on the far side of the valley to the west-northwest, up toward the Whale. It was a little compound of mud huts, almost like a ranch area, where the people kept their donkeys and such.

A few days earlier, when they'd been out of ammo, glassing and feeding coordinates to their fast air assets for air strikes, they had noticed quite a bit of movement over in that area, and they'd wanted to shut it down. But even if they'd had ammo they knew they wouldn't be able to reach it, even with their .50. They had called in some fast air in that area, but hadn't quite been able to nail it.

Now they spotted a three-man team heading out from that little compound, walking not exactly toward them but on an oblique angle to them. They were way out there, about three kilometers, or nearly two miles.

Stop for a second just to contemplate that.

Forget about shooting: just *seeing* someone at that range is an extreme accomplishment. If you've ever gone hunting or bird-watching with a decent set of binos, you know what it's like trying to zero in on an object at hundreds of feet, maybe even hundreds of yards. We're talking here about something at *two miles*.

The three suddenly shifted direction, altering their path so that they were now walking directly toward the Canadians.

"Hey," said Tim, "one of those guys has an RPK." Sure enough, one of the three walked with an RPK, a light machine gun, slung back over his shoulder. They kept watching, figuring that if the trio continued walking in their direction they might eventually come within range, and they could then possibly take them out.

But the walkers soon shifted course once again, now walking on a more oblique path, almost directly perpendicular to the snipers. If they continued on that path, they wouldn't be getting any closer.

They continued on that path.

Tim ranged them with his laser range finder. They were at about 2,430 meters.

At that point the two had been occasionally shooting at targets moving up toward that range, in the high 2,300s, even right up to 2,400. At these extreme ranges, though, a lot of what they were doing boiled down to what you'd call harassing fire: shots whose main purpose was to rattle the bad guys and get them moving out of there. But to actually *hit* the guys they were aiming at, at distances like those? Crazy. Insane. Nuts.

Saying it out loud wasn't even necessary. They both had the same thought.

Let's take him.

Husaybah, 2004

Every react asset the marines had was already out in the city, so the group headed out on foot, Lieutenant Awtry up in front with Lima 2, Kilo 1 following at a short distance, and Jason, Mavica, and DelFiorentino hanging back toward the rear where they could maintain the broadest perspective and be most effective as overwatch.

The column started out down West End and hoofed the mile down past the 440 to Route Train, where they took a left and began heading eastward along the bottom edge of the city. Jason assumed they were going out to help out some marines with cover fire. In fact, though he didn't know this yet, they were actually heading out to raid another stronghold that had been identified as a major trouble spot on the southwestern edge of the city.

After they'd gone a few hundred yards, Awtry called out to Jason. "Delgado!" he said. "C'mere."

Jason ran over to where he was standing. "What's up, sir?"

Awtry pointed over to the north, up at a rooftop of an apartment building one or two streets in. "What is that, up there? That someone on the roof waving a goddamn flag?"

Jason peered through his scope and saw a young kid standing on top of a rooftop water tank, waving a stick around with a white plastic bag tied to it.

He told the lieutenant what he saw.

Lieutenant Awtry looked at him and said, "It's your call, Sergeant. You can drop him, if you want, if you think there's something funny going on there."

Jason thought there was something funny going on, all right, and he didn't like the feeling of it. He knew better than anyone how common it was for the enemy here to use kids as intel assets. At the same time, he'd also seen local children doing something vaguely similar to what this kid was doing as a way of training pigeons.

For all his trigger-happy reputation, the truth was, Jason was fairly conservative with his shots. He was ready to kill without hesitation—but only the people he was sure needed a good dose of killing. This kid looked like he was about ten years old. And what if he really was just messing around with a bird?

"Sir," he said, "I don't feel comfortable dropping him. For right now let's just keep pushing. If something happens, then I'll take him out."

"All right," said Awtry. He looked back at the two platoons, then back at the city to the north, then back at Delgado. "I don't like this," he murmured. He turned around and looked behind them. Off to the south, a long trash ditch ran parallel to and a few yards south of the Iraqi Republic Railroad train tracks. It looked nasty in there.

Lieutenant Awtry nodded in the direction of the tracks and called out, "I want everybody inside that trash ditch for cover. We'll follow the ditch out into the city."

"Roger that," said Delgado.

It was, as he would later say, the single best battlefield decision he ever witnessed.

The men left the road and walked down to the train tracks, crossed over them, then dropped down into that funky trash ditch.

The air hung foul and heavy in the blistering Iraqi heat, the relative silence broken only by the *swish swish swish* of guys slogging their way through the trash and sewage and the sporadic muttered crack. "Hope like hell this is worth it." "Jesus Mary mother of God, this shit is rank."

And then the sky opened and poured down bullets.

Helmand Province, 2009

Just then Nick heard the putt-putt-putt of a small engine, and to his horror saw a guy riding down that north–south dirt road on a little moped, heading in the direction of Second Platoon and the target building.

Fuck! Nick was now staring at one of those classic dilemmas, like Marcus Luttrell and his team in the *Lone Survivor* mission. What could he do with this guy? If he just let him go on he would run right into the platoon as they made their way toward the main objective. That could blow the whole op. Worse, for all Nick knew he could have a suicide vest on and be heading there intentionally to blow them all up. While that admittedly sounded unlikely, it wasn't out of the question. These people had an extremely efficient grassroots intel network and could very well have foreknowledge of the rangers' approach. But if Nick made any move to stop the moped guy or ward him off course, he would be giving away his own group's position.

Risk the mission; possibly risk lives in the main element; or risk themselves.

No contest. He needed to stop the guy.

Nick raised his rifle and put his AN/PEQ-15's visible red laser dot on the guy's face.

The moped rider noticed the dot right away and came to a halt. A look of fear flitted across his face, which a moment later gave way to something like disgust, like he was thinking, "Oh, shit—*you* guys are here?"

He stood there on his moped for a few moments, peering around. It was clear that he couldn't see Nick or Pemberton; both of them had pretty well tucked themselves down into the dirt, hidden by tufts of grass.

Now Nick moved the laser dot down to his chest.

The guy looked at the dot, then slowly backed his moped up a little, turned around, and started off in the other direction, westward, toward the village Nick had seen waking up.

Fuck! Nick knew he was going back there to tell everyone the Americans were here. But he couldn't just shoot a guy putt-putting along on his moped. Even his ROEs didn't have room for that.

There was nothing to do but lie there and wait.

They lay there and waited.

After another ten minutes, Pemberton got Nick's attention. "Dude," he whispered, and nodded in the direction of the little village. "Big meeting going on."

Nick crawled over closer to Pemberton and looked over in the direction he was looking. They saw eight or nine guys in a huddle, what looked to be a gathering of elders or some similar sort of strategic pow-wow. The men peered over in their direction, much as the moped guy had done, as if they were trying to see exactly where they were. It didn't seem like they had located the snipers yet, but the direction they were looking in was pretty much spot on. They went back to their little huddle, then broke apart and headed out in different directions, each going out to his respective area of the village. *No doubt to go grab up their arms and get ready to fight,* thought Nick.

"Dude," he whispered to Pemberton, "we're about to get attacked."

He looked back toward Derek, the recce team leader, with a *Can I shoot now?* look. Derek looked back and shook his head.

"Hey, man," Nick called over quietly. "These guys don't have weapons, but I know what they're doing, and we're about to get attacked. Permission to engage?"

"Fuck!" said Derek, clearly torn. "No, man, you can't," leaving unspoken the self-evident corollary, *But I sure as shit wish you could.*

Nick said, "All right, roger that. But we're gonna get hit."

Derek thought for a moment and then said, "Hey, everyone, I've got a really bad feeling about this. Let's start getting really, really low."

Nick and Pemberton were already sprawled about as low against the ground as they could be; they couldn't get any lower. The recce operators start getting down on their stomachs, very slowly.

Less than thirty seconds later Nick heard a single shot go *sssnap!*—and then they were surrounded by a cacophony of gunfire.

13

IMPACT

Experience had taught me that warthogs who tough it out are better in combat than your natural gazelles.

—Richard Marcinko (founder of SEAL Team 6), *Red Cell*

Mogadishu Airport, 1995

Okay, thought Alex, *this is now officially going down.* Mr. Army Shirt was aiming his RPG tube up the runway, directly toward them.

Alex had his .50 cal up on the sandbags with his spotter right behind and to the left. Sitting on an ammo can with the Beast resting at about shoulder height, he found himself wishing he had cut a notch out of the sandbags so he could have rested the gun directly on the wall itself and gotten that solid bone-on-bone support. As it was, he was having to muscle it. That fucker weighed twenty-four pounds dry (just two pounds less than Furlong's big TAC-50), and it was virtually impossible to hold the gun completely steady.

This would also be the first time he had ever aimed at another human being and pulled the trigger, and his heart was pounding.

Perched right at the edge of the Indian Ocean, there was a fairly good, constant wind blowing. His spotter ranged the target at six hundred yards. Alex got his dope dialed in.

Mr. Army Shirt had his RPG tube cocked back. The rules of engagement were clear: they were taking fire, so they should have been clear to fire back. But everyone was still somewhat paranoid about those damned ROEs.

"Hey," Alex called out to his OIC. "Am I clear and hot? Am I clear and hot?"

"Hold on," the OIC shouted back, "I've got to call it in!" He got on comms, spoke a few words, then called back over to Alex. "Yeah, man, if they're preparing to shoot, you're good to go."

Alex had been in the armed forces now for eight years, but even long before that—for as long as he could remember, in fact—he had had dreams about being in this situation. I don't mean "dreams," as in ambitions or aspirations. I mean he had actual *dreams*: lying in bed asleep and having the vivid experience of being right here, right now, dreams of being in a place of mortal threat and facing the enemy, of being the one in a position to take out that threat. Of being the big-game hunter of the military, about to take down his prey.

Sometimes, though, those dreams would turn into nightmares. Those were the ones where he would see himself miss the shot.

He lined up on Mr. Army Shirt.

He would not miss this shot.

He squeezed off a round. *BOOM!* The monster Mark 211 bullet flew downrange, and the backblast from the .50 blew the binos clean out of his spotter's hands and nearly knocked the man off his feet. Fortunately there was another teammate up there with Alex, also watching with his binos. Alex shouted back to him, "Did I get a hit?"

"No," the guy called back. "You missed."

Shahikot Valley, 2002

Based on the previous two days' experience, Rob and Tim now had some decent dope for the extreme distances they were shooting with their new ammunition. Still, this particular shot was so far beyond maximum effective range, both for the rifle and for the scope, that they would have to do some serious improvising. Rob describes a lot of the 2,300-plus shots as being 60 percent skill and 40 percent luck—or possibly the other way around. But to go out 2,430 meters? That seemed more like 90 percent skill—and another 90 percent luck.

The tangle of complications is staggering when you break it down, strand by strand.

First, of course, was the sheer distance, which was so extreme that not only was the scope's normal capacity to adjust for elevation way beyond maxed out, but even the dope they had collected over the past few days was of only limited help.

Then there was the severe angle. They were, at this point, up at about nine thousand feet, and the little band of Taliban gunners were walking along the valley floor at probably eight thousand feet or so, so they were looking down on them at a fairly steep angle, about 40 degrees. Even if they'd had good dope for such a distance as 2,430 meters, it wouldn't work for this shot: if Rob used it the round would overshoot the target, because of the angle.

The angle was actually a help in one sense, in that it would allow Rob to shoot a little bit farther than if he and his target were both on level ground. Because he was shooting downward, the bullet could travel farther in its trajectory; you could say it was actually falling toward the target. Yet at the same time (just as when Jason Delgado would have to take out a crazed gunman in the streets of Baghdad a year later from the top of one of the city's tallest buildings) it added one more layer of complication.

There was also the altitude. The air was significantly thinner than it would be at more normal elevations. At Wainwright, back in Alberta, where they had first worked up their skills on the .50 a few months earlier, elevation was a little over two thousand feet above sea level. Here they were at nine thousand feet. Thinner air means less resistance, which translates into greater stability when the round enters the transonic range.

In the course of its flight, the bullet from a sniper rifle will start out in supersonic speed, then slow to transonic, that is, about the speed of sound. At this point its center of pressure shifts forward, causing a loss of dynamic stability. This can make it start to wobble like a slowing top, or even to start tumbling end over end. Once it slows further into the subsonic range it can become more stable again, but that transonic phase is a bitch. The thinner air to some degree mitigates this effect, adding up to good conditions for a further and more accurate shot.

The thinner air also means the bullet encounters less friction as it pushes its way through the atmosphere, which allows it to travel farther. Like the steep angle, this was actually another boon—but also another complication. Every thousand feet up you go means essentially a whole new set of equations. As the air thins, muzzle velocity increases, which increases both the velocity and precise arc of the round. It's a slightly different flight path—but that slight difference is enough to generate a complete miss on a human target on the other end.

Spin drift, at normal ranges an irrelevancy, also became a critical distorting factor at this extreme distance. By the time a bullet has traveled a thousand yards, its gyroscopic spin will have caused it to drift slightly in the direction of rotation—that is, clockwise—by about one minute of angle (MOA). At 1,000 yards, 1 MOA means 10 inches. This shot was more than two and a half times that distance (2,430 meters is about 2,657 yards), meaning that spin drift could have caused that bullet to veer as much as *two feet* to the right.

Then there's the Coriolis effect, the slight discrepancy created by the fact that the target (and everything else on the ground) is actually shifting its position in space as the earth rotates on its axis while the bullet is in flight. Coriolis has the most impact toward the poles, and the least at the equator; the Shahikot Valley lay just south of the 34th parallel, roughly on a par with Los Angeles. Not equatorial, but not exactly Siberia. The Coriolis effect is also most pronounced when shooting due north or south, least when shooting east or west. Rob was shooting in a mostly westerly direction. At least this was one complication that wouldn't be much of a factor here.

Added to all the other influences was the classic sniper's nemesis: the wind. Between Rob and his target were swirling not one, not two, but three competing crosswinds, each of which would blow his round off-course—in a different direction.

And his target was walking. It would take nearly four seconds for the round to reach the Taliban gunner's neighborhood on the other side of the valley. You might be surprised at just how far a guy walking at a good clip can travel in four seconds. Even if Rob's aim was perfectly calculated to match all the imperfections of flight so that the bullet landed precisely where the man was, by the time it got there, *he* wouldn't be there anymore.

In other words, he had to craft his aim to precisely compensate for:

- the bullet's drop over a mile and a half distance
- at a downward angle of about 40 degrees
- through air thinner than the thinnest air he'd ever shot in before
- with the wobblingly unstable impact of spin drift
- through the dragging effects of three separate and distinct crosswinds
- with ammo that behaved differently than what he was used to
- at a target he could only see, even through the rifle's scope, as a flyspeck
- and not at where that target was but where it *would* be roughly four seconds in the future

In a word, or rather two words: *rocket science.*

To all these factors, Rob himself added in one more, one that he knew should work in his favor: the sun.

If it was bitter cold at night in the Afghan mountains, it warmed up considerably during the day. In that high mountain desert terrain, they baked and broiled under direct sunlight all day long. Which had reminded Rob of that mental note he'd made back in 1999 when he was competing in Australia before he blew out his shoulder.

Laying the ammo out in the sun for a while before taking the shot.

High tech meets high touch: he had set out that hot-tempered copper-jacketed ammo to sit steeping in the hot sun, knowing it would heat the rounds' propellant and allow him to eke out just a fractional bit more distance. It might be just that fractional bit he would need.

Husaybah, 2004

Machine gun fire and AK bullets rained down on the marines from multiple directions, raking the lip of the garbage ditch they'd all just jumped into seconds before, the air suddenly filled with flying clods and spray of dirt.

They all froze. For a good ten seconds, nobody moved. To Jason Delgado and his teammates it could have been ten minutes or ten hours. No one did a thing or moved a muscle, just crouched there in that trash ditch, processing the fact that they had walked into a massive ambush.

Jason instantly understood what had happened. For weeks, the insurgents had been carefully tracking their every movement, learning their patterns, gathering intel, watching and waiting. The spatters of violence, like the small series of attacks three days earlier, were in part an effort to take out some of their key personnel; Colonel Lopez had been shot at, Jason's sniper, Thompson, wounded and put out of action. But more than inflicting harm, those skirmishes were further intel operations—probing, testing, weighing, and watching the Americans' responses.

They knew damn well there would be some kind of unit coming out to storm that stronghold. And they'd been ready for them.

Shit, thought Jason. That little kid with the flag had been signaling, all right. He'd been telling his handlers that a big juicy column of marines was down here on Route Train, primed and ready for the killing. The marines had been goldfish in a bowl. And an awful lot of them would probably be dead right now—except that the marines had done one thing the architects of this ambush had not expected.

They'd gotten down into that funky garbage ditch.

That sudden move to the ditch had been either a brilliant tactical move on Aaron Awtry's part, or a gut response to one hell of a premonition. Maybe both. It had for sure saved their lives. If they hadn't gotten off the road and jumped down into that trench when they did, they would still be sitting on Route Train right now, reduced to shredded mounds of flesh.

At the same time, that trench now also held them captive. Wherever the shooters were, they didn't appear to have enough angle to shoot directly *into* the ditch, but they sure as hell were chewing away at the edge of the thing. The marines had to keep their heads down. Even poking up to barely peek over the edge was a potentially fatal risk.

The stronghold site they'd been heading for was an apartment building, the largest of a cluster of five or six such buildings, located at the southern edge of the city about 250 yards down Route Train to the east. The marines' formation now stretched out through most of that 250 yards.

Jason heard someone cry out. A marine near the front of the formation, closer to the stronghold building, went down, hit by a round coming from the stronghold building itself.

A moment later a second marine was hit. This was bad. They were taking injuries.

They wouldn't last much longer.

Helmand Province, 2009

The sheer enormity of the noise was overwhelming. Nick Irving couldn't tell where the rounds were originating. It seemed like they were coming at them from every direction at once. Nick had been through dozens upon dozens of firefights, but never in all his deployments had he heard this much gunfire going off all at once. There were machine guns and AK-47s, RPKs, a few RPGs—it seemed like they were throwing an entire battalion's worth of arsenal at them.

Nick and Pemberton both jumped to their feet and scrambled. They knew exactly what to do: run like hell for that little hole in the ground Nick had pointed out a few minutes earlier when they'd been walking in here, and throw themselves in. It sure wasn't much, but what else could they do? Nick got there a split second before Pemberton and dove in, Pemberton piling in on top of him. Derek, the leader of the recce team, came running from the other direction and jumped on top of Pemberton. The other recce operators slammed themselves down against the dirt just around the edge of the hole.

Nick took stock of their situation.

The depression was about two feet deep. He was lying on his stomach, with two guys lying on top of him, but he could turn and raise his head slightly, just enough to see that the grass poking over the lip of the hole was getting torn up by gunfire. Dirt splashed up a few inches away from his face.

"Dude," he had to shout to be heard over the din, "we're going to die out here. That's a fact."

Both his and Pemberton's comms were still out, but Derek's (miraculously) had some functionality. He called over to the main element to see if they could come help them out with some suppressive fire.

"Sorry, guys," the answer came back, "but we're fucked right now, too. We're in a three-hundred-sixty-degree ambush."

Okay. So for the moment, at least, they were on their own.

In the process of diving into the hole and squirming around to avoid the gunfire, they had gotten themselves into what looked like a strange game of Combat Twister. Nick was now on his back, lying on top of Derek's legs, and Pemberton was sprawled out on top of him. He flipped over onto his stomach again and managed to get Dirty Diana up into position. He very briefly peeked his head up over the lip of the depression, caught some motion on top of one building about five hundred meters to the north, then ducked down again.

It looked like three guys, doing something. Something like setting up a machine gun. He needed a better look.

He started raising his head once more to peek out over the lip of their little foxhole. Just as he did he heard an extremely loud *sssssnap!* just to the left of his left ear.

He dropped back down on his stomach, face in the dirt.

As loud as that *snap* was, that round had to have come within inches of his head. And it was a high-speed round. No question about that. Nothing else cracked open the sound barrier in that intimate, immediate way, like a sniper round.

Was there a sniper out there?

Very, very carefully, he started raising his head just enough so his eyes could peek back over the lip again—and immediately the same thing happened: *sssssnap!*

Son of a bitch.

The Chechen.

Mogadishu Airport, 1995

The Army Shirt guy downrange was clearly startled by Alex's shot, and his reaction cost him a few precious seconds.

"Correction!" shouted Alex. "Give me a correction!" he called to the guy behind him with the binos as he went to reload the Beast:

Pull out the bolt—
Eject the spent brass—
Slide in a new round—
Slam in the bolt—
Ratchet it in and down and ready—

It felt like it was taking an hour.

Mr. Army Shirt now had his RPG tube shouldered again and was once again preparing to launch.

The SEAL with the binos said, "Shit, man, I can't give you a correction—I couldn't see where it impacted."

Motherfuck! thought Alex.

It was his nightmare come true. Not only had his first shot missed, but he also had no idea in what *direction* he had missed, and nobody could give him the correction he needed. And his fucking gun took roughly twenty years to reload.

Okay. The .50 was now reloaded. Alex got back on his scope.

Mr. Army Shirt was now seconds away from launching his grenade directly at them.

With no correction to go by, Alex had no clear information on which to base the second shot. He wasn't sure he'd get a third. There was nothing he could do but go by his gut.

When Alex went through the NSW course they started the students out on iron sights, just like Delgado's marine course. They had some civilian service rifle instructors there, who right from the start taught them a mental shooting program, something like the checklist a pilot will do just before takeoff.

"Front sight focus, front sight focus, front sight focus," they'd repeat, "breath, breath, breath, squeeze, squeeze, squeeze—" And then somewhere in there they'd suddenly shout *"Break!"*—and *Boom!* The shot would practically take itself. Alex had made that practice part of himself at the cellular level. It not only served as a solid checklist, it also calmed his mind, almost like a mantra in meditation, and helped ensure that the round would go where he needed it to.

Without thinking, he ran through his mental program: *Front sight focus, front sight focus, breath, breath, squeeze, squeeze . . . —BREAK*.

He took the shot.

Shahikot Valley, 2002

The scope mounted on the big .50 cal was a fixed 16x. Rob and Tim had selected that particular scope because it provided 120 minutes of adjustment, which at the time was extremely high-end precision. But that 16x magnification limit was now a serious handicap. Staring at the spot Tim was describing, all Rob could see was a tiny grouping of three specks. He couldn't make out any details whatsoever. If Tim had said, "The guy with the beard" or "the one with the long sash" it would have been meaningless to Rob. In fact, "the guy with the machine gun over his shoulder" was already more detail than Rob could make out.

The three men looked literally like three ants, crawling along the valley floor. Or maybe, three flies.

Tim, on the other hand, could see everything. He could tell that the guy in the middle, the one with the backpack, was carrying the machine gun. It was a classic shooter-spotter scenario.

"Okay," said Tim, "lead guy, not our target. Rear guy, not our target. Our target is center man."

Okay, the fly in the middle, thought Rob. *Let's see if we can hit that fly.*

"Confirm center man," repeated Tim.

"Yah," replied Rob. "Center man."

Tim lased him again with the Vectronix and gave Rob the exact range.

Using the mil dots in his scope, Furlong aimed at a point 4 mils high (about fifteen feet above the target) and 4 mils to the left (fifteen feet to the left of his target).

He sent a round downrange.

"Miss," he heard Tim say.

No surprise. And he wasn't worried. They weren't having any first-round hits now anyway, not with this new ammunition and at these extreme distances.

Tim followed the round's vapor trail, bringing every ounce of his concentration to bear on the tiny field of vision through that spotting scope. The sand of the Shahikot Valley floor was almost like fine flour, and when they hit it with a round, it would send up a distinctive *POOF!* of dust. Sure enough, Tim saw the splash as the .50 cal round hit the ground near the gunner.

Using the Vectronix's click-and-drag feature, Tim fed Rob a correction. Rob couldn't actually enter that data anywhere, because every adjustment he had was already well past maxed out, but he took what Tim gave him and translated it into an adjustment plotted to the reticle inside his scope.

Furlong ejected the spent cartridge from the first round, slammed a second round home into the chamber, then reset his aim, sent a second round downrange—and waited patiently for his round to soar across the valley.

One Mississippi, two Mississippi . . . or rather: *One Anaconda, two Anaconda . . .*

And saw the three scatter for cover.

"Fuck," said Tim. "I think you hit his backpack."

Wow, thought Rob. *Damn close.*

Although the Tali fighters scattered, they didn't do so very effectively. Confused about where the bullets were coming from, they were all still trying to scan locations out beyond them, in the opposite direction from where the Canadians lay. It must have never occurred to them that such accurate shots could possibly be coming from clear across the valley. So when they made for cover behind some dirt mounds, they actually placed themselves between their cover and the snipers, putting their backs to the hunters who were watching them.

Rob figured he had one more chance. After a third miss, chances were good it would finally dawn on his targets just where these shots were coming from, and if they then scrambled and put effective cover between them and him, the match would be over.

This one had to be it.

This time Tim didn't have to feed any data to his partner. Rob now knew his dope was solid. He knew everything he needed to know. He didn't need any further corrections. It was all up to him now.

He looked through his scope again.

For a moment he had a weird image. It felt like he was in the clouds, looking down at the earth—like he was in a passenger plane, looking out the window at cars crawling like ants across the plains below, only they weren't cars, and they weren't ants or flies, they were three people, crawling along the foot of a mountain ridgeline opposite the one on which he sat.

He squeezed the trigger.

Husaybah, 2004

As gunfire continued raking the edge of the trash ditch, Jason Delgado struggled to get a clear assessment of just where the enemy forces were located.

A barrage of machine gun fire was coming at them from the east, from inside the stronghold building itself, which, because it was the southernmost building of its little complex, had an unimpeded view of Route Train. The insurgents had set up a machine gun nest there with multiple machine guns, so that anyone who came down that road was going to get lit up in a big way. The gunners' view into the trash ditch wasn't perfect, because the ditch didn't line up exactly parallel with the building's location, but close enough to give them way too much visual access. The marines, especially those closest to the stronghold complex, couldn't hide in there forever. Two had already been hit by machine gun rounds.

And that wasn't all. They were taking significant fire from at least one other direction.

Jason crept up on the berm, and managed to take a split-second look around before ducking down again.

In that brief glimpse, he spotted two men on a rooftop, perched on a building due north from his location, that is, right across the tracks and Route Train and a few buildings into the city. One held an AK, the other a machine gun. Jason was in no position to range them carefully, but if he had to wager on it, he'd put them at about 230 yards. It was the same rooftop where that kid had been waving his little flag.

So that was it.

The enemy's plan was clear now. The marines would walk down Route Train toward the stronghold building while the guys on the machine guns to their east watched them advance, waiting until they drew just level with this second machine gun nest, the one to the north, before giving the signal to open fire.

A classic L-shaped ambush.

It was a solid plan, and if it had worked, it would have taken out more than two entire platoons of marines, plus the new company CO, since Lieutenant-now-Captain Neal was in the mix with Kilo 1. It would have been a devastating blow to the Americans.

Except that Awtry's decision to hit the ditch had saved their asses.

Still, they couldn't last long where they were. The ditch was giving them cover, but not complete cover. It wasn't that deep, and at the angle they had, sooner or later the shooters would walk their aim in closer and nail them. Plus they had fire coming at them from two directions, at basically 90 degrees from each other, pinning them into a vise that kept them at least partially exposed no matter what they did—and gunfire from additional fighters scattered everywhere in onesies and twosies only added to their exposure.

They needed some leverage of movement here.

What was the weakest chink in the enemy's armor? It had to be the machine gun nest directly across from them. Jason had to neutralize the two shooters manning the position to the north.

But these two guys were maddeningly elusive, moving around like crazy up there on that rooftop. When Jason first spotted them they were at the western edge of the roof they were on. Their building was adjacent to another, slightly taller building, which looked to Jason like they'd been planning to use for cover. In fact, they had probably been hunkered down behind that taller building when Lieutenant Awtry spotted the boy with the flag.

At the same time, that had also most likely prevented the two shooters from seeing what Awtry did when he moved his whole column down into the trash ditch. Jason now realized that the shooters may have been surprised when they realized the marines were already passing them in the ditch. They were expecting them to appear on the road.

In any case, now it came down to a duel. The machine gunner and AK gunner were ripping into the column but they were also moving around so constantly that it was extremely difficult to get a fix on them. They, on the other hand, now had a clear fix on Jason, and from the way their fire was focused right at his position, they had clearly made him their primary target. Classic battle tactics: target officers and snipers first.

Which made targeting them even more difficult, because now it wasn't just a matter of getting hit by random fire. They were expecting him and gunning for him.

The one thing going for Jason was, they didn't have the accuracy he did. They had an AK-47, a solid workhorse but not much of a gun for range or accuracy, and a machine gun, which was great for raking an area with random fire but not so great for target shooting.

He had his bolt-action M40A3.

Popping up and down, doing his meager best to maintain evasive action by being at least marginally unpredictable, running the math in the back of his head to account for the upward angle, Jason kept at it, trying to maneuver his way into a kill shot. It was maddening, like trying to thread a needle with gloves on while sitting on a bucking bronco. It felt to Jason that it took forever.

Finally, for a split second, he got the machine gunner in his scope.

This was the opposite of that high-angle shot in Baghdad. There he'd been aiming down at a target on ground level from fifty-plus stories up. Now he was at sub-ground level himself, aiming upward.

To compensate, he moved his point of aim to slightly above center mass.

And squeezed.

The gunner flew back from his weapon, dead before he hit the roof.

A perfect one shot, one kill.

Delgado racked another round.

And took the guy on the AK with his second shot.

Helmand Province, 2009

Irving figured the enemy sniper must have been observing them before the firefight broke out, because he seemed to know exactly where they were. And he wasn't shooting at anyone else. He had a clear strategy. He was going after Nick.

Nick knew the number one rule for a sniper in combat: the first person you want to target and kill is another sniper. The Chechen obviously knew that rule, too.

And he was pretty well dialed in on them. Every time Nick moved, another shot skimmed past him. The rest of the fusillade of bullets didn't bother Nick that much, because it was mostly machine gun fire scattering at them from what appeared to be either at or fairly near to ground level, and those rounds weren't coming in at enough of an angle to get down into their shallow hole.

This guy, though. This guy had to be in an elevated position, because those bullets were finding their way in.

Nick needed to pinpoint just where this shooter was located. Derek was a trained recce operator, a master of reconnaissance and observation. If they both took a quick glance at the same time, splitting up the general area where Nick figured the shots had to be coming from, they might be able to triangulate. And presenting two targets simultaneously might also have the effect of forcing the sniper to pause for a fraction of a second as he decided which target to go for. It was worth a try.

He communicated this idea to Derek. They crouched down together and prepared to work fast and in perfect synchronization.

They both raised their heads up slightly, about six inches apart—
sssnap! another high-speed round tore through the air right between
their two faces.

They both slammed down into the dirt again, Derek screaming, *"Are
you hit? Are you hit?"* and Nick screaming at the same moment, *"You
okay? You okay?"* until they each realized the other was shouting, too.

"No, man," shouted Nick. "I'm good, I'm good. Are you good?"

"Yeah," said Derek. "I'm good."

Okay, that wasn't going to work. This sonofabitch had them completely pinned down.

Still, he wasn't hitting them, at least not yet, which was good. Not
only did it mean they were still breathing, it also meant that his view of
them was not perfect. He could catch glimpses of them coming up over
the lip of the hole, and he was getting rounds on them down there, but
he couldn't peer down into the hole enough to see their bodies and fix
their individual locations well.

Meanwhile, Nick was still thinking about that group of three fighters he'd seen.

From the shots the Chechen had taken so far, Nick knew at least
roughly what direction he was shooting from: a little off from due north.
Call it north-northwest.

Nick told Pemberton to start shooting his big .300 Win Mag in that
direction, and to aim high. Suppressive fire—worth a shot.

Pemberton started cranking off round after round; BOOM, BOOM,
BOOM. He wasn't hitting anything but at least it gave Nick a chance to
grab another glimpse.

"Okay, slow down, man," he told Pemberton. Their ammo wasn't
going to last forever, and it looked like they might be out here a while.
If they lived that long.

In that brief glimpse he'd seen that little knot of three guys again,
huddling together on a rooftop at maybe five hundred yards, just to the
right of due north. It was definitely a machine gun team: gunner, ammo
bearer, and ammo loader. *Damn,* he thought, *that's exactly how we'd do
it.* They had just unloaded a belt of 7.62s at the Americans and were
setting back up to shoot some more.

"Hey," Nick shouted to Derek, "I've got three guys up here with a
machine gun!"

Derek's reply was eloquent in its economy. "Shoot them!"

Being down in the depression, with those three guys on the rooftop
of a fairly tall building, Nick already had Dirty Diana positioned at a
pretty good upward angle and didn't really need to raise his head to

shoot. He just pushed his gun barrel up over the lip of the hole and nuzzled it through the grass there, his scope sticking up just enough so that he could get a line of sight.

He got the three guys on his scope and dialed in. He thought it had to be the most uncomfortable, unorthodox firing position he'd ever shot from.

He squeezed the trigger.

And missed. High and to the right.

He compensated for elevation and windage, and fired again. His second shot connected with the gunner right in the upper corner of his chest. He spun away from the gun and disappeared.

Now a second member of the team jumped into the first guy's place behind the machine gun, placing himself right in the spot Nick already had dialed in. *Thank you very much,* thought Irving, *And have a nice day,* as he squeezed the trigger and watched this round slam into the second guy and hurl him backward, too. *Next in line, please?*

But the third member of the machine gun team wasn't playing. He started grabbing a few ammo belts. From his cramped and contorted firing position, Nick knew he probably wouldn't hit this one, but he put a few rounds up there anyway, just to say, *Hey, don't come back to this position again. Leave the gun. And don't take the cannoli.* The guy ran.

Other than those three up on the rooftop, Nick wasn't able to locate any other shooters visually, but he sure could hear a hell of a lot going on, as the thunderstorm of gunfire continued.

This wasn't just a massive force of guys with guns. They were *good.* They had foreign professionals in there working with them, Chechens, Uzbeks, Pakistanis, hard-core fighters who trained them in how to work together as an effective fighting force. To Nick, it was eerie, almost as if they were fighting another ranger platoon, their movements were so efficiently organized.

At one point he heard footsteps slapping the ground very close by, and someone screaming *"Allah akbar!"* They were closing in.

Time to call in the bombs.

Derek grabbed his radio, fortunately (and miraculously) still functional, and keyed in his CO's RTO.

"Hey, we need air support, now! We're about to get captured or killed. Repeat: We are in immediate danger! Multiple enemy positions, request ordnance drops on all."

And now they came face-to-face with what may be the Spec Ops warrior's greatest enemy, worst nightmare, and true nemesis:

Rules of engagement.

This was 2009, remember. The American public was tired of war. Our economy was in the tank. Resources, patience, and political will were all stretched paper-thin. At this point the political leadership wanted the war to wind down, not escalate. We were supposed to be helping these people rebuild, not messing up their infrastructure.

Which meant that, even though Nick and his group were ridiculously outnumbered by a massive enemy force and all about to be killed, they couldn't get an air strike—because it would hurt too many buildings.

"Sorry," came the answer, "we can't drop any bombs there because we can't accept anything over a point-one percent collateral damage." In other words, there couldn't be a building even anywhere in sight of where they dropped a bomb.

Now Derek was cursing a blue streak over the radio. But they wouldn't budge.

Derek called back up and said, "Hey, drop bombs right here, right on us. We're a minimum safe distance from those buildings. Just drop on our position."

What the hell, he figured, they were going to die out there anyway, at least this way they could take some of these bad guys with them. But they wouldn't do that, either. Instead, they sent in a B-2 stealth bomber and an F-16 to fly some three hundred feet overhead and drop a few flares.

That was it. That was the air support.

Nick couldn't believe this was happening. What was a quick over-flight supposed to do, frighten the enemy into dropping their guns, picking up their skirts, and running away? What were they *thinking*?

Of course it had no effect whatsoever.

The pace of the attack intensified.

Mogadishu Airport, 1995

That second shot felt good to Alex. He had the fleeting thought, *I had to have gotten close that time*—but he hadn't had time to follow the round in his scope. The moment the shot was away he had to pour himself into the mechanics of the reload—

Pull out bolt—
Eject spent brass—
Slide in new round—

Slam bolt home—
Ratchet, in and down—

The comms guy had by now grabbed the spotting scope and moved a little farther away so he would be safely out of the Beast's backblast. His eye was glued to the glass, watching Alex's shot go downrange.

As Alex went through the whole reload routine he heard small arms rounds coming in overhead—*dg, dg, dg, dg, dg, dg, dg, dg*. Slamming the Beast back down onto his sandbag rampart to get ready for a third shot, he called back to the comms operator, "Gimme a correction."

The comms guy said, *"Son of a bitch."*

"What's the correction, man?" repeated Alex. "Give me a fucking correction!"

Instead of answering, the comms guy just said, "God . . . *damn.*"

"Where'd the round hit?" shouted Alex. He reached over with his hand and gave the guy a whack. He needed that correction!

The comms guy wasn't even hearing him. He was glued to that spotting scope. "Man, that *had* to hurt."

"What do you mean?" Alex shouted. *"What* had to hurt?"

"That guy is *down,*" the comms guy said. Alex's second shot—the one he'd made with no data to go on, no correction, on pure sniper's instinct—had nailed the guy dead center. The RPG tube lay on the ground where it had dropped. Mr. Army Shirt was history.

It was Alex's first kill shot, and if it had come half a minute later, it might have never come at all.

But there was no time to reflect on that, or reflect on anything, for that matter. The men around Mr. Army Shirt were now opening fire on the Americans.

He got back on the gun.

Shahikot Valley, 2002

Furlong's .50 cal emitted one more BOOM as his third round exploded from the barrel, traveling at 2,700 feet per second, nearly 2,000 miles per hour, well more than twice the speed of sound. Yet even at that blinding speed the copper-jacketed slug would be flying for nearly four full seconds on its long arced journey over the valley floor below . . .

One Anaconda . . .

. . . pulled first in one direction by the first crosswind, then another by the second, and still another by the third, arcing up, up, up like a two-thousand-mile-an-hour pitch from a pitcher's mound toward a home plate a mile and a half away, too far for the naked eye to see . . .

Two Anaconda . . .

. . . up, up, up until it reached a point, a little past midway, at which its trajectory flattened to zero arc and it began its inevitable downward arc . . .

Three Anaconda . . .

. . . now plummeting to meet that point where the imperfection of aim meets the corruptions of air and gravity to cancel each other out in a fraction of a second of calculated perfection—

Husaybah, 2004

Delgado had taken out the machine gun nest directly across the street, neutralizing the short end of the isosceles triangle that had the entire platoon pinned down. That at least bought them some slight freedom of movement. But the barrage of gunfire coming from the east, from the stronghold building, was a bigger problem. There were too many guns in that building for Jason to locate, let alone to take out one by one. And they were all still being shot at from multiple other directions, too.

Something big needed to happen, or they were all going to die. It was that simple.

They needed bigger guns.

What Jason really needed now was not his rifle but his radio. But Josh Mavica, who was serving as his RTO, was tens of yards away, hunkered down in the ditch like everyone else.

"Mavica," Jason yelled. "Come to me, bitch! 'Cause I'm sure as hell not going to you!"

Someone by his shoulder laughed—DelFiorentino, probably. Delgado laughed, too. Hey, there was an excellent chance they would all be dead within the next ten to fifteen minutes. Sometimes you just have to laugh; it's the only thing that keeps you going.

He heard Mavica say, "Oh, *shit,*" then yell out, "Okay!"

"Wait!" shouted Jason. He turned to DelFiorentino and yelled, "Pop smoke!" They popped off some high-concentrate smoke right there in the ditch and tossed it out into the street. That HC smoke is amazing stuff, it can give you a football field's worth of total visual obscurity. Jason hoped he'd created enough of a temporary curtain to hide his RTO's next move.

The moment after they popped those two HC smokes Jason saw

Mavica lurch to his feet and make a Medal of Honor run toward him, bullets smacking the desert hardpack on either side of him as he ran, and the next moment he was sliding into Jason on a skid of trash like a base runner making an extremely close inside-the-park home run.

Jason got up close to Mavica and together they called for 81mm light mortar fire. (81mm is considered "light"; "heavy" mortar rockets are 120mm and bigger.) The light mortar platoon, back at Camp Husaybah a solid mile-plus away, responded.

The first few rounds hit a few hundred yards long.

Jason grabbed their Vectronix range finder—nearly identical to the one Rob Furlong and Tim McMeekin had used two years earlier in the Shahikot Valley—and trained it on the splash where those mortar rounds were hitting, double-clicked the Vector, went back to the main machine gun position they were trying to take out, clicked on that, and had his correction.

"Drop two hundred, fire for effect!"

Jason didn't know how in God's name they did it, but the mortar guys had their shit so dialed in that, out of that whole apartment complex, they managed to hit that one building dead on.

When the mortar rounds hit, something inside the house—propane tanks, Jason guessed or possibly munitions—detonated sympathetically. The house became a raging inferno.

In the temporary lull that followed the explosion of the stronghold building, they needed medevac for their wounded, and they needed it fast, because even though the machine gun nests were gone there was still a constant hail of gunfire coming their way, and it was already picking up steam again.

But all their medevac assets were gone. All that was left back at the camp was a lone Humvee and a seven-ton, which was a logistics vehicle. Word came back that the seven-ton was on its way—and then they saw it, hurtling down West End and banging a left at Route Train. It reached them and rolled up to the head of the line, where the wounded were, and pulled to a stop.

As it did, a rocket-propelled grenade streaked across the way and slammed into its fuel tank.

Everybody braced for the explosion.

Nothing happened.

Incredibly, even though the RPG had pierced the truck's fuel tank, it somehow failed to ignite the fuel. Now, however, the truck was spraying fuel everywhere. The marines hastily loaded their injured onto the seven-ton. The truck turned around and started making its way back westward. As it drove past Jason and the others, it doused them with gasoline.

To this day, says Jason, he tends to freak out every time he smells gasoline.

They were now in a good news, bad news situation.

The good news was, they had now neutralized both arms of the L-shaped ambush's pincers, Delgado's two shots taking out the machine gun nest across the street, and the mortar assist destroying the nests in the stronghold building.

The bad news was, they were still pinned down. Because by this time a mob of fighters had mobilized in multiple locations and were raking them with gunfire from rooftop after rooftop after rooftop. They were being hit from every direction imaginable. It seemed to Delgado that the city was suddenly alive with eyes, all attached to fingers on automatic weapons, and all trained on them. This was beyond the snipers' capacity to shoot at, beyond the capacity to call in mortar fire on. They were being shot at by an entire city.

So that was it. *This is where you put your head down between your legs,* thought Delgado, *and kiss your ass good-bye.*

Helmand Province, 2009

Once again, Nick took stock. Their platoon was pinned down in their own firefight a thousand yards away and couldn't come help them. They couldn't get any air support. They really, truly were on their own. Completely.

Okay.

Chess.

Who do you need to take off the board, Irv? Queen? Bishop? Knight?

Sniper.

Despite the barrage of gunfire coming at them from multiple directions, the single greatest threat they faced right now was that sniper, because he was targeting them more accurately than anyone on the board. He had to deal with the Chechen. Which presented a challenge: he didn't know exactly where the guy was located. And he couldn't get on ground level with eyes and scope long enough to scan the area and find him.

Countersniping: going sniper to sniper. In all his training, they really hadn't spent much time on this topic. The speech Nick remembered getting in one of his sniper schools went something like this:

"If you ever find yourself up against a serious sniper, number one, you're a lucky son of a bitch, and number two, just drop a JDAM on 'im. Don't ever go out there and try to duke it out with the guy, 'cause you have no idea what his skill set is."

Good advice.

No help here.

There weren't any JDAMs coming their way, and as far as whether to go up and duke it out with the guy, Nick didn't have the luxury of choice. He was in a corner and on his own—up against a sniper who'd been picking off Soviet soldiers years before Nick was born.

Nick had always wanted to follow in Carlos Hathcock's footsteps.

Well, here he was.

Only for the next few moments he *wasn't* here. He was back at home in Jessup, Maryland, a high school sophomore, watching a video of an old documentary from the sixties. Staring at the TV set, he was listening to a grizzled old sniper talk on-screen about the snap-bang theory.

"When you hear that snap," the guy was saying, "you start counting from one to five in the space of one second, 1-2-3-4-5. Whatever number you land on by the time you hear the bang is how far away the guy is."

A quick-and-dirty method of ranging by ear, the guy explained, this works exactly the same way as judging the distance of a thunderstorm: when you see the lightning flash, you count until you hear thunder—counting the seconds, in other words, until the sound waves from the lightning catch up to the speed of light. Only in this case, you're counting fractions of a second.

Because the sniper's bullet travels faster than the speed of sound, the *sssnap!* of the bullet cracking the sound barrier as it passes your ear (the "lightning") happens well before the *bang* of the rifle's report—that is, the initial explosion of powder that started the bullet's journey: the "thunder"—reaches your ear. Exactly how long that gap is depends on the exact speed of that particular bullet. A typical sniper round will leave the muzzle at a velocity of about 2,700 fps, or 900 yards per second, but start slowing almost immediately. This equation was supposed to work up to about five hundred yards, by which point the bullet will have slowed down to more or less 1,800 fps, depending on altitude and other environmental conditions. The way the math and physics work out, you can estimate that the gap between bullet's flight and sound's flight will be about one hundred yards per one fifth of a second.

Thus: when you hear the *ssssnap!* you count to five in the space of one second, and when you hear the *bang,* you've got your range.

What the hell. Nick decided to give this snap-bang theory a shot.

To do it, he needed to get the Chechen to shoot at him once more. Which was insane, because he'd been getting closer and closer with each shot.

The shooter's elevation was spot on. The only reason he hadn't hit one of them yet was that his rounds were missing them laterally, to the right or to the left. Nick understood that the only thing messing with the Chechen's perfectly placed shots was the wind.

They'd been out there for a few hours now, and the hot desert sun was well over the horizon. As it struck the ground at different points and heated up different features of the landscape at different rates, this produced temperature differentials that generated a variable wind, what the snipers called a "shift wind." It was the hardest kind of wind to read correctly, because it was fishtailing and constantly changing.

So far, it had saved their lives. Had it been high noon, when it would become completely calm, they would have been dead already.

And at that, it wouldn't save them long, because the Chechen was missing only by inches. Every shot got closer and closer. Two inches. An inch. A half inch. Within another five or ten minutes, without question, he would connect with at least a body part, if not a head.

For all Nick knew that five or ten minutes might already be up; the sniper might have finally gotten him perfectly dialed in. Or he might just get lucky this time. But Nick didn't see any other option. He needed the shot to take the range.

Here goes.

He poked his head up again, and the moment he did he heard another loud *sssnap!* of another supersonic round creasing the air right next to his head. As he ducked back down he immediately started his rapid count:

One–two–three–four–fi—

Boom! He heard the thunder of the sniper rifle's report just before completing his five-count.

Shit. This guy was barely five hundred yards away. For a machine gun nest, five hundred yards was pretty far. For a sniper, it was like reaching across the dining room table. This was bad.

Okay, he had range: five hundred yards. But five hundred yards, where? There were dozens of buildings out there. And he couldn't exactly pop his head up to scan them all.

But then, he didn't have to pop his head up, did he? He didn't need to physically look at all those buildings. He already had them all stored in his brain.

Keep in memory.

This was just like the KIMS games in sniper school. Although pulling off memory tricks when you're sitting in Fort Benning is one thing. When you're pinned to the ground like a bug by expert sniper fire, after five days of no sleep, things are a little different. And the barrage of gunfire was continuing around him without letup. He was dimly aware that Pemberton sighted a guy on a rooftop at about a thousand yards, ten football fields. Boom. He dropped him. *Nice work, Mike.* But Nick wasn't thinking about that. He couldn't afford to think about any of it right now.

Never mind. Just get the job done.

Irving lay back in that hole and closed his eyes. He let the image of the entire scene come up, and scanned it in his mind:

Over there, at about one o'clock, was where the machine gun nest was that Nick took care of . . . but the Chechen's shots didn't come from there, did they? No. Scanning left, scanning left . . . there!

He recalled one tall building, about two hundred yards to the left of center. Its window was open, covered by a black curtain. That looked like an excellent position.

If it were me out there, he thought, *that's where I'd be.*

He smiled.

I've got you, he thought.

He opened his eyes.

He quickly detailed to Pemberton where the building was and told him to train his Win Mag scope on that window. "I'm going to make a bunch of movement. If you see something happening there, shoot it."

He wasn't about to pick his head up again, but he didn't think he needed to. He would just start moving around in his foxhole, making it look like he was about to get up, jump to his feet and start running or something, and as he did—*sssssnap!* A round smacked the ground right behind him.

"I saw him!" Pemberton yelled. "I fucking saw him!"

Just before the round hit Pemberton had seen the curtain move and a little flash go off.

They'd found him.

Nick leapt up and they both started putting rounds on that window. A moment later one of Pemberton's big .300 rounds hit the curtain and made it move again. He'd put a round right through it.

But the Chechen wasn't there anymore.

He was still shooting at them, and doing a damn decent job of keeping them pinned down, if not quite as well as before. How could he be shooting at them if he wasn't there?

Nick knew exactly what he'd done. He'd pulled back to a position deep in that room, and instead of firing at them through the window he was now firing through a small hole in the wall somewhere.

It's called "loophole shooting." It was damnably difficult but not really new: in principle, it was essentially the same thing as medieval archers shooting through the tiny slits in a castle's crenellated walls. Only with the archer sitting maybe ten or twelve feet back. At a target five football fields away. And being pretty damn spot on.

This was one of the many innovations Eric and I learned about at the NSW course, when we would debrief our graduates as they rotated back from deployment. By 2006 we were showing our guys how to build shooting loopholes, and how to defend against them. By the time Nick was being pinned down in Helmand Province, this feature had already shown up on the menu at other sniper courses, too—including some of the advanced courses Nick went through. Later that year, the fall 2009 International Sniper Competition would feature a loophole shooting event for the first time, testing marksmen's ability to shoot from a third-story rafter through a three-inch hole and strike a target 150 meters away.

Meanwhile, the Chechen was practicing his own version of that competition event, with Nick as target. And while he wasn't doing bad, it was a losing proposition. After having Nick backed into a corner for hours, Nick had now turned the tables and backed him into a corner himself.

There was no way they were going to nail that sniper now, but at least they'd located him and forced him back into the depths of his aerial hide. They hadn't bought their safety, but they'd at least bought a little freedom to move.

And perhaps another few minutes to live.

Mogadishu Airport, 1995

Alex's team was now taking heavy fire from the Somalis gathered down to the southwest. He scanned the fighting position just to the left of the man he'd just shot. Nobody there.

He swung the .50 a little to the right to check the fighting position on the guy's other side. There! The man with the PKM had his big machine gun rested on the top of a sandbag, a huge muzzle plume emanating from it like a corona around a lunar eclipse.

Alex did some quick mental calculations and put his crosshairs smack in the middle of the muzzle plume. He forced himself to relax and ran his mental program: *frontsightfocusfrontsightfocusfrontsightfocusbreath-breathbreathsqueezesquee BREAK—*

He sent a round downrange.

No time to see where it landed—

Pull bolt—
Eject brass—
Slide round—
Slam bolt—
Ratchet in—

He got his gun back up on the sandbag, got on the scope, and took a look. The picture had changed. The big PKM machine gun was now a twisted, mangled piece of metal spilling out over the front of the sandbag. There was a big divot in the sandbag where the guy had been standing. The guy himself had fallen out to the side. He was torn nearly in half, still alive.

Alex watched.

The man lay there on the ground, propped up on one elbow, looking down at himself in shock and disbelief. His guts were spilling out of him.

An image popped into Alex's mind: it looked like one of those gag spring-loaded snakes that pop up out of a can.

Two of the guy's buddies went over and grabbed hold of him, but as they did he went completely limp.

Alex's shot had destroyed both the machine gun and the man shooting it.

Shahikot Valley, 2002

For nearly four full seconds the long, copper-plated .50 cal bullet arced up and over the Afghan valley and down, pushing against the air and weaving back and forth through the crosswinds—

—and IMPACT.

"Holy shit," whispered Tim, almost reverently. Rob's third round had torn into the man's torso on the far side of Shahikot Valley and flung his lifeless body onto the desert floor.

This time there was no ambiguity or hesitation in the others' reaction. The man's two companions took off like a pair of spooked hares, scrambling into a nearby wadi. There would be no chance of engaging them.

Tim and Rob looked at each other, stunned, as the improbability of what they'd just done sunk in. This was no harassing fire. They'd ranged an enemy fighter, aimed, adjusted, and delivered a surgically precise kill shot at a distance of more than a mile and a half. Yes, in the past few days they'd taken some crazy-long shots. But this was far and away the farthest kill shot they'd taken.

What they didn't realize at the time was this: it was the farthest kill shot anyone had *ever* taken.

Husaybah, 2004

. . . *and kiss your ass good-bye*, thought Delgado—

And just at that moment, the roaring of twin Bushmaster machine guns erupted just behind him. He turned and looked, saw nothing. Then looked *up*.

Two Bell AH-1 Cobra attack helicopters hovered in the air just yards above them, unleashing their full fury on the southern edge of Husaybah. This attack bird is one vicious machine, with its 20mm cannon, 70mm (2.75-inch) rockets, and handful of TOW missiles. The two Huey Cobras hovered directly overhead like avenging angels, unloading into the city with their cannons and rockets. Delgado felt his hair standing up.

For a moment, the marines forgot all about being under fire themselves. They all started clapping and howling and jumping around. They were just so happy to see those killing machines.

It didn't take long for the two Cobras to clear the area and give the marines the chance to finally climb out of that garbage ditch and get on the move. They hoofed due east to the site of the stronghold complex, snipped the wire fence surrounding it, and approached the building itself. Fire was still raging inside.

The lieutenant in charge of Kilo 1 turned to a marine who had an AT4 84mm antitank rocket, a monster of a thing, and said, "Hey, launch that shit in there just for GP"—GP meaning *general purpose,* that is, just to be damn sure. The kid launched his AT4 into the building. It damn near collapsed the thing.

The marines kept walking eastward, heading to the Iraqi Republic

Railroad train station to rendezvous with the rest of Third Battalion. The day was far from over.

And their war was just getting started.

Helmand Province, 2009

At this point Nick Irving and his buddies had been mired in a continuous firefight for close to three hours. Good news: the assault team had successfully gotten their HVT. Time for exfil. Bad news: one of their snipers from Second Platoon, a guy named Walkens, had been hit. Not too bad, he was only hit in the foot, but it still sucked.

Worse news. Nick and Pemberton may have pushed the Chechen sniper back into a corner, but they were still being ground down by the ongoing barrage of overwhelming forces—and running low on ammo themselves. They were, in fact, in deep shit and it was getting deeper by the minute.

Over the din of gunfire Derek shouted, *"Listen. I've got a grenade and I've got smoke."*

He didn't have to explain. The looks on their faces told Nick that the others got the idea. If things got truly hopeless, if they reached the point of no return—which was pretty much where they were now—they could all jump on Derek's grenade, he'd pull the pin, and they'd call it a day. That was Plan A.

Plan B? He could pop smoke and they could all leap to their feet and just run the hell out of there. Like Butch Cassidy and the Sundance Kid making their last stand against what sure as shit looked like the entire Bolivian army.

What was Butch's last line again?

For a moment there, I thought we were in trouble.

At that point, either one of those plans sounded okay to Nick. Make a last stand, or eat the grenade: either way meant their time was up.

"What the hell," shouted Nick. Pemberton looked back at him, agreeing with his eyes. They'd pop smoke and make a run for it. The two friends bumped fists and nodded at Derek.

Time to go.

14

DELIVERANCE

How did I escape? With difficulty. How did I plan this moment? With pleasure.

—Alexandre Dumas, *The Count of Monte Cristo*

Mogadishu Airport, 1995

Now all hell broke loose on the Mogadishu Airport runway.

Another jeep showed up with a DShK on a pintle mount on back,
the dude manning the thing shooting directly at them—*DNK, DNK,
DNK, DNK, DNK!* Those .51 cal DShK rounds made a hell of a racket,
and they were landing damn close, *too* close. No time for careful aim.

Alex swung the Beast and rushed a shot at the guy.

The jeep took off.

"You hit the sidewall," called his spotter, "right above the tire, between the gunner's legs." Good enough.

A moment later someone behind Alex shouted, "Everybody down!"

As they all ducked down an RPG shot straight over their heads,
barely a meter above them. To Alex it sounded like a jet plane flying
directly overhead. It exploded in the air behind them.

They were now also taking fairly effective small arms fire from several directions. The scene had degraded into full-out hostilities. Pepper spray and foam were most definitely not going to cut it.

Alex looked down to the southwest. *All right,* he thought, *what's the
biggest threat?* Quickly scanning the area, he spotted a Somali with an
RPG, running low along the tarmac and heading for a building. Cover
and concealment. If he reached the building he would be safe, and he
could wreak havoc on them.

He tried to lead his target, but there just weren't enough mils in the scope to lead this guy. He was running full speed, and he was *fast*.

Alex gave it his best from-the-hip estimate and sent off a round.

"Hit behind him," shouted his spotter.

"Building is at seven hundred yards!" called out another teammate who had a range finder on the spot.

As quickly as he could, Alex dialed in the dope, reloaded—*bolt, eject, slide, slam, ratchet*—and got back on the gun. Through his eyepiece, he just managed to catch sight of the guy as he disappeared behind the corner of the building.

He took a breath, placed his crosshairs about 1 mil back from the corner of the building, about three feet off the ground . . . and waited.

Five seconds.

Ten seconds.

Fifteen . . . twenty . . . Alex stayed frozen as a statue, holding the Beast as steady as he could . . . *twenty-five . . .*

At about thirty seconds the man with the RPG stepped cautiously out from around the corner. His pelvis was directly in Alex's crosshairs. He dropped carefully to one knee, raised his RPG tube, and aimed it directly toward Alex. Now Alex's crosshairs were directly on his sternum.

BOOM!

The round cracked and sped away.

An instant later a bright spark flew up from the man's chest: the incendiary round exploding as it made contact. The RPG gunner was gone.

And that was it.

Like a ferocious spring thunderstorm suddenly abating, the deadly spatter of small arms fire began to dry up and disappear.

A few minutes later some little kids ran out onto the runway, picked up the RPG tubes lying there, and started pointing them at the Americans. Alex didn't know if they were just kids, screwing around, or if this was a conscious tactical ploy on someone's part, an attempt to get the American intruders to shoot a kid, thus inflaming the locals and sparking off another Battle of Mogadishu.

Whatever it was, they didn't fall for it.

The kids soon tired of their game and left.

Shahikot Valley, 2002

By day nine, the majority of the fighting in the Shahikot Valley was over, and entire units of American soldiers were being recalled from the valley. Operation Anaconda was winding down. Tim and Rob were up on the ridge, lying prone, side by side, glassing distant enemy positions, looking for whatever targets might still be there.

Suddenly Tim grabbed Rob's head and smashed it down into the ground. "Stay down!" he shouted.

Rob just had time to wonder what the hell Tim was doing when he heard a loud THUD.

After a moment, they both lifted their heads and looked around. About thirty meters away a massive bomb was lodged in the ground, tail up.

"Jayyyy*suss*!" said a voice emerging from a nearby trench: B Company, U.S. 101st Airborne. An American soldier climbed out, walked over to the thing, and kicked it.

"Whoa, whoa, whoa!" Rob called out. "We don't have to tempt fate here, do we?"

It was a five-hundred-pound American bomb, the kind a B-52 might drop. The kind a B-52 *had* dropped, just now. On them. For whatever reason Rob will never know, it just hadn't gone off.

He looked at Tim, both of them thinking back to the American sniper round that zipped right between them their second day in the valley, missing them both by inches. Friendly fire. Blue on blue.

The closest they'd come to dying had been at the hands of their own team.

Husaybah, 2004

By the time Jason's team and the two platoons, Lima 2 and Kilo 1, reached the train station at the southern edge of the city, the rest of the battalion had just arrived from Al Qaim, and CAAT teams were loading up to move into the city to sniff out and stamp out pockets of the armed offensive.

Jason and his team started hitting the rooftops, moving through the city as overwatch for their platoon. It was a complex and exhausting sequence. They would come off a roof to kick down doors with the platoon, help out where they could at the street level, make sure no one was coming up on their backs, then hop back up onto the roof again to scout the area. And it was a moving element, combing through the city, so in a short time the platoon would move on to a new area of influence—at which point the snipers would have to scramble down off that rooftop, run and slingshot past the platoon, always keeping their own 360 degrees of immediate danger in consideration, and get to high ground so they could cover the unit as they entered their new location . . . a game of leapfrog as played in hell.

And it lasted for hours, nonstop, right through the hottest part of the day, when temperatures hit 110 degrees—running up and down stairs, jumping across rooftops and ledges, climbing into small windows, and always covering, always maintaining security, always watching. Jason had never before experienced such a grueling gauntlet. Hell Week in sniper school now seemed like a summer day's fun at Coney Island.

Armed skirmishes continued throughout the day.

When nightfall came, they switched to NVGs (night vision goggles) and kept going.

The shift in visibility made identification much harder. With close to two thousand troops moving through the thickly settled square mile of the city, not everyone was on the same radio frequency. It was chaos at times.

These guys had been briefed in Al Qaim that they were coming in to pull this company out of a major offensive. Things tend to get exaggerated when you're briefed on something like this. No doubt they'd heard, "Shit's going down, blowing up everywhere, bodies everywhere!" They were hyped as hell rolling in there, and anyone on a rooftop was going to be in one dangerous position. Marines tend to shoot first and then ask questions, especially in a situation like this one.

At one point Jason, Mavica, and DelFiorentino suddenly found themselves hugging the concrete as automatic rounds tore at the lip of the roof they were on, saying, "Please, God, let them stop." A CAAT team had seen silhouettes moving around up there on the rooftop and started lighting everything up with their .50 cals.

Getting these guys to stop was easier said than done. Reaching them meant getting on the radio with the snipers' watch commander, who would get in communication with another guy, who would get in communication with the guys in the CAAT. Jason didn't have a lot of confidence in that whole telephone game. Instead, they popped some chem lights and started yelling, "Hey, stop shooting at us!"

That seemed to work.

It wasn't the last time that night they were shot at by friendlies. And they were shot at by quite a few *un*friendlies, too. It was a long night.

They stayed out in the city, fighting block to block, until close to midnight, when things finally calmed down enough so they could come back to the rear to resupply. They'd shot a lot of rounds and needed to restock on ammunition, as well as get some water and chow.

By the time they arrived back at base, there were orders waiting for them to go back out again with another platoon. Command had broken the city down into distinct areas of responsibility for each company and unit. Battalion was going to stay, and all roughly two thousand marines were going to spend the next day doing a complete sweep of the city, building by building, door to door.

At this point, the snipers had been fighting for about fourteen hours straight. They were just getting started.

Helmand Province, 2009

After hours of crouching in that cramped, shallow hole in the ground, fighting for their lives, Nick Irving and Mike Pemberton were just about to jump to their feet and make a run for it when Derek, the recce operators' team leader, said, "Hey, we've got some guys coming in!"

A machine gun team from Second Platoon who'd been hearing their calls over the comms had decided to break away from the firefight and come help get them out of there.

Nick looked over his left shoulder and saw them coming, five guys, two with M4 rifles and three with Mark 48 machine guns, screaming and laying down a blanket of gunfire even as they ran at full sprint.

That's one seriously brave bunch of dudes, he thought.

The five rangers came plowing in to where they lay, rolling on the ground. Nick recognized the lead gunner, a buddy of his named Ben Kopp. He couldn't remember ever being so happy to see another human being. He'd have to remember to tell him that, later on when things calmed down and they were out of this mess.

The machine gun team bought them a little more time and some serious firepower. Without Kopp's team roaring in for that epic save, Nick doubts they would have been alive more than another few minutes. But they were still sitting ducks, and they still had to get out of there. Time to make the dash, back to where the machine gun team had just come from. They were back at the Butch-and-Sundance, Bolivian-army option—but at least this time they had Ben Kopp and his machine gun team with them.

Derek quickly organized their sequence, who would go first, who next, right on down the line to Irving and Pemberton, who would be the last two in line. He pulled out his smoke grenade, popped and tossed it—and Nick watched in disbelief as the gusting wind caught at the billow of smoke and pulled it away in exactly the wrong direction.

So much for cover.

Not that it mattered: by the time the machine gun team and recce operators had all taken off and it was finally his and Pemberton's turn to go, the smoke was long dissipated anyway. And they were still being pounded by overwhelming firepower.

They were pretty much back where they'd been just a few minutes ago. They looked at each other with looks that said, *Okay, time to die.*

"Hey, tell my wife I love her," Pemberton said.

"Fuck that, man," replied Nick. "You tell her yourself."

They pounded fists a second time, then lunged to their feet and began running for their lives. As they started sprinting they heard the sounds of a very specific gunfire within the din of the ongoing firefight—*sssnap! sssnap! sssnap!* That wasn't just the continuing barrage.

It was the freaking Chechen.

Fuck! thought Nick. *Probably back at his window again, now that we're were on the run.*

When you're being sighted by a sniper you don't want to run in a straight line, because if you do, all you're doing is helping him estimate your lead so he can drop a bullet out just ahead of you on your path so that by the time it reaches your distance, you've just run smack in to meet it. Instead, you have to move in as unpredictable a pattern as possible. Which goes completely against your instincts, because doing that also means you're significantly slowing down your forward movement, prolonging the amount of time you're exposed. Which is crazy—but you have to, because if you just make a beeline and run like hell, you'll be dead for sure.

As they ran Nick repeated the mantra to himself, *Zigzag! Zigzag!*

The two ran as fast as they could, over rocky hardpan laced with muddy irrigation ditches, the worst kind of terrain for running; Nick says he doesn't remember his feet ever touching the ground. It felt like they flew over the whole eight football fields' worth of zigzag sprint, *sssnaps!* and splashes of dirt all around them.

They stopped running when they reached a small ditch, where they joined up with a small element of ten rangers from the platoon. The rest of the force was back inside a safe house they'd commandeered about two hundred yards farther to the southeast, most of them up on the roof, engaged in firefights. The Alamo, they'd dubbed the place. Nick lived in San Antonio. He'd seen the real Alamo up close and personal and knew its history. Not an encouraging image.

"You got any water?" Nick panted. "I need water, bad." He'd had nothing to drink since running out of water on that endless march through the sand the night before.

Kopp pulled some water from his backpack. Nick drank half and gave the rest to Pemberton. *Another one to thank you for later, Kopp.*

They started moving. Nick saw a guy with an AK-47 pop his head around a corner about fifty yards away. He grabbed Pemberton and plopped Dirty Diana right down on his shoulder, using him as a human bipod. Pemberton understood and stayed still. Nick watched his inhale and exhale and timed his own breathing to his partner's to make sure he could compensate correctly for the rising and falling of the gun barrel.

BOOM.

The AK guy went down.

"Hey, man," said one of the machine gun team, "take formation."

Nick ran up to the front of formation and started leading the twenty-odd guys—recce operators, Kopp's machine gun team, and the ten rangers they'd met up with—out to the Alamo.

From this spot they had about one hundred yards left to get to the safe house. *It's only a hundred yards,* he thought. *We can make it. We've come this far.* The days of no sleep, the hours of constant gun battle, were all catching up with him, and he made a critical miscalculation: he led them along a small ridgeline with a ravine in front and a line of trees behind it.

They were silhouetting themselves along a tree line.

Husaybah, 2004

The citywide sweep began at first light. Lieutenant Colonel Lopez was not going to let up even for a moment, and he was not pulling any punches. No more killing 'em with rainbows, no more soccer-ball diplomacy, and definitely no more looking for goat milk smugglers. They were locking this place down, tight. *Show of force.*

Before long, Jason's group found a carefully planted 105mm shell. He radioed the EOD (explosive ordnance disposal) team, and they set up their position and waited. And waited.

No one had expected or planned for any kind of operation near this size or scope, and battalion had only one EOD team for the entire battalion. That's *one* team, two guys and two little bomb-disposal robots, for a citywide door-to-door sweep involving more than 1,600 marines and a population of 100,000. And there were IEDs stashed throughout the city.

So they waited. And waited. As the sun rose, it became insanely hot, Iraqi hot.

The longer they waited there in position, the more time some insurgent was out there with his hand on the trigger, and this guy was no doubt calling up *his* reinforcements, saying, "Okay, they found the IED but they're held up here, so get some guys over here right now, they're sitting targets."

Sure enough, soon men were creeping up on them and taking shots.

Close to three hours later, the EOD team finally showed up, looking exhausted and absolutely wasted. Delgado felt bad for these guys. They'd been hoofing around the city, blowing up four or five other calls in different locations before they got to this one. They'd lost one of their robots, so now they were just two guys and *one* robot.

They examined the situation, carefully blew up the IED, then gathered their robot and other equipment, mounted up, and headed off to their next appointment.

Just as they left, a barrage of machine gun fire opened up. Evidently the explosion had telegraphed their position. Time for another gunfight.

Still, this was nothing like the day before. It was clear to Jason that the insurgents had lost their prime advantage, which was their efficient and highly integrated web of communication. Now, rather than being a well-prepared and highly coordinated citywide force, the insurgents had been buttoned up into isolated pockets. The massive number of IEDs planted around the city were all bombs they had planned to detonate the day before at strategic moments as their offensive unfolded. There were also caches of additional weapons hidden in multiple locations throughout Husaybah, waiting for the mujahedeen to grab and use throughout the day. But the American response—far swifter and far more ferocious than the enemy had expected—had crushed them before they could do so. While they had resupply pockets stashed all around the city, they couldn't get to them in force.

Jason and his snipers continued taking small arms fire throughout the day, as they methodically swept through, block by block, going door to door like an urban police force on a TV procedural. ("Sergeant Delgado, Third Battalion Fourth Marines, ma'am, open the door, we just want to talk to you." Yeah, right.) Later that day they found a second

IED and had to halt their part of the sweep to stay on station and baby-sit the bomb, while the EODs ground through their workload.

Jason estimates they must have gone through two hundred blocks of C-4 that day.

Helmand Province, 2009

As soon as Nick's group hit that little tree-lined ravine—*POP-POP-POP-POP-POP!*—they were ambushed. These were no high-speed rounds breaking the sound barrier, these were machine gun rounds exploding at them from no more than thirty-five meters away. Danger close.

Nick did an immediate cartwheel into the ravine. They all dove in. The thing was full of funky water and filth, but it was better than being shot.

Dirty Diana was now completely submerged and full of water. Nick spotted one fighter over the lip of the ravine, really close, put the crosshairs on his face, and squeezed the trigger—and a stream of water flew out of the barrel. Fortunately, a bullet came out with it, and nailed the guy.

Then there were more guys, and more guys. Nick realized they were literally coming out of the ground—they had established *underground positions*. Was this real, or some nightmarish vision?

It was real, and it was like playing Whac-A-Mole. Fighters kept pouring out of the ground, and Nick kept shooting them. He couldn't even see exactly where they were, he just saw flashes come out of the ground and shot them. The rangers were all floundering around in the water.

Suddenly Nick heard an extremely loud *sssssNAP!* right next to his ear. For an instant he thought one of his team had fired with his rifle right next to Nick's head, and he was about to scream at the guy to back off, but then realized there was no one there. It wasn't someone shooting an inch from his head. It was a solo high-speed round snapping past an inch from his head. If he'd been standing an inch or two to the left, he wouldn't have a face anymore.

That fucking Chechen.

He was still out there. He'd followed their escape path and was zeroed back in on Nick. He was now more than seven hundred yards away, and he was still popping head shots at that distance. This fucker was *good*.

And in the next moment Nick realized it wasn't him the sniper was after, not anymore. Now it was the machine gunners.

He heard a loud THUD, like the sound you'd get if you swung a baseball bat hard into a punching bag, and then he heard a scream that curdled his blood.

"Fuck, I'm hit! I'm hit!"

You can tell when someone's been nicked, and when someone's been hit bad. This guy was hit bad.

Nick looked over to his left and saw Ben Kopp, about twenty feet away, a twenty-foot arc of blood spraying from his femur. He went down.

The medic on the recce team, a tall guy named Melvin, took off toward Kopp, half running and half swimming. Bullets snapping all around his head, completely ignored them. "Bravest guy I've ever seen," recalls Nick. He took off his medical kit, threw it toward Kopp, and let it float there so he could move faster. He reached Kopp moments later, opened his bag, and went to work.

Nick waded over to the platoon leader, Kent, and said, "Sir, we've got to get the fuck out of here—you want us to move out and secure you to Alamo?" To make himself heard over the gunfire he had to get up close and yell right in Kent's ear.

As he spoke, he felt a warm splash hit him.

His first thought: bullets hitting water, sending up a spray.

His second thought: no, that wasn't it. A high-speed round had hit Kent in the upper chest. That was Kent's blood splashing up onto Nick's face.

The Chechen was systematically taking out their key personnel.

Nick froze: went into shock.

Pemberton took one look and saw what was happening, sloshed over, and stuck his finger in the bullet hole. Melvin came over and now started working on Kent, who was meanwhile screaming at Nick, *"Dude, fucking kill these guys."*

Nick snapped to, turned back around, and started engaging targets.

The water around them was turning red from Ben Kopp's blood. Melvin had gotten one tourniquet on him, but that wasn't doing it; he wrapped on another. Kopp asked for morphine but Melvin couldn't give him any; he'd already lost too much blood. He wrapped the gunner in a sort of carry bag and strapped him on.

They told Nick to take up the rear formation, make sure no one came up behind them, and started spraying up their back side. Pemberton took point. They had to get Kopp to the safe house, pronto.

They set off along the ravine, still getting shot at, made about eighty yards, until they reached a point where the Alamo was right in front of them, no more than twenty yards away—but it was all open, completely naked terrain. No cover at all.

Twenty yards.

Nick and Pemberton told the others to wait there with Kopp, who was by now fading in and out, while they cleared the way to the Alamo. They looked at each other. There was no cover, nothing but flat open ground between them and the safe house. Their clothes felt incredibly heavy now, soaked with water and filth and blood. They knew they were probably not going to make it all the way across.

Butch. Sundance. Bolivian army.

Time to go.

"Hey, man," said Nick, "let's get this over with."

For a third time: the fist bump.

Once again: they ran.

The moment they got out in the open it felt to Nick like an earthquake struck. They had run straight into another major ambush! He hit the ground and screamed out, "Shit!"

Pemberton looked back at him. "Dude, are you hit? Are you all right?"

"Yeah, man," shouted Nick. "I'm all right, get down! We're getting hit!"

And Pemberton said, "No, you crazy bastard, those are *our* guys. That's cover fire."

Nick looked up. From the rooftop of the Alamo an entire line of machine guns from the platoon had all opened up at once, making the earth shake. Pemberton laughed as Nick picked himself up. Nick was laughing a little, too.

Husaybah, 2004

After the second IED had been dispatched, Jason Delgado slipped away from the main group and skirted off to a side street. He'd heard what sounded like harassing gunfire, from fairly close by, and wanted to shut it down.

He popped his head around the corner. The side street sloped upward, leading up a small hill. Jason slipped out, low to the ground, and hid behind a small pile of trash on the corner. Using the trash as an ad hoc ghillie suit, he began slowly creeping up the street.

After he'd gone a fair distance he cautiously came around the edge of his mobile trash heap and peered down his scope.

There.

He found the source of the gunfire: a lone guy peeking out from a cement gate ledge in front of a house and shooting sporadically down the street at a unit of marines from the platoon Jason was attached to.

Jason sized up the situation. For two days now he'd been banging around in ditches, running up and down cement stairs, and jumping on and off of rooftops. He had no idea if his M40's zero was still solid or not. This guy was a serious hazard; he hadn't hit anyone yet, but if he kept hiding out there and shooting away, it was only a matter of time. Delgado did not want to lose this guy. He wanted to take him down with his first shot.

He needed to shoot something first, to make sure his boomstick was on point.

There was a lamp on a cement post right at that guy's range, in fact, just a few feet away from the guy. He took a shot at the lamp. It exploded. Incredibly, the guy didn't seem to notice; he was too busy ducking in and out to avoid the marines firing back downrange in his direction.

The lamp had told Jason his zero was right on. All he had to do was watch and wait.

A half minute later, the man peeked out around the corner of that ledge.

Jason let a round fly and, just like the lamp, the man's head exploded.

Jason called his unit over, staying where he was while they came, watching to make sure nobody else crept up on them. By the time the marines made their way down to the man's house and he had joined up with them, there was no body there to be found, nothing but a blood trail where the body had been dragged away.

Two women came out of the house making a lot of noise and tried to keep the marines from entering. They went in anyway, and found a huge cache of weapons—RPKs, RPGs, explosives, a shitload of AK-47s.

They arrested the two women and brought them back to the base. It was the first time they'd arrested any women.

In the course of their door-to-door searches that day they found a lot of dead bodies inside houses, wounded fighters whose time ran out before their women could stitch them up successfully. This was war, Jason figured, and they had their own corpsmen, too. They just weren't as good as ours.

By the end of that second day, April 18, the marines had killed an estimated three-hundred-plus insurgents in the city. They also finally tore down the infamous former Baath Party headquarters building, where Jason and his snipers had their first experience of the insanity of Husaybah months earlier, and where Captain Gannon had been killed along with four of his marines just the day before.

They laid C4 all around its foundation and blew the whole damn thing to pieces, took it to the ground.

A few days later the two women Jason arrested were released.

He was never again investigated for any shots he took.

Helmand Province, 2009

The Alamo was a big house with a ten-foot wall around it, big blue metal gates for the front door and back door. A ranger with a combat camera snapped a few shots of Nick's and Pemberton's faces as they came bursting in through that big blue gate, both covered in blood, faces white with fatigue and shock.

The machine gunners on the roof covered the rest of the group as they made the twenty yards in safely.

They managed to get a medevac in to take out Kopp, Kent, and Walkens, the sniper who'd been hit in the foot.

The rangers had held off the incoming fire like the pros they were for the last hour or however long they'd been there, but there were a lot of unhappy Taliban out there, and they needed some snipers to come in and take out targets for them. Nick and Pemberton were only too happy to oblige. They clambered up a makeshift ladder out onto the roof and started engaging targets.

Fought for another hour or so.

They talked about staying through the night, when their night vision would give them the advantage. But they were just about out of ammo. Nick was down to five or six rounds. Time to get out of there.

It was right about then that they got some disconcerting news.

There were no helicopters coming. The area was too hot; too much gunfire.

Time for backup: call the marines. When the marine commander was told their location he said, "Holy shit, you guys are in *that* area? Sorry. We can't go in there with anything less than a brigade."

Are you fucking kidding me? thought Nick. *A brigade: that's a few thousand men!* So they'd been fighting it out there for close to eight hours now, about forty of them, and this guy was saying he couldn't go in without a *brigade*? Nick stood there, trying to get this to compute. It wasn't working.

"Sorry," the message came back again. "We just can't go in there. We can drive over to a rendezvous point nearby, but you'll have to run out to us."

The rendezvous point they gave was about one mile south of the Alamo.

"So let me get this straight," Nick said out loud to nobody in particular. "Now, after all this, we have to leave our safe house and run a mile, through a hail of enemy gunfire, to go meet our rescuers with their trucks? Is that the deal?

That was, in fact, the deal.

Nick didn't see how he could run a mile. He was so completely used up, he didn't see how he could run a meter. And that mile was all through open terrain.

"Fuck it," said one of the other guys. "We've gotta do it. Irv, you've got point. Pemberton, you cover our six."

So Nick would be the first guy out of the safe house, the first guy to break into that sprint through a full mile of pure open terrain. Sure, why not?

They opened up that big blue metal door and Nick took off like a jackrabbit.

In an instant he started hearing it—*sssnap! sssnap! sssnap!*—all around him. A stray thought shot through his mind: *I guess I'm about to find out how fast I can run a mile.*

When you're running past people in the middle of a firefight, you have to make split-second decisions as to whether they're combatants or just ordinary citizens who happen to live there. They were running through a scatter of rural villages. There were people out there in the middle of the fields, with shovels and hoes, planting their carrots or poppies or whatever the hell they were doing, and Nick and his friends were staggering along, running for their lives while being shot at from behind, and they had to take the time and care to PID (positive-identify) these people.

Nick saw a guy pop up about fifty yards beyond the house, slipping out of a doorway with a rifle.

Guy with rifle. Roger that.

He broke formation, stepping out to the left, dropped down to one knee, and shot the guy while everyone ran past him.

Got back on his feet, took off, caught back up.

Saw another guy—*guy with rifle*—broke out, dropped to a knee, shot him. Caught up again.

And repeated that sequence a few more times throughout the run.

Finally they reached the waiting marines and their five Humvees. Five vehicles for forty guys. Okay. They piled in, Nick lying across four guys' legs with a few more guys sitting on *his* head and legs and the Humvee's marine machine gunner standing on his chest. Some of the rangers clung to the outsides of the Humvees.

They drove.

As they bounced along, Nick realized he wanted one thing: a dying man's last cigarette. Only he wasn't dying, he figured, he'd already died many times over that day. But he could still have the cigarette, right?

One of the marines lit a Marlboro Light and gave it to him. He smoked practically the whole thing in a single drag. When he tried to put it out, it fell inside his shirt and caught on fire. *I'm on fire. Sure, why not?* One of the rangers he was lying on top of reached up, poured out the contents of his CamelBak all over Nick's back, and put him out.

Later on that afternoon, Alex Morrison noticed a Somali civilian walking out across the runway with four others trailing along behind him. The man was not armed, so the SEALs and marines left him alone, but they watched him carefully. When he hit the concertina wire the marines had set out as their defensive position, he followed it to where it dropped down a ten-foot cliff face behind them. He followed it down the cliff—and then started climbing *over* the concertina wire.

Crazy bastard. What the hell was he trying to do?

Some marines went over there with some pepper spray and a card with Somali phrases printed on it. They started calling out to the guy in Somali, trying to get him to back the fuck up.

He started yelling back at them, but then a wave hit him, pulling him down off the beachhead and into the water. Everyone assumed he could swim, but this turned out not to be the case. The man flailed around in the water for a short time, and then the water got really choppy and started carrying him farther out. There was nothing the marines or the SEALs could do but watch. They had been given strict orders not to go in the water, which was amply populated with sharks.

Whatever the man might have been hoping to accomplish, it didn't happen. After another few minutes, he drowned, about fifty yards offshore.

As he floated there on the surface, Alex noticed seabirds landing on him. They weren't eating him. They just looked happy to have something to sit on that wasn't being blown up or shot at.

Late that night Alex and the others boarded an LCAC, climbed into their metal shipping container, took their benches in the dark, and felt themselves slip back out to sea.

Rob Furlong was struck by how different things felt when they got back to Bagram. When they'd first been there getting their orders some ten days earlier, they'd been just one more entity in the Coalition, a handful of unknown Canadians, anonymous in the crowd. Now they were practically celebrities. They found they could walk around into any tent lines, talk to any of these guys, and everyone knew who they were.

Rob was no military buff. Unlike Nick Irving, who idolized Carlos Hathcock and knew the details of his career the way a pro baseball fan knows his favorite player's stats, Furlong was only dimly aware of the name, and certainly hadn't memorized the stats. He didn't know that Hathcock had held the world record for longest confirmed kill shot, at 2,250 meters, for decades. The idea that he'd just broken some sort of world record never occurred to him.

Ironically, the record Rob broke that day was *not* that set by Hathcock during Vietnam. The legendary marine's record had already been smashed just two days earlier—by Arron Perry, Rob's counterpart on 63 Alpha, the other Canadian team, when Perry took out a Taliban machine gunner manning a gun from the back of a truck at 2,310 meters.

"We'll make you proud," Ragsdale had told Colonel Stogran.

No idle threat.

Between the five of them, the Canadians had had a huge impact on the course of the operation and had earned enormous respect from their Coalition peers, and with it a powerful sense of brotherhood, a bond that carried on throughout their tour. Their performance in Anaconda also earned them all Bronze Stars, the medal for bravery that the U.S. military typically awards to outstanding warfighters from foreign units who serve alongside American troops.

"Their professionalism was amazing," Lieutenant Overbaugh reported, calling the Canadians "a very large asset to the mission."

Based in part on their experience in Anaconda, the Canadian sniper program incorporated detailed instruction in how to call in direct fire and close air support into their sniper training.

Less than twenty-four hours after arriving at Bagram, they were airborne again, on their way to another mission.

* * *

I asked Jason Delgado, after the whole battle was over, when all the smoke had cleared, what did the city of Husaybah look like? Like London after the Blitz?

"Believe it or not," he said, "it looked exactly the same as before we started. Exactly the same."

That's the thing about Iraqi architecture: it's solid concrete. Concrete stairways coming out of concrete walls. Concrete floors, concrete roof.

"You can send rockets into these fucking houses," he said, "and they'll stay on their foundations."

Seemed like a hell of a metaphor.

After their two-day sweep of the city, things were relatively quiet for the next week and a half or so. Then it started raining 155mm mortar shells again. Soon IEDs were blowing up throughout the city and the pace of attacks accelerated. Jason saw a good deal more carnage over the following months. By his count, they lost thirty-two marines during his time there.

When their deployment came to an end a few months later, Jason and his teammates turned down their ride, choosing to avoid the main roads and instead slog their way through the desert the long way around to get to Al Qaim, where helos would ferry them to Al Asad to meet their flights home. Even so, they didn't expect to make it out.

They'd seen too many of their guys hit by rockets and blown up by IEDs, says Jason. Why should they be any different?

Nick Irving says he still doesn't know how they managed to survive the gauntlet of that last one-mile run to the marines' Humvees. When they got back to that remote marine base and all started inspecting themselves for damage, every last one of them found multiple bullet holes in their clothes, yet somehow, with the exception of Ben Kopp and Kent, the platoon leader, none of them had actually been hit.

Later that afternoon Nick sat waiting for a transport bird to pick them up and take them back to rejoin their own platoon. There was still so much adrenaline coursing through his system that he was too buzzed to sleep. Finally, he started to drift off.

SSSSSNAPPP!

Nick sat bolt upright as a supersonic round whipped past, within inches of taking his head clean off at the shoulders. He grabbed Dirty

Diana and leapt to his feet in a single clean movement and looked around at the other guys—

Who all sat stock-still, staring at him like he'd just shouted "Cocksucker!" in church. No sounds but the rasp of his own panting breath.

He slowly sat back down and tried to let himself drift off again.

Irving was finally out of the battle. It would be a long time for the battle to be out of him.

V.
THE KILL

When the right moment arrives, you will act without hesitation to stop the beating heart of another human being. The next day, or the next minute, or even seconds later, you will do it again, and then again. You will do so without hesitation, remorse, or passion, as a pure and unquestioned expression of your mission and of your craft.

When you are finished you will return to the society you have just risked your life to protect, and live among those who will never say "Thank you" or "Well done!" nor, in fact, have any idea what you've done.

15

TAKING LIFE

It's a hell of a thing, ain't it, killin' a man. You take everythin' he's got, an' everythin' he's ever gonna have.

—Will Munny (Clint Eastwood), *Unforgiven, by David Webb Peoples*

The instructor leaned in close to his sniper student and pointed across the field toward the plywood hut. Guy sitting there, tied to a chair, trying to keep his face from fidgeting, clearly nervous as hell. Didn't know what was about to happen to him. Or maybe he did.

Hence the anxiety.

"See that guy?"

The student nodded.

"The CIA gave us that guy. They were going to kill him." The student shrugged. The instructor continued. "Why let a good kill go to waste, when it could have instructional value? So they're letting us do it."

He looked pointedly at the student.

"'Us' meaning *you*." He nodded in the direction of the hut. "Shoot him."

The student looked over at the hut, then back at the instructor. "Wait. Seriously?"

The instructor nodded. Seriously.

"Are you sure? 'Cause in five seconds, I'm pulling the trigger."

The instructor's face was passive. He just nodded again in the direction of the hut.

The student stared at the instructor for a few long seconds, then looked over at the man in the chair again. He took a long breath, and let it out. Then raised his sniper rifle, took aim, let his breath out slowly, and squeezed the trigger. A jet of flame spurted out the end of the barrel. The man in the chair grunted, spun, and toppled over. Lay motionless on the ground, still tethered to his chair.

The man was not dead, of course. As great a plot point as it might be for a paranoid-thriller Hollywood film, the CIA doesn't actually turn over fresh-caught bad guys to military sniper courses for target practice. The "prisoner" was simply a projected image, albeit a damned realistic one. Whether or not the student realized that, I couldn't say for sure. He probably did. Still, I could see that the realism of it freaked him out.

And that was exactly the point of the exercise: to give him the chance to experience how he would react in a situation where he was required to point his weapon at a live human being, another person of flesh and bone, blood and thought, a person with parents and friends and probably children, too, and snatch their breath away from them forever.

Nothing can prepare a student sniper for the cold reality of fixing a human target in the crosshairs and knowing that a light squeeze of the index finger will stop his heartbeat. Yet we *have* to prepare our students for exactly that reality.

That was the whole point of the rural-program hunting trips in our advanced sniper training, where we took our new graduates up into the mountains to hunt: it was so they would have the chance to genuinely kill something. No movie cameras, no projectors, no actors. They were by this time absolute masters of the rifle, experts of marksmanship—but they were not yet masters of killing. When you shoot a deer, gut it, and haul it out of the woods, getting blood and guts on your hands, it's an experience that stays with you.

I remember the first time I cleaned a fish, when I was thirteen. It was a very weird experience. And I remember gutting that first deer I shot. *Man,* I thought, *this is gnarly.* But you do it a couple of times, and it becomes just something you now know how to do.

And killing other human beings? Yes, that's different. Of course it is. But at the same time, it really isn't. You do it a couple of times, and it becomes just something you now know how to do.

Not everyone can do it, no matter how good the training.

Nick Irving recalls the battery of strange questions he and his ranger colleagues had to answer just to qualify for sniper school. Two of those rangers didn't make it through that test and were not even allowed into the course. Not because they were crazy or unstable. They just didn't meet the profile.

To be a sniper, you have to have a certain psychological capacity. Lots of soldiers and sailors and airmen kill other people in war, but it's different when you're a sniper. When you're tearing through a room at a dead sprint, and it's pitch black, and someone suddenly pops up with a gun and you shoot him, it's not really that big a deal. You shoot him and you move on.

As a sniper, you sit there and watch the person through a scope for anywhere from seconds to minutes to hours, and then calmly shoot him. It's very conscious and deliberate. The psychologists testing Nick's class wanted to make sure their snipers wouldn't freak out or get scarred in some crazy way, that they weren't going to end up on a bell tower somewhere eating peanut butter and jelly sandwiches and shooting people.

At Kandahar Airfield, before Rob Furlong and the other Canadian snipers flew up to Bagram to launch into Anaconda in March 2002, an American master sergeant named Cunningham came to have a talk with them. He took them privately, one at a time, probably so he could gauge the mind-set of each shooter he'd be working with. If he found anyone he judged as not ready to kill, or not to have that capacity at all, he was ready to yank him out then and there.

Rob waited while Sergeant Cunningham talked to McMeekin. Then it was Rob's turn.

Cunningham didn't waste a lot of time with pleasantries.

"Furlong," he said, "you ever kill anyone before?"

Nope, replied Rob, he hadn't.

"Well, when you do, you're going to have a reaction. And exactly what reaction you have is going to determine how you handle it."

This is a weird conversation, thought Rob. Nobody had ever spoken to him about this aspect of military life before—not in basic, not in battle school, not in airborne, not in recce, not in any of his sniper school training. Hell, Canada hadn't even been to war since Korea, and that was a quarter century before Rob was born. So far, he didn't think he'd ever actually talked to anyone in his entire military career who had killed people in combat.

Cunningham had.

"You may feel something," he went on. "Emotionally, mentally. Some guys go into, I guess you'd say, almost a kind of shock. Where this strange feeling'll come over you."

He paused, his eyes never leaving Rob's face.

"Or," he said, "you can look past it, and just keep doing your job."

He looked at Rob as if he'd asked a question, so Rob nodded, like he got it. Which, he supposed, he did.

A few days later he was lying prone on a mountainside at nine thousand feet peering through his scope, watching his .50 cal bullet slam into a man's back. Watching him die.

The fact that he'd just killed another human being had no noticeable impact on him, not at the time. When you're engaged in contact there's no time for reflection. You're so switched on while you're in the middle of it, your level of alertness is so high, that your mind doesn't want to go anywhere but into the intense focus on what you're doing. Especially when you've spent years training and honing that focus to a laser point.

Although one thought did briefly pass through his mind as he watched his killing shot find its target: he thought of September 11, of the thousands of innocent people going about their mundane lives when those hijacked planes crashed into the towers. The thought flickered for a moment, then was gone. Rob was busy looking for the next target.

It was only later, that night, when he started thinking about the day, that it began to sink in. Lying on his back on the mountainside, wrapped in his ranger blanket with the custom zipper, he thought, *I killed a man.*

Yes. Yes he did. And he would kill more men the next day, and the day after that. And he would look past it. Just keep doing his job.

When I described that early morning skirmish a few of us had in Zhawar Kili in January 2002, a few months prior to Anaconda, the one where we called in a JDAM drop on that little knot of fighters, there was one detail I didn't mention: in the last few seconds before the bomb fell that obliterated them all, we heard the last thing anyone would have expected in that situation: the sound of a baby crying.

Those fuckers, I thought. They had brought family there with them. They had brought *babies* onto the battlefield. I had just called out coordinates for dropping a five-hundred-pound bomb . . . on a baby. Any illusions I had about the nobility of armed battle, of Hector and Achilles duking it out under the hot sun for the honor of their countries, evaporated. War isn't noble, it's brutal and it's ugly.

But when it's there, it has to be done, and done well, or your people die.

It was not a good moment. I lived with it by doing what military fighters have done for millennia: I compartmentalized it. You could say, I put it in perspective. My first son had just been born; in fact, I hadn't even met him yet. I had deployed before having that opportunity. And I was going to do whatever the fuck it took to do my job, protect my brothers, and get my ass safely home to meet my little boy. If I had to kill two people, twenty people, or two hundred people to achieve that, so be it. Stack up the bodies. And if they brought their own families onto the battlefield with them? I sure as shit wasn't happy about it, but it was their call. I had a job to do: stay alive and get my brothers home.

A few days later while patrolling out in the valley we came upon a small convoy of fighters and captured them. A big discussion followed: what do we do with them?

We were already many days into a mission that was supposed to be no more than twenty-four hours and, just like Furlong's experience in Anaconda, with no idea how long we would still be out there. We were stretched thin just feeding ourselves. And now we had prisoners we would have to feed, watch carefully, and take with us back to Kandahar. Some of us, frankly, were quite prepared to take these guys out into the bush and take care of them. By which I mean, terminally.

I know that sounds cold and brutal, and I might feel differently about it today. But you get in a certain frame of mind when you're in a situation like this. You become hardened. It's war; it's kill or be killed. And these guys were seriously bad dudes who had a lot of killing of innocent people on their agenda. I am a certified California surfer, son of two hippie children of the sixties—and I would not have hesitated to waste these guys where they stood. Would have done it and slept well that night, in fact.

Of course, that didn't happen. Protocol and rule of law outweighed battlefield pragmatism. But it could have.

Hunters are used to getting their hands bloody.

It becomes just part of your job, like dressing out a deer. You're a professional, and you do the job.

Which is not to say it doesn't have an impact. Does killing change you? It does. Of course it does. How could it not?

Nick Irving, who earned the nickname The Reaper for his exceptionally lethal record overseas, recalls how weird it was to be surrounded by killing.

"I was raised in a Christian family," he says, "where we learned Thou Shall Not Kill, and here I was, with an awful lot of killing going on. In a way you get used to it; you have to. But in another way, you never get used to it."

In 2005 Nick Irving was a brand-new gunner serving his first deployment in Tikrit. No ranger tab yet, no sniper training, no experience in the field, that terrible jump when his chute dragged him down the airstrip and shredded his uniform just a few months behind him.

He wasn't The Reaper yet; he was just Nick Irving, the warfighter formerly known as Stick Figure.

His job at the time was to man the remote weapons system (RWS) for one of his unit's six Strykers. The Stryker is a light tank (if you want to call forty tons "light"), designed as a more maneuverable and easily deployable armored vehicle than tanks like the Abrams or Bradley. The RWS operator sits inside a little pod, staring at a video display and working a joystick. You are playing, in other words, a videogame. Except that your joystick is operating a very real and very big gun. Some of the rangers' Strykers sported a 105mm or 20 mic-mic (20mm) cannon. Nick's system worked a .50 cal.

As a trained Stryker driver and RWS operator, Nick had learned all about how to maintain this system, connect the .50 cal to all the electronics, and operate it with all the proficiency of Jason Delgado's PIGs playing *Grand Theft Auto: San Andreas* on their Xboxes. The zoom on that video display was insane; you could see a fly on a wall a mile away. It was extremely accurate.

But so far he had not yet fired it at another human being.

Until one morning, when he happened to be the RWS operator in the lead Stryker in his convoy, and a guy in a car came charging straight at them. Was the car wired to explode? Was it a suicide run? No way of knowing, but Nick had seen the look in the guy's eyes with that uncannily accurate zoom, and whatever he was doing, it was deliberate as hell and dangerous as hell, and Nick got the order to shoot, and he did, fired off a burst of .50 cal rounds and watched on his screen as they stitched up the front of the car, blasted out the windshield, and obliterated the man behind the wheel, vaporizing him into a sloppy mess of pink mist and chunks of bone.

The car, it turned out, was indeed loaded with munitions and primed to blow, which made the kill feel both justified and inevitable—but did not stop the dead man from haunting Nick's dreams that night.

Irv had his own room, no roommate, which suited him fine. Growing up, he always tended to keep to himself. Other than his best friend, Andre, he was never much for socializing. Unlike most of the other guys in his unit, he didn't bring over DVD players or Xboxes, had no television. In his room he kept just the bare minimum: a couple of uniforms, socks, T-shirts, and his thoughts. Downtime, for Nick, was lying on his cot, in the dark room.

That night he was lying on his back, staring at the ceiling, and then there was a ceiling fan slowly turning up there, and then the fan's four blades were the dead man's arms and legs, and in the center those deliberate killing eyes, dead eyes, stared at him, and then the man's mouth opened and he began to scream . . .

Nick didn't sleep a lot after that.

Every day they rode out on the Strykers was pretty much similar to that day. He doesn't even know how many men he killed with that joystick; he didn't keep count. It was quite a few.

One day there was a guy who kept stalking them in his car. Finally he gunned it, heading in their direction. Nick was guarding over a unit of rangers who were inside a compound capturing a target, and this guy was now piling straight for them at high speed. Nick put a burst of .50 cal rounds into the driver's side of the vehicle. This was the third or fourth time Nick had shot someone with his RWS and it was already second nature. The car swerved back and forth wildly and came to a stop when it hit a wall. One of the closest rangers to the scene went over and opened the driver's-side door, and a stream of jellylike liquid poured out. The man's body had been liquefied. Yet as vivid as it was, the image of that kill didn't bother him, didn't come back to him later, didn't haunt his dreams.

It was that first one, always the first one.

The nightmare persisted for weeks, months. In fact it's still a recurring dream he has, though now no more than once or twice a year.

Nick also describes often feeling an odd sense of connection to the target he was about to shoot.

"I became, for that split second, very attached to that person, and when I shot him, it's almost like you watch the soul just go away and leave behind this body. I would feel a coppery, metallic taste in my mouth, like when you suck on a penny, followed immediately by a strange hollow feeling, as if I'd been kind of emptied out a little bit. Like a part of *me* had left, too.

"I know it sounds weird. But that's how it feels to me. I don't know what it's like for other guys. Some will probably tell you they don't feel anything at all, but I would call bullshit on that. You feel something."

In the summer of 2009, about the time Nick Irving and his spotter, Pemberton, were fighting their way out of a 360-degree ambush in Helmand Province, Alex Morrison and about sixty other SEALs slipped into nearby Marjah with an Army Green Beret unit.

Their target was an area of four square blocks, centered around the intersection of two main thoroughfares. The place was laid out like a gigantic plus sign, with its two streets, running north-to-south and west-to-east, lined with buildings. Just beyond the streets the place opened out immediately into wide-open fields, with acres and acres of crops—wheat, barley, mungbeans, melons . . . and poppies. Lots of poppies.

Marjah was the focal point of the Taliban's heroin economy and considered the heart of darkness in Helmand. As far as the rest of the world knew, no U.S. or other Coalition forces had been there (the world didn't know Irving and Pemberton had already inserted numerous times, lancing pockets of Taliban leadership like a hot needle). Which was an advantage, in one major way: it gave them the element of total surprise. They went in fast and hard and the Taliban never saw it coming.

They inserted at night by helo. Alex's element made their way to their preplanned blocking position, in a large compound located to the west of the plus sign's center, on the east-bound route in. They cleared the compound, kicked out everyone who was in there, got set up, and waited. The moment the sun came up, they started taking small arms fire—typical for Afghanistan.

Meanwhile another element had landed near them and gone in the opposite direction, clearing to the center of the intersection and then turning to the north, heading for their own designated blocking position. They were using hand grenades to clear buildings. It was full-out urban warfare.

As that team continued northward, Alex caught a glimpse of an Afghan out in the fields with an AK-47, maneuvering his way toward the Americans. Helmand Province is heavily forested, and even in the open fields there were ample trees to provide concealment—and this guy knew what he was doing. As he moved, he kept slipping into dead space, in classic stalk fashion, so that he would be visible for a few seconds, then disappear, then appear again, then disappear.

Alex ranged him. About three hundred yards away. *Okay,* he thought, *I have got to zap this fucker.*

As he worked to get the man on sights, suddenly a younger guy appeared from the west, running up to the guy with the AK. The second guy looked to be about fifteen years old. As he got closer, the older man turned around and started shooing the kid away.

It didn't take more than a second to figure out what was going on. This was the man's son, and the AK guy was yelling at him the Afghan equivalent of, "Go! Get the fuck out of here!"

He chased his son away, then turned back and started heading east again to get within shooting distance of the Americans—but his son came back again. Once more, he stopped and waved the boy off. This time he got the son to back up maybe twenty yards, at which point the boy stopped and refused to budge further.

Now the guy headed east again, again appearing and disappearing behind the landscape features. Then he popped up in a spot dangerously close to the thoroughfare. Finally Alex got a clear view as the man shouldered his AK and started shooting.

Alex already had his .30 cal sniper rifle up and ready. Three hundred yards: not a difficult shot. He quickly got the man in his crosshairs and *BOOM,* rolled him up. Hit him high in the shoulders and knocked him off his feet.

One shot, one kill.

Except that the scene didn't end there. As Alex continued watching through his scope he saw the son come running toward the downed fighter, screaming what Alex assumed was his father's name. Alex couldn't tear himself away; his right eye and scope were glued to the spot. He couldn't stop watching the man's son standing there, freaking out, wailing and screaming. Because Alex had just killed his dad.

When he described it to me, Alex got so choked up at this point that he had a hard time going on.

"It was intense," he said. "You've got kids. You know what it's like."

I did.

The op escalated and ended up being a pretty intense firefight that stretched out over four days. When it was all over, the Americans had captured something in the neighborhood of eight thousand pounds of opium and eight hundred pounds of refined heroin, all packaged in vacuum-sealed bags with a scorpion logo printed on them. It was the biggest drug seizure to date, estimated at about $100 million. But the celebratory feeling barely touched Alex.

That scene between the Tali fighter and his son kept echoing around the inside of his skull.

Alex had killed plenty of other people, going all the way back to his first kill on the Mogadishu Airport runway fourteen years earlier. But all those other times, says Alex, it was almost like a cartoon, and not truly real. "As a sniper, you get the luxury of killing people from a distance; you can keep that distance between yourself and the kill."

But that moment in Marjah took away that distance. In that moment, he says, those people he killed became human beings to him.

"If I had to do it over," he adds, "I would do it again—and again, and again, because I had buddies that guy was about to shoot. Hell, he was *already* shooting at them. But I'd never really stopped to consider that the guys I was shooting were people just like me, who had families just like I do. When we got back from that op, first thing I did was call my son and express to him how much I loved him, how much he meant to me."

I told him his story reminded me of my experience in Zhawar Kili, when we heard a baby crying just before our bomb dropped.

"It was fucked up, man," I told him. "It still haunts me."

"Yeah," he said. Then he added, "And you know what? It *should*. If it doesn't haunt me and I just 'deal with it,' then I'm an asshole."

I didn't say anything. I guessed I could agree with that.

"But at the end of the day," he went on, "this is what we do, that's what they do, and that's how it turns out. And it's horrible, but it's the law of the jungle, or the earth, or whatever it is. It's just a cold, hard fact that has no emotion.

"But it does make you reassess things."

As I said earlier, most snipers you talk to will say it's not about the people they killed, it's about the people they kept from being killed. Sometimes that happens in an extremely vivid way, and a sniper will find himself vested with an almost godlike power over life and death. To inflict a death; to prevent a death from being inflicted.

On April 6, 2003, as Jason Delgado and his fellow snipers provided overwatch from a small bell tower for a column from India Company, Third Battalion, Fourth Marines, approaching the Diyala River Bridge on the outskirts of Baghdad, someone fired an RPG at one of India's vehicles. The grenade did not explode, but it touched off a sequence of events that led directly to one of the more tragic events of the invasion.

Evidently enemy forces, composed at this point of both Republican Guard and other, less readily identifiable fighters, had planned to wait until the company crossed the bridge, then blow the bridge with artillery, thereby separating the battalion's forces, and ambush them on both sides. Their artillery was already in place on the far side of the river, aimed at the bridge, waiting for the right moment. But their timing was thrown off by one overeager soldier with a loaded tube on his shoulder.

When the RPG went off and firefights erupted, the Americans had not quite reached the bridge itself. As the skirmishes continued, though, someone in Saddam's army must have realized their plan was out the window and given the signal to commence the attack.

The artillery went off, firing over the river onto the column of meched-up units and destroying an AAV. A handful of rounds fell short and hit the bridge itself, destroying one pylon and doing enough damage on the bridge's roadway surface that it would now be impossible for the marines to cross by mech.

As the fighting continued, an order came down from Colonel McCoy, the battalion commander, sending two companies to cross the bridge on foot and secure the other side, so they could then send over engineers to set up a pontoon bridge that would allow them to get their armored vehicles across the river. McCoy would be damned if he was going to let the other side sabotage their passage by blowing a few holes in a bridge.

Jason and his fellow snipers were sent up on point, the first to cross the bridge, the line platoons of India Company on their heels and Kilo Company following them. As they ran they could look down through holes in the roadway and see bodies and body parts floating in the water—dead Iraqi civilians, blown to pieces by Iraqi artillery as they tried to escape the impending carnage by fleeing over the bridge.

Partway across the bridge the snipers were hit with mortar fire. Jason peeled off to the right into a small grove of palm trees. Dirt kicked up all around him as he ran into the trees, whether from further mortar fire or land mines, he didn't know and didn't stop to wonder.

He started yelling at his teammates. "Hey, this area may be booby-trapped. We gotta get out of the groves."

They all ran out of the trees and into a nearby street to find a building where they could take cover. Most of India Company had now made it across the bridge and Kilo Company was just arriving. Kilo Company split off to the left, with a three-man sniper element. Jason and Jesse Davenport, his spotter, split to the right with India Company, all of them facing into Muaskar al Rashid Street, the main road that led all the way to Baghdad.

A call came over their comms: battalion had intel that the enemy had hijacked an ambulance truck, recognizable by the crescent moon and star logo on its side, loaded it with explosives, and planned to drive it headlong into the Americans' position.

This went out over battalion-wide comms, so *everyone* heard it.

A few days before, one of their tanks (an *Abrams*!) had been blown up by a suicide driver with a truck bomb. And ever since Beirut 1983, marines are *very* sensitive about being blown up by truck bombs. They had just been ambushed, had artillery fired on them, and lost some of their men. They had now pushed across a bridge on foot, their vehicles unable to follow. This was as desperate, as focused as combat gets. They were all in that bubble now, that zone, the infamous fog of war, that place that says *Do not fuck with me, this is kill or be killed*.

And in the chaos of the moment, "Possible ambulance coming toward you with explosives" became "Don't let *anyone* come near you!"

Kilo Company was already dug in, their machine guns in place, ready for this fight. India followed suit.

Any vehicle that came in their direction got mowed down.

Jason saw a few uniformed soldiers approaching in the distance, saw their weapons, and BOOM! BOOM! BOOM! took them out. Jesse was acquiring targets as well. They were doing their job and doing it well. Protecting their boys and saving their own asses, too.

And then Jason noticed something. There were still a lot of civilians coming toward them, streaming out of the city, trying to get away from the war.

Shit!

Jason and Jesse and the other three snipers all had an advantage over their comrades from India and Kilo Company: they had good scopes. Jason was now on the M40, Jesse had his spotting scope out, and the three snipers on the other side of the thoroughfare had similar equipment. But all the rest of the marines were on M16s, equipped with nothing but iron sights. You look down the barrel of your rifle and see a 240 Golf coming toward you from four football fields away, and you've got nothing to look through but iron sights—your unaided eyesight, in other words—and you can't tell a thing about who's driving. All you know is, there's a vehicle heading toward you, and you've just been told there are vehicles coming toward you with bombs. What do you do?

You shoot.

And the marines of Kilo Company did just that: they shot and they shot and they shot. Some of the people they shot were enemy fighters storming the bridge. Some were enemy fighters dressed as civilians. Some, as would later be claimed, may have been civilians coerced into storming the bridge. But an awful lot of them were simply people trying to get away, people caught in a tragically impossible situation.

All five snipers started shooting engine blocks and tires, doing their best to keep the trucks and cars from approaching the bridge and being shot at. It went on for hours. They didn't dare stop to sleep, or even to rest. Jason started getting scope fatigue, his eye twitching out of control; they switched off on the long gun, and the same happened to Jesse. They pushed themselves and kept going anyway, staying up throughout the night and into the morning, shooting engine blocks and tires, keeping people away, or at least as many as they could.

It was only hours earlier that Jason and Jesse had both had their own very first kill shots. They had trained for years, and they were very good—*marine* good—at what they did. They were graduates of the Killing School, but they had not actually killed, not until that day. And now, just hours later, the meaning and impact of killing changed for them.

"Up until that point," says Jason, "we were pretty savage. We were hungry. At that moment, though, we realized the humanity of what we were doing—or make that the *in*humanity of it. That night-long battle was what turned us into experienced, responsible snipers."

They started choosing their shots with great care. Now, instead of shooting to kill, they were shooting to *prevent* killing.

The battle continued well into the afternoon of the following day. They ran out of food; they ran out of water. With the exception of the marathon at Husaybah on April 17 and 18 a year later, it was the longest continuous firefight Jason ever experienced.

The morning after the shooting stopped, Jason was one of the first men privy to see the aftermath. Quite a few civilians' lives were saved that day because of the snipers' efforts. Many more were lost, as the stilled, bullet-ridden vehicles and scatter of corpses attested. The picture still sits in Delgado's head; it's something he struggles with to this day.

On July 18, 2009, a week after that endless firefight deep in Helmand Province, Nick Irving got the phone call he'd been dreading. "Ben Kopp didn't make it." Irving's friend had survived long enough to get home and see his mom, and not much longer after that.

"That fucking hurts," says Nick. "The only team that could come in and save us, and the guy ended up dying for it."

People ask, what is it like to take another man's life? They never ask, what is it like to *lose* another man's life? To have the life of someone you know, someone you respect, admire, even love, ripped away and be powerless to prevent it from happening? Because you really can't separate the two questions. In war you're confronted with the brutal reality of sudden death, and death is not something you can bargain with or persuade to fight for your side.

Death is like the wind: it blows where it wants to blow.

Furlong thinks about the sight of that enemy fighter walking along the distant ridgeline wearing the dead American's BDU and helmet. "I hope like hell we killed those guys," he muses.

Just how many people *did* he and Tim kill out there in the Shahikot Valley? Thirty, maybe more? And if you include all the air strikes they glassed and called in? Who knows. He certainly doesn't lie awake at night thinking about it. The number he thinks about, the number no one can quantify and he can only speculate on but which means a hell of a lot more to him, is the number of lives they saved.

To take just one example: that RPK gunner he and Tim took out with their historic 2,430-meter shot. How many wives would be widows today if they'd missed, and that gunner had continued on with his mission? How many kids would be fatherless?

"I don't know," says Rob to that question. "I know this. If we saved one, that was one guy who got home, who got to see his family again. If we saved one guy, then it was worth it."

Delgado still thinks about Rick Gannon, the best CO he ever had. After the battle of April 17 and 18, Camp Husaybah was renamed Camp Gannon, and the captain was awarded a posthumous Silver Star and promoted to major. These are worthy honors and meaningful gestures. But they don't make him any less dead. And Van Leuven, Gibson, Smith, and Valdez. Jason Dunham, who never came out of his coma. Jesus Medellin and Andrew Aviles, who both died in the attack over the Diyala River Bridge, and Mark Evnin, the sniper who was killed in Al Kut three days earlier. And so many others.

"With every good man you lose," says Delgado, "you have people like us who assume the guilt of what happened, and the responsibility of knowing what these great men could have achieved if they were still here. That makes us driven. We'll never rest until we achieve greatness. Gotta do it for your boys."

Nick Irving says he was never quite the same person after his stint in Helmand Province. What plagues him, though, is less the people he killed, and more the people he could not prevent from being killed. He still thinks every day and dreams every night about what else he could have done to change the outcome of that terrible firefight. What else he might have done that would cause Ben Kopp to still be here today.

"Call it survivor's guilt, if you want," he says. "For me, it's not guilt so much as memory. These aren't things I can't forget. They're things I don't *want* to forget. Things I choose to take with me until it's my time to recover under the dirt."

Rob Furlong left the service not long after Anaconda and served on the Canadian police force for a few years before joining the private sector. His longest-kill-shot record stood until 2009, when it was surpassed by a British sniper, Sergeant Craig Harrison, in Afghanistan. To this day the two small teams of Canadian snipers are respected and widely viewed by U.S. military as having played a strong role in the success of Anaconda. Today he runs his own training center in Alberta, Canada, Rob Furlong's Marksmanship Academy.

Jason Delgado was in Husaybah for six months before returning to the States. After getting out of the service he went back to school, majoring in media technology, produced an award-winning film, did some private contract security work, and nearly joined the NYPD, but instead decided to pursue his passion for art. He started his own tattoo business, GunMetal Ink, in Bridgeport, Connecticut.

"It was surreal, man, surreal," he says. "To this day, I still can't believe that was me over there, doing that shit."

After leaving the army behind, Nick Irving did a few turns overseas as a private contractor before settling down for good in San Antonio with his childhood sweetheart, who is also his wife. He teaches precision shooting in South Texas and is founder of HardShoot.

Irving still has that snapshot his fellow ranger took of him and Pemberton standing in the Helmand Province safe house they called the Alamo, just after making their epic run from the ravine. In the photo you can see the stains on his and Pemberton's uniforms, filthy ditch water mixed with the blood from two of their men. Whenever he's in what feels like a difficult situation, whenever things seem a little tough, he thinks back to his time as a ranger, and especially to the day that picture was snapped.

In 2011, two years after that last deployment in Helmand Province, Nick was back in Iraq again, this time doing private contract work in Baghdad. One morning when he went to check his e-mail he found a message from a guy he'd known briefly in the Australian Special Air Service (SAS). It read:

"Hey, just to let you know, mate, we got that fucking Chechen for you."

Nick wrote back: "Roger that."

He never heard back from that SAS commando again, but that was okay with Nick; he didn't need to. He'd already gotten the e-mail he'd hoped for.

EPILOGUE: ALIVE

Death smiles at us all; all a man can do is smile back.

—Marcus Aurelius

About six months after returning from Afghanistan, I went to my brother-in-law Wayne's wedding. At the reception, I was seated at the same table with a woman with olive tan skin and piercing brown eyes. Both gorgeous and smart. A killer combination, in my book.

We got talking, the usual dinner-table talk. What do you do? and so forth. I told her I was in the service. That I was a sniper, recently back from Afghanistan. She, it turned out, was an air force pilot. "I fly an F-16," she said. And nodded in answer to my unasked question: "Afghanistan." We clinked glasses in a wordless toast. *To making it back alive.*

"You guys are amazing," I said. "You're like snipers in the sky. I had the chance to call in some air strikes with an F-16 and it blew me away how accurate you are. . . ."

We kept talking, but my attention split in two. Part of me was sitting in the chair in the California hotel ballroom, surrounded by champagne and good cheer. Another part of me was crouching in the low desert scrub of Zhawar Kili.

On our fifth day out my shooting partner, Toby, and I set off into the valley just before dawn to spend the day reconning the area. On our way in we come within a few yards of being badly ambushed. By pure providence, we missed a small pocket of armed Taliban (was there any other kind?) by a hairsbreadth. (If we'd hit our location there ten minutes later or ten minutes earlier, someone else would've had to write this book, because I'd be fourteen years dead now.)

By day six, we decide we need to do something.

We know there are plenty of fighters out there in the valley watching us. We've rounded up a bunch of them on the roads, confiscated their vehicles, taken them prisoner. But most of these guys are staying well off the roads. The two of us talk it over and decide we can't take these people on our terms. We have to go hunt them on their terms.

We need to get outside the box.

We ask our CO, Lieutenant Chris Cassidy, if we can go out there, alone, and hunt these people, just the two of us, no support, no backup, no comms. He gives us the thumbs-up. We spend the night planning out the op.

We dress like locals. I have dark coloring and thick black eyebrows and could easily pass for Afghan; Toby is of Turkish descent, and looks it. At a distance or in poor light we could both pass for Taliban. (Maybe.) We take no ID with us. I bring my MK13 .30 cal bolt-action sniper rifle, Toby his SR-25 semiauto. Toby has his sidearm, and so do I: my Heckler & Koch, a USP (universal self-loading pistol) compact .45, with three mags of .45 rounds plus one chambered, and probably a hundred rounds for the .30 cal. And water. A small notebook to write in and a stub of pencil.

Water, paper, guns, bullets. That's about it.

We set out before dawn, using the cover of darkness to slip unseen from our camp up on the mountain. It's just one day from new moon; pitch black in the valley.

It takes us thirty minutes to get down the hill. At the bottom Toby and I look at each other and I whisper, "Did Jack notify the TOC about us?"

Jack, our comms guy, was given the task of notifying our tactical operations center as to what we'll be doing. The area we'll be operating in is a gunship kill box; air assets are free to shoot or bomb any heat signature that pops up in this grid. We've seen the videos, a blacked-out screen with tiny little green trails zipping around—people fleeing for their lives—and then disappearing in a blip. We call it Murder TV. Here we are, dressed in local garb, don't even have IR glint tape on us, nothing whatsoever that identifies us. Jack has shown up as less than reliable in a few instances.

"Fuck it," says Toby. "We're not going back up this hill." I agree. I just hope Jack has done his job.

We start out at the south end of the valley, find our way up to a goat trail that runs along about three quarters of the way up the mountain ridge. Our plan is to follow that trail as it winds its way roughly north-northeast up through the whole valley, and hunt.

We start tracking.

It sounds arcane and exotic, but it's really pretty basic if you just pay attention. You look for any disturbed ground, broken twigs, anything out of place. It's amazing how clumsy and sloppy human beings are, compared to animals. A guy will drop a shell casing out of his pouch, drop bits of paper, spit somewhere out in the open. You say, Oh, this guy stopped to take a piss here. You pretty quickly put together a picture: how many people there are, what direction they're going, what they're doing.

Of course, the people we're tracking are not so lazy. They know the area really well, and they know how to hide. Still, we have no trouble finding trace. Our prey hides out and sleeps at night; when daybreak comes they roll up their stuff and stash it in the grass or the bushes. We find some bedrolls and simple camping gear. A teapot, still warm. We stop and glass, get out our binos, scan the area. Mark the position in our notebook.

Every now and then we stop and whisper back and forth. Mostly, though, we communicate with hand signals. We continue tracking, stopping, glassing.

I see a guy.

The valley population is in the hundreds, but by now the bombs have chased them all out. All the regular inhabitants are gone, for now. Any people we see are here for a reason, and it's the same reason we're here. We're all on the hunt.

There is a mix of Taliban and Al Qaeda out here. It isn't hard to tell them apart. The Talis are grizzled, hardened by the natural environment. The Arabs have a softness to them; a lot of them come from wealthy Saudi families and grew up in a fairly easy environment, and have only recently signed up to fight a jihad. The Taliban guys are as old as the mountains.

This guy is Taliban. I have him in my sights. He doesn't know I'm here. I could shoot him. I could shoot him right now.

We are absolutely itching to take down some live targets. But if we start taking shots, this whole valley is going to know it.

I don't shoot him. We mark the position and keep going. We trace a path throughout the valley, one full sweep up and one full sweep back down. We mark some six or seven positions. We leave virtually no trace. No one sees us.

We get back to camp that night, report in, meet up with our two air force combat control techs, CCTs. One of them says, "Hey, you want to do this yourself?"

Normally you would go to a JTAC (joint terminal air controller) training course to learn how to do this. But they train us up right on the spot: here's how the nine-line works, here's how you call in each one, and so on, and a few minutes later I am on the radio with an F-16.

A sniper in the sky.

"Reaper 1, this is Red Devil 1. I have multiple enemy in the vicinity, would like to request ordnance drops on all."

The pilot responds with available resources.

"Roger that," I continue. "First position, four enemy at . . ." and I read off the coordinates in latitude and longitude of the first position we marked in our notebook. "You are clear to fire. Fire when ready."

I'm watching the valley below on my spotting scope. It is now dead-on new moon, total blackness out there, but here and there faint flickers betray hints of campsites being sparked to life. I know which one I'm looking at.

Then, BOOM! a brief fireball.

"That's a direct hit," I report to the pilot, and I call in the next set of coordinates.

And the next.

And the next.

We kill them all.

We ended a lot of lives that night. Toby and I and our faceless companion, the voice in the sky, the one who actually dropped those bombs and did our killing for us.

I'm back at the California table. Someone's put a champagne glass in my hand. And then I remember one more detail from that night. The voice coming over the radio, the F-16 pilot's voice—it was a woman.

I look at the woman sitting next to me. She smiles faintly, and nods again.

"Yeah," she says. "That was me."

We don't say anything for a moment. Then both raise a glass to the bride and groom.

A toast to the living.

Afterword: A Spec Ops Sniper in Civilian Life

In 2006, thirteen years after my first day in navy boot camp as an eighteen-year-old recruit, I left the U.S. military service. I spent a year doing private-contract security work in Iraq, but that wasn't the life for me. I wanted to be home in the States, close to my kids. And I wanted to apply the skills I learned, maybe learn some new ones, and see what I could do as an entrepreneur to serve my fellow snipers and other Spec Ops warriors here at home. My first business effort crashed and burned. (Call it *business boot camp*—undergrad work in the School of Hard Knocks.)

Then, I found my calling.

Hurricane Group, Inc.

In 2012 I started SOFREP.com, a Web site devoted to serving the Special Operations community, both vet and active duty. The site exploded and soon it grew into a full-fledged digital media company, which I dubbed Force12 Media, from terminology for gauging the ferocity of nautical storms. On the Beaufort scale, 12 denotes hurricane strength—and a hurricane is exactly what the next few years felt like. Starting from that first single site, we grew into multiple sites serving a range of readerships, including FighterSweep (aviation), The Loadout Room (guns and gear and lifestyle blog), The Arms Guide (self-explanatory), and The SpecOps Channel (original video content), which we launched online as a subscription channel featuring reality shows and documentaries aimed at taking on the largest networks on traditional television. (As SEALs say, "The only easy day was yesterday.") In 2016 I formally changed the company's name from Force12 Media to Hurricane Group, Inc.

During those early years we also stood up SOFREP Radio, the number one podcast in its iTunes category (Government); a publishing arm, with *New York Times* bestsellers on its list, and then our own publishing imprint; a Spec Ops–focused book-of-the-month club; and Crate Club, a tactical and survival gear club. And on SOFREP, we expanded into hard news and op-ed pieces on military and foreign policy, and began taking the lead in breaking quite a few stories, starting with the events surrounding the attacks in Benghazi on September 11 and 12, 2012, that took the life of my best friend, Glen Doherty.

Which brings me to my other venture.

RED CIRCLE FOUNDATION

Back in 2000, Glen and I went through the SEAL sniper course together as shooting partners. We'd been teammates at SEAL Team Three for some time already, but sniper school was where our bond really formed. They say the closest relationships are ones forged with those you go through a crisis with together, like floods, earthquakes, and other natural disasters, or war. Going through sniper school is something like that. Glen and I came out the other end as close as friends could be, and for the next twelve years we were never far apart.

My life was forever altered in September 2012. One day, Glen and I were shooting e-mails back and forth about edits on a book we were working on together. The next day he was gone. Part of a small group responding to the attacks on an American compound in Benghazi, Glen was one of four who died heroically in the course of those attacks.

Earlier that year my SEAL memoir, *The Red Circle,* had come out, and not long after its release I formed the Red Circle Foundation, in order to create a nonprofit organization that I knew I could trust and give to personally. At the time, I had no clear idea on how to establish our unique turf within the already crowded nonprofit sector. For a few short months, the Foundation worked to get its bearing and define its mission. Then Benghazi happened.

When Glen died, our mission suddenly gained a very personal focus. Here was a former Navy SEAL sniper and accomplished CIA contractor who'd just died promoting and protecting American interests abroad—and while the government shipped the body back home, it took zero responsibility beyond that point . . . not even basic burial costs. Since Glen wasn't married and had no kids, the CIA-mandated life insurance policy he'd carried was deemed void. On the plane flying home from the memorial, I wrote a tribute to Glen, a personal good-bye letter to my friend, which *The New York Times* published in full the next day. (It appears, reprinted in full, in my book *Among Heroes,* which

John Mann and I were working on at the time.) Glen's passing garnered a lot of public attention, which I totally appreciated. But it didn't pay the Doherty family's bills.

Witnessing firsthand how Glen's family was left hanging (for years, as it turned out!) with their memorial expenses and how stressed it made them to have to deal with this financial burden, on top of the deep wounds of personal loss, made our foundation's purpose suddenly very real. The Red Circle Foundation, I realized, existed for situations exactly like this. It existed to bridge the gap—to help families of Spec Ops warriors in times and situations when government funds or assists from other private sources were either too slow in coming or not there at all.

We made our first payout to the Doherty family for about $11,000. It didn't cover everything, not by a long shot (a group of his friends and I covered the rest), but it helped. I'll never forget how great it felt to cut that check.

As I write these words in the fall of 2016, America has been at war for fifteen years straight—far and away the longest stretch of continuous warfare in our nation's history. Nobody has felt the stress of that more than our Spec Ops warriors—people like Alex Morrison, Rob Furlong, Jason Delgado, Nick Irving—and their families. In past eras, snipers and other Special Operations Forces were used sparingly and on only special occasions, for specific operations that were deemed, as the term implies, *special*. The more massive companies of regular forces carried out the bulk of the battles waged. In the twenty-first century, that equation has been turned on its head. In today's asymmetrical warfare, Special Operations has become the tip of the spear, and Spec Ops fighters have suddenly been in demand as at no other time in our history.

This has been an indescribably tough burden to bear—especially for the families. Which is why the Red Circle Foundation exists.

The Red Circle Foundation is what we in the military call a QRF—a *quick reaction force*. When these families are hit with memorial costs or emergency medical expenses, they are hit suddenly and hit hard. Private organizations typically have nothing like the molasses-slow bureaucracy of the Veterans Administration, but still, they often move way too slowly. It can take weeks to months before funds are disbursed to help people in need. This is where the Red Circle Foundation comes in. We make decisions within hours to provide immediate assistance, and in the process make a huge difference in people's lives. The Foundation also provides scholarship funds to send children of Spec Ops parents to schools, camps, and other enrichment programs.

The Foundation channels every penny of its general contributions to Special Operators and their families. Which means that whether you give $30 or $30,000, every penny of that money goes directly to a military family who needs it. (Our operational costs are covered by business donors, large and small.)

I invite you to visit the Foundation's Web site, at redcirclefoundation.org, and consider making a contribution. You don't have to be wealthy or give large amounts for it to be genuinely meaningful. Even the smallest donations can make a huge difference.

And it sends them a message, too: that their sacrifices are not forgotten.

Brandon
September 11, 2016

Acknowledgments

Every book project is like a massive, eighteen-month stalk. We go in with a general idea of where and what our target is, but have to cover a hell of a lot of unknown ground getting from here to there. And authors are like snipers in this way: they may look like solo operators, but there's always a vast unseen team behind them working to help put them on point. Our thanks especially:

To Marc Resnick, our editor and solid champion at SMP, as great a publishing partner as you could hope for. Marc, you're the best.

To Steve Cohen, EVP and COO at Macmillan, SMP's parent company, whose peerless deal-making savvy is matched only by his sense of humor.

To our literary agent, Alyssa Reuben, for carrying our concepts around the canyons of Manhattan and helping them find their ideal homes.

To Jason Kenitzer, for the excellent map renderings, and to David Glazier at GoodTone Studios, for his expert work with us in creating the audiobook version.

To Chris Martin, for the superb research and groundwork behind his excellent *Modern American Snipers*.

To Jack Murphy and Benedetta Argentieri: it's too bad we ended up not using that fantastic material on the women snipers of the YPJ (Kurdish People's Defense Units); that book is crying out to be written, and we hope you write it.

To Glen, my best friend and NSW sniper school partner; you are missed by many, Bub. And to Chief Dan Goulart, for tapping two FNGs (fuckin' new guys) to go through the NSW school.

To Glen's family and Sean Lake for their steadfast class in the face of extreme adversity.

To Eric Davis, my partner in redesigning the NSW course, and to Chief Bob Nielsen and Chief Jay Manty, for trusting the two of us to do this crazy thing.

To Lanny Bassham for his pioneering work in mental management.

To all those SEAL snipers who graduated Eric's and my course, many of whom have quietly surpassed most known confirmed kills of record.

To *all* military snipers. Only you know the level of attention to detail that goes into the craft, and what it means to sight in and pull the trigger under extreme mental pressure.

Finally, and most importantly, to Alex Morrison, Rob Furlong, Jason Delgado, Nick Irving, and all the others who serve in the craft. No matter how many words get put to paper, the world will never fully grasp the sacrifice you guys have made to keep the world a safer place.